IMPROPERLY OBTAINED EVIDENCE IN ANGLO-AMERICAN AND CONTINENTAL LAW

This is the first book to offer an extensive cosmopolitan, cross-cultural insight into the perennial controversy over the use of improperly obtained evidence in criminal trials. It challenges the conventional view that exclusionary rules are idiosyncratic of Anglo-American law, and highlights the 'constitutionalisation' and 'internationalisation' of criminal evidence and procedure as a cause of rapprochement (or divergence) beyond the Anglo-American and Continental law divide. Analysis focuses on confessional evidence and evidence obtained by search and seizure, telephone interceptions and other means of electronic surveillance. The laws of England and Wales, France, Greece and the United States are systematically compared and contrasted throughout this study, but, where appropriate, analysis extends to other Anglo-American and Continental legal systems. The book reviews exclusionary rules vis-à-vis the operation of judicial discretion, and explores the normative justifications that underpin them. It attempts to reinvigorate the idea of excluding evidence to protect constitutional or human rights (the rights thesis), arguing that there is significant scope for Anglo-American and Continental legal systems to place a renewed emphasis on it, particularly in relation to confessional evidence obtained in violation of custodial interrogation rights; we can locate an emerging rapprochement, and unique potential for European Court of Human Rights jurisprudence to build consensus in this respect. In marked contrast, remaining divergence with regard to evidence obtained by privacy violations means there is little momentum to adopt a reinvigorated rights thesis more widely.

Improperly Obtained Evidence in Anglo-American and Continental Law

Dimitrios Giannoulopoulos

·HART·
OXFORD · LONDON · NEW YORK · NEW DELHI · SYDNEY

HART PUBLISHING
Bloomsbury Publishing Plc
Kemp House, Chawley Park, Cumnor Hill, Oxford, OX2 9PH, UK

HART PUBLISHING, the Hart/Stag logo, BLOOMSBURY and the Diana
logo are trademarks of Bloomsbury Publishing Plc

First published in Great Britain 2019
First published in hardback, 2019
Paperback edition, 2020

A catalogue record for this book is available from the British Library.

Library of Congress Cataloging-in-Publication data
Names: Giannoulopoulos, Dimitrios, author.
Title: Improperly obtained evidence in Anglo-American and
Continental law / Dimitrios Giannoulopoulos. Description: Oxford [UK];
Portland, Oregon: Hart Publishing, 2019.
Identifiers: LCCN 2018044755 (print) | LCCN 2018045927 (ebook) |
ISBN 9781509923250 (Epub) | ISBN 9781849463829 (hardback)
Subjects: LCSH: Admissible evidence—United States. | Evidence, Criminal—United States. |
Exclusionary rule (evidence)—United States. | Evidence, Criminal. |
Conflict of laws—Evidence. | International criminal courts.
Classification: LCC KF9662 (ebook) | LCC KF9662.G53 2019 (print) | DDC 347.06—dc23
LC record available at https://lccn.loc.gov/2018044755

ISBN: HB: 978-1-84946-382-9
PB: 978-1-50994-532-0
ePDF: 978-1-50992-324-3
ePub: 978-1-50992-325-0

Typeset by Compuscript Ltd, Shannon

To find out more about our authors and books visit www.hartpublishing.co.uk.
Here you will find extracts, author information, details of forthcoming events and
the option to sign up for our newsletters.

To my parents
To Yiola, Panagiotis and Nina

PREFACE

The inspiration for this book has come from the unique opportunity I had to study, research, practice or teach law in four different legal systems, two in Continental Europe (France and Greece) and two in the Anglo-American world (England and the United States). I cannot trace it back to a particular moment in time or particular jurisdiction. I have *not* from the outset set my mind upon undertaking a legal cosmopolitan study. The book was rather the product of experiencing in practice our cosmopolitan legal order.

I do have a vivid recollection, however, of my first encounter with the law of improperly obtained evidence, as an undergraduate law student at the University of Athens. A leading constitutional law scholar – who later became the Greek Ombudsman with responsibility for the protection of individual rights in the public and private sectors – Prof Georgios Kaminis, introduced our final year 'individual rights' class to the challenging perennial dilemmas facing criminal procedure when evidence has been obtained in an unlawful, unconstitutional or otherwise improper way. His rigorous defence of constitutional or human rights in this context has stuck with me since, shaping, considerably, my understanding of the topic. It has also helped me conceive the improperly obtained evidence doctrine as a litmus test for measuring the level of protection afforded to constitutional or human rights in the criminal process. I have sought to consistently apply the test when studying, teaching or researching the English, French, Greek and United States criminal procedure systems following those formative years in Athens.

The book started its life as a doctoral thesis, which I have written in French and successfully defended at the University of Panthéon-Sorbonne (Paris I) (receiving the *félicitations du jury*), and I owe a profound debt to my supervisor, Geneviève Giudicelli-Delage, for her unfailing support, the constant direction she has provided and for instilling in me a passion for comparative legal studies. In Paris, I was also fortunate to immerse into comparative criminal justice research next to renowned experts Christine Lazerges and Haritini Matsopoulou at the Sorbonne, and found invaluable inspiration in Mireille Delmas-Marty's teachings at the Collège de France, where she occupied the Chair in Comparative Legal Studies and Internationalization of Law. Research I had previously undertaken in the United States, at Columbia Law School, Yale Law School and Harvard Law School, had played a crucial part in my doctoral work, and, to this day, I remain thankful to George Fletcher, Debra Livingston, the late Richard Uviller, Kate Stith and Philip Heymann, for their kind reception there. My time as a trainee barrister in Greece, in the chambers of criminal law scholars Argirios Karras and

Aristotelis Charalambakis, had also given me a flavour of criminal law and procedure in action and influenced the direction of this project.

But it was a highly rewarding experience to relaunch the improperly obtained evidence project with a UK publisher, as an academic in the UK. As I had done much of the heavy lifting, methodologically speaking, when undertaking the French PhD, I now had complete freedom to concentrate upon analysis of the most challenging comparative and normative perspectives. Since my time at the Sorbonne, my viewpoint had also changed as to how far one could go in advocating a model exclusionary rule, exclusionary discretion or system of exclusionary rules and discretions for that matter. This book does not have such an ambition. It rather invites Anglo-American and Continental legal systems to review domestic solutions in the light of the comparative and normative conclusions it offers, and to adjust these solutions accordingly, if needed, to ensure that rights considerations are given due weight when determining whether improperly obtained evidence should be used in the criminal process.

In completing this book, I have been very fortunate to benefit from the insights of a large number of people. I am particularly thankful to Liz Heffernan, Paul Roberts, Charles Weisselberg and the Judge at the European Court of Human Rights, Julia Laffranque, who have read chapters in draft form, offered invaluable advice and have been very generous with their words of encouragement. A big thanks is likewise owed to Jaimee Campaner, Yvonne Daly, Thom Dieben, Kelly Pitcher and Vania Costa-Ramos, who have assisted me with updates on improperly obtained evidence developments in their domestic legal systems. I am equally very appreciative of the support of former Brunel University colleagues, notably Liat Levanon, Ben Chigara, Abimbola Olowofoyeku, Alexandra Xanthaki, James Knowles and Zahir Irani. I must specifically thank my former Head of School, Javaid Rehman, for his valued guidance and touching collegiality, and his concrete support for this project. I am also appreciative of the opportunity I have had to teach the Law of Evidence, often with a focus on improperly obtained evidence, to many generations of Brunel University final year students. I am thankful to them for their thoughtful engagement with the subject.

My warmest thanks also go to Jackie Hodgson, at Warwick Law School, for her invitation to present an analysis of tentative ideas in my book at Warwick's annual Criminal Justice Centre research seminar series (in January 2014), and to her colleagues, for their feedback. I have particularly appreciated the email exchanges with Victor Tadros, which have followed on from that presentation. I have also spoken to themes central to the book at City Law School's Centre for Criminal Justice Research seminar series (in March 2016), at the invitation of fellow comparative criminal justice expert, and enthusiast, Riccardo Montana. It was the last time we met – and I will have a lasting memory of that visit – before he very sadly passed away a few months later. Similar fora were offered to me at the 7th Panhellenic conference organised by the Hellenic Criminal Bar Association in Patras (April 2016), at the 'Fair Trials' judicial remedies working group meeting in Lisbon (in January 2017) and at the annual conference of the Legal Experts Advisory Panel (LEAP) in Athens (in March 2017). I am very appreciative of the opportunities I have had to discuss the book with criminal procedure scholars and criminal justice professionals on these thought-provoking occasions.

I am also very thankful to the Honourable Society of the Inner Temple for their wonderful support to me as an academic fellow. In the context of this fellowship, it was a unique privilege to discuss my improperly obtained evidence research with former Justice at the UK Supreme Court, Lord Hughes, Sir Geoffrey Nice QC and Alison Levitt QC among others. Gratitude is also owed to the general prosecutor at the Court of Cassation (Arios Pagos) in Greece, Charalampos Vourliotis, and the Director of the Hellenic Criminal Bar Association, Ilias Anagnostopoulos, for their insights on the practice of improperly obtained evidence there. My collaboration with the 'Fair Trials' organisation has been equally advantageous in allowing me to engage with criminal defence practitioners in various European jurisdictions. Acting as an academic adviser on a Fair Trials research project that addressed judicial remedies for violations of suspects' rights in Europe was particularly rewarding in that respect, and I want to thank Fair Trials' director, Jago Russell, and his team, for this opportunity.

Writing this book also offered the opportunity to revisit and further explore some of the ideas I had originally developed in previous work, particularly in the following two articles: 'The Exclusion of Improperly Obtained Evidence in Greece: Putting Constitutional Rights First' (2007) 11 *The International Journal of Evidence & Proof* 181–212 and 'Strasbourg Jurisprudence, Law Reform and Comparative Law: A Tale of the Right to Custodial Legal Assistance in Five Countries' (2016) 16 *Human Rights Law Review* 103–29. I want to thank the journal editors at the time of publication, Paul Roberts and David Harris respectively, for nurturing these ideas.

I must also add that I am deeply grateful to Andrew Choo, for his advice and support over the years, first as a supervisor, then as a colleague and mentor, and for his critical engagement with this project. Andrew was a sounding board and an inspiration, as I was engaging with theoretical arguments and empirical observations, and provided crucial input on many aspects of the book, including editorial perspectives. We have a long-lasting friendship and scholarly connection, which I value enormously.

I am, of course, also greatly indebted to my editors at Hart Publishing, for their expert guidance and unremitting dedication to this book. A big thanks is, first of all, owed to Richard Hart, for the enthusiasm he has shown from the start for the comparative improperly obtained evidence project. Rachel Turner, Bill Asquith and Francesca Sancarlo have taken me through the first stages of the process. Vicki Hillyard has meticulously dealt with copy-editing, Linda Staniford provided excellent support with proofs, while Emma Platt and Rose Wood very diligently handled marketing aspects. But I must especially thank Rosamund Jubber, for her direction, patience and encouragement, when I was bringing the project to completion. I am equally thankful to the anonymous referees for their most useful feedback.

I also want to acknowledge my gratitude to friends and relatives, for their constant backing with, and interest in, the book: Nina, Anthony, Eugenia, Sissy, John, Chris, Dimitris, Aris, Julian, and to Fani, for all the above and her generous assistance with the cover.

I must add a special dedication to Geoffrey Woodroffe, who has always been there for me and my loved ones, and who, I know, would have been proud to see this book published.

The deepest debt of gratitude is owed to my parents, Panagiotis and Ioanna, for their unconditional love and support, their sacrifices, their unshakable belief in the human capacity to achieve great things. I am forever grateful to them for their constant efforts to cultivate in me, from a young age, the value of integrity, respect for individuality, the ability to wholeheartedly dedicate oneself to a particular project, a zeal for writing, debating, for education, a passion for travel and independence, for exploring other languages, countries, ideologies and cultures. This book would never have happened without their tremendous inspiration, their nurturing of independent and critical thinking, their example. I owe them everything.

Finally, for the love, fulfilment, stability, motion, passion, amazement, the sheer joy that they bring every day in my life, I am greatly indebted to my wonderful wife, Yiola, and my two exceptionally loving, loveable, children, Panagiotis and Nina. I have no words to thank them for their patience, their unceasing encouragement, their affection and support, their enthusiasm for, and pride in, this project. They mean everything to me.

Dimitrios Giannoulopoulos
London
September 2018

TABLE OF CONTENTS

TABLE OF CASES

Australia

Belgium

Canada

England and Wales

European Court of Human Rights

France

Cour de cassation:

International criminal tribunals

Israel

Italy

Ireland

Netherlands

New Zealand

Portugal

Singapore

Spain

United States

TABLE OF LEGISLATION

Australia

Belgium

Canada

European Convention on Human Rights

European Union Directives

France

Greece

International Criminal Court

Italy

Netherlands

Portugal

Spain

Switzerland

United Kingdom

United States

1

Introduction

Whether improperly obtained evidence should be used in criminal trials has proven to be one of the most tortuous, convoluted and perennial questions of criminal evidence and procedure across the Anglo-American and Continental legal cultures and beyond.[1] Whereas a number of legal systems have quickly drawn the link between the unlawful, unconstitutional or unfair *obtaining* of criminal evidence and their *use* in court, other legal systems have isolated the criminal trial from irregularities taking place at the pre-trial stage and often implicitly taken the approach that the exclusion of improperly, but reliable, evidence is a counter-intuitive process, and that the public interest in the investigation of the crime reigns supreme, even where constitutional or human rights have been breached. The ideological dichotomies caused by the improperly obtained evidence debate within these legal systems have been no less noteworthy,[2] and the supreme and cassation court judgments generating them have been replete with symbolism, extending far beyond the technical question of whether the fact-finder should be barred from accessing tainted information. Several major constitutional law and human rights 'landmarks' can be located within the relevant jurisprudence.[3]

From this angle, it can be argued that there has long existed significant scope for cross-cultural dialogue in this area, as a means to investigate approaches to improperly obtained evidence presenting alternative solutions to those adopted by domestic law. But legal systems have taken a predominantly unilateralist approach here, paying little attention to exclusionary rule developments happening outside their domestic jurisdiction, even where these were occurring within

[1] See generally R Traynor, 'Mapp v Ohio at Large in the Fifty States' (1962) 3 *Duke Law Journal* 319; J Stribopoulos, 'Lessons from the Pupil: A Canadian Solution to the American Exclusionary Rule' (1999) 22 *Boston College International & Comparative Law Review* 77; O Tsolka, *The 'nemo tenetur se ipsum prodere/accusare' principle in the criminal process* (Athens, PN Sakkoulas, 2002) 213 (in Greek).

[2] See generally R Uviller, *Virtual Justice: The Flawed Prosecution of Crime in America* (New Haven and London, Yale University Press, 1996) 63.

[3] See, eg, *Mapp v Ohio*, 367 US 343, 81 SCt 1684, 6 Led2d 1081 (1961) and *Miranda v Arizona* 384 US 436 (1966), in the United States or *A and others v Secretary of State for the Home Department (No 2)* [2006] 2 AC 221, in England and Wales. See the Israeli Supreme Court decision that recognised a discretionary exclusionary rule in 2006, which was 'hailed by many as a revolution in Israeli evidence law'. See B Blum, 'Doctrines without Borders: The "New" Israeli Exclusionary Rule and the Dangers of Legal Transplantation' (2008) 60 *Stanford Law Review* 2131; CrimA5121/98 *Issacharov v Chief Military Prosecutor* [2006]. See also the 155,000-word long judgment of the Irish Supreme Court in *DPP v JC* [2015] IESC 31.

the same family of law,[4] let alone where these could only be observed within a foreign legal culture.[5] The accessibility of foreign sources, and the linguistic and conceptual obstacles intrinsic in the comparative study of law, may to some extent provide an explanation for this state of affairs, though it will be far less convincing an explanation today than it would have been 20 or 30 years ago, for instance, considering the rapid growth of technology in legal research and the explosion of cosmopolitan legal studies. It seems more plausible to suggest that misconceptions about the origins of the exclusionary rule, and its relationship with Anglo-American and Continental law, may have blocked wider cross-cultural interactions in this domain. A view of the exclusionary rule as idiosyncratic of Anglo-American law,[6] coupled with an exaggerated understanding of the central role that free proof plays in Continental law, may therefore account for a lack of interest towards solutions offered by Continental legal systems. Conversely, glossing the exclusionary rule as part and parcel of the adversarial tradition may be discouraging Continental observers, versed in the inquisitorial tradition, from concentrating upon the simultaneous development of the exclusionary rule as a constitutional and human rights doctrine (and, ultimately, from identifying important similarities with Continental constitutional and human rights law). Similarly, if Continental observers continue, erroneously, to view the common law as revolving predominantly around exclusionary rules, leaving no room for the deployment of free proof, it is likely that they will be equally discouraged from investigating potential

[4] For examples of cross-referencing of exclusionary rule jurisprudence between Supreme Courts in the common law see, however, *Attorney-General's Reference No 3 of 1999* [2001] 2 AC 91; *R v Shaheed* [2002] 2 NZLR 377; *DPP (at the suit of Walsh) v Cash* [2007] IEHC 108.

[5] Noteworthy examples of cross-cultural exclusionary rule studies include: C Bradley, 'The Exclusionary Rule in Germany' (1983) 96 *Harvard Law Review* 1032; W Pakter, 'Exclusionary Rules in France, Germany and Italy' (1985) 9 *Hastings International and Comparative Law Review* 1; G Kaminis, *Illegally obtained evidence and constitutional guarantees of human rights (the exclusion of evidence in criminal and civil proceedings)* (Athens-Komotini, AN Sakkoulas, 1998) (in Greek); Y Ma, 'Comparative Analysis of Exclusionary Rules in the United States, England, France, Germany and Italy' (1999) 22 *Policing: An International Journal of Police Strategies & Management* 280; C Bradley, 'Mapp Goes Abroad' (2001) 52 *Case Western Reserve Law Review* 375; SC Thaman, '*Miranda* in Comparative Law' (2001) 45 *Saint Louis University Law Journal* 581; SC Thaman, '"Fruits of the Poisonous Tree" in Comparative Law' (2010) 16 *Southwestern Journal of International Law* 333; SC Thaman (ed), *Exclusionary Rules in Comparative Law* (Heidelberg, Springer, 2013).

[6] Fletcher and Sheppard, for instance, consider the exclusionary rule an American invention. G Fletcher and S Sheppard, *American Law in a Global Context: The Basics* (Oxford, Oxford University Press, 2005) 261. Chief Justice Warren noted in his dissenting opinion in *Bivens v Six Unknown Named Agents of Federal Bureau of Narcotics*, 403 US 388, 415 (1971) that the exclusionary rule was 'unique to American jurisprudence'. See also Office of Legal Policy, *Report to the Attorney General on the Search and Seizure Exclusionary Rule*, Truth in Criminal Justice Report No 2, 26 February 1986 (1988–1989) 22 *University of Michigan Law Reform* 573, 579. The report states that '[n]o other nation, including those with a common law heritage, has adopted an American-style exclusionary rule solution to the problem of illegally seized evidence'.

rapprochement with the common law with regards to the latter.[7] Coupled with the above, the normative question arises of whether, in establishing the principles relating to the law of improperly obtained evidence, primacy should be given to the objectives and values central in domestic law – the domestic legal, social and political environment more generally – or whether the legislator and domestic courts should also be taking into account shared values within a particular legal culture or across legal cultures, or consider universal values entrenched in international human rights law.[8] Depending on how a legal system answers this question can influence how quick its reflexes might be to future developments in comparative law, and if it is going to take an interest in them in the first place. We must note, in this regard, that the desire to protect legal culture from external influences is perhaps nowhere demonstrated with more force than in the area of criminal evidence and procedure,[9] and that this may therefore provide an additional explanation of a certain myopic view of domestic jurisdictions as far as the comparative dimensions of improperly obtained evidence are concerned.

By undertaking detailed analysis of the exclusion of improperly obtained evidence across the Anglo-American and Continental legal traditions, this book aims to fill the gaps identified above. Through the adoption of a cosmopolitan approach to improperly obtained evidence, it will attempt to tackle misconceptions about the role of truth discovery and evidence admissibility in Anglo-American and Continental law. This approach takes as its point of departure the development of the law of improperly obtained evidence within the domestic legal and socio-political environment. But it goes further than that to pinpoint new vistas of possibility for cosmopolitan legal thinking when addressing one of the most enduring enigmas of comparative criminal evidence and procedure.

I. Four Comparative Law Pillars

The book relies on four comparative law pillars with the aim of constructing a bridge that will enhance communication and mutual understanding between Anglo-American and Continental law solutions on improperly obtained evidence.

[7] See P Roberts, 'Science, Experts and Criminal Justice' in M McConville and G Wilson (ed), *The Handbook of the Criminal Justice Process* (Oxford, Oxford University Press, 2002) 258; A Psarouda-Benaki, Parliamentary debates, 13 May 1996, 6269 (in Greek).

[8] See generally *Law Society of Singapore v Tan Guat Neo Phyllis* [2007] SGHC 207, [2008] 2 SLR(R) 239 [58]; *People (AG) v O'Brien* [1965] IR 142, 158.

[9] A Garapon and I Papadopoulos, *Juger en Amérique et en France* (Paris, Odile Jacob, 2003) 29. See also M Delmas-Marty, 'The Contribution of Comparative Law to a Pluralist Conception of International Criminal Law' (2003) 1 *Journal of International Criminal Justice* 13, 19; G Fletcher and S Sheppard, *American Law in a Global Context: The Basics* (Oxford, Oxford University Press, 2005) 531; R de Gouttes, '*L'encadrement de la procédure pénale par la norme internationale: quelle norme? quelle cohérence? quel encadrement?*' in Cour de cassation, *La procédure pénale en quête de cohérence* (Paris, Dalloz, 2007) 171.

The exclusionary systems of England and Wales, France, Greece and the United States present the observer with fascinating synergies and divergence that go beyond the conventional Anglo-American and Continental law divide. These come to the surface primarily when evidence obtained in violation of the right to privacy is in question; as it will also be argued, there is a wider, emerging, rapprochement around self-incriminating evidence obtained in violation of custodial interrogation rights. All this will be analytically explored in chapters two and three, on the exclusion of evidence obtained in violation of the right to privacy, and chapter four, on the exclusion of confessional evidence. It can still be briefly explained here that, faced with violations of the human right to privacy, English and French law adopt converging, non-automatic, discretionary, solutions, on the one hand, and that Greece and the United States opt for automatic exclusionary rules, on the other. We are, in other words, presented with converging solutions that traverse the Anglo-American and Continental legal cultures, and diverging approaches taken within legal systems belonging to the same legal culture. This provides an interesting point of departure when seeking to place new emphasis on the cross-cultural study of the law of improperly obtained evidence. The argument can be reinforced if one looks at the vastly different procedural frameworks that set the United States and Greece apart, or the diverging legal histories, legal culture and institutions that differentiate France to England and Wales.

On this point, we may observe, for starters, that first acquaintance with the idea of undertaking a full-blown comparison between the United States and Greece will probably puzzle comparative law experts conscious of the substantial socio-political, cultural, institutional and economic gap that separates the two countries, the different composition of their populations, the infinite geographical disparities and diametrically opposed geopolitical roles or, perhaps more importantly, their serious differences in terms of incarceration and criminality rates and the nature of such criminality. But, from this angle, the United States will probably be viewed as exceptional in comparison to most, if not all, countries in the Western world anyway.[10] In fact, the rising criminality and harsher law enforcement policies that have resulted from the current socio-economic crisis in Greece[11] lend themselves to a quite timely comparison with the United States, given the high crime rates and law and order policies that are characteristic of the American criminal justice system.

[10] D Nelken, *Comparative Criminal Justice* (London, Sage, 2010) 29.

[11] For the association between socio-economic conditions, especially unemployment, and criminal activity see, eg, R Fadaei-Tehrani and T Green, 'Crime and Society' (2002) 29 *International Journal of Social Economics* 781; MS Habibullah and AH Baharom, 'Crime and Economic Conditions in Malaysia' (2009) 36 *International Journal of Social Economics* 1071; R Cox, 'Crime, Employment and Incarceration in Light of the Great Recession' (2010) 37 *Review of Black Political Economy* 283. For its manifestations in Greece in the current socio-economic environment see C Kollias and SM Paleologou, 'Labour Market Conditions and Crime in Greece' (2012) 39 *International Journal of Social Economics* 983.

A comparison between England and France will be much more in tune with conventional comparative law practice. The contrasting procedural traditions of common law adversarialism and Continental inquisitorialism that they have respectively long embedded are still leaving their mark on the two sides of the Channel.[12] It suffices to take note of the vastly different organisation of the police and the prosecution service, the antithesis between reliance on professional magistrates in France and lay justice in England and Wales or the divergent roles of the defendant, the victim, prosecutors and judges in the criminal process, in which there is an opportunity to participate to markedly variant degrees.[13] Equally notable are disparities as to the parties' access to criminal evidence, such as those encapsulated in the comparison between continuous access to the case file – the 'dossier' – in France and the arguably more limited access through 'disclosure' in England and Wales.[14] Differences as to codification of the law,[15] the role of legislation and jurisprudence, and ensuing variations as to how actively judges seek to develop the law,[16] or discrepancies concerning the status of judges, law professionals and academics,[17] play no less an important role in England and France continuing to take different directions in the organisation of their criminal processes. All these differences exist despite the fact that important convergence mechanisms have long been in action, especially in the European Union and in international criminal tribunals, and are now pushing the common law and Continental law traditions closer together.[18] But, on the other hand, persisting idiosyncrasies should not obstruct one's view of the modern transformations of English and French criminal justice, which have as a consequence that systemic

[12] See JR Spencer, 'Evidence' in M Delmas-Marty and JR Spencer (ed), *European Criminal Procedures*, Cambridge Studies in International and Comparative Law (Cambridge, Cambridge University Press, 2005) 635. See also R David and CJ Spinosi, *Les grands systèmes de droit contemporains*, Précis Dalloz, 10th edn (Paris, Dalloz, 1992) 253.

[13] See J Hodgson, *French Criminal Justice – A Comparative Account of the Investigation and Prosecution of Crime in France* (Oxford and Portland, Hart Publishing, 2005); J Bell, *French Legal Cultures* (London, Butterworths, 2001).

[14] See A Ashworth and M Redmayne, *The Criminal Process*, 4th edn (Oxford, Oxford University Press, 2010) 259.

[15] J Hodgson, 'Codified Criminal Procedure and Human Rights: Some Observations on the French Experience' [2003] *Criminal Law Review* 165.

[16] See G Canivet, 'The Practice of Comparative Law by the Supreme Courts – Brief Reflections on the Dialogue Between the Judges in French and European Experience' in B Markesinis and J Fedtke, *Judicial Recourse to Foreign Law – A New Source of Inspiration?* (London, UCL Press, 2006) 309, 315.

[17] See JR Spencer, 'Introduction' in Delmas-Marty and Spencer (ed), *European Criminal Procedures* (2005) 27–37.

[18] See, eg, B Markezinis, 'Learning from Europe and Learning in Europe' in B Markezinis (ed), *The Gradual Convergence – Foreign Ideas, Foreign Influences, and English Law on the Eve of the 21st Century* (Oxford, Clarendon Press, 1994) 30; DM Amann, 'Harmonic Convergence? Constitutional Criminal Procedure in an International Context' (2000) 75 *Indiana Law Journal* 809; J McEwan, 'Ritual, Fairness and Truth: The Adversarial and Inquisitorial Models of Criminal Trial' in A Duff, L Farmer, S Marshall and V Tadros, *The Trial on Trial – Volume 1: Truth and Due Process* (Oxford, Hart Publishing, 2004) 51, 51–52.

differences in the two legal systems are beginning to lose their explanatory force.[19] It may be a dangerous, stereotypical, oversimplification to emphasise the divergent attitudes of England and France, while losing sight of contemporary reform that may indicate gradual convergence.

II. Linguistics

The fact that the book seeks to amalgamate normative analysis, legislation and jurisprudence from a range of legal systems across the Anglo-American and Continental legal cultures gives rise to an interesting, preliminary, linguistic issue. Whereas in the common law we speak of the 'exclusion' of improperly obtained evidence, the focus, in Continental law, is on the procedural act that may have enabled the improper obtaining of the evidence. Most Continental European legal systems use the term 'nullity' to denote the procedural sanction that applies to acts that are devoid of validity,[20] acts that are 'null and void', where they have been performed in breach of relevant procedural standards. We also come across the concept of 'evidentiary prohibitions', the *Beweisverbote* of German law, or non-usability, the *inutilizzabilità* of Italian law. We are therefore confronted with a linguistic plurality that may initially confuse the comparative observer.

Now, where a nullity has been pronounced, the act does not produce its legal effects. Where the police have undertaken a search of premises or questioned the suspect, for instance, in violation of the relevant provisions in the Code of penal procedure, a nullity will be pronounced and the act will not produce the legal effect of the discovery of evidence or the obtaining of self-incriminating statements respectively. In practical terms, this often means that the evidence obtained through an invalidated procedural act must be removed from the investigation dossier. This is not always the case, as a pre-trial procedural act may also be invalidated by the trial judge, who is also the fact-finder in the continental tradition and will necessarily become aware of its content; the evidence is still excluded from the consideration of the fact-finder, and the court cannot base its judgment on it.

We see, in other words, that though 'exclusion of evidence' and 'nullity' in principle exercise the same functions – the 'exclusion' of improperly obtained evidence from the consideration of the fact-finder – and can therefore be compared and contrasted despite the linguistic divergence that at first sight sets them apart, caution is warranted in making sure that we do not obtain a monolithic

[19] See generally R Colson and S Field, *The Transformation of Criminal Justice: Comparing France with England and Wales; Les transformations de la justice pénale: une comparaison franco-anglaise* (Paris, L'Harmattan, Bibliothèques de droit, 2011).

[20] See Garraud, *Traité théorique et pratique d'instruction criminelle et de procédure pénale*, t III, 1912, n 1099, 421. See also L Liberopoulos, *The flaws of the procedural act and sanctions in the criminal process: nullities in criminal procedure* (Athens-Komotini, Sakkoulas, 1993) 37 (in Greek); P Tonini, *Lineamenti di diritto processualle penale* (Milan, Giuffrè Editore, 2004) 106.

understanding of their operation in practice. This requires moving the discussion, in this introductory chapter, to the procedural idiosyncrasies that influence the practical application of exclusionary rules and nullities in Anglo-American and Continental legal systems. The key questions here are 'who excludes', 'when' (at what stage of the criminal process) and 'what happens after exclusion'.

III. Who Excludes?

Nowhere is analysis of procedural divergence between Anglo-American and Continental law more pertinent to understanding how exclusionary rules operate in practice than in relation to the divide between Anglo-American bifurcated and Continental unitary courts.[21] In Continental unitary courts, a professional judge has the dual role of deciding whether particular evidence should be used in a criminal trial and undertaking the factfinding exercise. By definition, then, when called upon to decide on guilt, the judge will also have knowledge of evidence that she may have previously formally excluded. In other words, the unitary structure of Continental trials does not, in principle, insulate the fact-finder from knowledge of tainted ('excluded') evidence. In this context, 'exclusion' of improperly obtained evidence simply means the fact-finder is obliged to ignore or disregard the tainted evidence which she has previously become aware of. She must not take it into consideration when deciding on guilt. Put simply, the judge must forget she has ever become aware of the evidence. In Anglo-American trials, on the other hand, the division of labour between trial judge and jury naturally lends itself to blocking the fact-finder's access to tainted evidence. The trial judge decides on the admissibility of evidence in a *voir dire* or pre-trial hearing, in the absence of the jury. The jury then decides on guilt entirely oblivious to evidence that may have been excluded.

The question that inevitably arises is how realistic it is to expect that a duty to disregard or ignore improperly obtained evidence in Continental unitary courts will in effect prevent the factfinder from drawing upon her knowledge of such evidence to inform the verdict. Damaška's powerful critique of the ability to enforce exclusionary rules against this procedural and institutional background merits special attention.[22] In 'Evidence Law Adrift' he sums up the problem perfectly, noting that 'where the same individuals decide the admissibility of evidence and the weight it deserves, the taint from the forbidden but persuasive information cannot be avoided: it always affects the decision maker's thinking'.[23] Damaška then goes on to conclude that exclusion under these circumstances 'easily produces an

[21] See M Damaška, *Evidence Law Adrift* (New Haven and London, Yale University Press, 1997) 46.

[22] See M Damaška, 'Free Proof and its Detractors' (1995) 43 *American Journal of Comparative Law* 343; Damaška, *Evidence Law Adrift* (1997) 47–52.

[23] Damaška (n 21) 47.

excursion into unreality'.[24] The trier of fact is asked to 'unbit[e] the apple of knowledge'. In painting the contrast with Anglo-American bifurcated settings Damaška seeks to demonstrate that, irrespective of how far reaching Continental exclusionary rules may appear to be, in reality they may offer only hollow protections, and that 'the occasional identity in the wording of Continental and Anglo-American exclusionary rules can thus be deceptive'.[25]

It is impossible not to acknowledge the intuitive force in Damaška's critique. Contemporary accounts provide further support. For Jackson and Summers, for instance, exclusion 'suggests more than simply the fact that the evidence cannot be used'. It rather signifies that 'the decision maker does not know of the substance or content of the evidence'.[26] This 'not knowing' is the essence of 'exclusion', they argue, and it provides a strong contrast with the Continental concept of 'non-usability' of evidence that the fact-finder already knows about. In citing an empirical study that seems to suggest that 'knowledge of the evidence which is to be excluded means that the judge will inevitably take this into account in the decision-making process',[27] Jackson and Summers then arrive at the logical conclusion that 'it is legitimate to question whether judges can really be expected to ignore evidence which they have already seen'.[28] Weigend develops the same line of thought, taking German law as an example. 'Trial judges – with the exception of lay assessors – will have read the dossier before the trial even begins', he explains; '[e]xclusion then means only that the evidence will not be discussed at the trial and that the court must not mention the evidence in the written reasons for the judgment', but, 'of course, the tainted information will still be present in the judge's mind'.[29]

The issue caught the attention of the European Court of Human Rights (ECtHR) in *Dvorski v Croatia*. In his concurring opinion, Judge Zupančič took notice of the divide between the common law and Continental law as regards 'the problem of excluding the contaminated evidence, ie with the exclusionary rule', precisely because in Continental unitary trials 'once the evidence had been presented, there is no way to exclude it from the cognitive range of the sitting judges'.[30] 'Once the genie is let out it is impossible to squash it back into the bottle',[31] he emphasised, providing as vivid a metaphorical illustration of the problem as that chosen by Damaška.

[24] ibid 48.
[25] ibid 49–50.
[26] JD Jackson and SJ Summers, *The Internationalisation of Criminal Evidence – Beyond the Common Law and Civil Law Traditions* (Cambridge, Cambridge University Press, 2012) 72.
[27] B Schünemann, 'Der Richter im Strafverfahren als manipulierter Dritter? Zur empirischen Bestätigung von Perseveranz- und Schulterschlusseffect' (2000) 3 *Strafverteidiger* 159–65.
[28] Jackson and Summers, *Internationalisation of Criminal Evidence* (2012) 73.
[29] T Weigend, 'Throw It All Out? Judicial Discretion in Dealing with Procedural Faults' in M Caianiello and J Hodgson, *Discretionary Criminal Justice in a Comparative Context* (North Carolina, Carolina Academic Press, 2015) 185, 189. See also B Blum, '"Exclude Evidence, You Exclude Justice": A Critical Evaluation of Israel's Exclusionary Rule After *Issacharov*' (2010) 16 *Southwestern Journal of International Law* 385, 397.
[30] *Dvorski v Croatia* (2016) 63 EHRR 7 per Judge Zupančič (concurring opinion) [11].
[31] ibid [8].

However, this criticism loses some of its force when one considers that Continental courts have to explain their findings through reasoned opinions. Damaška recognises that this feature allows 'exclusionary rules [in Continental trials] to retain some residual effect even though technically inadmissible information remains lodged in the fact-finder's mind'.[32] Since professional judges have to indicate the evidentiary basis for their findings of guilt, appellate courts are well-equipped to check whether prohibited evidence has indeed been relied upon; all the more so if one considers that appellate review takes place as a matter of routine in most Continental systems.[33] From this angle, it can be observed that an effective system of appellate review reduces the significance of procedural divergence between Anglo-American and Continental systems in relation to improperly obtained evidence.

The critic may still argue that the reasoned opinion of the court can simply omit reference to evidence that judges have taken into account in spite of their duty to disregard. Pointing specifically to the operation of exclusionary rules in Germany, Bradley drew attention to cases where 'the suppressed evidence is not obviously necessary to support a finding of guilt but is in reality the dispositive factor in the minds of the fact-finders'.[34] Judge Zupančič's opinion in *Dvorski* similarly characterised reliance on a duty to disregard tainted evidence as 'naïve',[35] noting that it is 'obviously not going to prevent the judge from ex post facto rationalizing his "intime conviction"',[36] where this has specifically been shaped by knowledge of the 'contaminated' evidence.

A recent example from Greece, on the other hand, indicates that exclusionary rules may not be as easy to bypass as the above criticism suggests. An exception to a strict exclusionary rule was recently introduced there, allowing for the use of improperly obtained evidence, including evidence obtained in breach of data protection laws, in prosecutions for financial crime. Commentators have been quick to point out that the exception was incompatible with the constitutional exclusionary rule for violations of the right to privacy, and that the government had enacted it through the back door, with no prior consultation, as a last minute amendment to an entirely unrelated Bill.[37] The reason for this, the press reported,

[32] Damaška, *Evidence Law Adrift* (n 21) 50.

[33] In France, for instance, the Court of Appeal acts as a second degree of jurisdiction, and defendants convicted at the court of first instance are ordinarily given access to it. See generally B Bouloc, *Procédure pénale*, 25th edn (Paris, Dalloz, 2016) 959. For an analysis of the contrast with the common law, where access to the Court of Appeal is exceptional, see P Béliveau and J Pradel, *La justice pénale dans les droits canadien et français* (Québec, Bruylant, 2007) 723.

[34] C Bradley, 'The Exclusionary Rule in Germany' (1983) 1064. For similar criticism of exclusionary rules in Italy and Greece see E Grande, 'Italian Criminal Justice: Borrowing and Resistance' (2000) 48 *American Journal of Comparative Law* 227, 248 and N Dimitratos, *Evidential prohibitions in the criminal process*, Poinika No 35 (Athens-Komotini, AN Sakkoulas, 1992) 71 (in Greek) respectively.

[35] *Dvorski v Croatia* (2016) 63 EHRR 7 [12].

[36] ibid [13].

[37] See, eg, I Anagnostopoulos, *Improperly obtained evidence in the criminal trial and (the state's duty to respect) fair trial guarantees*, Public debate at the Athens Bar Association, 19 January 2016; Hellenic

was to allow for the use of unlawfully intercepted private data in a series of serious tax avoidance cases that would have to be abandoned otherwise.[38] The cases related to the infamous 'Lagarde list', which contained unlawfully leaked data from more than 100,000 clients of HSBC's Swiss private bank.[39] Among these were the names of 1,991 Greek citizens with bank accounts in Switzerland, allegedly used for tax avoidance and tax evasion purposes. One may deduce from this that the judges' ability in continental unitary proceedings to freely draw upon contaminated evidentiary sources may be somewhat exaggerated. In the Greek case at hand, the effect of the exclusionary rule was perceived to be so far-reaching as to make redundant the emblematical 'Lagarde list', seemingly leaving the government with no choice but to bring forward a drastic amendment to the exclusionary rule.

The extent to which Continental judges draw upon contaminated evidence in practice is, of course, an empirical question. But the issue can also be approached from a purely theoretical perspective. We can start with Damaška's explanation as to how the jury trial's deliberative context can give meaning to judges' requests to the jury to disregard inadmissible information. The importance of exchange and deliberation in the jury room leads Damaška to conclude that a request to jurors to disregard contaminated evidence retains its force. This is so 'because jurors are often uncertain about what to decide, waiting to make up their minds in the course of exchanges in the jury room', which means that 'the foreclosure of an effective line of argumentation can make a difference'.[40] It may be argued, however, that the same deliberative context applies to non-jury trials in the Continent, where decisions on guilt are taken by panels of judges (normally comprising three professional judges),[41] and where the deliberative element extends to considering the opinion of the prosecutor. Now professional judges may be more reassured than jurors in their findings, but they still have to use effective lines of argumentation to also convince their colleagues in the panel or to support a verdict that goes against the opinion of the prosecutor. This means that, if the foreclosure of a line of argumentation is meaningful in a jury trial in the common law world, then it can in theory also be meaningful in bench trials in the Continent. In fact, one might

Criminal Bar Association, *Press release on improperly obtained evidence in the criminal trial (art 65 Law 4356/2015)*, www.hcba.gr/news/announcements (in Greek).

[38] See, eg, P Tsimpoukis, *Amendment for the use as evidence of the Lagarde list by financial crime prosecutors*, Proto Thema, 22 December 2015, www.protothema.gr/politics/article/538586/tropologia-gia-tin-axiopoiisi-tis-listas-lagard-os-apodeiktikou-mesou-apo-tous-oikonomikous-eisaggeleis (in Greek).

[39] C Barrett and J Aglionby, *Famous names had HSBC Swiss accounts*, Financial Times, 9 February 2015, www.ft.com/cms/s/0/c4f77d36-b04e-11e4-a2cc-00144feab7de.html#axzz48kkiRKPu.

[40] Damaška, 'Free Proof and its Detractors' (1995) 351.

[41] See, eg, the *tribunal correctionnel* in France and the Court of first instance in Greece, whose composition includes three professional judges (unless the offence in question is a more trivial one, in which case there is one judge only). The graver criminal offences go to the *Cour d'assises* in France and the mixed tribunal in Greece, which comprise professional judges and jurors, with professional judges in the minority (three judges and six lay members in France, three judges and four lay members in Greece). See art 398 CPP (France) and arts 5 and 8 CPP (Greece).

argue that it can be even more meaningful in Continental bench trials, where the Court of first instance judges will be acutely aware that their reasoned opinions will be routinely checked by their more senior colleagues at the appellate level and by legal commentators producing case comments.

To continue with this argument, it can also be pointed out that to easily accept that judges take no account of procedural law's direct mandate to ignore tainted evidence is perhaps equivalent to stripping judges of the capacity for dispassionate factfinding. In other words, this logic deprives judges of one of the key attributes of their professional selves, the ability to apply the law against their better judgement on guilt or innocence. This logic also seems to stipulate that a judge's view on the appropriate outcome of a case is shaped uniquely by reference to substantive criminal law values, in other words the question whether the defendant has indeed completed the *actus reus* with the required *mens rea* or whether a defence applies. This logic stipulates, in other words, that the judge's knowledge that the defendant has committed the offence prevails over any other consideration and in particular procedural considerations such as the fairness of the proceedings or the integrity of the criminal process. This view of the institutional party who more than anyone else is versed with the responsibility to ensure that the criminal trial is aligned with key procedural values may be myopic.

IV. At What Stage of the Process is Evidence Excluded?

We can now turn our attention to how the prototypical divide between the common law's 'day-in-court' trial and the episodic trial of Continental law also affects the application of exclusionary rules in practice.[42] Here I want to focus on the different emphasis that Anglo-American and Continental law place on the judicial scrutiny of procedural acts at the pre-trial stage. In Continental law, the criminal trial tends to be the culmination of a sequence of procedural acts undertaken at the pre-trial stage. Typically, pre-trial judicial chambers are given responsibility for the examination of the legality of these procedural acts.[43] The parties can apply directly to them and can appeal their findings, with an appeal often going as far up as a

[42] Though we must at the same time pay attention to modern transformations of criminal justice that are bridging this gap. Damaška, *Evidence Law Adrift* (n 21) 59.

[43] In Greece, for example, the judicial chamber at the Court of first instance is a panel of three professional judges of a court of first instance (art 5, para 1 and 305 CPP Greece). It decides on committal to trial following the culmination of the investigation phase. The most usual avenue for a procedural act to be nullified is by appealing the judicial chamber decision that takes the case to trial. However, a nullity application can also be made during the investigation phase, prior and independently of the committal decision. See judicial chamber of the Court of Appeal of Athens 1716/2000, 3 *Poiniki Dikeosini* 838. The judicial chamber most often decides in the absence of the parties.

chamber of the Court of cassation.[44] The judicial chamber then has the power to declare the act null and void, which, in principle, bars the use of evidence obtained through that act in the remainder of the proceedings. Since inadmissible evidence then normally has to be suppressed from the investigation dossier, the fact-finder will not obtain any knowledge of it.

With this in mind, we can revisit the criticism discussed in the previous section according to which in unitary Continental trials the judge is often influenced from knowledge of tainted evidence. Even if we take this criticism at face value, we can now explain that it only applies to situations where a party seeks to have evidence admitted for the first time during the trial phase, where there has been no previous opportunity to challenge its admissibility. This in Continental systems, however, is rarely the case, and occurs mostly in relation to trivial offences that are taken directly to trial in lower courts.[45] In relation to all other offences, and certainly in serious offences, Continental procedure generally provides parties with the opportunity to contest the admissibility of evidence at the pre-trial phase, usually by a nullity application to the judicial chamber responsible for supervising the pre-trial investigation. In fact, the parties are often *required* to challenge the admissibility of evidence before the pre-trial stage culminates. Failing to submit a nullity application before the commencement of the trial precludes the parties from raising the admissibility issue altogether (with the exception, of course, of nullity and admissibility issues that occur in the trial itself).[46] Put simply, this means that in practice nullity and admissibility of improperly obtained evidence issues are often exhausted before trial, and this by definition prevents the fact-finder from accessing such contaminated procedural acts and the evidence deriving from them.

[44] In Greece, the decision of the judicial chamber is subject to appellate review by a judicial chamber of the Court of Appeal (art 478 CPP Greece). The Court of cassation (*Arios Pagos*) also reviews pronouncements of nullity (art 482 CPP Greece), even ex officio, at the cassation level (art 171 CPP Greece).

[45] In France, this happens with some of the less serious offences that are taken directly to the Court of first instance (*tribunal correctionnel*). See art 385 al 4 CPP (France).

[46] See, eg, arts 178 and 179 CPP (France), which state that the decision of the investigating judge that commits the case to the *tribunal de police* or the *tribunal correctionnel* respectively has the effect of correcting any existing 'vices' of the (pre-trial) process. In other words, the parties cannot apply for nullity past the point of committal to trial. See similarly art 595 CPP (France). In addition, once one of the parties has applied to the judicial chamber (*chambre de l'instruction*) for nullity, all other parties are also required to raise nullities. They otherwise lose the right to apply for nullities at a later stage (art 198 CPP France). Legislative reform in 2000 has also provided for a six-month deadline for applying for nullity, from the time of the interrogation of the suspect by the investigating judge. Beyond this point, the suspect or other relevant party cannot raise the nullity or admissibility issue (art 173-1 CPP France). These are illustrations of how strictly the process of applying for nullity is regulated in France, meaning that nullities of the pre-trial stage cannot generally be raised during the trial. We come across a similarly strict regime for the pronouncement of nullities in Greece, where the parties are required to raise nullities up until the end of the pre-trial phase (art 173 para 1 CPP Greece), and this applies even to 'public interest nullities' (known as 'absolute nullities'), which apply to grave breaches of defendants' rights and other serious procedural violations. These must be raised up until the moment when the committal to trial has become definitive (art 173 para 2 CPP Greece).

From this viewpoint, judicial chamber review during the pre-trial phase exercises the same function as the application of exclusionary rules at the Anglo-American *voir dire* or pre-trial hearing. In both cases, the fact-finder will not have access to the tainted evidence and there will be no risk of the tainted evidence exercising an effect on his mind. Any views of Continental exclusionary rules as pure rhetoric on grounds of the unitary court setting must therefore declare this as a caveat.

V. What Happens after Exclusion?

A final question relating to the procedural context needs to be asked: what happens after evidence has been 'excluded'? Is there any chance to recover – and thus render usable – the evidence 'excluded', and does 'exclusion' leave any traces that could reveal to the fact-finder the tainted evidence? Discussion in the preceding section constitutes a good platform from which to launch these inquiries. This is because excluding the evidence at a *voir dire* in a common law setting or even at the trial stage in a Continental law setting can have very different ramifications compared to a Continental judicial chamber pronouncing the nullity of a procedural act in the course of pre-trial proceedings. An act that is declared null and void at the pre-trial stage does not produce its effects, which means that any evidence obtained through that act cannot be taken into consideration during the trial. This, however, is not necessarily the end of the matter.

Let us take a few illustrations from French and Greek law. To start with the former, under the *Code d'instruction criminelle*, the nullification of procedural acts was originally not producing any consequence other than an instruction to judges to disregard evidence produced via procedural acts declared null and void.[47] However, as a result of reforms that were introduced with the *Code de procédure pénale* 1958 and legislation enacted in 1993, the French Code of Penal Procedure now specifically mandates that any nullified or invalidated acts, and evidence obtained through them, should be removed from the case file.[48] It also strictly prohibits judges and lawyers from using any information contained therein, and provides for disciplinary action against lawyers and judges who may do so.[49] Case law extends this prohibition to any procedural or evidentiary device that might bring the tainted evidence into court through the back door.[50] A reversal of older Cour de cassation jurisprudence has also more recently led to a prohibition to use the tainted evidence in a different process, even where it concerns an unrelated

[47] See *Crim* 22 June 1905, *Bull Crim* n 302, (1909) *Recueil Dalloz* 1, 431 and *Le Poittevin, Code d'instruction criminelle*, ann Loi 1897, art 12, n 39.

[48] Art 174 al 3 CPP (France), introduced with *Loi* n 93-13, 24 August 1993.

[49] ibid.

[50] *Crim* 30 June 1981, *Bull Crim* n 224; *Crim* 23 January 1990, *Bull crim* n 42; *Crim* 16 January 2002, appeal n 01-81.054; *Crim* 26 February 2014, *Bull crim* n 56.

case.[51] This may reassure the critic about the ability of Continental law to 'acoustically separate' the fact-finder from discussions relating to the tainted evidence,[52] at least where a nullity has been declared at the pre-trial stage.[53]

Other aspects of this regime are a cause for concern though. If a procedural act is partially invalidated only, then it is *not* removed from the case file, rather the invalidated parts are 'cancelled', which means they are erased from the report or simply made illegible, but the court can still access the remaining parts of the report.[54] Similarly, where only one of the parties has applied for nullity, the effects will only apply to that party. Put simply, this means the tainted procedural act will remain in the case file, the fact-finder will obtain full access to the evidence obtained with the act and will be able to draw upon it when deciding on the culpability of other parties in the process.[55] Though the evidence will formally be deprived of any probative value against the particular party who will have applied for nullity,[56] it hardly needs emphasising at this stage that it may be a tall order for the fact-finder to ignore it. A survey of the relevant provisions of the Greek Code of Penal Procedure further highlights the problem of the use of tainted evidence in unitary proceedings. There is no provision there[57] equivalent to that which requires the tribunal to cancel the partially invalidated acts in French law, nor an explicit requirement in the Code that invalidated acts should be removed from the case file.

What is more, the Greek Code of Penal Procedure instructs the Court to repeat the tainted procedural acts, if there is a realistic prospect to obtain the tainted evidence.[58] The same is true in France, where it is possible to repeat the invalidated act subject to the nullity having been pronounced at the pre-trial stage.[59] How wide scope there is to repeat the invalidated acts is key to understanding the scope for exclusion in practice. Continental nullities that may at first sight appear strict and absolute may well have little effect in practice, if procedural authorities

[51] *Crim* 7 December 2005, *Bull crim* n 327; *Crim* 7 June and 31 October 2006, *Bull crim* nn 166 and 233; *Crim* 16 February 2011, *Bull crim* n 29.

[52] See Damaška (n 22) 352.

[53] The Code of Penal Procedure also requires that any evidence that is removed from the case file should be stored in an archive at the local court of appeal. There is nothing to suggest that this allows the fact-finder to get access to it. See art 174 al 3.

[54] Art 174 al 3 CPP (France). See also Bouloc, *Procédure pénale* (2016) 800. See a recent case, however, where the Cour de cassation held that 'cancellation' could not cure the procedural defect and invalidated the entire act (a police interrogation in which the suspect had made self-incriminatory statements). *Crim* 16 June 2015, *Bull crim* n 149.

[55] *Crim* 11 December 1984, *Bull crim* n 396; *Crim* 5 September 1990, *Bull crim* n 310; *Crim* 12 February 1991, *Bull crim* n 68, (1991) *Recueil Dalloz*, summary 209, obs Pradel.

[56] ibid.

[57] See arts 170–176 CPP (Greece).

[58] In the exact words used by the Code, the Court 'orders that the acts that have been found null are repeated, if it considers it necessary and achievable'. See art 176 para 2 CPP (Greece).

[59] Art 206 al 3 CPP (France).

are given unfettered power to repeat them.[60] Only empirical evidence can, of course, shed light on how this procedural difference between Continental and Anglo-American systems shapes the nature of exclusion of improperly obtained evidence there. Where this is not available, observers should proceed to comparison cautiously, with this important caveat in mind.

VI. Organisation of the Book

This book seeks to offer an extensive cosmopolitan, cross-cultural, insight into the perennial controversy over the use of improperly obtained evidence in criminal trials. It will challenge the conventional view that exclusionary rules are idiosyncratic of Anglo-American law, and highlight the 'constitutionalisation' and 'internationalisation' of criminal evidence and procedure as a cause of rapprochement (or divergence) beyond the Anglo-American and Continental law divide. Chapters two and three will concentrate on evidence obtained by search and seizure, telephone interceptions and other means of electronic surveillance. Chapter two will bring to the surface surprising convergence between the United States and Greek exclusionary rules. Chapter three will offer the contrasting view of discretionary exclusion, endorsed by France and England and Wales. Chapter four will highlight emerging rapprochement in relation to the exclusion of confessional evidence obtained in violation of custodial interrogation rights, whilst chapter five will pinpoint unique potential for European Court of Human Rights (ECHR) jurisprudence, in parallel with EU legislation, to build consensus in this respect.

The book will systematically review exclusionary rules vis-à-vis the operation of judicial discretion, and will explore the normative justifications that underpin them. In chapter six, the book will attempt to reinvigorate the idea of excluding evidence to protect constitutional or human rights, arguing that there is significant scope for Anglo-American and Continental legal systems to place a renewed emphasis on it, particularly in relation to confessional evidence obtained in violation of custodial interrogation rights, in light of a unique combination of developments in domestic and international law, with recent ECHR jurisprudence and EU procedural rights directives showing the way. This will be in marked contrast to remaining divergence with regards to evidence obtained by privacy violations, leading to the conclusion that there is little momentum to adopt a reinvigorated rights thesis more widely.

It must be added that the book adopts a rights-centred approach, but does not push forward a model exclusionary rule. Recognising that different legal systems have different stress resistance levels to human rights pressures for reform, it

[60] Béliveau and Pradel make this point in the context of a comparison between Canadian and French law. P Béliveau and J Pradel, *La justice pénale dans les droits canadien et français* (2007) 206.

simply aspires to generate a renewed interest in the rights thesis and calls upon legal systems to give rights considerations due weight when determining the admissibility of improperly obtained evidence, regardless of whether they rely on exclusionary rules or exclusionary discretion.

The law of England and Wales, France, Greece and the United States will be systematically compared and contrasted throughout this book, but, where appropriate, analysis will extend to other Anglo-American and Continental legal systems, including Belgium, Canada, Germany, Ireland, Portugal, Switzerland and international criminal courts. The wider ambition of the book is for the contextual analysis undertaken in connection with these legal systems to provide a case study in, and generate further reflection on, the place and role of constitutional and human rights in the criminal process, and facilitate cross-cultural dialogue in that respect.

2

Exclusionary Rules for Evidence Obtained in Violation of the Right to Privacy: Greece and the United States

In one of his more recent, ever fascinating, excursions on Anglo-American and European Continental law, Mirjan Damaška observed that some national criminal procedure systems adopt a 'very strict' approach to improperly obtained evidence, 'demanding that credible but illegally obtained evidence be automatically rejected, no matter how important and reliable it might be'.[1] Damaška cited Greece as an example of this strict legal regime on the European Continent, observing that it would be worth exploring '[w]hether Greek (and some other) courts always follow this approach in processing most serious crimes'.[2] He also quickly pointed out that the vast majority of national criminal procedures, either Anglo-American or Continental, opt instead for a balancing approach.[3] In *Evidence Law Adrift*, Damaška had similarly observed that the rejection of illegal evidence was seldom mandatory in Continental countries, and that the Continental fact-finder's freedom of proof levelled a powerful argument against rejection of illegally obtained evidence.[4] In this lack of a mandatory approach in Continental systems, Damaška saw 'a significant difference vis-à-vis the exclusionary regime of many common law jurisdictions'.[5] The comparison of the automatic exclusionary rules of Greece and the United States in this chapter will put into perspective Damaška's empirical observations. Though the discussion will not offer an evaluation of the exact popularity of automatic exclusionary rules in comparative law, it will address the possible misconception that they are a rare local peculiarity.[6] In bringing to

[1] M Damaška, 'The Competing Visions of Fairness: The Basic Choice for International Criminal Tribunals' (2011) 36 *North Carolina Journal of International Law and Commercial Regulation* 365, 384.

[2] ibid 384.

[3] ibid 385.

[4] M Damaška, *Evidence Law Adrift* (New Haven and London, Yale University Press, 1997) 23–24.

[5] ibid 24.

[6] Amongst American commentators in particular, there is a strongly held view that the automatic exclusionary rule is idiosyncratic to the United States, an American innovation that has influenced the development of similar rules in other foreign legal systems. See, eg, J Kaplan, 'The Limits of the Exclusionary Rule' (1974) 26 *Stanford Law Review* 1027, 1031; J Langbein, *Comparative Criminal Procedure: Germany* (St Paul, Minnesota, West Pub Co, American Casebook Series, 1977) 69; Office of Legal Policy, *Report to the Attorney General on the Search and Seizure Exclusionary Rule*, Truth in Criminal

light the significant automatic exclusionary rules of Greece, this discussion will also challenge the conventional view that exclusionary rules are idiosyncratic to Anglo-American law and adversarial criminal procedure, or that the Continental principle of 'free proof' leaves no space for exclusionary rules in European countries rooted in the inquisitorial tradition,[7] allegedly leading to illegally obtained evidence being generally admitted there.[8] This discussion will also bring to light the variable nature of such exclusionary rules and the exclusionary rationales that underpin them, the significant differences in application in practice and the effect of resistance – judicial and political – to the continued operation of automatic exclusionary rules.

I. Prolegomena on the Link Between Constitutionalisation and Automatic Exclusionary Rules

The legal systems of the United States and Greece derive from distinct legal traditions, the former being a significant representative of the Anglo-American

Justice Report No 2, 26 February 1986, available in (1988–1989) 22 *University of Michigan Law Reform* 573, 579; CM Bradley, *The Failure of the Criminal Procedure Revolution* (Philadelphia, University of Pennsylvania Press, 1993) 96; L Crocker, 'Can the Exclusionary Rule Be Saved?' (1993) 84 *The Journal of Criminal Law & Criminology* 310; M Reynolds, 'Why Stop Halfway?' (1995) *National Review* 59, 60; A Liptak, 'American Exception – US is Alone in Rejecting All Evidence if Police Err' (2000) *The New York Times*, 19 July; G Reamey, 'The American Exclusionary Rule Experience' in F Höpfel and B Huber, *Beweisverbote in Ländern der EU und vergleichbaren Rechtsordungen, Exclusion of Evidence Within the EU and Beyond*, Europäisches Kolloquium Wien, 18–20 September 1997 (Freiburg, Iuscrim edns, 1999) 191, 201; M Bloom and E Dewey, 'When Rights Become Empty Promises: Promoting an Exclusionary Rule that Vindicates Personal Rights' [2011] *Irish Jurist* 38; D Gray, 'A Spectacular Non Sequitur: The Supreme Court's Contemporary Fourth Amendment Exclusionary Rule Jurisprudence' (2013) 50 *American Criminal Law Review* 1, 14; C Slobogin, 'The Exclusionary Rule: Is it on Its Way Out? Should It Be?' (2013) 10 *Ohio State Journal of Criminal Law* 341, 353. See also Chief Justice Warren Burger's dissenting opinion in *Bivens v Six Unknown Named Agents of Federal Bureau of Narcotics*, 403 US 388, 411 (1971), where he stated that the exclusionary rule is 'unique to American jurisprudence'; *Sanchez Llamas v Oregon*, 548 US 331, 343–44 (2006), citing approvingly Burger's opinion in *Bivens* and noting, in addition, that the exclusionary rule is 'a remedy that nearly all [countries] refuse to recognize as a matter of national law'. But there are notable exceptions of American scholars, such as Craig Bradley, Stephen Thaman and, more recently, Charles Weisselberg who have undertaken significant comparative studies of exclusionary rules in Continental countries. See generally CM Bradley, 'The Exclusionary Rule in Germany' (1983) 96 *Harvard Law Review* 1032–66; CM Bradley, '*Mapp* Goes Abroad' (2001–02) 52 *Case Western Law Review* 375; SC Thaman, '"Fruits of the Poisonous Tree" in Comparative Law' (2010) 16 *Southwestern Journal of International Law* 333; SC Thaman (ed), *Exclusionary Rules in Comparative Law* (Heidelberg, Springer, 2013); C Weisselberg, 'Exporting and Importing *Miranda*' (2017) 97 *Boston University Law Review* 1235.

[7] Jackson and Summers describe, and argue against, this 'dichotomy' that is 'commonly invoked by evidence scholars'. JD Jackson and SJ Summers, *The Internationalisation of Criminal Evidence – Beyond the Common Law and Civil Law Traditions* (Cambridge, Cambridge University Press, 2012) 28. For an early account of the view that exclusionary rules are unique to the common law see JB Thayer, *A Preliminary Treatise on Evidence at the Common Law* (Boston, Little, Brown, 1898) 2.

[8] See, eg, Langbein, *Comparative Criminal Procedure* (1977) 69.

tradition and adversarial criminal procedure,[9] while the latter takes its roots in the Roman-German legal tradition of Continental Europe,[10] relies on a pre-trial criminal process that is symptomatic of inquisitorial or non-adversarial procedure,[11] and has no history of an 'Americanisation' of its criminal procedure system; on the contrary, we can trace strong resistance to incorporating elements of the American criminal process, with plea bargaining a notable example.[12] It is therefore the unexpected convergence of Greece and the United States around automatic exclusionary rules that provides the main justification for their analytical comparison in this chapter.

More specifically, the two countries have long adopted identical exclusionary rules for evidence obtained in violation of the right to privacy; rules that were constitutional, automatic and absolute, and that gave the court no leeway to admit reliable evidence once a breach of the constitutional right to privacy had been established. As this chapter will thoroughly document, the development of these converging solutions was underpinned by a dynamic process of constitutionalisation of criminal procedure, whereby constitutional legislation and jurisprudence influence the development of criminal procedural rules.[13] In the United States, exclusionary rules have emerged under the undeniable influence of the Bill of Rights, 'this great American legal text',[14] whose applications to criminal law means it can be perceived as a 'mini-Code of criminal procedure'[15] and whose key objective is 'to limit and qualify the powers of government', to use the words of James Madison.[16] These rights guard 'sometimes against the abuse of the executive power, sometimes against the legislative, and, in some cases, against the community itself; or, in other words, against the majority in favor of the minority'.[17] In Greece,

[9] R David and CJ Spinosi, *Les grands systèmes de droit contemporains*, Précis Dalloz, 10th edn (Paris, Dalloz, 1992) 329; A Garapon and I Papadopoulos, *Juger en Amérique et en France* (Paris, Odile-Jacob, 2003) 47; H Patrick Glenn, *Legal Traditions of the World*, 2nd edn (Oxford, Oxford University Press, 2004) 248; G Fletcher and S Sheppard, *American Law in a Global Context: The Basics* (Oxford, Oxford University Press, 2005).

[10] S Vrellis, *Comparative law* (Athens-Komotini, AN Sakkoulas, 1988) 75 (in Greek); X Deligianni-Dimitrakou, *Introduction to comparative law* (Athens-Thessaloniki, Sakkoulas, 1997) 77 (in Greek).

[11] A Karras, *Penal procedural law*, 4th edn (Athens, Nomiki Bibliothiki, 2011) 18 (in Greek).

[12] See generally N Androulakis, 'A change of paradigm in the criminal trial?' (2016) 7 *Poiniki Dikeosini* 545 (in Greek).

[13] J-F Seuvic, 'Forces et faiblesses de la constitutionnalisation substantielle et formelle du droit pénal' in Cour de cassation, *La procédure pénale en quête de cohérence* (Paris, Dalloz, 2007) 111, 112. See also K Martin-Chenut and F De Melo e Silva, 'La constitutionnalisation/conventionnalisation du droit de la preuve' in G Giudicelli-Delage (ed), *Les transformations de l'administration de la preuve pénale: perspectives comparées* (Paris, Société de législation comparée, 2006) 31.

[14] Garapon and Papadopoulos, *Juger en Amérique et en France* (2003) 47.

[15] Martin-Chenut and De Melo e Silva, 'La constitutionnalisation/conventionnalisation du droit de la preuve' in Giudicelli-Delage, *Les transformations de l'administration de la preuve pénale* (2006) 37. See also S Simmons, 'The Warren Court and Civil Liberties' (1973–75) 18 *Howard Law Journal* 610, 626.

[16] James Madison, Speech proposing the Bill of Rights, 8 June 1789 in *American History – From Revolution to Reconstruction and Beyond*, www.let.rug.nl/usa/documents/1786-1800/madison-speech-proposing-the-bill-of-rights-june-8-1789.php.

[17] ibid.

exclusionary rules have likewise derived from within a robust Bill of Rights culture, which conceptualised individual rights as 'limits of the rights of the State against the individual' or guarantees of 'individual liberty against arbitrary interference' by the State.[18] A culture of individual rights dates back to the time of the Revolution against the Ottoman empire, nearly 200 years ago, and the enactment of the constitutional charters that followed it.[19] With the exception of the period of dictatorship by the Colonels, nearly all Greek constitutional charters reinforced that Bill of Rights culture, with the individual rights provisions of the Constitution of 1975, which are currently in action, seen as providing 'pioneering protection vis-à-vis all European constitutions'.[20] This culture has impacted so drastically upon the principles, spirit and institutions of Greek criminal procedure[21] that we now perceive the latter as 'applied constitutional law'.[22]

It is in this Bill of Rights context that the supreme courts in both the United States and Greece devised an improperly obtained evidence theory as early as the end of the nineteenth century, taking the major step of reading a strict exclusionary rule into the Constitution. Their jurisprudence marks the first stage in the historic development of exclusionary rules there. But in a second stage, the exclusionary rule was in both countries separated from the Constitution. This second evolutionary stage manifested itself in different eras in the United States and Greece: between the 1950s and the beginning of the 1960s in the former, between the 1960s and the beginning of the 1990s in the latter. The United States was then first to enter a crucial third stage in the constitutionalisation of the exclusionary rule, marked by the recognition of the constitutional nature of the Fourth Amendment exclusionary rule with the seminal Supreme Court judgment in *Mapp v Ohio*.[23] This was a momentous development that was emphatically reproduced in Greece 40 years later, with the introduction in 2001 of a strict exclusionary rule into the text of the Constitution (article 19, para 3). Despite happening at different moments in time, these three stages in the evolution of exclusionary rules in Greece and the United States speak volumes about the level of converging solutions conceived there, and, more generally, provide an illustration of the constitutionalisation phenomenon as a cause of convergence of evidential regimes beyond the common law and civil law divide.

This historic perspective also allows for the identification of the reasons for the existence of some fundamental differences between the Greek and United States exclusionary rules today, in relation to scope, theoretical underpinnings and law

[18] N Saripolos, *Constitutional law system*, Tome B (Athens, 1923) 25–26 (in Greek).

[19] The Constitutions of Epidaurus of 1822, Astros of 1823 and Trizina of 1827. See K Chrisogonos, *Individual and social rights*, 2nd edn (Athens-Komotini, AN Sakkoulas, 2002) 8 (in Greek).

[20] I Varvitsiotis, Parliamentary debates archives, Period I, Session A, 24 January 2001, 96.

[21] K Konstantinidis, *Criminal law and human dignity* (Athens-Komotini, AN Sakkoulas, 1987) 33 (in Greek); A Charalampakis, 'Constitution and criminal law' [2000] *Syntagma* 93 (in Greek).

[22] N Androulakis, *Fundamental notions of the criminal process*, 2nd edn (Athens-Komotini, AN Sakkoulas, 1994) 33 (in Greek).

[23] *Mapp v Ohio*, 367 US 343, 81 SCt 1684, 6 Led2d 1081 (1961).

in action. This divergence is mainly due to the United States entering a fourth – and final until now – evolutionary stage in the constitutionalisation of the exclusionary rule (a deconstitutionalisation stage). This was initiated with the transition from the Warren Court to the Burger Court, and the relentless assault that the Burger, Rehnquist and Roberts Courts have waged against the Fourth Amendment exclusionary rule, radically transforming its nature, reach, theoretical basis and effect. The exclusionary rule devised in *Mapp* has now long been deprived of its Fourth Amendment constitutional basis, while its application has been subjected to wide-ranging exceptions deriving from the ever-present – and ever-devouring of the rule's 'original' scope – deterrence rationale. In fact, many commentators in the United States view the recent exclusionary rule jurisprudence of the Roberts Court as signalling the beginning of the end for *Mapp*.[24] Even those optimistic enough to argue that the rule will survive the continued attacks of the Supreme Court do recognise that the rule has reached the nadir of its long constitutional history.[25] Against this backdrop, Greece offers a timely counterpoint of a Continental legal system that has written into the Constitution a strict and protective rationale-orientated exclusionary rule, even though here too we will find resistance. This observation might intrigue American commentators, especially those critical of the Supreme Court's departure from the spirit of *Mapp*. The study of the Greek exclusionary rule might thus reveal a previously hidden vista from which to analyse current developments in the United States. Conversely, Greek commentators supporting a turn towards a more qualified approach to exclusion will find a helpful point of reference in the United States.

The comparison between the contemporary – more limited – version of the exclusionary rule in the United States and the more far-reaching exclusionary rules in Greece will also shed light on some of the different types of categorical exclusionary rules that exist in comparative law today. In addition, the comparison will bring into focus the procedural, institutional and historical context in which automatic exclusionary rules evolve, and the different 'protagonists' – parties and types of evidence – that take centre stage in this process, while it will underline the constant movement towards and away from the rigorous exclusionary position, mainly as a result of changing judicial and legislative attitudes and the mutating socio-economic and political conditions that underpin them. Put differently, it will be demonstrated here that the link between constitutionalisation and automatic exclusionary rules is not linear. The relationship is equivocal. Changes in the balance of powers in a supreme court or in the political equilibrium more

[24] See, eg, E de Golian, '*Davis* and the Good Faith Exception: Pushing Exclusion to Extinction?' (2011–12) 63 *Mercer Law Review* 751; CM Bradley, 'Is the Exclusionary Rule Dead?' (2012) 102 *Journal of Criminal Law & Criminology* 1; AE Taslitz, 'Hypocrisy, Corruption and Illegitimacy: Why Judicial Integrity Justifies the Exclusionary Rule' (2013) 10 *Ohio State Journal of Criminal Law* 419, 420.

[25] See, eg, TK Clancy, 'The Fourth Amendment Exclusionary Rule as a Constitutional Right' (2013) 10 *Ohio State Journal of Criminal Law* 357, 358.

generally, from more to less liberal and vice versa, calibrate the effect of constitutionalisation upon the nature – automatic or otherwise – of the exclusionary rule.

II. Reading the Exclusionary Rule into the Constitution

The Fourth Amendment protects citizens against intrusions into their privacy.[26] Article 19, para 1 and Article 9 of the Greek Constitution, respectively, protect the right to secrecy of correspondence and the sanctity of a person's home and inviolability of their private and family life. The United States Supreme Court (hereinafter Supreme Court) and Arios Pagos – the Cassation Court in Greece – have read the automatic exclusionary rule into these broadly based privacy rights, through a series of pivotal decisions dating back to the end of the nineteenth and the first part of the twentieth century. This 'original' exclusionary rule jurisprudence is of paramount importance for the analysis of the modern transformations of the exclusionary rule.

A. The Original Jurisprudence

The long history of the Fourth Amendment exclusionary rule starts in 1886 with *Boyd v United States*,[27] where the Supreme Court held that the admission in evidence of a shipping invoice that the defendants had been ordered to produce, in breach of the Fourth and Fifth Amendments, was erroneous and unconstitutional, and this despite the fact that, as the Court recognised, this case lacked many of the aggravating factors of unreasonable search and seizure.[28] This, the Court insisted, was the only way to adhere to the rule that 'constitutional provisions for the security of person and property should be liberally construed'.[29] In fact, the liberal construction of the Fourth and Fifth Amendments was seen as so progressive in this case that – a whole 80 years later – Justice Hugo Black did not hesitate to call it 'one among the greatest constitutional decisions' of the Supreme Court.[30] And yet, in the immediate aftermath of *Boyd*, state courts remained faithful to the general admissibility rule that had been established under the common law,[31] while, in 1904, the Supreme Court reaffirmed the common law

[26] C Whitebread and C Slobogin, *Criminal Procedure – An Analysis of Cases and Concepts* (New York, University Textbook Series, 2000) 17.

[27] *Boyd v United States*, 116 US 616 (1886).

[28] ibid 635.

[29] ibid.

[30] *Schmerber v California*, 383 US 757, 776 (1966), *per* Black J (dissenting opinion).

[31] See, eg, O Fraenkel, 'Concerning Searches and Seizures' (1920–21) 34 *Harvard Law Review* 361, 368–69; JH Wigmore, 'Using Evidence Obtained by Illegal Search and Seizure' (1922) 8 *American Bar Association Journal* 479.

position in *Adams v New York*.[32] As Justice Potter Stewart noted, writing extra-judicially, this development 'seemed to bury the exclusionary rule – even before its birth was recognised'.[33]

But the effect of *Adams* proved too ephemeral to put a halt to the development of the exclusionary rule thesis. In *Weeks v United States*,[34] the Supreme Court broke new ground, by reading the rule into the Fourth Amendment, without this time having to rely on the 'intimate relation'[35] of the Fourth and Fifth Amendments. In *Weeks*, the evidence in question had been obtained 'in direct violation of the Constitutional rights of the defendant',[36] as a result of the police entering into the house of the defendant without a warrant, in his absence, and seizing private papers and other property.[37] The Court reversed the conviction, on the basis that the use of the unconstitutionally obtained evidence had led to 'a denial of the constitutional rights of the accused'.[38] Put differently, the unconstitutional obtaining of the evidence was necessarily resulting in its unconstitutional use. The use was in itself a violation of the Fourth Amendment. It 'posed an inherent contradiction to the Fourth Amendment itself, reducing the right to a nullity'.[39] Justice Brennan perfectly summarised *Weeks*' 'original basis' for the exclusionary rule, by observing that the Fourth Amendment 'comprises a personal right to exclude all evidence secured by means of unreasonable searches and seizures. The right to be free from the initial invasion of privacy and the right of exclusion are coordinate components of the central embracing right to be free from unreasonable searches and seizures'.[40] In other words, the rule's original understanding was that the exclusionary rule is inherent in the Fourth Amendment.

Weeks' emphasis on the need to preserve constitutional rights against governmental intrusions through exclusion was not welcome in all quarters, though. One of the most prominent critics of the exclusionary rule, Dean Wigmore, spoke of a misplaced individualistic sentimentality towards the Fourth Amendment, stimulated by the repressive war measures of the years 1917–19.[41] In his view, there was no justification, either historic or normative, for the Supreme Court's departure from 'the fundamental principle that *an illegality in the mode of procuring evidence is no ground for excluding it*'.[42] Here, it is evident that the controversy surrounding the American exclusionary rule is as old as the rule itself. In this first period of historic development of the rule though, it did not seem to affect the

[32] *Adams v New York* 192 US 585 (1904).

[33] P Stewart, 'The Road to Mapp v Ohio and Beyond: The Origins, Development and Future of the Exclusionary Rule in Search-and-Seizure Cases' (1983) 83 *Columbia Law Review* 1365, 1374.

[34] *Weeks v United States*, 232 US 383 (1914).

[35] *Boyd v United States*, 116 US 616, 633 (1886).

[36] *Weeks v United State*, 232 US 383, 398 (1914).

[37] ibid 384.

[38] ibid 398.

[39] Gray, 'A Spectacular Non Sequitur' (2013) 15.

[40] *United States v Leon*, 468 US 897, 935 (1984), *per* Brennan J (dissenting opinion).

[41] Wigmore, 'Illegal Search and Seizure' (1922) 480.

[42] ibid 482.

Supreme Court's willingness to provide a solid constitutional foundation for the latter. In the 1920s, the Court first removed some procedural limitations of the doctrine – notably the requirement for a timely pre-trial application for the return of the unconstitutionally seized property[43] – then directly extended its scope,[44] and it continued to develop the exclusionary rule around *Weeks*' original understanding until the beginning of the 1950s.[45] During this period, the exclusionary rule was a sanction *provided by law* against the flouting of the Fourth Amendment.[46] The Court recognised that the 'striking outcome' of *Weeks* was that, although not referring to the use of evidence in court, the Fourth Amendment 'really forbade its introduction, if obtained by government officers through a violation of the amendment'.[47] Exclusion was 'compelled' by 'a direct constitutional command'.[48] No other justification was required.

Like in the United States, the origins of contemporary Greek exclusionary rules can be traced back to nineteenth-century case law developed in the context of the right to privacy. Faced with the question of whether unconstitutionally seized private letters could be used in court, Arios Pagos held for the first time in 1871 – 15 years prior to the decision of the Supreme Court in *Boyd*[49] – that the use of such evidence was forbidden by the constitutional right to secrecy of correspondence,[50] a specific expression of the right to privacy.[51] Put differently, Arios Pagos read into the right to secrecy of correspondence an automatic exclusionary rule of evidence obtained in violation of this right.[52] Considering that the question of the way in which evidence had been obtained could not be separated from the question of its evidential use, Arios Pagos repeatedly reached this conclusion in many cases that

[43] See *Gouled v United States*, 255 US 298 (1921); *Amos v United States*, 255 US 313 (1921).

[44] The *Weeks* exclusionary rule was no longer limited to documentary evidence. See *Amos v United States*, ibid; *Agnelo v United States* 269 US 20 (1925). After the decision of the Supreme Court in *Silverthorne Lumber Co v United States* 251 US 385 (1920), which instituted the fruit of the poisonous tree doctrine, *Weeks* also applied to unconstitutionally obtained derivative evidence.

[45] See *Goldstein v United States*, 316 US 114, 120 (1942); *Harris v United States*, 331 US 145, 155 (1947); *United States v Wallace & Tierman*, 336 US 793, 799 (1949).

[46] *McDonald v United States*, 335 US 451, 453 (1948).

[47] *Olmstead v United States*, 277 US 438, 462 (1928) *per* Taft CJ.

[48] *United States v Leon*, 468 US 897, 938-39 (1984), *per* Brennan J (dissenting opinion).

[49] 116 US 616 (1886).

[50] Arios Pagos 89/1871, 6 Ellinikoi Kodikes 165.

[51] The right is protected by art 19 of the Constitution, which states that 'the secrecy of letters and all other forms of free correspondence or communication shall be absolutely inviolable'. See generally P Paulopoulos, 'Technological evolution and constitutional rights: the modern adventures of secrecy of correspondence' (1987) 35 *Nomiko Bima* 1511 (in Greek); S Tsakirakis, 'Secrecy of correspondence: absolutely inviolable or a wish of the legal order' (1993) 41 *Nomiko Bima* 995 (in Greek); G Kaminis, 'Secrecy of telephone communication: constitutional protection and its application from the criminal law legislator and the courts' (1995) 43 *Nomiko Bima* 505 (in Greek); P Tsiris, *The constitutional protection of the right to secrecy of correspondence* (Athens-Komitini, AN Sakkoulas, 2002) 72–73 (in Greek); D Giannoulopoulos, 'Protecting the Right to Secrecy of Correspondence: Constitutional Myths and Reality in Modern Greece' (2006) 9 *Mediterranean Journal of Human Rights* 119.

[52] G Kaminis, *Illegally obtained evidence and constitutional guarantees of human rights (the exclusion of evidence in criminal and civil proceedings)* (Athens-Komotini, AN Sakkoulas, 1998) 23, 25 (in Greek).

followed.[53] As succinctly put by the General Prosecutor of Arios Pagos, the original jurisprudence of the Court meant that the right to secrecy of correspondence forbade 'the seizure or unsealing of letters as well as the use of their content with the aim of discovering and proving the commission of crimes'.[54] The similarities with the jurisprudence of the Supreme Court are striking: neither the text of the Fourth Amendment nor the text of the Greek Constitution provided for exclusion, but an exclusionary rule was seen as constitutionally mandated in both cases. The exclusionary rule was part and parcel of the constitutional right to privacy.

At the same time that Arios Pagos was recognising a progressive exclusionary rule, however, it was reading the right to secrecy of correspondence narrowly. The seizure of unsealed letters was held not to amount to a breach of the right to secrecy of correspondence,[55] while the right ceased to produce its protective effect after the delivery of a letter to its addressee, particularly where it was demonstrated that the addressee had become aware of its content.[56] In other words, Arios Pagos' pro-exclusion rhetoric was deprived of much effect in practice. An analogy can be drawn with the *Weeks* exclusionary rule whose scope was also quite limited when the rule was first instituted. However, this takes nothing away from the novel and liberal jurisprudence that introduced these exclusionary rules. It suffices to take note of the position of the common law at the time that the United States and Greece first recognised an extrinsic constitutional exclusionary rule, which was that the method of obtaining criminal evidence was in no way connected to admitting evidence in court.[57] With all their weaknesses, the first judgments of the Supreme Court and Arios Pagos on unconstitutionally obtained evidence had made significant theoretical advancements away from this position.

B. The Original Jurisprudence Abandoned

The *Weeks* exclusionary rule was limited to federal prosecutions only. The Fourth Amendment was not applying to the states at the time *Weeks* was decided, and so

[53] See, eg, Arios Pagos 70/1891, B′ Themis 345; 169/1893, Δ′ Themis 388; 76/1894, E′ Themis 278; 23/1909, K′ Themis 130; 102/1935, MΣT′ Themis 857.

[54] K Kollias, Legal opinion No 31/1952, 3 *Poinika Chronika* 457.

[55] See Court of Appeal of Athens 235/1920, ΛA′ Themis 484: 'It is not permitted to seize or adduce evidence of letters in court … and it is not possible to make any use of their content … However, this strict version of the inviolability [of the right to secrecy of correspondence] doctrine does not apply in relation to letters in possession of the addressees who can adduce them as evidence'. See also Arios Pagos 70/1891, B′ Themis 345; Arios Pagos 169/1893, Δ′ Themis 388; Arios Pagos 76/1894, E′ Themis 278; Arios Pagos 23/1909, K′ Themis 130; Arios Pagos 96/1919, Λ′ Themis 298; The Court of first instance of Athens 357/1923, KΓ′ Themis 14; Arios Pagos 347/1924, ΛE′ Themis 535; Arios Pagos 189/1933, MΔ′ Themis 724; Arios Pagos 102/1935, MΣT′ Themis 857; Arios Pagos 581/1939, NA′ Themis 181; Arios Pagos 861/1947, NH′ Themis 581.

[56] N Saripolos, *Constitutional law system* (Athens-Komotini, Classic Legal Library, 1987) 94; originally published in 1923 (in Greek).

[57] *R v Leatham* (1861) 8 Cox CC 498, 501.

the exclusionary rule could not apply either. But even when the Fourth Amendment was finally incorporated in the Due Process Clause of the Fourteenth Amendment with *Wolf v Colorado*,[58] and was thus made applicable to the states, the Supreme Court rejected *Weeks'* central notion that the exclusionary rule was an integral part of the Amendment. In this way, the Supreme Court incorporated and applied the Fourth Amendment without the exclusionary rule. Justice Frankfurter, who wrote the opinion of the Court in *Wolf*, justified this outcome by noting that the ruling in *Weeks* 'was not derived from the explicit requirements of the Fourth Amendment', but was rather 'a matter of judicial implication'.[59] Justice Black likewise denied the constitutional nature of the federal exclusionary rule, by noting that it was 'not a command of the Fourth Amendment, but … a judicially created rule of evidence which Congress might negate'.[60] Put differently, in *Wolf* the Supreme Court abandoned its original exclusionary rule jurisprudence, and continued to rely on the states to give effect to the Fourth Amendment through adopting or rejecting the exclusionary rule. As Lewis Katz put it, this meant that 'in about two-thirds of the states, police were free to violate fundamental constitutional rights without consequences',[61] since about two-thirds of the states had not adopted, at the time of *Wolf*, an exclusionary rule under their own constitutions.[62] In fact, this curious coexistence of a strict exclusionary rule at the federal level with exclusionary remedies of variable nature and application at state level quickly undermined the effect of *Wolf*. A number of important decisions in the 1950s,[63] coupled with relevant jurisprudential developments in the states,[64] opened the way for the reaffirmation of *Weeks* and the extension of the constitutional exclusionary rule to the states with *Mapp v Ohio*,[65] the 1961 Supreme Court decision that until this day is at the centre of Fourth Amendment exclusionary rule jurisprudence.

In Greece, the rise of telephone communication and greater availability of technology facilitating the covert recording of private conversations, telephone or other, in the 1950s led to an explosion in the use of covertly obtained recordings in civil and criminal trials.[66] It is at this time that Arios Pagos abandoned the original jurisprudence, turning conformity with criminal law, rather than with

[58] *Wolf v Colorado*, 338 US 25 (1949).

[59] ibid 28.

[60] ibid 40.

[61] L Katz, 'Mapp After Forty Years: Its Impact on Race in America', Symposium on the fortieth anniversary of *Mapp v Ohio* (2001) 52 *Case Western Reserve Law Review* 471, 472. See also F Allen, 'Federalism and the Fourth Amendment: A Requiem for Wolf' (1961) *Supreme Court Review* 1.

[62] See *Wolf v Colorado*, 338 US 25, 38 (1949).

[63] See *Rochin v California*, 342 US 165 (1952); *Irvine v California*, 347 US 128 (1954); *Elkins v United States*, 364 US 206 (1960).

[64] See, eg, *People v Cahan*, 44 Cal2d 434 (1955).

[65] *Mapp v Ohio*, 367 US 643, 81 SCt 1684, 6 LEd2d 1081 (1961).

[66] See A Psarouda-Benaki, 'The tape recorder in the criminal trial and the need to protect oral speech' (1965) 15 *Poinika Chronika* 397 (in Greek).

the Constitution, into the main criterion for admissibility.[67] More specifically, telephone taps and recordings of face-to-face private conversations were admissible in court under the condition that they had not been obtained by the commission of a criminal offence. Article 370A of the Penal Code proscribed the covert recording of conversations between third parties, but, crucially, this provision did not extend to recordings made by one of the parties to the conversation.[68] When it was one of the parties that covertly recorded the conversation without the consent of the other(s), the recording was admissible, since no criminal offence had been committed.[69] Such recordings were not barred by the Constitution either, after Arios Pagos held, in an important decision in 1969, that the right to secrecy of correspondence did not have horizontal effect. It limited the state only and did not apply to interference by private individuals.[70] The above developments thus contributed to a regime of wide admissibility of tape-recorded conversations in criminal[71] and civil[72] trials, which remained intact until the beginning of the 1990s.

The departure of Arios Pagos from its original jurisprudence was underpinned by the development of a so-called 'theory of balancing'. Following German legal doctrine on this point (*Abwägungslehre*), Greek criminal law scholars accepted that the exclusion of improperly obtained evidence should be determined upon a balancing of competing interests. The interest in not-condoning rights-violations should be balanced against the interest in efficiently combating crime,

[67] A Charalampakis, 'The punishable nature of interceptions' (2002) 50 *Nomiko Bima* 1061, 1065 (in Greek).

[68] Arios Pagos 717/1984, 34 Poinika Chronika 1030, 1031.

[69] Kaminis, *Illegally Obtained Evidence* (1998) 29–30.

[70] See Arios Pagos 60/1969, 17 Nomiko Bima 562. See also General Prosecutor of Arios Pagos, Legal Opinion No 8/1972, 20 Nomiko Bima 1120; Arios Pagos 1002/1977, 27 Poinika Chronika 456. Many commentators argued, contra, that the act of covertly recording private conversations was always a violation of the Constitution, independently of whether it was the State or private individuals who were responsible for it. They were deducing from this that covertly obtained recordings should not be used in court. See K Stamatis, Opinion of the Prosecutor of the Court of Arios Pagos in Arios Pagos 717/1984, 34 Poinika Chronika 1030 at 1033. See also Court of Appeal of Thessaloniki 189/1981, 32 Poinika Chronika 552 at 553, where the Court of Appeal held that 'a voice recording without the knowledge of the person whose words are recorded – irrespective of who undertakes it (a private individual or a public service, ie the military, the police etc) and irrespective of its objective – constitutes an illegal means of evidence'.

[71] See Arios Pagos 85/1962, 12 Poinika Chronika 338; Arios Pagos 139/1963, 13 Poinika Chronika 345; Arios Pagos 571/1970, 21 Poinika Chronika 159; Arios Pagos 240/1974, 24 Poinika Chronika 53; Arios Pagos 717/1984, 34 Poinika Chronika 1030; Arios Pagos 1283/1985, 36 Poinika Chronika 283; Arios Pagos 26/1986, 34 Nomiko Bima 586; Judicial chamber of the Court of Appeal of Athens 187/1985, 33 Nomiko Bima 1467; Judicial chamber of the Court of first instance of Kilkis 50/1986, 11 Armenopoulos 1002; Arios Pagos 1150/1989, 37 Nomiko Bima 1264.

[72] Covertly obtained recordings were being regularly admitted mainly in divorce proceedings until the beginning of the 1990s. See Arios Pagos 673/1983, 14 Diki 445; Arios Pagos 381/1987, 36 Nomiko Bima 563. See also Charalampakis, 'The punishable nature of interceptions' (2002) 1065; Tz Iliopoulou-Stragga, 'The use of illegally obtained evidence to prove the defendant's innocence after the revision (2001) of the Constitution' (2002) 2 *Poinikos Logos* 2175, 2180–81 (in Greek).

on a case-by-case basis.[73] This balancing exercise would give courts flexibility, allowing them to avoid 'predetermined legal formulae'[74] incapable of tracking the infinitely variable circumstances of relevant cases. Some commentators were also of the view that the Constitution itself dictated a balancing approach,[75] and that truth discovery was a principle of constitutional nature,[76] leading to the argument that the conflict between the pursuit of truth and the protection of individual rights could not be resolved *ex ante* and *in abstracto*, but only through a judicial balancing exercise *in concreto*.[77]

In abandoning their original 'constitutional exclusionary rule' jurisprudence in this second stage of historic development, both the Supreme Court and Arios Pagos left the exclusionary rule in limbo. In the United States, the protection of the Fourth Amendment was left upon the discretion of the states, which could either adopt a version of the federal exclusionary rule or opt for alternative sanctions. In Greece, the use of improperly obtained evidence now entirely depended on how widely or narrowly the legislator would define the scope of relevant criminal law offences. The above offer a first glimpse of the influence of changing judicial attitudes and socio-political conditions on the character and effect of the exclusionary rule, and the variability of responses to the exclusionary rule dilemma thus generated. The constitutionalisation of criminal procedure can create the conditions for the alignment of constitutional rights-based exclusionary rules across legal cultures, but much will ultimately depend on the socio-political conditions on the ground. This is further illustrated by another U-turn in American and Greek exclusionary rule jurisprudence. Entering a third stage of historic development, the supreme jurisdictions of both nations turned their back to graduated and flexible responses, and adopted instead the categorical constitutional exclusionary rules that control the use of improperly obtained evidence still today.

[73] See A Kostaras, 'Do the ends justify the means? Or the procedural evaluation of illegally obtained or illegally used criminal evidence' (1984) *Efimerida Ellinon Nomikon* 169, 178 (in Greek); D Spinellis, 'Evidential prohibitions in the criminal process' (1986) 36 *Poinika Chronika* 865, 880 (in Greek); S Papageorgiou-Gonatas, 'The problem of illegally obtained indirect evidence in the criminal process' (1989) 39 *Poinika Chronika* 545, 554 (in Greek); N Dimitratos, *Evidential prohibitions in the criminal process*, Poinika No 35 (Athens-Komotini, AN Sakkoulas, 1992) 39 (in Greek); Androulakis, *Fundamental notions of the criminal process* (1994) 181 (in Greek); A Tzannetis, 'Evidential prohibitions and alternative legal obtaining of evidence' (1995) 35 *Poinika Chronika* 5, 11 (in Greek); Ch Satlanis, 'Tape recordings as evidence in the criminal process (a parallel contribution to the evidential prohibitions doctrine)' Poinika No 48 (Athens-Komotini, AN Sakkoulas, 1996) 57 (in Greek); Th Dalakouras, 'Prohibited evidence: doctrinal foundations of evidential prohibitions in the criminal process' in Hellenic Association of Criminal Law (ΕΕΠΔ), *Evidence in the criminal process*, Proceedings of the 6th panhellenic conference (PN Sakkoulas, Athens, 1998) 60 (in Greek).

[74] See Kostaras, 'Do the ends justify the means?' (ibid) 178.

[75] On the basis of art 96, para 1 and art 25, para 1 of the Constitution. See Spinellis, 'Evidential prohibitions' (1986) 880; Androulakis, *Fundamental notions of the criminal process* (1994) 181; G Triantafillou, 'Evidential prohibitions and the proportionality principle' (2007) 57 *Poinika Chronika* 295 (in Greek).

[76] Androulakis (ibid).

[77] See Dalakouras, 'Prohibited evidence' (1998) 60.

III. Constitutional Exclusionary Rules

In *Mapp v Ohio*, the Supreme Court recognised a constitutional, automatic and absolute exclusionary rule for Fourth Amendment violations. Greece experienced the same development, though with a forty-year delay. The legislator wrote an automatic and absolute exclusionary rule into the Constitution, explicitly for violations of the right to privacy.

A. The Constitutional Exclusionary Rule of *Mapp v Ohio*

Mapp is arguably one of the most famous and controversial decisions in the history of the Supreme Court.[78] By overruling *Wolf* and returning to *Weeks* and its liberal exclusionary rule jurisprudence, *Mapp* marked the end of an era and the beginning of a new one in the history of the American exclusionary rule.[79] Its significance extended long beyond the confines of the Fourth Amendment. As the first decision to apply to the states the same constitutional criminal procedure standards that restricted the federal government, *Mapp* is rightly seen as the decision that began the Warren Court's criminal procedure revolution of the 1960s,[80] while it was also at the centre of the counter-revolution that followed, this time as a result of Supreme Court decisions that undermined *Mapp's* original meaning.[81]

In *Mapp*, Justice Clark, the author of the six-to-three majority opinion, started his analysis by attacking *Wolf's* main proposition that the exclusionary rule was not part of the Fourth Amendment. 'The plain and unequivocal language of *Weeks* – and its later paraphrase in *Wolf* – to the effect that the *Weeks* rule is of constitutional origin', and not a simple rule of evidence, 'remains entirely undisturbed', he declared.[82] This provided the foundation for the Court's finding that the exclusionary rule was an 'essential part of the right to privacy',[83] which should also be 'insisted upon as an essential ingredient of the right newly recognized by the *Wolf* case'.[84] The exclusionary rule was 'an essential part of both the Fourth and

[78] See J Gallaway, *Criminal Justice and the Burger Court* (New York, Facts on File, 1978) 122; G Calabresi, 'The Exclusionary Rule' (2003) 26 *Harvard Journal of Law & Public Policy* 113; RJ Rychlak, 'Replacing the Exclusionary Rule: Fourth Amendment Violations as Direct Criminal Contempt' (2010) 85 *Chicago-Kent Law Review* 241, 242.

[79] Y Kamisar, 'Does (Did) (Should) the Exclusionary Rule Rest on a "Principled Basis" Rather Than an "Empirical Proposition"' (1983) 16 *Creighton Law Review* 565.

[80] See CM Bradley, *The Failure of the Criminal Procedure Revolution* (University of Pennsylvania Press, Philadelphia, 1993) 18; T Maclin, *The Supreme Court and the Fourth Amendment Exclusionary Rule* (Oxford, Oxford University Press, 2013) 85.

[81] See section V A and B below.

[82] *Mapp v Ohio*, 367 US 343, 349 (1961).

[83] ibid 656.

[84] ibid.

Fourteenth Amendments',[85] the Fourth Amendment's 'most important constitutional privilege'.[86] It was therefore no longer possible to separate the Fourth Amendment from the exclusionary rule. The former applied to the states, and so should the latter, 'by the same sanction of exclusion as [was] used against the Federal Government'.[87] In view of the above, the Court concluded that 'all evidence obtained by searches and seizures in violation of the Constitution [was], by that same authority, inadmissible in a state court'.[88] The exclusionary rule was dictated by the Fourth Amendment, and was a direct product of the constitutionalisation of search and seizure.

The grounding of the exclusionary rule on this direct constitutional mandate meant that no additional theoretical justification was required for its application. Justice Clark still underlined the exclusionary rule's deterrent[89] and judicial integrity[90] purposes. He also characterised alternative sanctions as 'worthless and futile'[91] and argued that the experience of the states with the exclusionary rule was impressive, and that there was no evidence that the application of the federal exclusionary rule for almost half a century had disrupted federal prosecutions.[92] This multiplicity of justificatory bases caused some normative confusion, even amongst 'defenders' of the exclusionary rule, leading them to think that rather than clearly reaffirm the original understanding of the exclusionary rule as defined in *Weeks*, *Mapp* could be read as resting the rule on an empirical foundation.[93] But Kamisar's interpretation – that in trying to 'secure maximum approval for the decision overruling *Wolf*, Justice Clark advanced 'as many reasons for the exclusionary rule as he could find, whether constitutional or pragmatic'[94] – is much more convincing. As he rightly pointed out, *Mapp's* message is that the exclusionary rule is 'a command of the Constitution'; *Mapp* reaffirmed 'the "original understanding" of the exclusionary rule, as explained in *Weeks* and its progeny, that … it is a constitutionally required rule, although not explicitly provided for in the text of the fourth amendment'.[95]

The exclusionary rule that *is* provided for in the text of the Greek Constitution perfectly encapsulates *Mapp's* original understanding.

[85] ibid 657.
[86] ibid 656.
[87] ibid 655.
[88] ibid.
[89] ibid 656, citing *Elkins v United States*, 364 US 206, 217 (1960).
[90] ibid 659, citing *Elkins* (ibid) and *Olmstead v United States*, 277 US 438, 462 (1928).
[91] ibid 652.
[92] ibid 660.
[93] For a detailed analysis see Kamisar, '"Principled Basis"' (1983) 565.
[94] ibid 622–23.
[95] ibid 623. See also B Wilson, *Enforcing the Fourth Amendment – A Jurisprudential History* (New York and London, Garland Publishing, 1986) 100–01.

B. The Greek Constitutional Exclusionary Rule

The 2001 revision of the Greek Constitution placed particular emphasis on the right to privacy.[96] Parliament introduced article 19, para 3 of the Constitution, which states that: 'Use of evidence acquired in violation of the present article [article 19 para 1] and of articles 9 and 9A is prohibited'.

Article 19, para 1 and articles 9 and 9A, respectively, protect the right to secrecy of correspondence, the sanctity of a person's home and inviolability of his private and family life, and place restriction on the use of his personal data. The use of evidence obtained in violation of any of these privacy rights (privacy *lato sensu*) is now constitutionally prohibited. The exclusionary rule contained in article 19, para 3 is an important innovation, when viewed in comparative perspective, since it simultaneously possesses the following three characteristics: it is written in the Constitutional text and is automatic and absolute.

Firstly, the fact that the exclusionary rule is now part and parcel of the Constitution means that the rule has become 'fundamental law' (higher order law) and cannot be abolished by statute or other act of government.[97] Conversely, any statutory legislation infringing this rule must be amended.[98] At a more abstract level, there is a strong symbolism attached to the incorporation of this rule in the constitutional text. Secondly, exclusion under article 19, para 3 is automatic. The rule of exclusion is applied mechanically once the relevant constitutional violation has been established, and the protection of fundamental privacy rights cannot be put in the balance with public interest values. Finally, the exclusionary rule is absolute.[99] The alternative of a less rigid rule was discussed in Parliament, but in

[96] An innovative right to be 'protected from the collection, processing and use, especially by electronic means, of personal data' (art 9A) has been added to the Constitution. Likewise, art 19, para 2 provided for the institution of an independent authority for the protection of secrecy of correspondence. Fourteen out of the 22 articles of Part B of the Constitution, which guarantees individual rights, have been amended. See generally K Chrisogonos, *Individual and social rights*, 2nd edn (Athens-Komotini, AN Sakkoulas, 2002) 12 (in Greek).

[97] Abolition or amendment is possible only through the complex process of constitutional revision. See art 110 of the Constitution. The Constitution of 1975 has so far been revised three times, in 1986, 2001 and 2008.

[98] Charalampakis, 'The punishable nature of interceptions' (2002) 1067; E Venizelos, '*The constitutional acquis*' – *The constitutional phenomenon in the 21st century and the contribution of the revision of 2001* (Athens-Komotini, AN Sakkoulas, 2002) 148 (in Greek); G Kaminis, 'The problem of illegally obtained evidence in the criminal process after the revision of Article 19 of the Constitution' in volume in honour of Ioannis Manoledakis, *Democracy – Liberty – Security* (Athens-Thessaloniki, Sakkoulas, 2005) 337, 345–60 (in Greek); D Kioupis, Comment on Arios Pagos 1317/2001, 1 *Poinikos Logos* 1822, 1829 (in Greek); G Tsolias, Comment on Arios Pagos 1568/2004, (2005) 8 *Poiniki Dikeosini* 295, 297–98 (in Greek).

[99] See K Kokkinakis, 'The importance of article 19 para 3 for the criminal process' (2001) 4 *Poiniki Dikeosini* 876 (in Greek); X Kontiadis, *The new constitutionalism and fundamental rights after the revision of 2001* (Athens-Konotini, AN Sakkoulas, 2002) 159 (in Greek); S Paulou, A Fountedaki and G Dimitrainas, 'Evidential prohibitions and adoption' (2002) 5 *Poiniki Dikeosini* 915, 921 (in Greek); Venizelos, '*The constitutional acquis*' (ibid) 147; S Papageorgiou-Gonatas, 'Evidential prohibitions as expressions of constitutional mandates' (2003) 3 *Poinikos Logos* 17, 25 (in Greek); Tsolias, Comment (ibid) 298.

the interests of more effective constitutional rights protection the balance tipped in favour of an absolute standard without any exceptions.[100]

The rule applies at all stages of the criminal process as well as to civil and administrative proceedings,[101] and to derivative evidence. 'Independent source' and 'inevitable discovery'-type exceptions are rejected, on grounds of the complexity of the *post-hoc* rationalisation that these require and the inability of such 'fruit of the poisonous tree' theories to redress violations of the right to privacy and return the defendant to the *status quo ante*.[102] Violations by private individuals are covered no less than violations of constitutional rights by the state, since constitutional rights in Greece apply *erga omnes*.[103] This is of great significance for Continental criminal procedure given that private individuals – especially crime victims – actively participate in criminal proceedings against the defendant as 'civil parties'[104] and can submit incriminating evidence to the court. Furthermore, the exclusionary rule applies even in cases where evidence has been obtained through a violation of the right to privacy of a person other than the defendant.[105] Finally, a conviction relying on evidence obtained in violation of the right to privacy will be quashed upon appellate review on grounds of nullity. When a conviction is quashed, the court will often order a new trial.

Thus, article 19, para 3 gives a categorical, and novel,[106] answer to the 'perennial dilemma'[107] at the centre of the debate on improperly obtained evidence. It puts primary emphasis on the protection of rights, communicating the idea that the pursuit of truth, though cardinal, is not an absolute principle of criminal procedure. More specifically, it signals that the right to privacy cannot be sacrificed in the name of the efficient investigation of crime, which must be pursued within the parameters prescribed by the Constitution.[108] Article 19, para 3 is a means to

[100] See Commission for the Revision of the Constitution, Proceedings of September 13, 2000. See also Kontiadis, *The new constitutionalism* (ibid) 158–59.

[101] Venizelos, *The constitutional acquis* (2002) 148.

[102] A Papadamakis, 'Evidential prohibitions and "fair" trial' (2016) *Poiniki Dikeosini* 449, 450 (in Greek); N Livos, 'Evidentiary use of derivative evidence' in Volume in honour of GA Magkakis (Athens, AN Sakkoulas, 1999) 525; Roxin, *Strafverfahrensrecht* (1998) 148.

[103] Article 25 of the Constitution states that constitutional rights 'also apply to relations between private individuals'. See D Giannoulopoulos, 'The Illusion of Privacy' (2006) 156 *New Law Journal* 572. *cf* Triantafillou, 'Evidential prohibitions and proportionality' (2007) 295.

[104] See Arts 63–70 Code of Penal Procedure (CPP) (Greece).

[105] Papageorgiou-Gonatas, 'Evidential prohibitions' (2003) 25–26.

[106] Iliopoulou-Stragga observes that art 19, para 3 is a 'European, if not universal, innovation'. Iliopoulou-Stragga, 'Illegally obtained evidence to prove the defendant's innocence' (2002) 2219.

[107] See A Zuckerman, *The Principles of Criminal Evidence* (Oxford, Clarendon Press, 1989) 343.

[108] For example, art 19, para 1 of the Constitution provides for interference with the right to secrecy of correspondence 'for reasons of national security or for the purpose of investigating especially serious crime', but the interference must be taking place in accordance with the relevant statutory scheme (Law 2225/1994 as amended with Law 3115/2003). This means that evidence obtained through interceptions authorised under this scheme is admissible. Article 19, para 3 is not a blanket rule of inadmissibility with the potential to 'harm' law enforcement beyond the extent mandated by the Constitution.

'reinforce the efficacy of constitutional provisions protecting private life',[109] reflecting the dominant view among Greek scholars that the exclusion of unconstitutionally seized evidence is inextricably linked with the protection of constitutional rights.[110] Article 19, para 3 translates the ideology of the protective rationale into concrete practice, and offers evidence of the strong link between constitutionalisation of criminal procedure and the emergence of categorical exclusionary rules.

Yet, for all its progressive character and wide scope, article 19, para 3 is at the same time unduly narrow. The rule applies only to violations of privacy, while the admissibility of evidence obtained in violation of other constitutional rights turns either on the exclusionary rule of evidence obtained by the commission of criminal offences, which we will examine below, or judicial interpolation of an evidential prohibition into particular rights. Treating privacy violations differently from other constitutional violations lacks rational grounding. Through article 19, para 3 the Greek Constitution provides the qualified right to privacy with more rigid protection than 'absolute rights'[111] such as the right against torture[112] or the right to respect for human dignity.[113] The effect of article 19, para 3 ought therefore to be extended through teleological interpretation to include the violation of any constitutional right. This would also pre-empt a possible argument *a contrario* that the use of evidence obtained in violation of constitutional rights other than the right to privacy is permitted.[114]

Article 19, para 3 of the Constitution is combined with a statutory exclusionary rule for evidence obtained by the commission of criminal offences, which results in an idiosyncratically rigorous exclusionary regime for evidence obtained by privacy violations, but also raises questions about coherent interpretation of the statutory and higher order constitutional exclusionary rules.

[109] Kontiadis, *The new constitutionalism* (2002) 159.

[110] See Kostaras, 'Do the ends justify the means?' (1984) 176; Spinellis, 'Evidential prohibitions' (1986) 879; Dimitratos, *Evidential prohibitions in the criminal process* (1992) 31; Satlanis, 'Tape recordings' (1996) 20–22; Dalakouras (1998) 30; Papageorgiou-Gonatas (2003) 21; Paulou, Fountedaki and Dimitrainas, 'Evidential Prohibitions and Adoption' (2002) 920.

[111] For a discussion of the division between 'absolute' and 'qualified' rights in the context of the European Convention on Human Rights see generally A Ashworth and M Redmayne, *The Criminal Process*, 3rd edn (Oxford, Oxford University Press, 2005) 35–37; F Sudre, 'La dimension internationale et européenne des libertés et droits fondamentaux' in R Cabrillac, MA Frichon-Roche and T Revet (ed), *Libertés et droits fondamentaux*, 11th edn (Paris, Dalloz, 2005) 32, 41–44.

[112] Art 7, para 2 of the Constitution.

[113] Art 2, para 1 of the Constitution. Androulakis argues that limiting the effect of the exclusionary rule of Art 19, para 3 to violations of the right privacy only is 'unjustified and absurd'. Androulakis, *Fundamental notions of the criminal process* (2007) 470.

[114] See D Giannoulopoulos, Comment on *Khan* v *United Kingdom* (2001) 6 *Poiniki Dikeosini* 614, 628 (in Greek).

IV. The Greek Exclusionary Rule for Evidence Obtained by the Commission of Criminal Offences

Although Greek law on improperly obtained evidence developed through judicial interpretation for most of the twentieth century,[115] Parliament's intervention at the beginning of the 1990s was ultimately decisive. Faced with widespread use of telephone intercepts outside the court, particularly by radio reporters and newspapers, and amidst intense political controversy,[116] Parliament introduced article 370Δ, para 1 of the Penal Code in 1991,[117] which extended criminal liability for covertly recording private conversations and acts not taking place in the public domain to include recordings made by a party to the conversation. This filled a substantial legislative gap that the courts had long exploited to secure the admission of covert recordings.[118] Crucially, a specific exclusionary rule was attached to this provision, prohibiting the use in any criminal proceedings, or in proceedings before an investigative or other public authority, of evidence obtained in violation of article 370Δ, para 1.[119] This was an absolute exclusionary rule that could 'guarantee more efficiently and *ex ante* the protection of privacy, without a balancing of competing interests by the court being necessary'.[120] In opting for such a radical solution, Parliament seemed determined to put an end to the use of illegally obtained tape-recordings in trials. In applying this rule, Arios Pagos held that 'the use of an illegally recorded conversation caused nullity of the judgment',[121] requiring the defendant's conviction to be quashed. However, only two years after coming into effect, this exclusionary rule was abolished. In its place, Parliament introduced a criminal defence condoning the use in court of covertly obtained recordings when intended to protect 'justified interests' of the parties (article 370A, para 4 PC).[122] This looked like the end of the road for automatic exclusion.

However, in 1996, the Greek Parliament took another U-turn in this tumultuous period for the development of the statutory exclusionary rule. Article 177, para 2 was inserted into the Code of Penal Procedure (hereinafter CPP) mandating

[115] This is an interesting feature of the law on improperly obtained evidence in Greece, if one considers the preponderant role of the legislator in the civil law tradition. See generally David and Spinosi, *Les grands systèmes de droit contemporains* (Paris, Dalloz, 1992) 84.

[116] See Tsakirakis, 'Secrecy of Correspondence' (1993) 995 and 1007.

[117] See art 31, para 1 of Law 1941/1991.

[118] See text to n 68.

[119] Art 370Δ, para 2 Penal Code.

[120] Th Dalakouras, 'The exclusionary rule for improper audio and video recordings under article 370Δ para 2 of the Penal Code (article 31 of Law 1941/1991)' (1992) *Iperaspisi* 25, 27 (in Greek).

[121] Arios Pagos 589/1994, 42 *Nomiko Bima* 1059. See also Arios Pagos 9/1994, 44 *Poinika Chronika* 215.

[122] Introduced with art 33, para 8 of Law 2172/1993 and amended with art 12, para 8 of Law 3090/2002.

the exclusion of evidence obtained through the commission of a criminal offence. It provided that:

> Evidence obtained by [the commission of] criminal offences or through such offences will not be considered with regard to the pronouncement of legal guilt, the imposition of criminal punishment or the determination of restrictive measures, unless [the process concerns] crimes where maximum punishment is life imprisonment and the court makes a judgment that specifically justifies [the consideration of such evidence].[123]

With article 177, para 2, the legislator introduced a strict exclusionary rule, which was wide in scope and did not concentrate on specified offences, applied at all stages of the criminal process and endorsed the 'fruit of the poisonous tree' doctrine,[124] though, on the other hand, it did not apply to serious offences.

The exclusionary rule was introduced in Parliament by Evangelos Venizelos, Professor of Constitutional Law and minister of justice at the time. Venizelos pointed out that article 177, para 2 had been inspired by Arios Pagos' original exclusionary jurisprudence on unconstitutionally seized letters.[125] This robust exclusionary rule was the direct outcome of the constitutionalisation of the law of criminal evidence. It was giving effect to the idea that 'evidential prohibitions stem from constitutional provisions and from provisions contained in international documents for the protection of individual rights',[126] and the idea that constitutional guarantees would be deprived of substance if they did not lead to evidential prohibitions.[127]

This was the first time that the legislator was attempting to deal with the problem of improperly obtained evidence in a systematic manner in contrast to previous fragmentary approaches related to particular types of evidence.[128] But the legislator also recognised that the use of illegally obtained evidence could be exceptionally justified when the defendant was charged with an offence punishable with a maximum sentence of life imprisonment. The exception covered offences such as murder, aggravated robbery, aggravated forms of drug offences, arson, causing explosions and constructing or possessing explosives, and constituted an important limitation to the exclusionary rule's ability to give full effect to relevant constitutional rights. Its inconsistency with the blanket exclusionary rule of article 19, para 3 of the Constitution, which recognised no exceptions, did not take

[123] Introduced with art 2, para 7 of Law 2408/1996.

[124] See A Karras, *Penal procedural law*, 2nd edn (Athens-Komotini, AN Sakkoulas, 1998) 638 (in Greek); A Tzannetis, 'The unlawful obtaining of evidence (interpretative approach of article 177 para 2 of the Code of Penal Procedure)' (1998) 48 *Poinika Chronika* 105, 107 (in Greek); N Dimitratos, 'The evolution of the institution of evidential prohibitions in Hellenic penal procedural law – simultaneously, a comparative review of the correspondent American and German law' (2001) 51 *Poinika Chronika* 5, 11 (in Greek).

[125] Parliamentary Debates, Proceedings of 7 May, 1996, 6042; 9 May, 1996, 6149.

[126] Parliamentary Debates, Proceedings of 9 May, 1996, 6149.

[127] ibid.

[128] Tzannetis, 'The unlawful obtaining of evidence' (1998) 105.

long to come to the surface though. The 'life imprisonment' exception was therefore removed with the legislative reform of July 2008,[129] and, in its amended form, article 177, para 2 provided that '[e]vidence obtained by [the commission of] criminal offences or through such offences will not be considered in the criminal process'.

Abolishing the 'life imprisonment' exception gave effect to the idea that the Constitution does not distinguish between individuals who are charged with serious crimes and those who are not, but protects rights of individuals in general. In fact, it is widely recognised that it is in relation to serious crimes, with correspondingly severe penalties, that constitutional protection is most needed.[130] On the other hand, it is notable that some Greek scholars would have liked to see the application of the 'life imprisonment offences' extended to other serious offences.[131]

The article 177, para 2 saga exposes the perennial controversies and strong political dilemmas surrounding the debate on improperly obtained evidence. These have recently been exacerbated with another radical reform, introduced by Alexis Tsipras' government of the left at the end of 2015, in the midst of, and in connection with, the continued economic crisis. More specifically, the government enacted, through the legislative back door and with virtually no consultation with stakeholders,[132] an exception to article 177, para 2 for serious tax and corruption offences.[133] Following this amendment, when the prosecution seeks to adduce evidence in trials relating to such offences, its admissibility will be determined by taking into consideration whether:

> (a) [T]he damage caused by the obtaining [of the evidence] is considerably less significant, in view of its nature, importance and extent, compared to the damage or risk caused by the act under investigation; (b) the discovery of truth would otherwise be impossible and (c) the act with which the evidence has been obtained does not violate human dignity.

[129] See art 10 of Law 3674/2008 of 10 July 2008 on the 'reinforcement of the institutional framework guaranteeing the secrecy of telephone correspondence and other provisions'. See also A Zigouras, 'Evidentiary use by private parties of improperly obtained evidence after the latest legislative reform' (2008) 58 *Poinika Chronika* 1013 (in Greek); G Kalfelis, 'Violation of the right to privacy and cameras' (2008) 58 *Poinika Chronika* 865 (in Greek); D Zimianitis, 'Unlawful video or audio recording and use of products of taps by the media' (2010) 13 *Poiniki Dikeosini* 1028 (in Greek).

[130] See A Ashworth, 'Excluding Evidence as Protecting Rights' [1977] *Criminal Law Review* 723; A Ashworth, *Human Rights, Serious Crime and Criminal Procedure* (London, Sweet & Maxwell, 2002) 112. See also P Mirfield, *Silence, Confessions and Improperly Obtained Evidence* (Oxford, Clarendon Press, 1997) 31–33, demonstrating that a 'serious offences' exception could not be justified under any of the exclusionary principles. *cf* J Kaplan, 'The Limits of the Exclusionary Rule' (1974) 26 *Stanford Law Review* 1027, 1046–49.

[131] See, eg, Triantafillou, 'Evidential prohibitions and proportionality' (2007) 295.

[132] The amendment was added to legislation relating to civil partnerships. See generally I Anagnostopoulos, Intervention, Athens Bar Association debate on improperly obtained evidence, 19 January 2016, available at www.youtube.com/watch?v=5PPQGgAiocY (in Greek).

[133] Art 65, para 1 of Law 4356/2015 on Civil Partnerships, the exercise of rights, criminal law and other provisions, ΦΕΚ 181, 24 December 2015.

The explanatory memorandum rested this new balancing exercise on a judicial integrity rationale, arguing that integrity is damaged when excessive restrictions are placed upon freedom of proof, particularly in tax and corruption offences where the search for truth is inherently complex.[134]

The 'tax and corruption offences' exception contradicts the higher order choices made by the constitutional legislator to prioritise the protection of constitutional rights and give effect to existing balancing of competing individual and public interest considerations, as reflected in article 19, para 3 of the Constitution. It is quite striking that the explanatory memorandum discusses article 177, para 2 in complete isolation from the constitutional exclusionary rule. Taking a cue from immediate criticism directed at the rule by criminal procedure scholars, and abolition in 2008 of the 'life imprisonment' exception, precisely due to its incompatibility with the constitutional exclusionary rule, it is difficult to see how Greek criminal courts will not find the 'tax and corruption offences' exception equally incompatible with the Constitution and therefore how they will be able to apply it in practice. It can be safely predicted that they will practically disregard it.

The furore caused by this latest legislative reform offers further insights into the politicisation of the exclusionary rule, and the intriguing ways in which domestic legal culture can shape its content and orientation. For a start, criminal procedure scholars have rightly criticised this reform as a knee-jerk reaction dictated by the need for the government to be seen – by the country's creditors, one suspects – to be doing something about economic crime. But taking such a selective approach, which prioritises truth discovery in relation to tax evasion, corruption and other serious economic crime, over violent offences against the person for instance, is counterintuitive and opposed to an imagined hierarchy of criminal law values. In this scheme of things, the public interest will justify setting aside the blanket rule of inadmissibility in order to investigate economic crime, but not to uncover truth in cases where the defendant may be suspected of having caused loss of life or to have perpetrated serious violations of the right to bodily integrity and sexual autonomy. 'Tax collection comes first, and individual liberty [of those who are victims of violent offences against the person] a far second', seems to be the message here.[135]

It is equally intriguing, on the other hand, to observe the extent to which the constitutional rights-based argument for exclusion is embedded in the Greek legal culture, particularly with criminal procedure scholars and criminal defence practitioners, as illustrated by nearly universal condemnation from their part of the executive's impromptu intervention in this domain. With this new exception, the Greek exclusionary rule was put on a slippery slope, creating the risk of further incursions into the absolute evidentiary prohibition, depending on law and order

[134] Explanatory memorandum, Addition to the 'Civil Partnerships, the exercise of rights, criminal law and other provisions' Bill, 22 December 2015.

[135] Papadamakis, 'Evidential prohibitions and "fair" trial' (2016) 449, 451.

priorities, warned Tzannetis, a criminal law scholar and barrister with expertise in economic crime. Anagnostopoulos, president of the Hellenic Criminal Bar Association and Professor of Criminal Law at the University of Athens, went so far as offer a reminder that it was in national socialist regimes that the public interest outweighed individual rights. In the same spirit, a prosecutor at the Court of Appeal sounded a note of caution that this reform was reminiscent of abuses of rights under the Colonels.[136] Such strong reaction to attempts from the executive to encroach upon the constitutional rights-based exclusionary rule speaks volumes about the role of constitutionalisation in shaping the contemporary Greek exclusionary rule, particularly in the context of recent memories of military dictatorship and abuse of fundamental rights.

To focus back on the wider operation of article 177, para 2, it can be pointed out that a rule that renders the commission of criminal offences the only criterion for exclusion risks generating incoherent evidentiary outcomes, given that 'the constitutional protection of individual rights and the criminal law protection of corresponding legal values do not necessarily coincide'.[137] In other words, an act that violates the Constitution is not always punishable by criminal law,[138] and the exclusionary rule may be letting unconstitutional acts slip through its protective net, particularly where the criminal offence by which the evidence has been obtained can be justified or excused under the application of a criminal law defence, such as the defences of necessity or self-defence. The absence of legal guilt in such a case means no offence has been committed. A classic hypothetical posits the victim of blackmail who secretly records his blackmailer's threats. If the act of recording this conversation can be justified as self-defence (and therefore as non-criminal), use of the evidence thus obtained would be admissible at trial.[139] In this hypothetical, the outcome seems morally acceptable. The question that arises is whether limiting the discussion to criminal liability can cause the issue of the scope of the constitutional right pass below the court's visibility radar. In other words, the court may never ask the question of how far the right to secrecy of correspondence should extend, or, more specifically, whether 'decadent' or negative manifestations of the right should fall outside its scope. More generally, it can be argued that, as far as privacy violations are concerned, the operation of article 177, para 2 has been made obsolete by the constitutional exclusionary rule of article 19, para 3. It is in relation to violations of rights which do not come under the umbrella of the latter that article 177, para 2 offers added protection.

[136] See generally Athens Bar Association debate (2016).

[137] D Spinellis, 'Legal values and their importance in the modern teaching of criminal law' (1971) 21 *Poinika Chronika* 812 (in Greek). See also N Livos, 'The criminal protection of traffic data of telecommunications' (1997) 47 *Poinika Chronika* 737, 742 (in Greek).

[138] Kaminis, *Illegally Obtained Evidence* (1998) 281.

[139] See generally Dimitratos, 'Evidential prohibitions in the criminal process' (2001) 13; Livos, 'Criminal protection of traffic data' (1997) 747; Tzannetis (n 124) 107.

In conclusion, the introduction of article 177, para 2 in 1996 sent a strong message that Parliament wanted to take a radical step in the direction of automatic exclusion. But the legislator was also influenced by public interest considerations that would necessarily qualify the exclusionary rule's effect, particularly as exhibited by the 'life imprisonment' and 'tax and corruption offences' exceptions.

V. Same Origins, Different Directions: The Deterrent and Protective Rationales in Action

The different philosophies underlying the contemporary versions of the American and Greek exclusionary rules, and the different directions that the two systems have taken as a result of them, despite a mutual process of constitutionalisation triggering the development of exclusionary rules in both countries, are quickly revealed if one contrasts the multiple deterrence-based exceptions to *Mapp*, on the one hand, with the protective rationale-based Greek constitutional exclusionary rule that is subjected to very few exceptions, on the other.

A. The Exceptions to the Fourth Amendment Exclusionary Rule

The '*good faith*' *exception*, first introduced in the 1980s and significantly expanded with the decisions of the Supreme Court in *Herring v United States*[140] and *Davis v United States*,[141] has played a major role in the undermining of the automatic effect of *Mapp's* exclusionary rule. The exception applies where the police have undertaken an unconstitutional search, but have reasonably relied on information provided by a 'third-party source', for example a magistrate, court clerk, or previous precedent.[142] This includes situations where the police have reasonably relied on a search warrant issued by a magistrate but ultimately found to be invalid,[143] situations where the police have acted in objectively reasonable reliance upon a statute authorising a warrantless search, which was subsequently found to violate the Fourth Amendment,[144] or situations where the violation of the Fourth Amendment had resulted from clerical errors of court employees, such as in a case where a court employee had not informed the police that the warrant upon which

[140] *Herring v United States*, 555 US 135 (2009).
[141] *Davis v United States*, 131 SCt 2419 (2011).
[142] See Slobogin, 'The Exclusionary Rule' (2013) 346.
[143] *United States v Leon*, 468 US 897 (1984).
[144] See *Illinois v Krull*, 480 US 340 (1987); *Michigan v DeFillippo*, 443 US 31 (1979); *Cardenas-Alatorre*, 485 F3d at 1114.

the search was conducted had been quashed.[145] *Herring* has now substantially widened the scope of the exception, by applying the same principle to cases where a mistake in informing a database that a warrant had been quashed was not due to a court employee or other third party, but a law enforcement officer. This was a crucial twist in 'good faith' exception jurisprudence, because pre-*Herring* the non-applicability of the exclusionary rule had mainly been justified on the basis that the person primarily responsible for the Fourth Amendment violation was not a law enforcement official but rather a judge, legislators or a clerk in the employ of the judiciary.[146] In *Davis*, the Supreme Court found that searches conducted in objectively reasonable reliance on binding appellate precedent were not subject to the exclusionary rule either, thus expanding the kind of law included within the good faith exception; not only defective warrants and subsequently invalidated statutes, but also case law that was binding at the time of the search.[147]

Herring's and *Davis'* main significance lies in the logic that underpinned them. In *Herring*, the Supreme Court held that the exclusionary rule did not apply because police mistakes leading to the unlawful search were 'the result of isolated negligence attenuated from the search, rather than systemic error or reckless disregard of constitutional requirements',[148] and that, contrarily, 'to trigger the exclusionary rule, police conduct must be sufficiently deliberate that exclusion can meaningfully deter it, and sufficiently culpable that such deterrence is worth the price paid by the justice system'.[149] *Davis* confirmed this line of reasoning, repeating and expanding upon its broad dicta.[150] Their combined effect is that, in good faith situations, the application of the exclusionary rule will now be limited to cases where the police exhibit 'deliberate,' 'reckless,' or 'grossly negligent' disregard for Fourth Amendment rights, as opposed to a whole range of cases where the unconstitutionally obtained evidence will be admitted, when police act with 'simple, isolated negligence'.[151] Here it suffices to take note of Justice Breyer's astounding prognosis, in his *Davis* dissenting opinion, that 'if the Court means what it now says [in *Herring* and *Davies*] … then the good faith exception will swallow the exclusionary rule'.[152]

[145] *Arizona v Evans*, 514 US 1 (1995).

[146] See generally W LaFave, 'The Smell of *Herring*: A Critique of the Supreme Court's Latest Assault on the Exclusionary Rule' (2009) 99 *The Journal of Criminal Law & Criminology* 757, 761; CA Nolasco, RV del Carmen and MS Vaughn, 'What *Herring* Hath Wrought: An Analysis of Post-*Herring* Cases in the Federal Courts' (2011) 38 *American Journal of Criminal Law* 221, 223.

[147] E de Golian, '*Davis* and the Good Faith Exception: Pushing Exclusion to Extinction?' (2012) 63 *Mercer Law Review* 751, 764.

[148] *Herring v United States*, 555 US 135 (2009).

[149] ibid 136.

[150] *Davis v United States*, 564 US 229 (2011), *per* Breyer J (dissenting opinion).

[151] ibid 257.

[152] ibid 258, *per* Breyer J (dissenting opinion). Justice Breyer paradoxically expresses hope here that the Supreme Court does not mean what it says. See, in more detail, T Maclin and J Rader, 'No More Chipping Away: The Roberts Court Uses an Axe to Take Out the Fourth Amendment Exclusionary Rule' (2012) 81 *Mississippi Law Journal* 1183, 1189.

In other words, if the Court really means that 'exclusion is unwarranted in all cases where the police reasonably believed their conduct complied with the law',[153] the outcome predicted by Breyer is indeed inevitable; the exclusionary rule will only (and rarely) be applicable in exceptional cases of egregious – purposeful, bad-faith – Fourth Amendment violations.[154] Maclin argues that the Court indeed means what it says, and he explains that *Herring* 'effectively adopts a general good-faith exception to suppression'.[155] Most critics seem to agree with this point.[156] From this perspective, it can be suggested that the exclusionary rule risks being given a final blow if lower courts adopt a broad interpretation of *Herring*, something that Breyer indicated is already happening to some extent.[157] Such a development would actually make redundant the need for the Court to go as far as overrule *Mapp* in the future. The exclusionary rule would already be obsolete. *Mapp* could remain in force on paper. But *Mapp* is not safe, even if lower courts resist the temptation to adopt this broad interpretation. Commentators read *Herring* as signalling the Supreme Court's intention, when an appropriate case reaches the Court, to make the 'quantum leap' away from *Mapp* and existing precedent, and hold that courts should generally not exclude evidence if the police conduct is simple negligence.[158] This would make the exclusionary rule applicable only 'on those very rare occasions when an officer behaves so brazenly that his or her conduct can only be characterized as "grossly negligent" or worse'.[159]

The 'good faith' exception constitutes the most important contemporary threat to the exclusionary rule.[160] But various other exceptions already limit its scope and effect to a considerable extent. First of all, unconstitutionally obtained evidence that does not trigger the 'good faith' exception, and is thus barred from the prosecution's case-in-chief, may nevertheless still be used to *impeach the defendant* (attack his or her credibility) if the defendant decides to take the stand.[161] Other exceptions limit the application of the exclusionary rule outside trial proceedings. The Supreme Court has thus held that the exclusionary rule did not apply in *grand jury proceedings*; a witness summoned to appear and testify before a grand

[153] Maclin and Rader, 'No More Chipping Away' (ibid) 1190.

[154] ibid 1209.

[155] ibid. See also Maclin, *The Supreme Court and the Fourth Amendment Exclusionary Rule* (2013) 336.

[156] See Nolasco et al, 'What *Herring* Hath Wrought' (2011) 224, citing relevant scholarly opinion (at fn 15).

[157] *Davis v United States*, 564 US 229, 258–59 (2011).

[158] M Vitiello, '*Herring v. United States: Mapp's* Artless Overruling' (2009) 10 *Nevada Law Journal* 164, 179. See also E Canter, 'A Fourth Amendment Metamorphosis: How Fourth Amendment Remedies and Regulations Facilitated the Expansion of the Threshold Inquiry' (2009) 95 *Virginia Law Review* 155, 202.

[159] DA Moran, 'Hanging on by a Thread: The Exclusionary Rule (Or What's Left of It) Lives for Another Day' (2011) 9 *Ohio State Journal of Criminal Law* 363, 379.

[160] This is also how its effect is perceived by the media. With reference to *Herring* see, eg, Editorial, Chipping away at the Constitution (2009) *Los Angeles Times*, 27 January; A Liptak, Justices step closer to repeal of evidence ruling (2009) *The New York Times*, 30 January; A Cohen, Is the Supreme Court about to kill off the exclusionary rule (2009) *The New York Times*, 15 February.

[161] See *United States v Havens*, 446 US 620 (1980).

jury could not refuse to answer questions on the ground that they were based on evidence obtained from an unlawful search and seizure.[162] The exclusionary rule did not apply in *habeas corpus proceedings*[163] or *parole revocation hearings* either,[164] whereas various decisions of circuit courts of appeal have equally recognised that it is possible to use evidence obtained in violation of the Fourth Amendment at the *sentencing stage*.[165] Such evidence can a fortiori be used in *civil proceedings*, for example in Internal Revenue Service[166] or immigration proceedings.[167] The exclusionary rule has also generally been held inapplicable in cases where the evidence has been obtained unlawfully by a *person acting in a private capacity*,[168] subject to that person being unconnected with the government,[169] and where search and seizure take place against aliens outside United States territory.[170] Finally, the exclusionary rule does not apply in cases where the evidence has been obtained in violation of the Fourth Amendment rights of a third person. By holding that such a person does not satisfy the *standing* requirement of the Fourth Amendment[171] the Supreme Court made obvious its willingness to avert a more widespread invocation of the exclusionary rule during criminal trials.[172] But the Supreme Court's jurisprudence did much more than simply limit the vicarious application of the exclusionary rule, effectively turning the standing rules 'into a sword to be used by the Government to permit it deliberately to invade one person's Fourth Amendment rights in order to obtain evidence against another person'.[173] The exclusion of derivative evidence obtained in violation of the Fourth Amendment ('fruits of the poisonous tree') is also subjected to significant exceptions – the 'attenuation' exception, which provides for admissibility when the connection

[162] See *United States v Calandra*, 414 US 338 (1974). The grand jury is both an investigative body, with wide-ranging powers to develop evidence against individual offenders and conduct broad-based examinations, eg of organised crime or government operations, and a screening body with the authority to refuse to return an indictment. C Whitebread and C Slobogin, *Criminal Procedure, An Analysis of Cases and Concepts* (New York, University Textbook Series, 2000) 584. It resembles the *jury d'accusation* that had been instituted in France after the Revolution with the law of 16–21 September 1791. See J Pradel, *Procédure pénale*, 10th edn (Paris, Cujas, 2001) 61–62.

[163] See *Stone v Powell*, 428 US 465 (1976).

[164] See *Pennsylvania Board of Probation and Parole v Scott*, 524 US 357 (1998); *State v Martin* 595 NW2d 214.

[165] See *United States v Ryan*, 236 F3d 1268, 1272 (10th Cir 2001); *United States v Acosta*, 303 F3d 78, 84-86 (1st Cir 2002); *United States v Torres*, 926 F2d 321, 324–325 (3d Cir 1991).

[166] *United States v Janis* 428 US 433 (1976).

[167] *Immigration and Naturalization Service v Lopez-Mendoza*, 468 US 1032 (1984).

[168] *Burdeau v McDowell* 256 US 465 (1921).

[169] For examples of cases where such a connection might be established, see, eg, Euller's analysis of private security personnel that acts independently in investigating crimes and pursuing evidence in preparation for criminal prosecutions. S Euller, 'Private Security and the Exclusionary Rule' (1980) 15 *Harvard Civil Liberties-Civil Rights Law Review* 649.

[170] *United States v Verdugo-Urquidez*, 494 US 259 (1990).

[171] See, eg, *Jones v United States* 362 US 257 (1960); *Alderman v United States*, 394 US 165 (1969); *Rakas v Illinois*, 439 US 128, 134 (1978); *United States v Padilla*, 508 US 77 (1993).

[172] *Rakas v Illinois*, 439 US 128, 134, 137 (1978).

[173] *United States v Payner*, 444 US 727, 738 (1980), *per* Justice Marshall (dissenting opinion).

between unconstitutional police conduct and the evidence is sufficiently remote or has been interrupted by some intervening circumstance,[174] the 'independent source' exception,[175] where, for example, despite an initial illegal search, the evidence is eventually discovered during a search pursuant to a valid warrant, and the 'inevitable discovery' exception,[176] where unlawfully obtained evidence would ultimately or inevitably have been discovered even if no violation of any constitutional provision had taken place.

These wide-ranging exceptions significantly minimise the protective effect of the a priori automatic Fourth Amendment exclusionary rule. In the eyes of American commentators, those critical of the rule's demise in particular, these exceptions are seen as either having already extinguished the essence of the rule or imminently threatening to do so. It was thus as early as 1980 that Former Supreme Court Justice, Arthur Goldberg, noted, writing extra-judicially, that 'without actually overruling *Mapp*' the Supreme Court had already 'riddled it so full of loopholes as to render its effect almost meaningless',[177] while soon thereafter Justice Brennan emphatically remarked, in his *Leon* dissenting opinion, that, in the ten years since *Calandra*, he had 'witnessed the Court's gradual but determined strangulation of the rule'.[178] It should come as no surprise then that, in view of the accumulated effect of the Supreme Court's attacks upon the exclusionary rule since *Leon*, the rule is seen today, in some quarters, as 'a mockery of the original version' established with *Mapp*.[179] Even those not prepared to go so far will probably find it difficult to disagree with the view that the Court's post-*Mapp* jurisprudence has substantially blurred the line between the rule and its exceptions.[180] The exceptions have consumed a very significant part of the rule. These exceptions were underpinned by a violent turn to applying a deterrence-based approach, which helped embed a new – much less ambitious – mission for the exclusionary rule, and which provides a strong antithesis to the protective principle-based Greek exclusionary rules that put safeguarding the constitutional right to privacy first.

B. The Deterrence Road to the Exclusionary Rule's Perdition

United States v Calandra was the first case to manifest the Supreme Court's new deterrence-based approach to exclusion.[181] In departing from *Mapp's* original

[174] *Hudson v Michigan*, 547 US 586, 593 (2006). See also *Utah v Strieff*, 579 US (2016).
[175] See *Segura v United States*, 468 US 796 (1984); *Murray v United States*, 487 US 533 (1988).
[176] See *Nix v Williams*, 467 US 431 (1984).
[177] Justice AJ Goldberg, 'The Warren Court and Its Critics' (1980) 20 *Santa Clara Law Review* 831, 838.
[178] *United States v Leon*, 468 US 897, 929 (1984).
[179] Slobogin (n 6) 348.
[180] L Heffernan, 'The Fourth Amendment's Exclusionary Rule: Blurring the Line Between Rule and Exception' (2011) 9 *International Commentary on Evidence* 2, article 3.
[181] In that way, '*Calandra* was a signal event in the Court's Fourth Amendment jurisprudence'. Gray (n 6) 20.

understanding, the Supreme Court held there that the exclusionary rule is: 'a judicially created remedy designed to safeguard Fourth Amendment rights generally through its deterrent effect, rather than a personal constitutional right of the party aggrieved'.[182]

'The purpose of the exclusionary rule' was not 'to redress the injury to the privacy of the search victim', noted the Court, rejecting a rights-based approach and explaining that 'the ruptured privacy of the victim's homes and effects cannot be restored'.[183] 'The rule's primary purpose' was instead to deter future unlawful police conduct.[184] The rule was calculated to prevent, not to repair.[185] Deterrence was then quickly seen not just as the prime but rather, effectively, the sole purpose of the exclusionary rule.[186] In *Leon*, the Court brought more precision to these points, by holding that the use of fruits of a past unlawful search or seizure worked 'no new Fourth Amendment wrong', that the violation of the Fourth Amendment was 'fully accomplished by the unlawful search or seizure itself', and that the exclusionary rule could not cure the invasion of the Fourth Amendment that the defendant had already suffered.[187] Further, the judicial integrity rationale, which had been advanced in *Mapp* as one of the justifications for the rule, was seen as consistent with the deterrence rationale and was, as a result, subsumed into the latter.[188] Thus, with the exclusionary rule's constitutional foundation removed, and its remedial and judicial integrity functions denied, the applicability of the exclusionary rule now only rested on a cost–benefit balancing test which weighed the rule's ability to deter future police illegality against the 'substantial social costs exacted by the exclusionary rule',[189] notably the significant cost of impeding 'unacceptably the truthfinding functions of judge and jury',[190] by precluding 'consideration of reliable, probative evidence',[191] thus creating the risk that 'some guilty defendants may go free or receive reduced sentences as a result of favorable plea bargains'.[192] It was by resorting to this cost–benefit analysis that the Supreme Court justified the introduction of the many exceptions to the exclusionary rule mentioned above, repeatedly finding that the 'substantial social costs' of exclusion

[182] *United States v* Calandra, 414 US 338, 348 (1974). The thesis that the exclusionary rule is not constitutionally mandated was confirmed in *Pennsylvania Board of Probation and Parole v Scott*, 524 US 357, 363 (1998).

[183] *United States v Calandra*, 414 US 338, 347 (1974).

[184] ibid, citing *Linkletter v Walker*, 381 US 618, 637 (1965).

[185] ibid, citing *Elkins v United States*, 363 US 206, 217 (1960).

[186] See *United States v Janis*, 428 US 433, 446 (1976).

[187] *United States v Leon*, 468 US 897, 906 (1984). The ability of the rule to cure the invasion already suffered was a remedial rationale which was previously seen as inherent in the constitutional nature of the exclusionary rule and which 'disappeared with the deconstitutionalisation of the rule' in *Calandra*. See Clancy, 'The Fourth Amendment Exclusionary Rule as a Constitutional Right' (n 25) 369.

[188] Clancy (ibid) 368.

[189] *United States v Leon*, 468 US 897, 907 (1984).

[190] ibid, citing *United States v Payner*, 447 US 727, 734 (1980).

[191] *Pennsylvania Board of Probation and Parole v Scott*, 524 US 357, 364 (1998).

[192] *United States v Leon*, 468 US 897, 907 (1984).

would outweigh the 'minimal',[193] 'small'[194] 'marginal or 'nonexistent'[195] benefits of deterrence. The Court justified such exceptions in cases where it found that no appreciable additional deterrence would be achieved, for instance, in *habeas corpus* proceedings, parole revocation hearings or when using unconstitutionally obtained evidence to impeach the defendant, and in cases where it questioned whether the exclusionary rule would have any deterrent effect at all, such as where the offending officers had acted in the objectively reasonable belief that their conduct did not violate the Fourth Amendment. The oxymoron here is that the Court made deterrence the exclusive basis for exclusion despite the fact that it was not convinced that the exclusionary rule had a deterrent effect.[196]

Nevertheless, the Supreme Court's reliance on the deterrence theory continues unabated and, as previously explained with reference to *Herring* and *Davis*, now risks consigning to oblivion *Mapp's* original logic, if not the decision itself as it applies today. The case that proves the point is *Hudson v Michigan*, which constituted the Roberts Court's first assault on the legitimacy of the exclusionary rule.[197] The issue in this case was whether a violation of the 'knock-and-announce' rule, which the Court had long recognised as a command of the Fourth Amendment, required the suppression of evidence found in the related search.[198] The Court held that it didn't, despite the fact that in this case it was the police – and not a third party, such as a magistrate or a court employee – that had breached a Fourth Amendment right. In conducting the usual balancing exercise, the Court first pinpointed the 'grave adverse consequence' of 'releasing dangerous criminals into society',[199] then identified the additional costs of over-deterrence[200] and the risk of new 'extensive litigation' on a question that could not be readily determined.[201] These were 'substantial social costs',[202] while 'deterrence of knock-and-announce violations [was] not worth a lot',[203] given that the police do not have a significant incentive to violate the knock-and-announce rule in the first place.[204]

[193] *Pennsylvania Board of Probation and Parole v Scott*, 524 US 357, 363 (1998).

[194] *United States v Calandra*, 414 US 338, 352 (1974).

[195] *United States v Leon*, 468 US 897, 922 (1984).

[196] Clancy (n 25) 370. In *Janis*, after reviewing relevant empirical evidence, the Court concluded that '[n]o empirical researcher, proponent or opponent of the rule, has yet been able to establish with any assurance whether the rule has a deterrent effect even in the situations in which it is now applied' (at fn 22), and only assumed that the rule is 'a substantial and efficient deterrent'. *United States v Janis*, 428 US 433, 453 (1976).

[197] *Hudson v Michigan*, 547 US 586 (2006).

[198] The 'knock-and-announce' rule is the 'common-law principle that law enforcement officers must announce their presence and provide residents an opportunity to open the door'. *Hudson v Michigan*, 547 US 586, 589 (2006) citing *Wilson v Arkansas*, 514 US 927, 931–32 (1995).

[199] *Hudson v Michigan*, 547 US 586, 595 (2006).

[200] The 'incongruent' exclusionary remedy would lead police to refrain from timely entry after knocking-and-announcing (ibid).

[201] For example, courts could not readily determine 'how many seconds' it would be reasonable for the police to wait before entering (ibid).

[202] ibid 596.

[203] ibid.

[204] ibid.

The outcome of the balancing exercise came as no surprise in this case. The same exercise had been typically undertaken in the post-*Mapp* jurisprudence introducing exceptions to the Fourth Amendment exclusionary rule. Far more noteworthy were the 'provocative dicta'[205] in the majority opinion of Justice Scalia that could 'portend an end to the Court's use of the exclusionary rule in other contexts outside the knock-and-announce area'.[206] Scalia argued that just because the Supreme Court had found that the exclusionary rule was 'necessary deterrence' when first introduced, it should not be assumed that it remained 'necessary deterrence' today.[207] Scalia explained that effective alternative deterrents had been developed since *Mapp*, such as civil rights lawsuits for Fourth Amendment breaches,[208] and placed emphasis on the 'increasing professionalism of police forces'[209] and 'increasing evidence that police forces across the United States take the constitutional rights of citizens seriously',[210] while he also made passing reference to 'the increasing use of various forms of citizen review [that] can enhance police accountability'.[211] This newly found faith on alternative remedies is troubling, irrespective of whether one agrees with Kamisar's view that 'the overwhelming consensus' in criminal procedure literature has traditionally been that these remedies are 'sadly inadequate'.[212] The fact that in its 45-year-old jurisprudence between

[205] M Cloud, 'A Conservative House United: How the Post-Warren Court Dismantled the Exclusionary Rule' (2013) 10 *Ohio State Journal of Criminal Law* 477, 513.

[206] C Totten and S Cobkit (Cheurprakobkit), 'The Knock-and-Announce Rule and Police Searches after *Hudson v. Michigan*: Can Alternative Deterrents Effectively Replace Exclusion for Rule Violations' (2012) 15 *New Criminal Law Review* 414, 424. See also Maclin (n 80) 328. Booker T Hudson's attorney, Prof David Moran, has repeatedly expressed the fear that the case that he 'managed to lose' would be the one to lead to abolition of the exclusionary rule: DA Moran, 'The End of the Exclusionary Rule, Among Other Things: The Roberts Court Takes On the Fourth Amendment' [2006] *Cato Supreme Court Review* 283, 307–09; 'The Supreme Court 2005 Term: Leading Cases' (2006) 120 *Harvard Law Review* 125, 178–83; 'Waiting for the Other Shoe: *Hudson* and the Precarious State of *Mapp*' (2008) 93 *Iowa Law Review* 1725, 1726; Moran, 'Hanging on by a Thread' (2011) 363. For a detailed analysis of the future of the exclusionary rule post-*Hudson* see J Tomkovicz, '*Hudson v. Michigan* and the Future of Fourth Amendment Exclusion' (2008) 93 *Iowa Law Review* 1819. Tomkovicz argued that the cost–benefit analysis adopted in *Hudson* was 'extraordinary' and therefore has 'enormous potential to diminish the scope of Fourth Amendment suppression. The logic and language evince palpable hostility toward the exclusionary rule, disagreement with its foundational logic, and an attitude that could ultimately lead to the dismantling of *Weeks* and *Mapp*'. On the other hand, Tomkovicz explained that, save for a change in the Court's composition that could make exclusion go either in the majority's or the dissenters' way, the consequences deriving from *Hudson* will probably fall between the two extremes of abolition of the exclusionary rule and *Hudson* being treated as a *sui generis* decision limited to 'knock-and-announce' situations. For criticism of the decision in *Hudson v Michigan* see generally DA Gutin, 'Technical Knockout: *Hudson v. Michigan* and the Unfortunate Demise of the Knock-and-Announce Rule' (2007) 44 *American Criminal Law Review* 1239; WR LaFave, *Search and Seizure: a Treatise on the Fourth Amendment*, 4th edn (Minnesota, Thomson West, 2011–12) s II.4, 52.

[207] *Hudson v Michigan*, 547 US 586, 597 (2006).

[208] ibid 597–98.

[209] ibid 598.

[210] ibid 599.

[211] ibid.

[212] Y Kamisar, 'Remembering the "Old World" of Criminal Procedure – A Reply to Professor Grano' (1989–1990) 23 *University of Michigan Journal of Law Reform* 537, 562. Kamisar referred here to

Mapp and *Hudson* the Supreme Court had never attached particular weight to such remedies speaks for itself. Be that as it may, *Hudson* threatened to make the exclusionary rule 'fall off the cliff' to which the Supreme Court had itself pushed it in the first place. Having elevated deterrence to the sole purpose of exclusion, it could subsequently extinguish the exclusionary doctrine by taking the 'simple' final step of finding that alternative deterrent remedies had removed the need for the deterrent effect exercised by the latter.

Outright abolition is arguably what Justice Scalia attempted in *Hudson*. As David Moran, the lawyer who argued *Hudson* at the Supreme Court, put it, Justice Scalia's opinion 'contained a full-frontal attack on the rationale of the exclusionary rule; and it treated *Mapp* as an outdated precedent' because of the alleged availability of alternative deterrent remedies and the increasing professionalism of the police.[213] Furthermore, Scalia's opinion stressed the need for causation between the violation of a Fourth Amendment right (such as the knock-and-announce rule) and subsequently discovered evidence,[214] while it also subjected suppression to a novel condition, namely that suppression should serve the interest protected by the Fourth Amendment.[215] In the end, all that stood between Scalia's determination to end the exclusionary rule and actual abolition was Justice Kennedy's swing vote. Justice Kennedy provided the key fifth vote, but, quite paradoxically, also wrote in a concurring opinion that 'the continued operation of the exclusionary rule, as settled and defined by [the Supreme Court's] precedents, [was] not in doubt'.[216] Kennedy's pithy words of support for the exclusionary rule, and their symbiosis with *Hudson*, have proved difficult for commentators to decipher,[217] all the more so after he joined the majority opinions in *Herring* and *Davis*.[218]

The exclusionary rule barely survived *Hudson* to live another day, but, in view of *Herring* and *Davis*, its continuous operation *may* now be short-lived. The trilogy of cases discussed here has surely planted the seeds for the exclusionary rule's final demise, but whether this development will actually happen cannot be predicted

alternative remedies such as 'civil suits, criminal prosecution, injunctions, review boards and internal police discipline'. In the oral reargument of *Hudson*, David Moran responded to Justice Scalia's comments about the availability of alternative remedies by noting that this view was 'inconsistent with *Mapp* in which the Court recognized that other remedies ha[d] proven completely futile in enforcing the (*sic*) Fourth Amendment'. See Moran, 'Waiting for the Other Shoe' (2008) 1732.

[213] Moran (ibid).

[214] *Hudson v Michigan*, 547 US 586, 592 (2006).

[215] ibid 594. Scalia argued that in the case of 'knock-and-announce' violations this would not be so. The interests protected by the 'knock-and-announce' rule were human life and limb, preventing the destruction of property and protecting aspects of privacy and dignity that would be violated by a sudden entry. These interests were distinguishable from the interests protected by the warrant requirement.

[216] ibid 603.

[217] See, eg, CM Bradley, 'Mixed Messages on the Exclusionary Rule' (2006) 42 *Trial* 56; Moran, 'The End of the Exclusionary Rule' (2006) 308; SL Davies and AB Scanlon, '*Katz* in the Age of *Hudson v Michigan*: Some Thoughts on "Suppression as a Last Resort"' (2008) 41 *University of California Davis Law Review* 1035, 1066.

[218] See, eg, Maclin and Rader, 'No More Chipping Away' (2012) 1191.

with any degree of precision; there are too many variables in the equation.[219] From a more empirical perspective, it must be remembered that the American exclusionary rule has already experienced many unexpected twists and turns: from *Boyd* to *Adams* to *Weeks'* federal constitutional exclusionary rule and abolition with *Wolf*, and from *Mapp's* constitutionalisation of an all-encompassing exclusionary rule to the contemporary narrow judicial remedy with the uncertain constitutional fate, who could predict, with some level of certainty, the next stage in the historic evolution of the iconic exclusionary rule? One thing is nonetheless certain. The deterrence theory that the Supreme Court has endorsed since *Calandra* has taken its toll, constantly mutating the exclusionary rule, to the extent that it is now unrecognisable in comparison to the rule originally conceived in *Weeks* and *Mapp*. Recent developments in American exclusionary rule jurisprudence thus appear to be diametrically opposed to recent legislative and jurisprudential developments in Greece. While the modern history of the American exclusionary rule has been one of constantly evolving exceptions, pushing the rule away from the original jurisprudence and threatening to abolish it altogether, that of the Greek exclusionary rule has been one of strictly applying the exclusionary remedies, removing existing exceptions (albeit the economic crisis leading to the addition of an exception for tax and corruption offences) and reinvigorating the original exclusionary rule jurisprudence, with the effect of further solidifying its protective effect.

C. The Greek Exclusionary Rules Strictly Applied

Evidence obtained in violation of the right to privacy has been excluded by lower courts – and its use in Courts of First Instance and Courts of Appeal has led Arios Pagos to quash the defendants' convictions – in several cases from the mid-1990s onwards.[220] The turning point was in 2001 when, prior to the introduction of

[219] As Tomkovicz notes, for instance, the difficulty to 'predict the fate of the exclusionary rule' can be attributed to 'Justice Kennedy's pivotal role, [the] genuine uncertainty about his willingness to participate in further efforts to prune the suppression tree, and [the] inability to know how the Court will change' in the future. Tomkovicz, 'Hudson v Michigan' (2008) 1886. With Brett Kavanaugh nominated to replace Justice Kennedy, and considering that Kavanaugh is no great supporter of the exclusionary rule, we may now be able to more accurately predict the rule's future. On Kavanaugh's approach to the exclusionary rule see, eg, American Enterprise Institute, 'From the Bench: Judge Brett Kavanaugh on the Constitutional Statesmanship of Chief Justice William Rehnquist', 18 September 2017, www.aei.org/wp-content/uploads/2017/08/from-the-bench.pdf.

[220] See Arios Pagos 9/1994, 44 Poinika Chronika 215, where Arios Pagos quashed a conviction for rape and ordered a new trial as a result of the use in court of recordings of telephone conversations between the victim and the defendant. The recordings had been surreptitiously obtained by the victim. See also Arios Pagos (in plenary) 17/1993, 43 Poinika Chronika 1105 (regarding exclusion in the context of an administrative process); Court of first instance (Athens) 3071/1997, 48 Poinika Chronika 294 (recording of a private conversation by one party in the conversation, the civil party in the relevant trial, without the consent of the other party, the defendant in the relevant trial); Arios Pagos 215/2000, 50 Poinika Chronika 688 (exclusion of four recordings obtained surreptitiously by the civil party).

article 19, para 3, Arios Pagos, in plenary, strongly condemned the use of such evidence. The Court held that the administration of justice did not justify the use of unconstitutionally obtained evidential means, that the surreptitious recording of a conversation violated the right to secrecy of correspondence and, therefore, that its evidential use was constitutionally prohibited.[221] The Court thus read an evidential prohibition into the Constitution, as it had previously done in cases of improperly seized letters, thus breathing new life into the original exclusionary rule jurisprudence.[222] This decision set the tone for the case law that followed.

In a 2002 case where the defendant had been convicted of bribery on the basis of a tape-recorded conversation, the conviction was quashed since it was not clear whether the recording had been lawfully obtained.[223] The defendant does not bear a burden of proof on contested evidence, and any doubts as to its provenance work in his favour.[224] In 2003, Arios Pagos held that a Court of Appeal had rightly excluded the transcript of a private conversation with the defendant which the civil party had recorded without consent.[225] The Prosecutor at the Court of Appeal of Thessaloniki issued a legal opinion the same year, prohibiting the use of unlawfully obtained audiotapes; unlawfully obtained tapes could be used exceptionally to demonstrate the defendant's innocence.[226] In a case from 2004, Arios Pagos quashed a conviction for insurance fraud,[227] where a witness had installed a listening device that allowed her to eavesdrop on the defendant's discussions from a distance of 100 metres.[228] The conviction was quashed on grounds of nullity, since the witness's testimony was derivative evidence arising from interference with the defendant's constitutionally protected private conversations. The time limits for prosecution having elapsed in this case, moreover, a new trial could not be ordered.[229] In a lower court case from the same year, private letters had not been seized in accordance with the provisions of the law allowing interference with the secrecy of correspondence. The court held that any evidentiary use of the letters was prohibited by article 19, para 3, despite the fact that they would be used against a third party.[230] In pre-trial proceedings in 2005, the judicial chamber of the Court of Appeal of Piraeus had committed the defendant to be tried on forgery charges,[231] relying on information derived from a recorded

[221] Arios Pagos 1/2001, 49 Nomiko Bima 1803; 42 (2001) Elliniki Dikeosini 374. See also Charalampakis, (n 67) 1066–67.

[222] See section II A above.

[223] See Arios Pagos 297/2002, 3 Praksi & Logos tou Poinikou Dikeou 33. For the offence of bribery, see arts 235–237 Penal Code.

[224] The view is taken in Greece that the *in dubio pro reo* principle and the presumption of innocence militate against burdens of proof, even evidential ones. See Androulakis, *Fundamental notions of the criminal process* (1994) 192–97.

[225] Arios Pagos 622/2003, 3 Poinikos Logos 640.

[226] B Theodorou, Legal opinion No 83–84/2003, 6 Poiniki Dikeosini 274.

[227] Art 388, para 1 Penal Code.

[228] See Arios Pagos 1568/2004, 8 Poiniki Dikeosini 295.

[229] The time limit for the prosecution of such an offence is five years. See art 111, para 3 Penal Code.

[230] Court of first instance (Piraeus) 7056/2004, 56 Poinika Chronika 459.

[231] Art 216 Penal Code.

conversation between the civil party and an employee of the defendant. Even though the recording had been obtained by an infringement of the rights of a third party – the rights of an employee of the defendant – Arios Pagos reversed the decision to commit for trial, since the use of the information obtained via the recording had breached article 177, para 2 of the Code of Penal Procedure.[232] In another 'fruit of the poisonous tree' case from 2005, the judicial chamber of the Court of Appeal of Athens committed the defendant to be tried for counselling fraud,[233] relying on an illegally intercepted conversation between the defendant's spouse and a co-defendant. The evidence had again been obtained in violation of the right to privacy of a third party, and Arios Pagos reversed the decision.[234] In a case in 2006, Arios Pagos held that illegally obtained audiotapes had rightly not been taken under consideration when determining whether the defendants would be taken to trial.[235] In a case from 2010, the Court of First Instance and the Court of Appeal had rejected the use of illegally intercepted conversations in a civil case connected with the issuing of a cheque with no funds for the amount of €47,000, while the claimant who had submitted the intercepts in court was prosecuted for the offence of a violation of the secrecy of correspondence.[236] In Arios Pagos, the defendant argued that the a priori unlawful act of the interception should be excused under the defence of necessity, but the supreme jurisdiction rejected this defence and affirmed the conviction, holding that the protection of the secrecy of correspondence outweighed the need to prevent the financial damage threatened in this case.[237] In a child custody case heard in 2009 by its civil division, Arios Pagos spoke very firmly about the evidentiary prohibition of conversations intercepted without the consent of one of the parties, irrespective of the place where the conversation takes place, even in cases where the evidence is adduced against a third party who has not suffered a violation of *his* or *her* constitutional rights. In addition to reflecting on the importance of protecting the secrecy of correspondence, the Court spoke in terms of judicial integrity and deterrence in this case, arguing that the administration of justice could not rest on an 'ends justify the means' ideology, and risking the prediction that, without the automatic exclusionary sanction, the constitutional right to secrecy of correspondence would be of limited effectiveness, despite the existence of a criminal sanction.[238]

It is clear from the above that Greek courts rigorously apply the exclusionary rule. This is also evident in the logic and structure of their judgments, which

[232] See Arios Pagos 1622/2005, 56 Poinika Chronika 426. The case was sent back to the judicial chamber to decide whether to proceed to trial or not.

[233] See arts 386 and 46, para 1(a) Penal Code.

[234] See Arios Pagos 2035/2005, 56 Poinika Chronika 538.

[235] Arios Pagos 570/2006, 9 Poiniki Dikeosini 1084.

[236] Art 370A, para 2 Penal Code.

[237] Arios Pagos 53/2010, 11 Praksi & Logos tou Poinikou Dikeou 200, 202.

[238] Arios Pagos 1092/2009, 57 Nomiko Bima 2356. See also Arios Pagos 1351/2007, 56 Nomiko Bima 178.

apply the exclusionary rules mechanically, as if they constituted a mathematical formula. These decisions typically open with reference to the constitutional and statutory bases for exclusion: mainly articles 19, para 3 of the Constitution and article 177, para 2 of the Code of Penal Procedure, article 370A of the Penal Code, which criminally sanctions violations of the secrecy of correspondence, the Constitutional provisions that protect human dignity and the right to privacy[239] as well as article 8 of the European Convention on Human Rights. It is in this way that Greek jurisprudence makes explicit that the exclusionary rule's sole purpose is to protect the specifically enumerated constitutional and international human rights. The protective rationale is dominant here. Other justificatory bases, such as deterrence and judicial integrity, are rarely offered, while, with a few exceptions only, no interests countervailing exclusion are taken under consideration. The critic might pinpoint the simplistic, perhaps unsophisticated, way in which exclusionary rules are applied in this context. One might, however, respond that it is the same 'simplistic' logic that supported *Weeks* and underpinned the original understanding of *Mapp*, and the replacement of which with a cost–benefit analysis in modern exclusionary rule jurisprudence remains today the cause of major disagreement in the United States. This would put the critic's view in a useful comparative perspective and would further underline the rigorous application of exclusionary rules in Greece.

There is no better illustration of Greek courts' strict application of the exclusionary rules than their jurisprudence on the use of improperly obtained *exculpatory* evidence. Arios Pagos initially interpreted article 177, para 2 as being compatible with the defendant's reliance on such evidence.[240] Greek scholarship concurred on this point.[241] However, the introduction by article 19, para 3 of the Constitution of an ostensibly absolute exclusionary rule was seen by some commentators as going so far as even prohibit the use of unconstitutionally obtained exculpatory evidence.[242] Arios Pagos then rightly held that preventing a defendant from using evidence that could prove his or her innocence would violate the overarching constitutional right to respect of human dignity (article 2, para 1 of the Constitution). The Court mentioned, at the same time, a proportionality requirement, that the gravity of the offence should be taken into account and, most importantly, that the evidence in question should be the only exonerating evidence available to the defendant.[243] Arios Pagos has in fact affirmed lower court decisions convicting the defendant in cases where the trial judge had rejected the use of improperly obtained but allegedly exonerating evidence, on the basis that this

[239] Article 2, para 1, art 5, para 1, 9, 9A and art 19, para 1 of the Constitution.

[240] Arios Pagos 1351/1997, 48 Poinika Chronika 965.

[241] See Kostaras (n 73) 180; Dimitratos (n 73) 52; Androulakis (n 113) 181; Kaminis, 'Secrecy of Telephone Communication' (1995) 518–19; Dalakouras (n 73) 55.

[242] See, eg, Iliopoulou-Stragga (n 72) 2204.

[243] See, eg, Arios Pagos 42/2004, 4 Poinikos Logos 66.

evidence was not the only evidence available to the defendant.[244] A murder case from 2007 clearly illustrates that the supreme court's jurisprudence on exculpatory evidence can in some cases push the exclusionary doctrine to its extremes. A mixed Court of Appeal had barred the defendant from adducing into evidence an illegally obtained recording of a private conversation with the victim which – the defendant argued – would prove his innocence (or, alternatively, his guilt for a less serious offence). The Court refused to admit the illegal audiotape and convicted the defendant. Then Arios Pagos affirmed the decision, on the basis that the defendant had adduced other exonerating evidence.[245] Here it must be stressed that exclusion under article 19, para 3 has been designed as a protection for the defendant. It prevents further violation of defendants' constitutional right to privacy, for example by barring the reproduction in court of an illegally obtained audiotape containing a private conversation of the defendant,[246] and returns the defendant to the evidentiary status quo ante. The use of article 19, para 3 to prevent defendants from proving their innocence is therefore inconsistent with its inherent protective function. It is not supported by historical interpretation either. To my knowledge, nowhere in the relevant parliamentary debates has exonerating evidence been raised as an issue relevant to the application of the constitutional exclusionary rule.[247]

The balancing exercise that Arios Pagos undertakes in such cases admittedly becomes much more complicated when the exculpatory evidence that the defendant (D1) seeks to adduce has been obtained by violating the right to privacy of a

[244] Arios Pagos 813/2008, 59 Poinika Chronika 321. The defendant in this case was being tried for libel, after he had accused certain individuals for blackmailing him to pay the amount of nine million drachmas. Following their acquittal for the relevant offences, these individuals pressed charges against the defendant for libel and participated in the process as civil parties. The defendant then surreptitiously recorded a private conversation with them, which, as he argued in court, would offer proof that he had indeed been blackmailed and that he had therefore not committed the offence of libel. The Court of appeal of Athens refused to adduce the tape recording into evidence and found the defendant guilty. Arios Pagos affirmed its decision, on the basis that the defendant had adduced other evidence and that the unlawfully obtained recording had therefore not been the only evidence available to him. The same outcome was reached in Air Force Tribunal (Larissa) 38/2008, (2009) 57 Nomiko Bima 652. See also Arios Pagos 2617/2008, 59 Poinika Chronika 2011, where the supreme jurisdiction found that the evidence had been rightly excluded by the Court of appeal of Athens: the defendant had not argued – let alone proved – that the illegal intercept was the only exonerating evidence that was available to him, while he had also called three witnesses to testify in his defence, which automatically proved that the audiotape was not the only exonerating evidence.

[245] Arios Pagos 1537/2007, 58 Poinika Chronika 216.

[246] See Androulakis (n 113) 214.

[247] See also Karras, *Penal procedural law* (2011) 692, who argues that the use of improperly obtained exculpatory evidence should never be prohibited. He points out (at p 700) the paradox inherent in the requirement that the improperly obtained evidence should be the *only* exculpatory evidence available to the defendant. When the trial judge makes the preliminary finding that the improperly obtained evidence is *not the only* exculpatory evidence, he works from the assumption that the defendant will be able to demonstrate his innocence by relying on other available evidence. In cases where the defendant fails to do so in the end, despite adducing such evidence, the excluded exculpatory evidence by definition and *ex post* becomes the *only* exculpatory evidence that was in reality available to the defendant, which then demonstrates why the trial-judge should not have excluded it in the first place.

co-defendant (D2), for example when D1 has covertly recorded a conversation with D2, which is exculpatory for D1 but inculpates D2. Arios Pagos indicates that such evidence is admissible: the fact-finder should take the exculpatory part into account when deciding on D1's guilt, but must then disregard the incriminatory part when deciding on D2's guilt.[248] However, D1 still has to argue that the evidence he or she seeks to adduce is the only exculpatory evidence available to him or her.[249] This jurisprudence effects a delicate compromise between respecting D1's right to human dignity, which would be seriously undermined if he or she were wrongly convicted as a result of not being able to adduce exculpatory evidence, and D2's right to privacy, which would be equally damaged if evidence obtained in breach of the relevant constitutional protection were admitted. Whether the fact-finder can realistically be expected to disregard the incriminating part of the evidence once she becomes aware of it is another question, which in these circumstances cannot be addressed through suppression of the evidence.

D. Contemporary Challenges to Greek Exclusionary Rules

While the above jurisprudence offers a stark demonstration of how unbendingly exclusionary rules for violations of the right to privacy are applied in Greece, other jurisprudence tends to undermine their protective effect, as a result of adopting narrow interpretations of the right to privacy. This jurisprudence must be seen in combination with direct challenges, coming from some judicial circles and strands of criminal scholarship, to strictly applying the exclusionary rules in all situations. But against this backdrop of post-2001 resistance to automatic exclusion, one must concentrate on the legislature's further strengthening of the statutory and constitutional exclusionary rules.

i. Narrow Interpretations of the Right to Privacy

Certain Arios Pagos decisions read the right to privacy so narrowly that the obtaining of the evidence is deemed constitutional and the exclusionary rules are not triggered. In a 2001 case, a video camera had been covertly installed in church premises where money and other items dedicated to the church were kept. A priest was charged with theft and 15 videotapes were submitted to court showing him stealing the money.[250] In a similar case decided in 2004, a video camera had been secretly installed in a shop. Twenty-eight video stills were produced

[248] See Arios Pagos 1351/1997, 48 Poinika Chronika 965.

[249] See Arios Pagos 42/2004, 4 Poinikos Logos 66. In this case a covertly recorded tape exonerating D1 was not admitted, since D2 objected to its use and D1 had in fact submitted to the court other exculpatory evidence.

[250] Arios Pagos 1317/2001, 1 Poinikos Logos 1822.

in court showing an employee committing theft.[251] In both cases, Arios Pagos concentrated on whether the evidence had been obtained by the commission of the offence of 'improperly recording non-public acts'.[252] It gave a negative answer to this question: the relevant acts were not non-public (private) since they were conducted 'in the context of administrative duties [which were] subject to public control and public criticism'.[253] Article 177, para 2 consequently did not apply and use of the recordings was lawful. These decisions have rightly been criticised for putting forward a restrictive interpretation of the notion of private life that pays no attention to where the right is exercised and whether there is an expectation of privacy from the part of the participants.[254] It could be argued, for instance, that in the above cases the recording was conducted in a place where the public had no or limited access, implying that acts taking place there were of a private nature.[255] In fact, Arios Pagos' interpretation is so narrow that conduct related to administrative duties would potentially not be protected even when undertaken in the privacy of one's home. Put differently, the effect of these interpretations is that conduct related to occupational activities falls outside the protective scope of the right to private life. A lower court decision from 2008 has rightly pinpointed the significant risks for the right to privacy inherent in this approach, and, in aligning its jurisprudence with criminal law scholarship on this question, adopted a broader interpretation that focused on whether those participating in the conversation had an expectation of privacy, irrespective of whether the conversation related to occupational or private activities.[256]

A 2009 legal opinion by the Prosecutor of Arios Pagos provides another example of this trend.[257] In response to queries raised by the Athens Police Department, the Prosecutor opined that the right to secrecy of correspondence did not cover correspondence taking place over the Internet, unless a private forum was used or similar precautions taken, and that telephone metadata did not fall within the scope of the constitutional right either, which meant the seizure of such electronic

[251] Arios Pagos 874/2004, 5 Praksi & Logos tou Poinikou Dikeou 229.

[252] Art 370A, para 2 Penal Code.

[253] Arios Pagos 1317/2001, 1 Poinikos Logos 1822; Arios Pagos 874/2004, 5 Praksi & Logos tou Poinikou Dikeou 229.

[254] See D Kioupis, Comment on Arios Pagos 1317/2001, 1 Poinikos Logos 1822, 1826 (in Greek). See also Iliopoulou-Stragga (n 72) 2201; Kaminis (n 98) 337, 361–62; E Symeonidou-Kastanidou, 'Journalism and secrecy of correspondence' (2006) 9 Poiniki Dikeosini 1297 (in Greek); E Symeonidou-Kastanidou, 'Article 370A Penal Code and recent announcements regarding its amendment' (2008) 4 Poiniki Dikeosini 462, 463 (in Greek).

[255] ibid 1827.

[256] See Naval Force Tribunal (Thessaloniki), 61 Poinika Chronika 425. The defendant, an officer in the coast guard, covertly recorded a conversation with two other officers that related to administrative issues and had taken place in the office of the commander of the coast guard during a formal meeting. The Court found that the conversation could not be considered as taking place in public simply because its content related to administrative issues. The meeting was not open to the public, the conversation was therefore private and, by surreptitiously recording it, the defendant had committed the relevant criminal law offence (art 370A, Penal Code).

[257] G Sanidas, Legal opinion No 9/2009, 45 Dikeomata tou Anthropou 187.

data by the police or other investigative authority was not subject to evidentiary exclusion.[258] An Arios Pagos decision from 2011 applied this interpretation to lists of incoming and outgoing telephone calls to uphold a murder conviction, in a case where the police had lawfully obtained these lists from the relevant telephone communication providers.[259]

A more welcome restrictive interpretation of the right to privacy has been adopted where the nature of a private correspondence is itself criminal, such as where a person has threatened or blackmailed another person during a telephone call, texting or other form of electronic communication. A surreptitious recording of such a conversation will not breach the Constitution and will not be subject to exclusion in a criminal trial. This is because, the argument goes, through the right to secrecy of correspondence, the Constitution protects positive expressions of one's personality and not the continuation of the decadent manifestations of the latter that have started with the commission of the offence.[260] Arios Pagos has explicitly acknowledged that it subscribes to this principle with regards to telephone calls and electronic texts containing threats of violence or demands with menaces.[261] A more far-reaching application can be seen in a case from 2010. The police had conducted a lawful search of the defendant's house and discovered videotapes containing nude and half-nude images of juveniles, including images of the defendant lying on his bed with two female juveniles and sexually touching them. The defendant took the case to Arios Pagos requiring that his conviction be quashed, as a result of a violation of the constitutional right that protects the individual against the collection, processing and use of personal data[262] and as a result of the fact that the statutory procedures for the authorisation of the collection of such data had not been followed.[263] However, Arios Pagos held that the videotapes were not covered by the relevant constitutional rights, and that subsequently the statutory authorisation procedure did not apply, and it followed from this that the Court of Appeal had been right to take the videotapes into consideration.[264] Though the opinion of the Court did not offer any explanation of why the private data were not covered by the right to privacy, Karras' analysis that this was because their content was a decadent manifestation – rather than a positive expression – of the defendant's personality is plausible.[265] We can open a parenthesis here. The Court's reasoning presents comparative law observers with

[258] This was despite the fact that a 2005 presidential decree had extended the protection of the right to secrecy of correspondence to the aforementioned means of correspondence. See Presidential Decree 47/2005.

[259] Arios Pagos 711/2011, Athens Bar Association Legal Database.

[260] Androulakis (n 113) 216.

[261] I Tentes, Legal Opinion of the Prosecutor of Arios Pagos No 12/2009, 53 Epitheorisi Dimosiou Idiotikou Dikaiou 1080 (bringing precision to Legal opinion No 9/2009, 45 Dikeomata tou Anthropou 187).

[262] Art 9A of the Constitution.

[263] Law 2225/1994, modified by Law 3115/2003 and 3666/2008.

[264] Arios Pagos 560/2010, 61 Poinika Chronika 193. See also Karras (n 124) 697.

[265] Karras (n 124) 696.

the interesting perspective of the admissibility of electronic records discovered during a search being determined in separation of the legality of the latter. In this case the police search had been conducted lawfully, yet Arios Pagos still had to determine whether the use of the evidence in court would have, on its own right, breached the relevant constitutional right. This offers an example of what is known in theory as an 'independent evidentiary prohibition', which applies irrespective of whether the evidence has been obtained in a lawful manner or not. The prohibition (or exclusionary rule) is justified by the fact that the evidentiary use itself would violate the constitutional right or related interest.[266]

To close the parenthesis, it must be noted that Arios Pagos' narrow interpretations of the right to privacy call to mind an important criticism of exclusionary rules. The inflexible way in which these are applied often lead courts to narrowly interpret the constitutional rights that the rules are supposed to protect. This is a well-known criticism of the exclusionary rules applying in the United States.[267] But one might quickly respond that inflexible exclusionary rules oblige the courts to reflect openly on the extent of constitutional limits, and that this is preferable to the courts disingenuously subscribing to constitutional rights rhetoric while validating the use of evidence obtained in violation of these very rights under a discretionary admissibility regime. It could also be pointed out that regimes of discretionary exclusion are not immune from the risk of narrow interpretations of the relevant constitutional rights and other 'avoidance techniques' either.[268]

ii. (Some) Resistance to the Exclusionary Rule's Reinforcement

As mentioned before, there was from early on wide consensus amongst Greek commentators that the constitutional legislator of 2001 conceived article 19, para 3 as instituting an absolute exclusionary rule. After this came into existence, Greek commentators also considered that pre-existing exceptions – the 'life imprisonment

[266] See generally Dimitratos (n 110); Triantafillou (n 75) 295. This terminology is widely used in German criminal procedure. See, eg, K Rogall, *Gegenwärtiger Stand und Entwicklungstendenzen der Lehre von den strafprozessualen*, ZStW 91 (1979).

[267] See generally AR Amar, 'Against Exclusion (Except to Protect Truth or Prevent Privacy Violations)' (1997) 20 *Harvard Journal of Law & Public Policy* 457, 465; Mirfield, *Improperly Obtained Evidence* (1997) 321–22; W Pizzi, *Trials Without Truth: Why our System of Criminal Trials has Become an Expensive Failure and What we Need to Do to Rebuild it* (New York and London, New York University Press, 1999) 39; D Ormerod, 'ECHR and the Exclusion of Evidence: Trial Remedies for Article 8 Breaches' [2003] *Criminal Law Review* 61, 72. See also MR Wilkey, 'A Call for Alternatives to the Exclusionary Rule: Let Congress and the Trial Courts Speak' (1979) 62 *Judicature* 351, 355, who points to 'one most salient vice of the exclusionary rule – [...] the judges are corrupted by the exclusionary rule'.

[268] See generally B Presser, 'Public Policy, Police Interest: A Re-Evaluation of the Judicial Discretion to Exclude Improperly or Illegally Obtained Evidence' (2001) 25 *Melbourne University Law Review* 757, 778; P Duff, 'Irregularly Obtained Real Evidence: The Scottish Solution?' (2004) 8 *International Journal of Evidence & Proof* 77, 90; S Optican and P Sankoff, 'The New Exclusionary Rule: A Preliminary Assessment of *R v Shaheed*' [2003] *New Zealand Law Review* 1, 3.

offences' exception and the partial defence that applied to telephone intercepts and recordings of private conversations – were incompatible with the constitutional prohibition and should therefore be abolished. The exceptions were statutory law that was conflicting with higher order constitutional law.[269] The Hellenic Data Protection Authority shared this view and, in 2002, issued a legal opinion recommending abolition.[270] Legislation introduced in July 2008 indeed abolished the exceptions.[271]

However, noteworthy strands of resistance, jurisprudential and doctrinal, can be identified both before and after the legislature's emphatic reaffirmation of the categorical exclusionary rules. Most characteristic is an Arios Pagos decision from 2006 which held that, in exceptional cases, the exclusionary rules of article 177, para 2 and article 19, para 3 do not apply even if evidence is admitted against the defendant. The court opined that:

> The reasonable use of evidence obtained in an illegal manner (for example, evidence obtained in violation of the right to privacy), either in favour or against the defendant, guarantees balance … in the evidentiary stage, in accordance with law's more profound logic, which is founded on balancing diverse interests and on their harmonious and proportional protection.[272]

It added that 'courts will take into consideration illegally obtained evidence against the defendant, when this is eventually the only evidence on which the victim can rely'.[273] This realignment with the theory of balancing is remarkable, considering the various legislative developments that had long turned the law of improperly obtained evidence in the opposite direction of categorical and unqualified exclusion. It is unsustainable too, as it has no foundation in either constitutional or common statutory law. It rather violates the expressions of both, in disregarding the exclusionary rules of article 19, para 3 and article 177, para 2. It must be explained, however, that the illegal intercept that would demonstrate the guilt of the defendant in this case would simultaneously demonstrate the innocence of a co-defendant, for the most serious offences of abduction and murder, and that this may have influenced the decision of the Court.

[269] See, eg, Charalampakis (n 72) 1067; Paulou, Fountedaki and Dimitrainas (n 99) 922; G Nouskalis, 'Some reflections on the extent of the protection of the secrecy of correspondence and private life, after amendment of articles 370A of the Penal Code and 7A of Law 2472/1997 and with Law 3090/2002' (2003) 6 *Poiniki Dikeosini* 8 (in Greek); G Papadimitrakis, 'The arrest of the suspect and house searches through the prism of the Fourth Amendment of the United States Constitution' (2007) *Poiniki Dikeosini* 1051 (in Greek); Triantafillou (n 75) 295. Iliopoulou-Stragga recognised the unconstitutionality of the 'life imprisonment offences' exception, but not that of the partial defence of art 370A, para 4 of the Penal Code. Iliopoulou-Stragga (n 72) 2196–98. Relating to the 'life imprisonment offences exception', Charalampakis was arguing that it was incompatible with the Constitution even prior to the introduction of art 19, para 3. See Charalampakis, 'Constitution and criminal law' (2000) 105.

[270] Hellenic Data Protection Authority, Legal opinion No 83/2002, 53 Poinika Chronika 80.

[271] Art 10 of Law 3674/2008 of 10 July 2008 on the 'reinforcement of the institutional framework guaranteeing the secrecy of telephone correspondence and other provisions'.

[272] Arios Pagos 611/2006, 58 Poinika Chronika 895.

[273] ibid.

Writing extra-judicially, the deputy prosecutor of Arios Pagos who sat in this case suggested that the exceptional use of improperly obtained evidence against the defendant will be limited to cases where the evidence has itself a criminal content. The hypothetical discussed concerned a defendant who has threatened the life of the son of the victim through numerous telephone calls, and it is argued that the use of the surreptitious recording of these calls would be legitimate.[274] Symeonidou-Kastanidou similarly recognised limited exceptions to the general prohibition to use evidence obtained in violation of the right to privacy. Her hypothetical involved using the secretly recorded telephone calls made by the defendant who has abducted the child of the victim and asks for ransom.[275] Both opinions criticised the 2008 reforms abolishing the two aforementioned exceptions to the exclusionary rule. They should not be read, however, as directly challenging the exclusionary rules' logic. They rather stress the need for a narrower interpretation of the right to privacy in the above two scenarios.

Taking these criticisms further, Kalfelis points out that the Greek exclusionary rule is antithetical to the approach taken by all countries in the Western world.[276] His attack on the exclusionary rule is reminiscent of criticism of the Fourth Amendment exclusionary rule as a sign of American exceptionalism. Both criticisms are significantly exaggerated, as already demonstrated in this chapter.[277] Kalfelis insists that Parliament's determination of the constitutional values whose protection should obtain priority is 'authoritarian' and 'paternalistic', and an interference with what should be the judiciary's prerogative. From this angle, he 'condemns' the July 2008 reforms as a deeply negative development.[278] A prosecutor at a Court of First Instance, writing extrajudicially, has, with equal force, attacked the latest legislative reinforcement of the exclusionary rules, suggesting that the use of improperly obtained evidence should instead be determined on the basis of a balancing exercise that would give weight to proportionality, necessity and the seriousness of the offence.[279] However, these views fail to take proper account of the Greek constitutional system (and the constitutional revision process), according to which it falls upon the constitutional legislator to make these judgments. The 2008 reforms simply affirmed that the article 177, para 2 exceptions were no longer consistent with the Constitution.

These criticisms cannot be ignored, but their effect so far seems limited in practice. Even with regards to improperly obtained exonerating evidence, Arios Pagos continues to require that strict conditions be met before the evidence can

[274] A Zygouras, 'The procedural use by private parties of illegally obtained evidence after the latest legislative reform' (2008) 58 Poinika Chronika 1013 (in Greek).

[275] Symeonidou-Kastanidou, 'Article 370A' (2008) 466.

[276] Kalfelis, 'Privacy and cameras' (2008) 866.

[277] See also ch 6 for other comparative examples that support this conclusion.

[278] Kalfelis (n 129) 865.

[279] D Zimianitis, 'Unlawful video or audio recordings and use of their products by the mass media' (2010) 13 Poiniki Dikeosini 1028 (in Greek).

be used in court, which is characteristic of the rigid approach it generally adopts in relation to violations of the right to privacy. But we must also not overlook that current criticisms of the rigid exclusionary rules in Greece generate significant risks for their continued operation in practice. As has already been discussed, the introduction in 2015 of a statutory exception in trials for corruption and tax offences marks a momentous U-turn in Greek exclusionary rule legislation, which one cannot help thinking risks creating the conditions for undermining the protective scope of exclusionary rules further, particularly if the recent legislative reform contributes to existing jurisprudential and doctrinal attacks obtaining new momentum.

VI. Caveats

There are important caveats to the preceding comparative law observations. First of all, Greek exclusionary rules are applied exclusively with respect to surreptitiously recorded private conversations. For all their wide scope, the rules have rarely been applied to other tangible evidence obtained in violation of the right to privacy. Isolated examples include application to the report of a medical examination that the suspect had been wrongly compelled to undergo[280] and unlawfully seized bank cheques that were protected by the secrecy of banking transactions.[281] But case law on the exclusion of evidence obtained by unauthorised police searches is virtually inexistent, despite the fact that the applicability of article 19, para 3 in this domain is not in doubt.[282] Compared to Fourth Amendment exclusionary rules, Greek exclusionary rules therefore entirely avoid arguably the most crucial area of police investigative activity, as far as the protection of the right to privacy is concerned. The reason for this is possibly that judicial supervision has replaced in practice the need for exclusion. It must be explained that the Constitution dictates that a judicial officer – a prosecutor or investigative magistrate – be present when police undertake a search of a house,[283] with the exception of preliminary investigations where there are exigent circumstances and the police act alone,[284] and that this is standard practice. Greek exclusionary rules still pale in comparison to the American one as regards impacting upon the day-to-day investigative activity

[280] CD Naïntos, Legal Opinion of the Prosecutor at the Court of first instance (Thessaloniki) No 6/20.3.2002, 62 Poinika Chronika 665.

[281] Arios Pagos 1713/2006, 55 Nomiko Bima 443. See also CD Naïntos, *Evidentiary prohibitions in the criminal trial* (Athens-Thessaloniki, Sakkoulas, 2010) 353–54 (in Greek).

[282] See D Tsatsos, A Papadamakis and K Chrysogonos, *The legality of house search and seizure in preliminary investigations and their consequences in the criminal trial (legal opinion)* (2003) 6 *Poiniki Dikeosini* 813 (in Greek); Androulakis (n 113) 308.

[283] Article 9 of the Constitution provides that '[n]o search of a private residence shall be made, except when and as specified by law and *always in the presence of representatives of the judicial power*' (emphasis added).

[284] Art 243, para 2 Code of Penal Procedure. For the ability of the police to undertake house searches in exigent circumstances see, eg, Arios Pagos 1328/2003, 54 Poinika Chronika 341.

of the police. The Fourth Amendment exclusionary rule poses a real exclusionary 'threat' to illegitimate police action, especially as it combines with a vast jurisprudence on the substantive protections that apply to search and seizure.[285] The Greek exclusionary rules, on the other hand, are seldom applied to search and seizure in practice,[286] while the substantive search and seizure protections they are supposed to enforce, though not much dissimilar to those provided by the Fourth Amendment,[287] remain widely unexplored in the jurisprudence of criminal courts.[288] The above observations are reinforced by the fact that in Greece it is nearly always the 'civil party' rather than the prosecution that submits the contested evidence. The Greek investigating authorities do not feel the 'heat' of exclusion for this additional reason. American law enforcement officers *do*, as their investigative action is routinely scrutinised by reference to the Fourth Amendment and its exclusionary rule.

A second caveat concerns the scope of exclusion in the United States. Analysis of United States law has so far concentrated on the all-important Fourth Amendment exclusionary rule. But emphasis must also be placed on the statutory exclusionary rule for illegal wiretaps and the exclusionary rules that apply under State Constitutions. To start with the former, the key point of reference is legislation that regulates the interception of wire, oral and electronic communications, Title III of the Omnibus Crime Control and Safe Streets Act 1968 (Title III).[289] Section 2515 (§ 2515) of this legislation contains a strict exclusionary rule that mandates the suppression of all illegally intercepted *wire* and *oral*

[285] For a brief description of search and seizure jurisprudence see CM Bradley, *Criminal Procedure: A Worldwide Study*, 2nd edn (Durham, North Carolina, Carolina Academic Press, 2007) 519.

[286] In a rare example of a search and seizure improperly obtained evidence case, Arios Pagos held in 2010 that art 19, para 3 mandates the exclusion of evidence obtained by residential searches in violation of the right to privacy in order to offer protection to the relevant constitutional values (the privacy of the house), and that this interest outweighed the search for truth and the existence of an efficient criminal justice system. On the facts of the case, the Court found that the relevant search was constitutional, as it had been conducted with the consent of the owner, and that the drugs discovered had subsequently been rightly adduced as evidence in the process before the Court of appeal. See Arios Pagos 1773/2010, 61 Poinika Chronika 688.

[287] Limitations of the ability of the police to undertake search and seizure are mainly provided by the Constitution in both the United States and Greece. In Greece, it is the Code of Penal Procedure that brings precision to the constitutional mandates, while judicial interpretations of the Fourth Amendment take priority in the United States. A judicial warrant issued by an independent and impartial judicial authority is central to both systems. There are also many similarities as to how widely the right to privacy is interpreted, especially with regards to residential and other types of premises that fall within its protective scope. See generally Papadimitrakis, 'The arrest of the suspect and house searches' (2007) 1051.

[288] The fact that the 'police searches' sections of the two most authoritative textbooks on Greek Criminal procedure contain no reference to case law, and are rather limited to an enumeration and critical discussion of the relevant provisions of the Code of Penal Procedure, speaks for itself. See Androulakis (n 113) 303–08; Karras (n 124) 487–94.

[289] Electronic communications were added to the protective scope of Title III with amendments introduced with the Electronic Communications Privacy Act 1986.

(but not *electronic*) communications.[290] More specifically, exclusion is automatic every time there is a breach of a provision of Title III that 'was intended to play a central role in the statutory scheme',[291] which means intercept evidence is admitted when *only* a 'technical' breach has been committed.[292] The rule is otherwise unqualified and has a much wider scope than the Fourth Amendment exclusionary rule.[293] Thus, its effect is not restricted to trial hearings, but extends to all types of proceedings, such as grand jury proceedings, bail and parole revocation hearings or proceedings before regulatory bodies and legislative committees.[294] More symptomatic of the rule's stringent application is the fact that it also applies to interceptions committed by private parties, even where the government, which introduces the intercept evidence in court, demonstrates that it was uninvolved in the wiretapping.[295] The Fourth Circuit of the Court of Appeals so held in 2009, in *United States v Crabtree*,[296] where it underlined that 'the protection of privacy was an overriding congressional concern' when Title III had been introduced with the aim of prohibiting private, non-consensual wiretapping, that the 'broad exclusionary rule of §2515 provide[d] the teeth to the prohibitions',[297] and that the protection of 'privacy interests sometimes outweigh[ed] law enforcement interests'.[298] The Court also found that exclusion was required despite acknowledging it would have no deterrent effect in cases such as this where the government was not involved in the illegal interception.[299] The primacy of the protective rationale in the Court's reasoning, as well as in the text of the statute and intent of the legislator more generally, presents a striking difference with the deterrence-based exceptions to the now contracted Fourth Amendment exclusionary rule, on the one hand, and an impressive resemblance with the strict exclusionary rules of

[290] US Code §2515. See also DT Fettig, 'When "Good Faith" Makes Good Sense': Applying *Leon's* Exception to the Exclusionary Rule to the Government's Reasonable Reliance on Title III Wiretap Orders' (2012) 49 *Harvard Journal on Legislation* 373, 380.

[291] *United States v Giordano* 416 US 505, 528 (1974).

[292] See *United States v Chavez*, 416 US 562 (1974). On the 'technical violation exception' see generally B Boerman, 'Beyond the Wire: An Analysis of Non-Telephonic Conversations under Title III' (2008) 3 *New York University Journal of Law & Liberty* 599, 623–26.

[293] See R Greenblatt, 'Violations of Electronic Eavesdrop Procedures Under Title III and the Exclusionary Rule' (1976–1977) 43 *Brooklyn Law Review* 1271, 1273–74. The rule is, however, subject to an impeachment exception. See *United States v Crabtree*, 565 F3d 887, 891–92 (4th Cir 2009), and Circuit Courts of Appeal case law mentioned there.

[294] See 18 USCA §2518(10)(a).

[295] See *United States v Crabtree*, 565 F3d 887 (4th Cir 2009). See generally J Hunter, 'Government May Not Introduce Evidence Derived from Illegal Private Wiretaps Despite Its "Clean Hands" – *United States v Crabtree*, 565 F3d 887 (4th Cir 2009)' (2009–2010) 43 *Suffolk University Law Review* 767. See also N La Forge, 'Hands Off: *United States v Crabtree* and the Proper Application of Title III of the Omnibus Crime Control and Safe Streets Act of 1968' (2011) 37 *New England Journal on Criminal and Civil Confinement* 123.

[296] *United States v Crabtree*, 565 F3d 887 (4th Cir 2009).

[297] ibid 889–90.

[298] ibid 890.

[299] The Court nonetheless opined that exclusion would have a deterrent effect on the private party intercepting the communication. ibid 891.

Greece, on the other. The fact that the latter are nearly exclusively applied with regards to illegal wiretaps also means that, in the end, convergence between the United States and Greece is, from the viewpoint of intercept evidence, even wider than originally meets the eye.

In the same vein, for the analysis of United States law to be reasonably comprehensive, the exclusionary rules that apply under state Constitutions require special attention. This is because the United States Constitution, as interpreted by the Supreme Court, defines only the minimum level of protection of individual rights required, leaving the states the freedom to extend these protections further.[300] The Supreme Court's jurisprudence on the Fourth Amendment exclusionary rule may thus provide the baseline for the application of the rule, but several state supreme courts have adopted exclusionary rules that extend much further. In many cases, this was in reaction to decisions by the Burger and Rehnquist Courts reducing the protective effect of the rule.[301] State supreme courts' resistance to *Leon* is a characteristic example. In rejecting the 'good faith exception', the supreme courts of Connecticut,[302] Delaware,[303] Georgia,[304] Idaho,[305] Iowa,[306] Minnesota,[307] New Jersey,[308] New Mexico,[309] New York,[310] North Carolina,[311] Pennsylvania,[312] Vermont,[313] Washington,[314] and Wisconsin[315] have adopted exclusionary rules that are more strictly enforced than that adopted under the Fourth Amendment.[316] Considering, in particular, the risks that modern 'good faith' Supreme Court jurisprudence generates for the continued viability of the exclusionary rule, this development cannot go unnoticed. In fact, some states go even further in adopting a version of the exclusionary rule that resonates strongly with, and in

[300] See Justice WJ Brennan Jr, 'State Constitutions and the Protection of Individual Rights' (1977) 90 *Harvard Law Review* 489, 491.

[301] R Bloom and H Massey, 'Accounting for Federalism in State Courts: Exclusion of Evidence Obtained Lawfully by Federal Agents' (2008) 79 *University of Colorado Law Review* 381, 383.

[302] *State v Marsala* (1990) 216 Conn 150; *State v Morrissey* (1990) 216 Conn 185.

[303] *Dorsey v State*, 761 A2d 807, 821 (Del 2000).

[304] *Gary v State*, 422 SE2d 426 (Ga 1992); GA CODE ANN § 17-5-30 (2007).

[305] *State v Guzman* (1992) 122 Idaho 981.

[306] *State v Cline*, 617 NW2d 277 (Iowa 2000).

[307] *State v Herbst*, 395 NW2d 399 (1986, Minn App).

[308] *State v Novembrino* (1987) 105 NJ 95.

[309] *State v Gutierrez* (1991, App) 112 NM 774, 819 P2d 1332.

[310] *People v Bigelow* (1985) 66 NY2d 417.

[311] *State v Carter*, 370 SE2d 553, 559 (NC 1988).

[312] *Commonwealth v Edmunds* (1991) 526 Pa 374, 586 A2d 887.

[313] *State v Oakes* (1991) 157 Vt 171, 598 A2d 119.

[314] *State v Crawley* (1991) 61 Wash App 29, 808 P2d 773.

[315] *State v Grawien* (1985, App) 123 Wis 2d 428, 367 NW2d 816.

[316] See generally JE Theuman, 'State Constitutional Requirements as to Exclusion of Evidence Unlawfully Seized – post-Leon case', 19 *American Law Reports* 5th 470, §12[b]. See also LA Morissey, 'State Courts Reject *Leon* on State Constitutional Grounds: A Defense of Reactive Rulings' (1994) 47 *Vanderbilt Law Review* 917; MJ Gorman, 'Survey: State Search and Seizure Analogs' (2007) 77 *Mississippi Law Journal* 417; Justice TJ Saylor, 'Fourth Amendment Departures and Sustainability in State Constitutionalism' (2012) 22 *Widener Law Journal* 1, 16–19; Clancy (n 25) 383–88.

some cases even surpasses, the protective effect of the rule originally conceived in *Mapp*. In New York, for instance, the exclusionary rule generally also applies to civil proceedings,[317] while in Texas there is no exception for evidence obtained by private parties.[318] Texas does not have an 'inevitable discovery exception' either,[319] same as Indiana.[320] What is more, in diverging from Supreme Court jurisprudence, some state supreme courts have taken a principled approach to exclusion, finding a strong constitutional basis for *their* exclusionary rules, placing emphasis on judicial integrity and taking distance from the logic of deterrence as the sole exclusionary rationale.[321] Though the majority of state exclusionary rules continue to mirror federal law, the disparity identified here once again changes the perspective. The analysis of post-*Mapp* federal jurisprudence painted a bleak picture of the automatic (but qualified) exclusionary rule as an effective remedy for violations of the constitutional right to privacy, and put it in contrast with the equally automatic (but unqualified) exclusionary rules espoused in Greece. But from the angle of those states which adopt a much more stringent version of the federal exclusionary rule, the exclusionary systems of the two countries appear to be much more closely connected. This is an important point, especially since analyses of the American exclusionary rule generally fail to take note of the liberal developments in some states, which often leads to myopic vision as to the rule's effect in practice. Put differently, the United States exclusionary doctrine is often seen as so heavily riddled with exceptions, and so deprived of its constitutional origins and remedial rationale, as to have no effect in practice. As regards many of the states that adopt their own exclusionary rules, this simply is not true.

VII. Concluding Thoughts

Exclusion for violations of the constitutional right to privacy is automatic in both the United States and Greece, but, while the American exclusionary rule is heavily qualified, leading, in a wide range of cases, to more elastic responses rather than mandatory exclusion, the Greek exclusionary rules are virtually absolute in theory

[317] *People ex rel Piccarillo v New York State Board of Parole* 397 NE2d 354 (NY 1979). See generally ML Spencer, 'Suppress or Suspend: New York's Exclusionary Rule in School Disciplinary Proceedings' (1997) 72 *New York University Law Review* 1494, 1507–09.

[318] Tex Code Crim Proc Ann art 38.23 (West 2011). See generally AM Gershowitz, 'Is Texas Tough on Crime but Soft on Criminal Procedure?' (2012) 49 *American Criminal Law Review* 31, 46–48.

[319] Gershowitz (ibid) 44–45.

[320] *Ammons v State*, 770 NE2d 927 (Ind Ct App 2002).

[321] See generally Clancy, 'The Fourth Amendment Exclusionary Rule as a Constitutional Right' (2013) 385–88. *Cf People v Goldston*, 682 NW2d 479 (Mich 2004), where the Supreme Court of Michigan held that '[t]he exclusionary rule in Michigan is a judicially created remedy that is not based on the text of our constitutional search and seizure provision' and that '[t]he purpose of the exclusionary rule is to deter police misconduct'. For criticism see generally A Woolworth, 'The Good Faith Exception: "What is it Good For?" The Michigan Supreme Court Overturns Twenty Years of Precedent Holding it Was Worth "Absolutely Nothing"' (2006) 83 *University of Detroit Mercy Law Review* 441.

and rigorously applied in practice. The comparison of the two systems usefully informs scholarly debate and reform. This is a timely exercise for the United States in particular, as the Fourth Amendment exclusionary rule has arguably reached the lowest point in its history – as supporters of the rule would criticise and fierce opponents would rejoice about – and may not be far from being consigned to oblivion, if not in theory, certainly in practice. If these are indeed *Mapp's* 'final hours', its supporters may in fact have no option but to resort to unconventional methods to save the rule. Where recourse to constitutional jurisprudence, legal history and criminal law doctrine may have previously failed, foreign and comparative law might succeed, even if their use is not exactly a popular choice in the United States these days,[322] all the more so when the comparison undertaken here – between one of the most iconic rules of the American adversarial system and similar rules adopted in a small European jurisdiction rooted in the inquisitorial culture – is itself unconventional.

And yet, it is precisely this contrast that may make the identification of the surprisingly robust exclusionary devices in Greece particularly noteworthy for the United States. The Greek exclusionary rule is written in the constitutional text and is strongly grounded on the protective rationale. Good faith does not render the rule inapplicable, while its use is not restricted to the criminal trial. The rule applies to derivative evidence and violations committed by third parties, and is even triggered by violations of the right to privacy against third parties. In other words, this is an enhanced version of the original rule conceived in *Mapp*. Naturally, it provides a strong contrast to *Mapp* as it applies today. What is more, despite its similarities with the original understanding of *Mapp*, the Greek constitutional exclusionary rule is the product of an indigenous and intuitive approach to unconstitutionally obtained evidence, not a foreign imported product stemming from a possible Americanisation of national criminal procedure; exclusion was first seen in Greece as inherent in the constitutional right to privacy a whole 15 years before *Boyd*, and this is still the position endorsed in contemporary exclusionary rule jurisprudence. It is equally noteworthy that the Greek exclusionary rule has passed from historical stages of evolution similar to those relating to the American exclusionary rule, with constant movement to and away from strict application, before emerging, virtually unscathed, in its current form. The American exclusionary rule has, on the contrary, come out of these evolutionary processes significantly transformed. More importantly, the Greek exclusionary rule does not rest on an empirical foundation, built on deterrence, but rather a principled approach based on constitutional analysis. Viewed from the States it can, therefore, help 'bring back into the debate a more constitutionally robust view of the [American]

[322] See generally AL Parrish, 'Storm in a Teacup: The US Supreme Court's Use of Foreign Law' (2007) *University of Illinois Law Review* 637.

exclusionary rule',[323] which, as Sandby rightly argues, has been 'obscured in the [Supreme] Court's formal doctrine since the Burger and Rehnquist Courts redirected the dialogue solely towards deterrence'.[324] Though unlikely to materialise, such a jurisprudential twist is 'worth contemplating as the Roberts Court appears to be rethinking the rule once again'.[325] Finally, there are lessons here for those who criticise the automatic Fourth Amendment exclusionary rule on the basis that it is an isolated example in comparative law.[326] Greece provides helpful guidance of an 'inquisitorial' system that adopts categorical exclusionary rules (constitutional and statutory), more rigorous than those recognised by the Supreme Court.

But right here it is as well to sound a note of caution. Though particularly wide encompassing in theory, Greek exclusionary rules are restricted to illegal wiretaps in practice, an area, in other words, in which an automatic and far-reaching statutory exclusionary rule already exists in the United States. This takes nothing away from the fact that Greece adopts robust exclusionary rules precisely in relation to the type of improperly obtained evidence most commonly adduced by the parties there. This is not the case in the United States, where it is search and seizure, not wiretaps, that is the epicentre of exclusionary jurisprudence. The critic might still question the desirability of looking at the example of a country with so heavily rights-centred remedies, especially when that country is facing ever-increasing threats to law and order, and until quite recently the threat of socio-political disorder in the context of brutal, long-lasting, economic crisis. Put differently, the critic might see Greek exclusionary rules as pinpointing an idealistic system detached from the realities of law enforcement. The critic might also draw attention to the legal system's 'neurotic' behaviour, to borrow a Freudian concept used in the criminal procedure context by Damaška. Narrow judicial interpretations of the relevant substantive rights might indicate such 'neurosis'. Faced with highly inflexible exclusionary rules that leave no scope for balancing, criminal courts in Greece may have had no choice but to start looking for ways to avoid their application altogether.[327] From this perspective, the American experience provides Greek law

[323] SE Sandby, 'Everyman's Exclusionary Rule: The Exclusionary Rule and the Rule of Law (or Why Conservatives Should Embrace the Exclusionary Rule)' (2013) 10 *Ohio State Journal of Criminal Law* 393, 411.

[324] ibid 394.

[325] ibid.

[326] Even supporters of the rule sometimes accept the validity of this argument, such as Bradley who argued that the fact that the American exclusionary rule is 'universally rejected by other countries' did 'give one pause about the need for a mandatory rule'. Bradley, 'Is the Exclusionary Rule Dead?' (2012) 22. Slobogin has similarly pointed to 'the fact that most countries in Europe and the former British Commonwealth rarely exclude illegally seized evidence and, when they do, it is usually only in cases where the police acted egregiously'. Slobogin (n 6) 353.

[327] As Krapac explains, this concept was developed by Damaška in his lectures in the Zagreb Law School in 2004 and 2005. Damaška drew the analogy with Freud's concept of a strong 'super-ego' that causes a person to behave neurotically. A procedural system that neglects efficient punishment to protect human rights risks causing the system to behave 'neurotically', including allowing for violations of the human rights it aims to protect in the first place. D Krapac, 'Some Trends in Continental

with a useful illustration of a more pragmatic response to improperly obtained evidence and a protracted engagement with the finer and more complex questions that arise in this field, such as the role of good faith, application to 'fruits of the poisonous tree' or the impact of exclusion in practice.

From a more holistic view, the contextual study of Greece and the United States also offers interesting insights about the exclusion of improperly obtained evidence in comparative law. For instance, it is intriguing that exclusion can manifest itself in different areas of police practice in different countries (search and seizure in the States, wiretaps in Greece), even when in theory there exist identical exclusionary mechanisms that revolve around the same constitutional right. This may be the result of better protections *ex ante* in different procedural areas in different countries, making the need for the exclusionary rule in these particular areas obsolete. This observation can help re-orientate the debate towards an approach that will place more emphasis on safeguarding suspects' rights *ex ante*, and away from a continued over-reliance on protection *ex post* through exclusionary remedies. On the other hand, the above observation may simply indicate the existence of more aggressive strategies used by different countries for the avoidance of the exclusionary rule in different procedural areas, which again can attract attention to the need for more effective protection, both *ex post* and *ex ante*. It is equally intriguing that the unlawful obtaining of evidence may have different protagonists in different countries (the police in the United States, private parties in Greece). This raises the question of whether significance should be attached to the acts of state representatives and private parties alike.

More importantly, the comparison between the United States and Greece provides a first glimpse of the different types of mandatory exclusionary rules that exist in Anglo-American and Continental systems: absolute or qualified, imposing mandatory exclusion or 'a more graduated response',[328] of varying scope and disparately solid constitutional foundations, attaching different weight to the protection of constitutional rights and the protection of the public interest in the conviction of the guilty, taking their inspiration in the contrasting protective and deterrent rationales, and being pushed, as a consequence, towards and away from the opposite ends of the exclusionary spectrum. Moreover, this comparison challenges the opinion that automatic exclusion is counter-intuitive. Damaška's view that '[t]he idea that the criminal defendant has a fairness-based claim to the automatic rejection of all illegally obtained evidence does not agree with ordinary perception of justice' may be convincing if the point of reference is the belief of 'ordinary people',[329] but it loses force if the ordinary perception of justice is taken to

Criminal Procedure in Transition Countries of South-Eastern Europe' in J Jackson, M Langer and P Tillers (ed), *Crime, Procedure and Evidence in a Comparative and International Context* (Oxford, Hart Publishing, 2008) 119, 122.

[328] RE Myers II, 'Fourth Amendment Small Claims Court' (2013) 10 *Ohio State Journal of Criminal Law* 567, 574.

[329] Damaška, 'The Competing Visions of Fairness' (2011) 386.

reflect that of the courts which are called upon to solve the exclusionary dilemma; for the justices of the supreme jurisdictions in the United States and Greece who have devised their indigenous exclusionary rules, automatic exclusion was historically the instinctive, intuitive, response to that dilemma, and, to different degrees, remains today the starting point in relevant debates there. The comparison also challenges the conventional view that exclusionary rules are idiosyncratic of Anglo-American law and that their genesis is linked with the adversarial culture or, more specifically, the influence of American law.[330] The example of Greece indicates that this may be an exaggerated view. Even more important in this chapter was the identification of impressive convergence between an Anglo-American system and a Continental system around automatic exclusionary rules. Despite their significant differences at the level of the exclusionary rationale and exclusion in practice, both the United States and Greece start from the premise that protection of the constitutional right to privacy mandates (in some contexts, always) exclusion. Identification of such convergence can help take the focus away from the traditional – arguably exaggerated – divide between the inquisitorial and adversarial cultures. This would then help minimise 'the nationalist tendency of states to differentiate themselves from others by classifying systems of evidence and procedure into [these] two discrete categories',[331] and promote a cosmopolitan approach to criminal evidence and procedure. Developing such a cosmopolitan approach requires us to shed more light on constitutionalisation as a factor of convergence beyond the Anglo-American and Continental law divide. This leads to an important postscript on the comparison between the American and Greek exclusionary rules.

VIII. Epilogue: Triggers for the Constitutionalisation of the Exclusionary Rule

As the above analysis of the backs-and-forths of constitutional exclusionary rule legislation and jurisprudence in the United States and Greece has vividly illustrated, the constitutionalisation of criminal procedure does not, in itself, necessarily generate constitutional, mandatory, exclusionary rules. The link between constitutionalisation and automatic exclusion is not linear. It rather fluctuates vis-à-vis changing socio-political conditions and transformations of institutional structures. To conclude this chapter, we must therefore take a closer look at the conditions that seem to have enabled constitutionalisation to open the way for categorical exclusionary rules in the United States and Greece.

[330] See, eg, Bradley, '*Mapp* Goes Abroad' (2001–2002) 375, where the author observes that '[s]ince *Mapp*, and partly because of it, the approach of the rest of the world to evidentiary exclusion due to police misconduct is changing'.

[331] Jackson and Summers, *The Internationalisation of Criminal Evidence* (2012) 6.

We can isolate four factors. First, the fact, quite simply, that the right to privacy is seen as the jewel in the crown of Bill of Rights protections in the United States and Greece. '[T]he right to be let alone' is 'the most comprehensive of rights, and the right most valued by civilized men', argued Justice Brandeis in *Olmstead v United States*;[332] 'an indispensable need for a democratic society', added Felix Frankfurter.[333] It is 'probably the most sacred right and [the right] most indispensable to human dignity', noted Svolos and Vlachos in Greece.[334] Saripolos described with equal force the intrinsic value of the right to secrecy of correspondence, 'one of the most important guarantees for liberty in general',[335] whilst 'excessive sensitivity' to the protection of this right[336] led Tsakirakis to opine that the Greek Constitution protects it 'more rigorously than the majority of countries in the world'.[337] The force with which the American and Greek Bill of Rights protected the right to privacy cannot therefore be easily – historically – separated from the recognition of rigorous exclusionary rules as an integral part of the constitutional right. Conversely, providing strong recognition to the substantive right and turning a blind eye on its procedural violations cannot be easily reconciled in practice, as is notably illustrated by the ability of the American exclusionary rule to resist, for over 40 years, the ferocious jurisprudential attacks upon its constitutional foundations, even if these have taken away much of its protective effect.

Second, the fact that the right to privacy had been reduced to empty words in practice, making the exclusionary rule the only effective solution that could prevent further degradation. To start with the example of the United States, it would be useful to explore the links between the reinforcement of the *Weeks* rule and the law enforcement excesses of the Prohibition era.[338] Or we could look at how pre-*Mapp* recognition of a categorical exclusionary rule in the State of California had been triggered by the proliferation of search and seizure practice inconsistent with the Fourth Amendment and the routine use of its evidentiary fruits in court.[339] From a wider angle, it is reported that, before the time of *Mapp*, state law enforcement officers were unaware of, and blatantly indifferent towards, Fourth Amendment requirements, and so arbitrary arrest, and search and seizure, were nothing out of the ordinary, notably when persons of colour and minorities

[332] *Olmstead v United States*, 277 US 438, 478 (1928). See also S Warren and L Brandeis, 'The Right to Privacy' (1890) 5 *Harvard Law Review* 193.

[333] *Harris v New York*, 331 US 145, 161 (1947).

[334] A Svolos and G Vlachos, *The Constitution of Greece*, Tome B (Athens, 1955) 311 (in Greek).

[335] Saripolos, *Constitutional law system* (1987) 143.

[336] K Tsiplakis, Parliamentary debates archives, Period I, Session A, 24 January 2001, 142.

[337] Tsakirakis, 'Secrecy of Correspondence' (1993) 995 (in Greek).

[338] See generally *Silverthorne Lumber Co v United States*, 251 US 385 (1920); *Amos v United States*, 255 US 313 (1921).

[339] See *People v Cahan*, 44 Cal 2d 434 (1955); Justice R Traynor, '*Mapp v Ohio* at Large in the Fifty States' (1962) 3 *Duke Law Journal* 319, 322; E Barett Jr, 'Exclusion of Evidence Obtained by Illegal Searches – A Comment on *People v Cahan*' (1955) 43 *California Law Review* 565.

were implicated.[340] This provided a strong counterpoint to the professionalism of the FBI, and federal law enforcement more generally, which *was* subjected to the operation of the federal exclusionary rule.[341] A similar story can be told in relation to the emergence in Greece of statutory exclusionary rules for unlawful telephone taps. These were born at a time when interference with the right to secrecy of correspondence was so ripe it had become banal. A market existed for the distribution of unlawful taps, with the press and television happily reproducing the unlawfully recorded tapes, exposing private conversations of businessmen, judges and members of political parties.[342]

The socio-political conditions that prepared the ground for reading the exclusionary rule into the constitutional right to privacy is a third crucial factor. In the United States, the passage from the constitutionalisation of the right against unreasonable search and seizure to the constitutionalisation of the exclusionary rule is the undisputed legacy of the *Warren* Court. It must be read in the context of the Court's 'criminal procedure revolution' that substituted a 'new world' of criminal procedure for the 'old world' that existed before,[343] with the exclusive aim of making real the protections inherent in the Bill of Rights.[344] This epoch-changing mission, which was executed by the *Warren* Court's revolutionary jurisprudence on defendants' rights, took its roots in the major social phenomena of that time: the fight against racial discrimination, improving access to justice – which was virtually prohibited for the poor – and battling against authoritarian law enforcement practice, at a time when memories of the second world war and Nazism were still very recent. The Court knew that to achieve equality it had to protect the rights of minorities, the rights of people of colour, poor people and people with

[340] See J Gallaway, *The Supreme Court and the Rights of the Accused* (A facts on file publication, 1973) 133; Y Kamisar, 'The Exclusionary Rule in Historical Perspective: The Struggle to Make the Fourth Amendment More than "an Empty Blessing"' (1979) 62 *Judicature* 337, 349–50; R Uviller, *Virtual Justice: The Flawed Prosecution of Crime in America* (New Haven and London, Yale University Press, 1996) 65; L Powe Jr, *The Warren Court and American Politics* (Cambridge, Massachussets and London, The Belknapp Press of Harvard University Press, 2000) 199; Katz, 'Mapp After Forty Years' (2001) 471.

[341] Uviller, *Virtual Justice* (1996) 66.

[342] P Paulopoulos, 'Technological evolution and constitutional rights' (1987) 1511-513 (in Greek); D Spirakos, 'The secrecy of correspondence – basic principles and choices to deal with the right to secrecy in law and politics' (1993) 3 *To Sintagma* 526 (in Greek); Tsakirakis, 'Secrecy of Correspondence' (1993) 995; F Kouvelis, Parliamentary debates archives, Period I, Session A, 24 January 2001, 106; Charalampakis, 'The punishable nature of interceptions' (2002) 1061 (in Greek); M Samatas, 'Studying Surveillance in Greece: Methodological and Other Problems Related to an Authoritarian Surveillance Culture' (2005) 3 *Surveillance & Society* 181, 184.

[343] J Grano, 'Introduction – The Changed and Changing World of Constitutional Criminal Procedure: The Contribution of the Department of Justice's Office of Legal Policy' (1988–1989) 22 *University of Michigan Journal of Law Reform* 395, 396. See also C Bradley, *The Failure of the Criminal Procedure Revolution* (Philadelphia, University of Pennsylvania Press, 1993); GF Cole and CE Smith, *The American System of Criminal Justice*, 8th edn (Belmont West/Wadsworth, 1998) 116.

[344] See generally S Simmons, 'The Warren Court and Civil Liberties' (1973–1975) 18 *Howard Law Journal* 610, 626; A Goldberg, 'The Warren Court and Its Critics' (1980) 20 *Santa Clara Law Review* 831, 837; M Horowitz, 'The Warren Court and the Pursuit of Justice' (1993) 50 *Washington and Lee Law Review* 5; R Fricker, 'The Warren Court: A Retrospective' (1995) 22 *Human Rights* 46.

no access to legal defence, and it did so by reinforcing suspects' rights.[345] These were the triggers of *Mapp's* legal earthquake and its many aftershocks (including *Miranda v Arizona*, of course). We can draw interesting analogies with the socio-political triggers for the recognition of exclusionary rules in Greece. We can take as our starting point the fact that the revision of the Constitution in 2001, which introduced the constitutional exclusionary rule of article 19, para 3 for violations of the right to privacy, brought forward vital innovations in individual rights protection, including, notably, in relation to the right to privacy.[346] The constitutional revision of 2001 continued in the ideological path of rights protection inherent in the Constitution of 1975, and its first revision in 1986. As the Constitution of 1975 symbolised the departure from the tortuous period of the military dictatorship and the path to restoring democracy in Greece, planting the seeds for the creation of a culture of individual rights and liberties became a key mission for the Constitution. The revision of 2001 was very rich in symbolism too. It happened at a time of unprecedented economic growth (quickly followed by disparaging economic crisis of course). The country was 'enjoying its most liberal period in recent history', marked by '[t]he modernization, democratization and the "Europeanization" of Greek society'.[347] It was preparing to host the Olympics and had just achieved the long-term ambition of becoming a member of the Eurozone, which 'signalled the beginning of a new era for [the] country'.[348] The constitutional revision was a marker for these successes, and a means to communicate them to Europe and the rest of the world: Greece was a liberal country, on the path of economic success, and its citizens were entitled the full protection of their fundamental rights. It is in this socio-political and economic context that the super charged, rights-centred, absolute, constitutional exclusionary rule for violations of the right to privacy was born.

We must isolate a fourth and final factor. We should not lose sight of the fact that the nexus between constitutionalisation and automatic exclusionary rules may also, ultimately, partly be due to historical coincidence. In the United States, *Mapp's* genesis was, in many respects, Justice Tom Clark's personal triumph. Dorin provides a convincing account of how Tom Clark metamorphosed *Mapp* in the

[345] See generally A Kurland, *Politics, the Constitutions and the Warren Court* (Chicago, The University of Chicago Press, 1970); E Warren, *The Memoirs of Chief Justice Earl Warren* (Lanham, New York and Oxford, Madison Books, 1977) 316; D Dripps, 'Beyond the Warren Court and Its Conservative Critics: Toward a Unified Theory of Constitutional Criminal Procedure' (1989–1990) 23 *University of Michigan Journal of Law Reform* 591, 592; Katz (n 61) 472.

[346] See generally E Venizelos, Parliamentary debates archives, Period I, Session A, 24 January 2001, 94; G Katrougkalos, 'Revision of classic rights and guarantees' in D Tsatsos, E Venizelos and X Kontiadis, *The new Constitution* (Athens, AN Sakkoulas, 2001) 55, 73 (in Greek); D Tsatsos, 'Constitutional revision and interpretation of the Constitution – the necessity for an interpretative theory preceding the Constitution of 2001' in Tsatsos, Venizelos and Kontiadis, *The new Constitution* (ibid) 28 (in Greek).

[347] M Samatas, 'Studying Surveillance in Greece' (2005) 181.

[348] As explained Gkikas Chardouvelis, one of the PM's closest consultants on economic matters. GA Chardouvelis, *The biggest challenge for Greece of the 21st century*, To Vima, 24 December 2000 (in Greek).

exclusionary rule case that it became, an outcome that no one would have predicted at the outset, considering that neither the defendant nor the prosecution had made any explicit reference to the exclusionary rule when the case was first discussed at the Supreme Court.[349] *Mapp* was 'a direct product of Clark's extraordinary actions', notes Dorin; '[s]eldom in the Court's history had one of its members so "seized the time" to change the very issues of the case before him in order to marshal the Court into a fundamental doctrinal change'.[350] In other words, perhaps *Mapp* would not have happened, or would not have happened in 1961, had it not been for the resolve of Justice Clark in making the Fourth Amendment protection real in the states. His unceasing belief in the Fourth Amendment, which provided unique momentum for the recognition of the automatic exclusionary rule, is perfectly encapsulated in extra-judicial writing he published shortly before he passed away:

> I myself think that the fourth amendment is the most valuable of all amendments because it does not matter what you have – if you have all the money in the world – unless you have the safety of your home and the privacy of your mind and heart, you have nothing. Nothing. Someone can take it away, regardless of what you have. So I say that the very foundation of our democratic system lies in the fourth amendment.[351]

Venizelos' leadership played a similarly pivotal role in the development of automatic exclusionary rules in Greece. As a distinguished Constitutional Law scholar, he approached the issue from a strict constitutional law perspective, prioritizing Arios Pagos' original jurisprudence which saw the exclusionary rule as inherent in the right to privacy. Venizelos rejected criminal law scholars' appeal to judicial discretion and balancing exercises as the appropriate remedies, arguing that these posed a threat for the effective protection of constitutional rights.[352] He led in Parliament both on the statutory legislation that created the article 177, para 2 exclusionary rule, for evidence obtained by the commission of criminal offences, and on the constitutional revisions that led to article 19, para 3. As he explained with regards to the latter, he engaged with this process drawing fully on his academic discipline and role as a Constitutional Law scholar.[353] Put differently, for all the institutional and cultural conditions calibrating the effect of constitutionalisation and making the ground fertile for the adoption of automatic exclusionary

[349] Powe Jr, *The Warren Court and American Politics* (2000) 196.

[350] D Dorin, 'Marshalling Mapp: Justice Clark's Role in Mapp v. Ohio's Extension of the Exclusionary Rule to State Searches and Seizures', Symposium on the fortieth anniversary of *Mapp v Ohio* (2001) 52 *Case Western Law Review* 401, 402.

[351] Justice TC Clark, 'Some Notes on the Continuing Life of the Fourth Amendment' (1977) 5 *American Journal of Criminal Law* 275, 276.

[352] E Venizelos, Parliamentary debates archives, Period I, Session A, 24 January 2001, 95.

[353] E Venizelos, 'The topical character of the constitutional phenomenon and the 2001 Greek revision approach' in Tsatsos, Venizelos and Kontiadis, *The New Constitution* (2001) 31 (in Greek).

rules, it took the fortuitous arrival of a charismatic Constitutional Law scholar at the ministry of justice, and his close involvement in the constitutional revision later on, for the statutory and constitutional, rights-centred, exclusionary rules to emerge.

These observations provide the backdrop for analysis in the following chapter of discretionary remedies for violations of the right to privacy, in a context where criminal procedure has mainly evolved with no apparent influence from a constitutionalisation process.

3

Discretionary Exclusion of Evidence Obtained in Violation of the Right to Privacy: France and England and Wales

Despite variations of degree in mandating the exclusion of real evidence obtained in violation of the right to privacy, the exclusionary rules of the United States and Greece studied in chapter two can be located on one side of the improperly obtained evidence spectrum, and, at first sight, provide the reverse image of discretionary, non-automatic, remedies on the opposite side of the spectrum. The debate on improperly obtained evidence has taken some interest in such discretionary remedies, with solutions adopted in Commonwealth countries, such as Canada, Australia and New Zealand, given attention by observers in the Anglo-American law strongholds of England and the United States.[1] This chapter's main contribution to the analysis of discretionary exclusion lies in the comparison of the discretionary remedies of England and Wales with the – little discussed in comparative law – discretionary remedies adopted in the Continental system of France,[2] and in providing a platform for the juxtaposition of the English and French solutions with the exclusionary rules already examined in this book, those of Greece and the United States. It is through these comparisons that this chapter will attempt to add further nuance to existing Anglo-American scholarship, bringing into focus the availability of remedies alternative to exclusionary rules.

[1] See, eg, R Pattenden, 'The Exclusion of Unfairly Obtained Evidence in England, Canada and Australia' (1980) 29 *International and Comparative Law Quarterly* 664; P Mirfield, *Silence, Confessions and Improperly Obtained Evidence*, Oxford Monographs on Criminal Law and Justice (Oxford, Clarendon Press, 1997); J Stribopoulos, 'Lessons from the Pupil: A Canadian Solution to the American Exclusionary Rule Debate' (1999) 22 *Boston College International & Comparative Law Review* 77; A Morrison, 'Application of the Canadian Section 24(2) Exclusionary Rule in U.S. Cases: Would It Make a Difference?' (2002–2003) 9 *Southwestern Journal of Law & Trade in the Americas* 149; A L-T Choo and S Nash, 'Improperly Obtained Evidence in the Commonwealth: Lessons for England and Wales? (2007) 11 *International Journal of Evidence & Proof* 75.

[2] But see, eg, W Pakter, 'Exclusionary Rules in France, Germany and Italy' (1985) 9 *Hastings International and Comparative Law Review* 1; R Frase, 'France' in C Bradley, *Criminal Procedure – A Worldwide Study* (Carolina Academic Press, Durham, North Carolina, 1999) 143; Y Ma, 'Comparative Analysis of Exclusionary Rules in the United States, England, France, Germany and Italy' (1999) 22 *Policing: An International Journal of Police Strategies & Management* 3, 280.

The chapter will first describe the converging general principles and corresponding legislative provisions that institute discretionary exclusion in English and French law (section I). It will then argue that their jurisprudential applications are unduly narrow in practice. Judges seem reluctant to undertake the balancing exercise that the discretionary powers provided to them seem to allow for. Even when they do, they give insufficient weight to human rights or judicial integrity considerations. As a result, English and French courts routinely uphold decisions allowing the use of real, non-confession, evidence, even if they establish that it has been procured through violations of the right to privacy (section II). The chapter will then look at recent developments in French law that indicate the emergence of a jurisprudential understanding of discretionary exclusion more in tune with the need to give effect to the right to privacy, especially when violations of the latter intersect with violations of the right against self-incrimination and the right to legal advice. This modern French jurisprudence might have interesting comparative ramifications for English law (section III). The study of the English and French solutions will also provide an opportunity to revisit the conclusions deriving from the analysis of exclusionary rules in the United States and Greece. Recent transformations, trends and related critical discussion in these four countries can be seen in a different light depending on one's comparative standpoint (section IV).

I. General Principles and Legislative Framework

The source of modern similarities between exclusionary discretion in England and France can arguably be traced in the common historic paths that the two criminal procedure systems have followed when dealing with improperly obtained evidence. English law has progressively moved from a position of general admissibility to recognising a limited exclusionary discretion. French law has from early on explored possible exceptions to *la liberté de la preuve* (free proof), but has not gone any further than recognise a narrow exclusionary discretion nonetheless. These discretionary powers were later formally incorporated – transformed to a smaller or larger degree – into contemporary legislation.

A. Recognising a (Limited) Discretion

The common law position on improperly obtained evidence that started to take shape from the mid-nineteenth century is seamlessly encapsulated in the, now legendary, phrase of Crompton J in the 1861 case of *R v Leatham* that 'it matters not how you get it; if you steal it even, it would be admissible in evidence'.[3]

[3] *R v Leatham* (1861) 8 Cox CC 498, 501. See also *R v Griffin* (1809) Russ & Ry 151; *R v Gould* (1840) 9 C & P 364; *R v Berriman* (1854) 6 Cox CC 388.

We find equally incontrovertible language in *Jones v Owens*, only a few years later: 'it would be a dangerous obstacle to the administration of justice if evidence obtained by illegal means could not be used against an accused person'.[4] The way in which evidence was obtained was 'strictly irrelevant'.[5] This remained the uncontested position of the common law for the first half of the twentieth century. The rare incursions into the freedom of proof principle did not go any further than bar the use of evidence whose prejudicial effect would outweigh its probative value.[6] This exclusionary rule left the use of improperly obtained *but real* evidence widely unaffected.

It was with the 1955 decision of the Privy Council in *Kuruma son of Kaniu v R* that English courts started to give recognition to the idea of fairness in the context of evidence admissibility. The Court opined that 'in a criminal case the judge always ha[d] a discretion to disallow evidence if the strict rules of admissibility would operate unfairly against an accused', explaining that a judge might properly rule out evidence 'obtained from a defendant by a trick'.[7] In *Gallis v Gunn*, it was admitted that exclusion on these grounds could arise 'if there was any suggestion of [the evidence] having been obtained oppressively, by false representations, by a trick, by threats, by bribes, [or] anything of that sort'.[8] Fairness was equated with ensuring that the impropriety did not affect the reliability of the evidence. Improperly obtained *but real* evidence, such as evidence obtained in violation of the right to privacy, did not fall within the scope of the newly founded discretion. '[A] number of experienced judges [were probably] quite ignorant of the possession of this discretion,' said the House of Lords in *Jeffrey v Black*. An unlawful search would only lead to exclusion in 'a very exceptional situation', where 'not only have the police officers entered without authority, but they have been guilty of trickery or they have misled someone, or they have been oppressive or they have been unfair, or in other respects they have behaved in a manner which is morally reprehensible'.[9]

The focus on reliability was even more acutely reflected in the development in common law – already from the eighteenth century – of an exclusionary rule for

[4] *Jones v Owens* (1870) 34 JP 759, 760.

[5] Archbold Criminal Pleading, Evidence and Practice 2015 (London, Sweet & Maxwell-Thomson Reuters, 2015) 1889 [15-457].

[6] See *R v Christie* [1914] AC 545, 559. See also *Noor Mohamed v R* [1949] AC 1242, 1256; *Harris v DPP* [1952] AC 694; *List* [1966] 1 WLR 9, 12; *Selvey v DPP* [1970] AC 304.

[7] *Kuruma son of Kaniu v R* [1955] 1 All ER 236, 239.

[8] *Gallis v Gunn* [1964] 1 QB 495, 502.

[9] *Jeffrey v Black* [1978] 1 All ER 555, 558–59, *per* Lord Widgery CJ. See also JR Spencer, 'Les limites en matière de preuve – Aspects actuels' (1992) *Revue de sciences criminelle* 42, 51. Sharpe comments that 'the judiciary acknowledged the possibility of excluding improperly obtained non-confessional evidence, but rarely applied their own rhetoric'. S Sharpe, 'Covert Policing: A Comparative View' (1996) 25 *Anglo-American Law Review* 163, 163–64.

involuntary confessions,[10] which provided a contrast with the limited discretion described above.[11]

Even this discretion to exclude on grounds of fairness was rejected with the seminal decision of the House of Lords in *R v Sang*. Lord Diplock noted, in an all too often-cited excerpt from the decision, that:

> save with regard to admissions and confessions and generally with regard to evidence obtained from the accused after the commission of the offence, [the trial judge] has no discretion to refuse to admit relevant admissible evidence on the ground that it was obtained by improper or unfair means. The court is not concerned with how it was obtained.[12]

One detects in *Sang* strong echoes of the strict admissibility principle that had been elaborated in *Leatham*, as far as non-confessional evidence, or evidence *not* obtained in violation of the defendant's right against self-incrimination, were concerned. Surprisingly little progress had been made in the nearly 120 years that had elapsed between what were probably the two most important judgments of the common law on improperly obtained evidence. Safeguarding the quality of the evidence remained the exclusive concern.[13] This outweighed the interest in the protection of individual rights, such as the right to be protected against unlawful searches, a matter seen as falling outside the scope of the law of Evidence.[14] Trial fairness, as a justification for exclusion, was defined narrowly.[15]

It is worth reminding here that the United States had, in the same period, rapidly moved from a common law admissibility position to a federal automatic exclusionary rule and then a strict constitutional exclusionary rule applying to all Fourth Amendment violations across the states.[16] Interestingly, the Privy Council in *Kuruma* showed awareness of the constitutional osmosis progressively leading to the adoption of the exclusionary rule in the United States, yet did not consider it 'necessary to examine [the relevant Supreme Court decisions] in detail', ascertaining instead that 'the common law did not reject relevant evidence' on the ground

[10] See generally C Tapper, *Cross & Tapper on Evidence*, 10th edn (London, LexisNexis Butterworths, 2004) 657. See *R v Warickshall* (1783) 1 Leach 263, 263–64; *R v Baldry* (1852) 2 Den 430, 444.

[11] But Uglow notes that, since the 1960s, the attitude of the judiciary had become particularly permissive, irrespective of whether it was confessional or real evidence that had been obtained in an improper way. S Uglow, *Evidence – Text and Materials*, 2nd edn (London, Thomson, Sweet & Maxwell, 2006) 152.

[12] *R v Sang* [1979] 2 All ER 1230.

[13] I Dennis, *The Law of Evidence*, 2nd edn (London, Thompson, Sweet & Maxwell, 2002) 73. See also Royal Commission on Criminal Procedure, *The Investigation and Prosecution of Criminal Offences in England and Wales, The Law and Procedure*, Cmnd 8092 (1981) [4.124].

[14] R Munday, 'Exclusionary Rules of Criminal Evidence in English Law' in JP Gardner, *UK Law in the 1990s*, UK Comparative Law Series (United Kingdom National Committee of Comparative Law, 1990) 360, 369.

[15] C Siyuan, 'The Judicial Discretion to Exclude Relevant Evidence: Perspectives from an Indian Evidence Act Jurisdiction' (2012) 16 *International Journal of Evidence & Proof* 398, 410.

[16] See ch 2.

of violation of constitutional rights.[17] In *Sang*, the House of Lords explained that civil remedies and disciplinary action were the appropriate remedies for the illegal or otherwise improper obtaining of criminal evidence, and that the function of the trial judge did not extend beyond ensuring fairness in trial proceedings.[18] This was diametrically opposed to the United States approach, where the Supreme Court remained for the largest part of the history of the exclusionary rule unconvinced that such remedies could substitute for exclusion, and where procedural fairness could not be separated from police behaviour in the investigation and pre-trial stage of the criminal process. Similarly to the United States, and in stark contrast to the English common law position, Greece had long recognised strict exclusionary rules for privacy violations. From early on both Greece and the United States rejected the view so central in *Sang*, that the court could not be concerned with how the evidence was obtained. In view of American and Greek early experiences with strict exclusionary rules, Ashworth's and Redmayne's view that '[t]he old common law approach was, basically, unsympathetic to the exclusion of [unfairly and improperly obtained] evidence'[19] is correct but an understatement. The common law strongly resisted the idea of exclusion.[20]

Now, English common law observers might have been able to find some comparative support for the common law position if they had looked across the Channel. French law followed a trajectory similar to that of the English common law, though it never went quite so far as endorse the principle encapsulated in *Sang*. Throughout the twentieth century, it explored the idea of non-use of improperly obtained evidence across the parallel lines of *loyauté* – a moral imperative, mandating the obtaining of evidence in accordance with ethical and legal standards,[21] which provides a rough equivalent to the 'fairness' basis for discretionary exclusion in the common law – and *legalité*, a principle mandating the obtaining of evidence in accordance with the rules and methods established by the Code of Penal Procedure (CPP).

[17] *Kuruma son of Kaniu v R* [1955] 1 All ER 236, 239–40.

[18] *R v Sang* [1979] 2 All ER 1230, 1231.

[19] A Ashworth and M Redmayne, *The Criminal Process*, 4th edn (Oxford, Oxford University Press, 2010) 438.

[20] See D Friedman, 'From Due Deference to Due Process: Human Rights Litigation in the Criminal Law' (2002) 2 *European Human Rights Law Review* 216, 226.

[21] The French dictionary *Le Robert* defines '*loyauté*' as keeping one's promises, obeying the rules of honour and probity. See generally P Lemoine, 'La loyauté de la preuve (à travers quelques arrêts récents de la chambre criminelle)' in Rapport annuel de la Cour de cassation, La vérité (La Documentation française, 2004) 141, 142, available at www.courdecassation.fr/IMG/pdf/rapport_annuel_2004_couverture.pdf. Similarly, de Lamy explains that the word 'loyal' has developed, by phonetic evolution, from the word *legalis*, 'conforming with law', and in the context of chivalry 'takes the meaning of honour, and probity'. B de Lamy, 'De la loyauté en procédure pénale. Brèves remarques sur l'application des règles de la chevalerie à la procédure pénale' in Mélanges offerts à Jean Pradel, Le droit pénal à l'aube du troisième millénaire (Paris, Cujas, 2006) 97, 98. See also VM Schwendener, 'L'action de la police judiciaire confrontée à l'exigence de la loyauté' (2005) *Actualité juridique pénal*, 267.

The eminent nineteenth-century French proceduralist, Faustin Hélie, described *loyauté* as imposing a high ethical standard in the obtaining of criminal evidence:

> No, the judge should not employ artifices and tricks to obtain disclosure [of evidence] … Justice which, as Domat says, is itself the truth, must put truth in all its actions. The judge is not allowed to employ means imprinted, to any degree, with theft or fraud. Taking a detour, showing reluctance, using circumlocution, calculated in advance, that is to trick the accused, to set a trap for him, to try to surprise him or even to inflict moral torture, if he becomes perceptive of [the judge's tactics]. Showing his acumen, the judge cannot but adopt a clear and legal position on all the questions that result from the conscientious study of the facts.[22]

It is as if Hélie had been able to predict the Cour de cassation's groundbreaking *Wilson* decision in 1888, where it was recognised that investigating judges should act in conformity with the *loyauté* principle. The investigating judge in this case had engaged in a telephone conversation with a suspect, hiding his true identity and pretending to be a potential client. This had 'compromised the dignity of the judge', said the Cour de cassation, in adopting a logic strikingly similar to that inherent in the contemporary judicial integrity principle; 'the [investigating] judge [had] employed a means which was doing away with the rules of *loyauté* that must be observed by every judicial investigation, and constituted, on this basis alone, an act that was contrary to the mandate and dignity of a magistrate'.[23] *Wilson's* effect was extended to police investigations ordered by an investigating judge, with the *Imbert* case in 1952. A police officer had 'provoked and intercepted a telephone call between the main witness and the accused with a view to leading the latter to make a confession'. The transcript of the telephone communication had been added to the case dossier and given judicial consideration by a Court of appeal, leading to a conviction for the offence of corruption. The Cour de cassation quashed the conviction, arguing that the actions of the police officer 'aimed, and had the result, of eluding the legal provisions and general procedural rules that an investigating judge, or his delegate, should not be unaware of without compromising the rights of the defence'.[24]

In more recent times, the principle was further reinforced with its extension to the police investigations stage of pre-trial proceedings, this time in the context of entrapment, which was perceived as 'machinations aimed to determine criminal acts' with the effect of 'vitiating the search and establishment of truth'.[25] Its application remains today broadly restricted to evidence obtained by entrapment

[22] F Hélie, *Traité de l'instruction criminelle*, Tome IV, 2nd edn (1866) n 1930.

[23] *Cass, Ch réunies*, 31 January 1888, S 1889.1.241.

[24] *Crim* 12 June 1952, *Bull crim* n 153.

[25] See *Crim* 27 February1996, *Bull crim* n 93; E Vergès, 'Loyauté et licéité, deux apports majeurs à la théorie de la preuve pénale' (2014) *Recueil Dalloz* 407, 408. For criticism of this development see J Buisson, 'Principe de loyauté dans la recherche de preuves et constat d'infractions' in *Journées d'études Dalloz*, Dossiers, Le nouveau procès pénal après la loi Perben II (Paris, Dalloz, 2004) 307, 308.

and other unfair means targeted to deceive the defendant, which can affect the reliability of the evidence. From this point of view, the *loyauté* principle resonates strongly with the fairness discretion recognised by the common law in *Kuruma* and *Gallis v Gunn*.

A much wider discretion to invalidate procedural acts – and thus 'exclude', make non-usable, evidence procured through them – was progressively developed in French law with the emergence, from the beginning of the eighteenth century, of the *legalité* principle, which was encapsulated in the recognition, with the Napoleonic *Code d'instruction criminelle* 1808,[26] of a first type of procedural nullities. These were known as 'textual nullities' (*nullités textuelles*), because they were specifically prescribed in the text of the Code. The sanction of nullity attached to particular provisions of the Code, mandating the invalidation of the relevant procedural acts when conducted in breach of these provisions. Significant progress was achieved here when French jurisprudence recognised a second type of nullities, 'substantial nullities' (*nullités substantielles*). Judges started to identify a range of 'substantial' procedural provisions where nullity was not mandated by the Code, and yet judges would proceed – in exercising their discretion – to invalidate procedural acts completed in breach of these provisions, especially where the procedural breach would have resulted in a violation of the rights of the defence.[27] These provisions primarily targeted the interrogation of the suspect, but, with time, nullities – 'textual', but also, importantly, 'substantial' – extended to search and seizure.[28] The distinction between 'textual' and 'substantial' nullities corresponded to a distinction between automatic and non-automatic, discretionary, nullities, and was formally incorporated into the *Code de procédure pénale* of 1958, which is the procedural Code still in force today. But while the Cour de cassation applied 'textual' nullities strictly, in relation to 'substantial' nullities it demonstrated significant restraint, with a few exceptions only of 'public order' provisions not linked with the protection of procedural rights.[29]

The preference for non-automatic, discretionary, nullity where defence rights were in action was solidified with the enactment of legislation in 1975 that introduced article 802 of the CPP. This article provides that, to pronounce a nullity, the judge must first find that the breach of a procedural guarantee has caused harm to the interests of the defendant. 'Public order' provisions, which are in principle not pertinent to the protection of individual rights, remain the only exception to this rule.[30] As a result of article 802, in addition to the first two levels of exercising discretion – where judges have the ability to classify a provision as 'substantial' or

[26] Art 408, para 1 *Code d'instruction criminelle* 1808.

[27] See P Bouzat and J Pinatel, *Traité de droit pénal et de criminologie*, 2nd edn (Paris, Dalloz, 1970) 1243.

[28] See, eg, the Laws of 7 February 1933 and 17 March 1935.

[29] J Dumont, *Nullités de l'information, Juris-Classeur Procédure Pénale*, arts 170–174 CPP (1997) 4.

[30] See generally MF Coutant, *Essai d'une théorie générale des nullités en procédure civile, pénale et administrative*, Doctoral thesis (Aix-Marseille, 1996) 11.

not, and then as of 'public order' nature or not, and accordingly determine whether its breach can trigger exclusion – there is a third level of discretion in French law, where judges determine whether an act conducted in breach of substantial procedural guarantees (of non-public order nature) must be invalidated in practice. For this to happen, the judge must make the *in concreto* finding that the defendant has suffered prejudice – a procedural 'harm' – as a consequence of the procedural breach. Article 802 has survived reforms of nullities attempted with legislation enacted – and then quickly abandoned for its most part – in 1993,[31] and provides today the backdrop of non-automatic exclusion in France, in relation to both violations of the right to privacy and improperly obtained confessional evidence. As we will see below, article 802 has been the subject of much academic criticism, especially in view of its ability to narrow, considerably, the scope for exclusion.

Despite their limitations, the discretionary powers originally recognised in English and French law have opened the way for the wider jurisprudential applications that we encounter today. These rest on the provisions of section 78(1) of the Police and Criminal Evidence Act 1984, as far as England and Wales are concerned, and articles 171 and 802 of the CPP in France.

B. Section 78(1) of the Police and Criminal Evidence Act 1984

The Royal Commission on Criminal Procedure, set up in 1977 and presided by Sir Cyril Philips, has done much of the groundwork for the enactment of the Police and Criminal Evidence Act 1984, this 'landmark statute in the development of the [English] criminal justice system'.[32] Its proposals on improperly obtained evidence reintegrated the 'narrowly defined discretion'[33] under the common law as crystallised in *Sang*.[34] The Commission was of the view that improperly obtained but reliable evidence should be admissible in court, and that even unreliable evidence should not be automatically excluded. It should rather be for the advocate for any accused to discredit the evidence of an unreliable confession, and trial judges should point out to the jury, and prosecutors should be advised of, the dangers of acting upon such evidence.[35] The Commission had first examined – and rejected – the options of automatic and presumptive exclusion. It surveyed the exclusionary

[31] See the Law of 4 January 1993, which was the collective work of the Delmas-Marty Justice Commission and was introduced by a government of the Left, and the Law of 24 August 1993, which was introduced by the new government of the Right and was designed to cancel the reforms that had been attempted with the January legislation, including a reform of the law of nullities which would see the list of textual nullities significantly expanded. See generally Y Roussel, 'Le régime des nullités de la procédure pénale après les lois du 4 janvier 1993 et du 24 août 1993' (1996) *Gazzette du Palais* 72.

[32] I Dennis, 'Editorial – Legal Advice in Police Stations: 25 Years on' [2011] *Criminal Law Review* 1.

[33] R May, 'Fair Play at Trial: An Interim Assessment of Section 78 of the Police and Criminal Evidence Act 1984' [1988] *Criminal Law Review* 722, 723.

[34] *R v Sang* [1980] AC 402.

[35] Royal Commission on Criminal Procedure, *Report*, 1981, Cmnd 8092 [4.133].

rules adopted by the United States.[36] Their deterrent effect, said the Commission, was contestable, creating the need for alternative remedies,[37] while there was also a risk of an increase in litigation, and in 'the patently guilty going free because of some minor procedural technicality'.[38] The organisational differences between the American and British police forces – the former lacking the central organisation and ministerial oversight characteristic of the latter – meant that English law did not need to resort to exclusionary rules to ensure the adoption of uniform police practice in the way that the Supreme Court did.[39] The Supreme Court also assumed the 'moral and political force' to mandate automatic exclusion 'from its responsibility to protect and interpret the rights of citizens of the United States that are enshrined in the Bill of Rights'. The reality in Britain was not necessarily the same, concluded the Commission.[40] We see in the above that the Commission confidently recited some of the arguments developed by those fiercely opposing the exclusionary rule – an anti-exclusion rhetoric quickly penetrating the Burger Court's jurisprudence at the time, the genesis of which we can observe in the early extra-judicial writings of Chief Justice Burger himself[41] – but, on the other hand, it showed little interest in exploring the exclusionary doctrine central to *Mapp* and the original exclusionary rule jurisprudence. In other words, the Commission's reading of the American exclusionary rule theory and jurisprudence was unduly selective. Its comparative law observations on the institutional differences with the United States also sound alarmingly self-reassuring. The Committee expressed confidence in the fact that the British police were not resorting to arbitrary methods, and there were no human rights guarantees in operation, equivalent to those in the American Bill of Rights. It would not be too long before the notorious wrongful conviction cases of the 1970s would come to light and prove the Commission wrong.[42] But, at the time, the Commission found on the above sufficient ammunition against the idea that English law possibly needed the exclusionary rule in order to discipline its police and protect defendants' rights; all members of the Commission except for one opposed the adoption of the American exclusionary rule.[43] A proposal for the introduction of a reverse onus exclusionary rule was equally rejected.[44]

[36] ibid [4.126]–[4.128].

[37] ibid [4.127].

[38] ibid [4.128].

[39] ibid.

[40] ibid [4.126].

[41] See, eg, *United States v Calandra*, 414 US 338 (1974). In making the point about the exclusionary rule's contestable deterrent effect, the Commission cited, from an article by Warren Burger published at a time when he was still a Judge of the Court of Appeals for the District of Columbia, an excerpt where the distinguished author suggested that 'the notion [of the exclusionary rule's deterrent effect] was never more than wishful thinking from the part of the courts'. W Burger, 'Who Will Watch the Watchmen?' (1964) 14 *American University Law Review* 12.

[42] See, eg, the cases of 'Guildford Four' and 'Birmingham Six'. See generally I Dennis, 'Miscarriages of Justice and the Law of Confessions: Evidentiary Issues and Solutions' [1993] *Public Law* 291.

[43] Royal Commission on Criminal Procedure, *Report*, 1981, Cmnd 8092 [4.128].

[44] ibid [4.129].

Following on the footsteps of the Commission, the Police and Criminal Evidence Bill that became the 1984 Act first did not go any further than integrate the limited discretion available under *Sang*. This reflected the Government's intention 'largely to re-enact [the] common law rules'.[45] Then Lord Scarman introduced an amendment proposing the adoption of a reverse onus exclusionary rule. The prosecution would bear the burden to prove, beyond reasonable doubt, that the evidence had been legally obtained. Alternatively, they could demonstrate that the violation had not been significant or that there was a public interest reason for admitting the evidence.[46] Lord Scarman's amendment was met with opposition by the government. The Home Secretary 'attacked' presumptive exclusion for risking the acquittal of the guilty.[47] The amendment still influenced, rather fortuitously, the development of modern exclusionary discretion in England and Wales. By making presumptive exclusion the starting point in the exclusionary debate, it left the government no room to manoeuvre, making a return to the 'common law admissibility' position that the Royal Commission had advocated untenable. The government rejected the reverse onus exclusionary rule, offering in its place the compromise solution of section 78(1) of the Police and Criminal Evidence Act 1984.[48]

Section 78(1) instantly became the epicentre of contemporary applications of discretionary exclusion, a provision that is 'by now known almost by heart by most people [in England and Wales] that have anything to do with the law'.[49] Section 78(1) provides that:

> In any proceedings the court may refuse to allow evidence on which the prosecution proposes to rely to be given if it appears to the court that, having regard to all the circumstances, including the circumstances in which the evidence was obtained, the admission of the evidence would have such an adverse effect on the fairness of the proceedings that the court ought not to admit it.[50]

[45] A Sanders, R Young and M Burton, *Criminal Justice*, 4th edn (Oxford, Oxford University Press, 2010) 702.

[46] Tapper explains that a simple violation of the Codes of Practice would thus lead to exclusion. Tapper, *Cross & Tapper on Evidence* (2004) 222. But this rests on the assumption that the prosecution would not be able to establish that a breach had not been significant in practice or locate a public interest reason mandating admission.

[47] HC Deb, 29 October 1984, vol 60, col 1014.

[48] As Ormerod and Birch put it, the reverse onus exclusionary rule was 'strong medicine', and section 78 was 'a knee-jerk reaction to' it rather than 'a measured response to the limitations imposed by *Sang*'. See D Ormerod and D Birch, 'The Evolution of the Discretionary Exclusion of Evidence' [2004] *Criminal Law Review* 767, 772–73.

[49] As stated in *Hudson v DPP* [1992] RTR 27, 34 *per* Hodgson J, cited by A L-T Choo, *The Law of Evidence, Text and Materials* (London, Longman, 1998) 433. Archbold describes section 78 as 'the most important provision in the PACE 1984, and the most often referred to in practice'. Archbold Criminal Pleading, Evidence and Practice 2015 (2015) 1872 [15-402].

[50] For a translation in French see Spencer, 'Les limites en matière de preuve' (1992) 50.

The introduction of section 78(1) signalled a possible radical departure from common law jurisprudence, and 'a major advance on *Sang*',[51] as the provision explicitly mandated giving consideration to the way in which the evidence was being obtained, irrespective of the nature of the evidence.[52] The discretion was not restricted to confessional evidence or 'evidence obtained from the accused',[53] or to a determination of whether the prejudicial effect of the evidence would outweigh its probative value.[54]

The 'entirely flexible and unstructured discretion',[55] which relied on the high-level concepts of 'adverse effect' and 'fairness of the proceedings', and dictated that regard should be given to 'all the circumstances, including the circumstances in which the evidence was obtained', could have enabled English courts 'to develop a fresh approach unencumbered by the common law'.[56] The provision's 'extreme generality'[57] would seem conducive to that. 'Ordinary principles of statutory interpretation' would logically create the expectation that the discretion would be exercised widely.[58] But perhaps expectations were put too high, considering historic scepticism in the common law about excluding improperly obtained evidence.[59] As analysis of section 78(1) jurisprudence on the exclusion of evidence obtained in violation of the right to privacy will demonstrate below, English courts still today exercise their discretion narrowly, focusing 'fairness' enquiries on reliability issues, in line with common law jurisprudence. Non-epistemic considerations antagonistic to reliability, such as judicial integrity and the protection of human rights, are given little attention in practice, with courts appearing unwilling to balance them with considerations relating to the cogency and quality of the evidence in question.[60] Here it suffices to take note of Lord Auld's observations in his seminal Review of the Criminal Courts of England and Wales:

> There is much uncertainty as to the ambit of section 78(1) and the common law power to exclude and as to their relationship one with another. The central problem is whether under section 78 and at common law the courts are generally confined to excluding evidence only on the ground of its quality, the 'reliability' principle of exclusion.

[51] Friedman, 'From Due Deference to Due Process' (2002) 225.

[52] HC Deb, vol 65, 1983–84, July 30–October 31, 1014.

[53] *R v Sang* [1979] 2 All ER 1230.

[54] See generally I Dennis, *The Law of Evidence*, 5th edn (London, Sweet & Maxwell, 2013) 95.

[55] Sharpe, 'Covert Policing' (1996) 165.

[56] A L-T Choo, *Evidence*, 3rd edn (Oxford, Oxford University Press, 2012) 172.

[57] Dyson Heydon, Justice at the High Court of Australia, *The Common Law of Evidence and Human Rights*, seminar at the School of Law, University of Nottingham, 21 February 2008 (on file with author).

[58] See Choo, *Evidence* (2012) 171. But *cf* May, who expresses the view that 'from the choice of language' in section 78(1), it might have been possible to deduce that 'the court's discretion should be narrowly confined'. The courts might have been able to do that by considering that 'the fact that the police behaved badly in obtaining the evidence can have no effect on the fairness of the trial'. R May, 'Fair Play at Trial' (1988) 726.

[59] See generally A Zuckerman, 'Illegally Obtained Evidence – Discretion as a Guardian of Legitimacy' [1987] *Current Legal Problems* 55.

[60] See generally K Grevling, 'Fairness and the Exclusion of Evidence Under Section 78(1) of the Police and Criminal Evidence Act' (1997) 113 *Law Quarterly Review* 667, 685; JR Spencer, 'Bugging

> An associated question, on which there is a division of judicial and academic views, is whether section 78, in requiring the court to have regard to 'all the circumstances, including the circumstances in which the evidence was obtained', widened the common law so as to require consideration of the propriety of obtaining of evidence as well as or regardless of its reliability. Of course, in those cases where the impropriety may affect the reliability of the evidence, there is no difficulty. The problem arises where the evidence, despite the impropriety, is potentially reliable and cogent.[61]

A whole 15 years after the enactment of section 78(1), Lord Auld's inquiries were still concentrated on whether the discretion extended at all beyond the limited common law discretion and the reliability principle.

In a similar fashion, French courts have historically shown little enthusiasm for applying procedural nullities broadly, to exclude improperly obtained evidence on extrinsic policy grounds, especially in relation to violations of the right to privacy.[62] But examples can be traced in recent jurisprudence indicating that this might be changing. These examples offer new vistas of possibility vis-à-vis the continued restricted operation of section 78(1), and supply impetus for exercising the discretion more widely. As an introduction to these issues, it is useful to note that French courts are in theory not in any way afforded a wider discretion than that enjoyed by their English counterparts.

C. Procedural Nullities in Contemporary French Criminal Procedure

Brief reference has already been made above to the 'textual' and 'substantial' nullities that were historically distilled from the *legalité* principle. These are still helpful today in indicating the sources – statutory and jurisprudential respectively – of procedural nullities in French law. Here, however, the focus will be on explaining how the conventional distinction has become obsolete in modern French criminal procedure, replaced by a distinction between 'public order'-based nullities (*nullités d'ordre public*), which are automatic, and 'private interest'-based nullities (*nullités d'intérêt privé*), which are discretionary and non-automatic. The latter provide the main focus when dealing with improperly obtained evidence. It must be clarified that the notion of '*ordre public*' should be understood here

and Burglary by the Police' (1997) *Cambridge Law Journal* 6, 7; A Keane and P McKeown, *The Modern Law of Evidence*, 10th edn (Oxford, Oxford University Press, 2014) 65–67; A L-T Choo, 'England and Wales: Fair Trial Analysis and the Presumed Admissibility of Physical Evidence' in S Thaman (ed), *Exclusionary Rules in Comparative Law* (Dordrecht, Springer, 2013) 352.

[61] Auld LJ, *Review of the Criminal Courts of England and Wales* (London, Stationary Office Books, 2001) ch 11 [108].

[62] A rule based on extrinsic policy grounds would be 'rejecting probative information for the sake of values unrelated to the pursuit of truth'. M Damaška, *Evidence Law Adrift* (Yale University Press: New Haven & London, 1997) 12.

as referring to issues pertaining to the 'administration of justice'. It should not be conceived in its traditional securitarian sense.

A good entry to these issues is to remind that 'textual' nullities were traditionally of limited importance in the French CPP. The fact that after legislation enacted in August 1993 there were only six provisions in the Code explicitly providing for a nullity speaks for itself.[63] Though the years 2000 have witnessed new legislative enthusiasm for these nullities, notably concerning organised crime and anti-terrorism provisions, textual nullities remain a rare occurrence in the Code.[64] Their development was in any case deprived of much significance in practice. The Law of 24 August 1993 subjected the previously automatic 'textual' nullities to the article 802 CPP requirement of making an *in concreto* finding of 'harm' before being able to pronounce a nullity. This requirement applies to 'textual' and 'substantial' nullities, according to article 171 CPP, which states that '[t]here is nullity when a breach of a substantial formality provided by the present Code, or other criminal procedure provision, has impaired the interests of the party that it concerns'.

'Textual' and 'substantial' nullities are definitively brought together, by article 802 CPP, which provides that:

> in case of violations of formalities provided by Law with the sanction of nullity, or [in case of] non-observance of substantial formalities, every jurisdiction to which an application of nullity is referred to – including the Cour de cassation – or [every jurisdiction that] examines the irregularity ex officio, can only pronounce a nullity when the irregularity has impaired the interests of the party that it concerns.

In other words, 'textual' and 'substantial' nullities are both non-automatic. They both depend on a discretionary finding of procedural 'harm', an impairment of the interests of the defendant. Only 'public order' provisions – irrespective of whether they are linked to 'textual' or 'substantial' nullities – are exempt from article 802, as Cour de cassation jurisprudence has quickly recognised,[65] under the influence of French criminal procedure doctrine.[66]

Pronouncement of nullity where 'public order' provisions have been breached is automatic. There is no need for an *in concreto* evaluation of the prejudice suffered by the defendant. The harm is presumed. The violation necessarily breaches the interests of the defendant. But this, generally, has little effect with regards to

[63] They were attached to arts 56, 56–1, 57, 59, 78–3, 100–07 CPP.

[64] J Buisson, 'L'annulation suppose le constat préalable de la violation d'une norme ou d'un principe' (2007) *Procédures*, comm 21.

[65] See *Crim* 25 June 1979, *Bull crim* n 253; 5 October 1982, JCP G 1982, IV, 369; 17 March 1987, D 1987, somm, 408, note J Pradel. See also J Pradel and A Varinard, *Les grands arrêts du droit criminel, Tome II – Le Procès, la sanction* (Paris, Dalloz, 1995) 171.

[66] See, eg, P Couvrat, 'Les méandres de la procédure pénale: commentaire de la loi n° 75. 701 du 6 août 1975' (1976) *Recueil Dalloz* 43; A Maurice-Hersant, 'Réflexions sur l'Article 802 du code de procédure pénale, loi n° 75. 701 du 6 août 1975 art. 19' (1976) *Recueil Dalloz* 117. See generally H Conchon, *L'évolution des nullités de l'instruction préparatoire* (Paris, L'Harmattan, 2002) 120–21.

improperly obtained evidence. This is because 'public order' provisions are mostly unconnected with violations of individual rights (and individual rights, in principle, form the backbone of exclusionary doctrines in comparative law). For the purposes of French law, 'public order' provisions are mainly those that relate to the organisation and functioning of criminal jurisdictions, and those that relate to the exercise of criminal prosecutions.[67] But the term 'public order' is vague and imprecise, lending itself to variable judicial interpretations.[68] In this way, it enables French courts to exercise discretion when called to determine the legality, and subsequent validity, of procedural acts, and when shaping in that way the conditions for the exclusion of improperly obtained evidence.

The above lead to one final practical distinction, the only one now required for an understanding of the contemporary French approach to procedural nullities. This is a distinction between 'public order' – automatic – nullities ('textual' and 'substantial') (*nullités d'ordre public*), on the one hand, and 'private interest' – non-automatic – nullities (again 'textual' and 'substantial'), on the other, that 'are established in the interest of the parties'[69] and 'concern the respect of the rights of individuals, of each person, and notably the rights of the defence' (*nullités d'intérêt privé*).[70] 'Private interest' nullities can be pronounced only where the Court makes an *in concreto* finding of 'harm' deriving from a procedural breach. The breach does not in itself lead to exclusion. The Court can invalidate the relevant procedural act, and make the evidence thus obtained non-usable in the criminal process, only in exercising its discretion. These non-automatic, discretionary, nullities have traditionally been most pertinent to the exclusion of improperly obtained evidence. French jurisprudence has categorised as such those concerning search and seizure, police interrogation, telephone intercepts and other forms of electronic surveillance, acts relating to the obtaining of expert evidence and those that relate to written records of procedural acts. Importantly, for the purposes of this chapter, violations of provisions regulating acts that interfere with the right to privacy have generally been deemed to generate 'private interest' nullities.[71]

[67] See JP Brouillaud, 'Les nullités de procédure: des procédures pénales et civiles comparées' (1996) *Recueil Dalloz* 99. Nullity for violation of public-interest provisions has been pronounced in cases relating to the jurisdiction of particular tribunals and the jurisdiction of the Investigating Judge, defects with the signing of formal procedural acts, oaths and expert evidence, but, importantly, also in relation to the *principe de loyauté*. See Juris-Classeur, *Procédure pénale*, Arts 170–174-1, fasc 20 (2003) 10–11. Perhaps we could draw an analogy here with 'abuse of process' in English law. The latter has important ramifications for the law of improperly obtained evidence, but its main function lies in the area of errors connected with the administration of criminal justice. See generally A L-T Choo, *Abuse of Process and Judicial Stays of Criminal Proceedings*, 2nd edn (Oxford, Oxford University Press, 2008).

[68] Juris-Classeur, *Procédure pénale* (ibid) 10.

[69] Conchon, *L'évolution des nullités* (2002) 122.

[70] Brouillaud, 'Les nullités de procédure' (1996) 99.

[71] ibid.

It is not outlandish to think that in the eyes of common law observers the above distinctions will appear highly technical and convoluted. French observers themselves find them complex and archaic.[72] But since the focus of this chapter will be on violations of the right to privacy – to which non-automatic nullities traditionally apply – exegesis of the above distinctions mainly serves to attract attention to the particular characteristics, and institutional gravity, of non-automatic, discretionary, exclusion in France. It is also important to emphasise the fact that, against their positivist Continental law background, these categorisations of nullities are exclusively jurisprudential in nature. As such, they continuously evolve, sometimes much more rapidly than one might expect. Strong evidence of this 'indeterminism' and 'fluidity' of procedural nullities[73] is provided by the fact that from the beginning of the 1990s, Cour de cassation jurisprudence has, on many occasions, transformed 'private interest' nullities into 'public order' ones, thus turning them from discretionary to automatic. Custodial interrogation rights have been at the centre of this development, but we are now beginning to witness similar movements – though of lower intensity – in the area of privacy rights. It is these contemporary transformations that much of the remainder of the chapter will set out to trace and analyse, in comparison with modern section 78(1) jurisprudence in England and Wales, with a view to identifying emerging divergence, and continuing convergence, between English and French law.

By way of concluding the analysis of the historic development and study of the contemporary framework of French procedural nullities, one cannot help but emphasise the seminal role of judicial discretion,[74] manifesting itself at three different levels; when determining 'substantial' provisions whose breach *may* trigger a nullity, when classifying between 'public order' and 'private interest' provisions, and, finally, when deciding whether a breach of a 'private interest' provision has prejudiced the defendant in practice, and whether the breach should therefore generate a nullity and evidentiary 'exclusion'. The 'exaggerated subjectivism'[75] of this system resonates strongly with the subjectivism inherent in section 78(1) of the Police and Criminal Evidence Act. The English concepts of 'fairness of the proceedings' and 'adverse effect' stemming from 'the circumstances in which the evidence was obtained' are no less abstract than their French counterparts of 'substantial provisions', 'private interest' and 'harm' or 'prejudice' caused by particular procedural breaches. Both systems rely on judicial discretion to help bring precision to these concepts, contextualise and apply them in practice. The extent to which this happens will now be explored through a study of the exclusionary jurisprudence for violations of the right to privacy in these two countries.

[72] See, eg, S Guinhard and J Buisson, *Procédure pénale* (Paris, Litec, 2000) 700.

[73] E Molina, 'Réflexion critique sur l'évolution paradoxale de la liberté de la preuve des infractions en droit français contemporain' (2002) *Revue de sciences criminelle* 266.

[74] See generally J Pradel, *Droit pénal comparé* (Paris, Dalloz, 1995) 423.

[75] R Merle and A Vitu, *Traité de droit criminel, Procédure pénale*, 4th edn (Paris, Cujas, 1989) 548–49.

II. Jurisprudential Applications: *Admitting* Evidence Obtained in Violation of the Right to Privacy

In contrast to Greece and the United States, where a long tradition of constitutional protection of the right to privacy transverses the legal system, recognition of the right to privacy is a recent phenomenon in English and French law. In France, the Conseil constitutionnel has taken this step in a 1977 case concerning a car search,[76] though the text of the French constitution still today does not explicitly provide for this fundamental right. In England and Wales, as recently as in the beginning of the 1990s, academic and judicial opinion were still in agreement that the right to privacy did not exist,[77] or, if it did, it was of limited importance in the English legal culture.[78] It was only through the medium of the European Convention of Human Rights (ECHR), and its incorporation with the Human Rights Act 1998, that English law began to give effect to a right to private life, deriving from Article 8 of the Convention.[79] As a consequence, there has been little or no constitutionalisation of aspects of criminal procedure engaging defendants' privacy expectations. It will be useful to keep this in mind when examining appellate and 'supreme court' jurisprudence on the exclusion of evidence obtained in violation of the right to privacy in English and French law, especially when confronted with the observation that this jurisprudence widely upholds decisions admitting evidence obtained in violation of the right to privacy.

A. Search and Seizure: An Inclusionary Approach Par Excellence

The French CPP subjects search and seizure to a rigorous system of procedural guarantees (rigorous from the viewpoint of French criminal law),[80] designed to

[76] *Cons const* 12 January 1977, *Pierre Joxe et autres*, D 1978, 1973. See L Favoreu, 'Le Conseil constitutionnel et la protection de la liberté individuelle et de la vie privée. À propos de la décision du 12 janvier 1977 relative à la fouille des véhicules', *Études offertes à Pierre Kayser*, vol 1, 411–25. See also *Cons const* 29 December 1983, JCP 1984.II.20160, which sanctioned the right of the inviolability of the house.

[77] See, eg, *Kaye v Robertson* [1991] FSR 62, 66; P Sieghart, *Human Rights in the United Kingdom*, Human Rights Network (London and New York, Pinter Publishers, 1988) 122.

[78] See, eg, D Feldman, *Civil Liberties and Human Rights in England and Wales* (Oxford, Clarendon Press, 1993) 381.

[79] A comparison between the 1993 edition of Feldman's work on *Civil Liberties and Human Rights* (ibid) with his 2002 edition provides a useful illustration. D Feldman, *Civil Liberties and Human Rights in England and Wales*, 3rd edn (Oxford, Oxford University Press, 2002) 546.

[80] See, eg, J Pradel, *Procédure pénale*, 10th edn (Paris, Cujas, 2000) 341. It is beyond the scope of this chapter to undertake an analytical review of French search and seizure provisions, but it can be pointed out that French law requires less scrutiny at the level of judicial authorisation in comparison to the United States or England and Wales. The Investigating Judge is not required to mention the specific location of a search that he will be undertaking for instance. See art 94 CPP and *Crim* 22 January 1953, *Bull crim* n 24.

alleviate the grave effects of police interference with the right to privacy, notably in cases of searches of residential premises.[81] A key provision of the Code mandates that police searches should take place 'in the presence of the person whose property is being searched', that, if this is not possible, the police officer undertaking the search must ask that person to nominate a representative and that, if this too proves impossible, the police officer should instruct two witnesses to be present during the search.[82] This provision has generated much jurisprudence on the question of the type of procedural nullities that should apply in this context.

The Cour de cassation's original interpretation of these provisions was that they were giving effect to 'public interest' nullities, which were pronounced without the need to demonstrate that the defendant's interests had been prejudiced by the relevant procedural breach.[83] However, the Cour de cassation now qualifies these provisions as of 'private interest', bringing them under the umbrella of article 802 CPP, which requires evidence of procedural 'harm' before a nullity can be pronounced. In theory this means that the relevant procedural act – in this case the police search conducted in breach of article 57 CPP – can still be invalidated, if the judge makes the ad hoc finding that the illegality has prejudiced the interests of the defendant. But neither the Code nor the Cour de cassation's jurisprudence provide the judge with any guidance as to the factors that he or she should be taking under consideration when making this finding. The outcome seems to depend entirely on the judge's discretionary judgment as to the factors that might tilt the balance in one direction or the other.[84] Pradel provides a pessimistic analysis of the law in action, taking the requirement for the ad hoc finding of 'prejudice' to mean that 'in reality [the pronouncement of nullity] is practically excluded'.[85] In his view, judges tend to disregard the breach, permitting the use of the evidentiary fruits of the relevant procedural act, in this case evidence obtained through illegal police searches. The examination of relevant case law will now shed light on the way judges exercise their discretion in practice.

Two Cour de cassation decisions from 1996 and 2000 offer a good introduction.[86] In both cases, the police failed to invite the defendants – who were detained at the police station while the police were searching their houses – to nominate a representative to attend the searches. The Cour de cassation found that the breach

[81] See M Guerrin, *Les irrégularités de procédure sanctionnées par la nullité dans la phase préalable au jugement pénal*, Doctoral thesis, Université Strasbourg III – Robert Schuman (1999) 94.

[82] Art 57 CPP.

[83] *Crim* 27 September 1984, *Bull crim* n 275; 7 December 1993, *Bull crim* n 372; *Crim* 23 February 1988, *Bull crim* n 91. See also C Vroom, 'La liberté individuelle au stade de l'enquête de police en France et aux Etats-Unis' (1988) *Revue de sciences criminelle* 487, 492.

[84] See *Crim* 17 September 1996, *Bull crim* n 316; (1997) *Revue de sciences criminelle* 149; *Crim* 4 November 2004, n 00-81-652; C Porteron, 'Nullité des perquisitions au cours de l'instruction' (2005) *Actualité juridique pénal* 143.

[85] *Crim* 15 June 2000, (2001) *Recueil Dalloz* 520, obs J Pradel.

[86] *Crim* 17 September 1996, (1997) *Recueil Dalloz* 144; (1997) *Revue de sciences criminelle* 149, obs J-P Dintilhac; *Crim* 15 June 2000, (2001) *Recueil Dalloz* 520.

of article 57 CPP had not prejudiced the interests of the defendants. The Court explained in one of these cases that 'even if the detained suspect had been invited to nominate a representative [...] the incriminating documents would still have been admitted'.[87] Underpinning the Court's logic here was a capacity for *post facto* rationalisation;[88] the incriminating evidence would have been discovered even if the defendants' representative had attended the searches. The procedural breach was inconsequential. One might ask, however, why the presence of two witnesses is mandated by the CPP if not to provide reassurance that evidence has been obtained in a lawful manner.

The same logic has been applied to breaches of CPP provisions relating to sealing evidence discovered during police searches. In one case, the police had made an inventory of evidence at the time of the search, but only placed it in sealed evidence bags six months later,[89] while in two other cases the evidence was sealed 24 hours and three hours respectively after the search.[90] The Cour de cassation did not pronounce a nullity in any of these cases. The Court emphasised in one of these cases that the defendant had not contested the discovery of the evidence, and that this demonstrated that his interests had not been prejudiced.[91] There was the same outcome in a case where the sealed evidence bag had been opened in the absence of the defendant as well as in a case where the police had not completed on site the report required for the verification of a search.[92] In both instances, the supreme jurisdiction underlined the need to demonstrate that the interests of the defendant have suffered a prejudicial effect as a result of the breach.

The Court provided explicit confirmation of the force of this jurisprudential line in a 2007 case,[93] by noting that 'no breach of the provisions on police searches, either substantive or technical, requires pronouncing a nullity of the police search and subsequent acts except if it has prejudiced the [defendant's] interests'.[94] Interestingly, the Court recognised an exception in the same case, qualifying provisions relating to the requirement to weigh seized drugs as of 'public order'. Breach of such provisions would give rise to a nullity and exclusion, without the need to demonstrate that the defendant had been disadvantaged by the particular breach. '[T]he implicit but certain objective' of the relevant provisions, noted the Court, was to 'avoid any dispute, in trial, of the authenticity of the evidence'.[95] But this is a rather isolated example. A case from 2013 proves the point. Though the supreme

[87] *Crim* 17 September 1996, (1997) *Recueil Dalloz* 144.

[88] A Choo, *Evidence* (Oxford, Oxford University Press, 2006).

[89] *Crim* 21 March 1995 (n 93-84-597).

[90] See respectively *Crim* 14 September 2004, n 04-83.754, (2005) *Revue de sciences criminelle* 389, obs Buisson; *Crim* 12 February 2008, n 07-87.753.

[91] *Crim* 21 March 1995 (n 93-84-597).

[92] See Porteron, 'Nullité des perquisitions au cours de l'instruction' (2005) 143.

[93] *Crim* 24 January 2007, n 06-88.351, *Bull crim* n 20; D 2007, 143, obs G Roussel.

[94] See J Buisson, 'Perquisition – saisie: nullité à grief – Pesée des stupéfiants: nullité d'ordre public' (2008) *Revue de sciences criminelle* 645.

[95] ibid.

jurisdiction admitted in this case that the defendant had been unfairly deprived of his entitlement to the right to privacy – on the basis that the search had taken place in the house of the defendant's parents, where the defendant nonetheless resided – it still refused to invalidate the search and exclude the evidence discovered by the police (a large amount of money). In doing so, it once again emphasised that these provisions came under the umbrella of article 802 CPP, and that the defendant therefore needed to demonstrate that his interests had been prejudiced by the police search.[96]

It is clear from the above that the Cour de cassation does not subscribe to a rights-centred logic. Violations of the right to privacy do not, in themselves, suffice to generate a procedural nullity. The violation must have also disadvantaged the defendant in a concrete way, by putting in doubt the authenticity of the evidence. This state of affairs may, of course, be due to search and seizure provisions in the CPP not necessarily drawing upon a specific constitutional right, in the way, for instance, that search and seizure provisions do so in the United States and Greece. Absent a constitutionalisation of procedural acts engaging the right to privacy, French courts seem comfortable to dismiss breaches of search and seizure provisions as inconsequential technical breaches. This must be seen in conjunction with a wider jurisprudential attitude aimed at increasing the opportunities for search and seizure. For example, the Court has classified various incidents as mere 'visual observations' (*constatations visuelles*), rather than search and seizure, in cases where the police were seemingly undertaking a search of premises.[97] Another example is recent jurisprudence that considers that communal areas in blocks of flats are freely accessible by the police.[98] A starker demonstration is provided by the Court's permissive attitude towards search and seizure in *cabinets d'avocats* (law offices)[99] and press offices,[100] which is arguably

[96] *Crim* 25 June 2013, *Gazzette du Palais* 13–15 October 2013, 38, note Fourment.

[97] Examples include discovering evidence in a cloakroom located in the premises of a fire service (*Crim* 17 May 1993, *Droit pénal* 1993, chron 59), a search taking place in a shop (*Crim* 4 May 1994, n 93.80-920, *Droit pénal* 1994, chron 59) and the spontaneous passing of medical records to a police officer in breach of CPP provisions mandating the seizure of such evidence only in the presence of a member of the Council of the relevant professional association (*Crim* 12 February 2008, n 07-87.862, (2008) *Recueil Dalloz* 924; *Actualité juridique pénal* 2008, 244, obs G Roussel; (2009) *Revue de sciences criminelle* 893, obs J Buisson).

[98] *Crim* 2 October 2013, n 12-87.976. See JL Capdeville, 'Possibilité pour les services de police d'accéder aux parties communes librement accessibles d'un immeuble' (2014) *Actualité juridique pénal* 138.

[99] In an example from 2013, the Court found that a search of a lawyer's house and office had been lawful, despite the fact that the lawyer had not yet been investigated for the offence, and that a personal agenda and other documents – seemingly covered by legal professional privilege and not associated with the relevant judicial investigation – had been seized. See *Crim* 25 June 2013, n 12-88.021. For a critique of the *Cour de cassation* judgment see V Nioré, 'Splendeurs et misères de la mission du bâtonnier au cours d'une perquisition chez l'avocat' (2013) *Dalloz avocats* 336.

[100] To take the example of a case from 2007, the Court rejected the defendants' request for nullity of a police search into a press office, which had been conducted with the direct aim of identifying journalistic sources. Rather astonishingly, the Court admitted that, although the law prohibited

at odds with legal professional privilege and journalistic confidentiality. This jurisprudential mindset offers a valuable insight into a critique that locates automatic exclusionary rules as the root causes of narrow judicial interpretations of the right to privacy. According to this account, courts limit the scope of the right to privacy in order to avoid the application of an exclusionary rule, in circumstances where a breach would necessarily generate exclusion.[101] In the case of France, the existence of a discretion to invalidate such breaches has not prevented the Cour de cassation from narrowing down the scope of the right to privacy.

The consequence of this is that judgments admitting evidence obtained through unlawful searches are not reversed at appellate and Cour de cassation level in France. A similarly generous approach to using evidence obtained by search and seizure, in the face of violations of the right to privacy, can be encountered in the English criminal justice system. The extent to which the discretion under 78(1) of the Police and Criminal Evidence (PACE) Act 1984 is exercised to exclude such evidence is highly questionable.[102]

A case to the point is *R v Wright*,[103] where the search had not been authorised in writing by an officer of the appropriate rank, a record of the search had not been made, and there had been no communication with the defendant, who was subsequently not present during the search, while the police had also failed to make a list of property seized. Despite various breaches of PACE[104] and the relevant Code of Practice,[105] the trial judge found that admission of the evidence – £16,000 in cash and a £9,000 gold necklace, which were relevant to the question of whether drugs found in the possession of the defendant were for supply to another – would not adversely affect the fairness of the proceedings. The trial judge had correctly

judicial authorities from compelling journalists to reveal their sources, it did not stop the police from undertaking searches of press offices with the objective to discover these sources themselves. See *Crim* 4 December 2007, n 07-86.086. See also J Buisson, 'Perquisition dans un local de presse: régie par les conditions de nécessité et de proportionnalité' (2008) *Revue de sciences criminelle* 648. In a 2012 case, the Cour de cassation similarly reversed a decision that had pronounced the nullity of the search of a press office and had ordered the return of the evidence seized. See *Crim* 11 January 2012, *Bull crim* n 8; (2012) *Recueil Dalloz* 213. The highly disproportionate character of such operations came to the fore with two decisions of the ECtHR in 2012 convicting France for violations of art 10 of the Convention. See *Martin v France* (Application No 30002/08, 12 July 2012; (2012) *Constitutions* 645, obs D de Bellescize; (2012) *Revue de sciences criminelle* 603, obs J Francillon) and *Ressiot and others v France* (Applications No 150554/07 and 15066/07, 28 September 2012; (2012) *Recueil Dalloz* 2282, note E Dreyer). These decisions can provide an explanation for the more recent U-turn taken by the Cour de cassation, as illustrated with a 2014 case, where the Court held that a similar operation had not been justified and that less onerous (for the 'freedom of the press') investigative measures should have been applied. See *Crim* 25 February 2014, n 13-84.761; (2014) *Recueil Dalloz* 609. See also J Pradel, 'Panorama – Procédure pénale juin 2013 – juin 2014' (2014) *Recueil Dalloz* 1736, 1740.

[101] See ch 2.

[102] See Archbold Criminal Pleading, Evidence and Practice 2015 (2015) 1889 [15–458], which notes that 'the mere fact that evidence is discovered in the course of an unlawful search is unlikely to render the admission of the evidence unfair'.

[103] *R v Wright* [1994] *Criminal Law Review* 55 (unreported).

[104] Sections 18 and 18(8) Police and Criminal Evidence Act 1984.

[105] Code of Practice B, Police and Criminal Evidence Act 1984.

exercised the section 78(1) discretion, opined later by the Court of Appeal. Breaches of the Codes of Practice had not been deliberate and the trial judge had taken into account everything that required consideration (and nothing that did not).

R v Stewart gives an equally convincing account of the Court of Appeal's trivialising approach to unlawful search and seizure. The relevant parties admitted in the *voir dire* that a number of breaches of the Code of Practice had been committed. The search led to the discovery of a 'mechanical apparatus' that the defendant had installed 'to divert both the gas and electricity supply so as to bypass the meters recording consumption'. But the Court of Appeal confirmed that the admission of the apparatus as evidence 'did not have any effect at all on the fairness of the proceedings', noting, in particular, that the evidence 'was there for all to see whether the entry was effected properly or not'.[106] Birch has perfectly captured the 'rather dubious' nature of this 'precedent'. 'After all', she rightly points out, 'real evidence is always "there to be seen" whatever the method of obtaining it, but it should not follow that the fruits of an improper search are always to be admitted'.[107] Accepting such an argument would be no different than to return to the common law archetype of 'it matters not how you get it'.[108] In the eyes of an American commentator, seasoned in the systemic exclusion of unconstitutionally obtained search and seizure evidence, the argument must look absurd; an upright rejection of the foundation of their exclusionary system. The American exclusionary rule critic on the other hand, might see this as a commonsensical escape from the suffocating constitutional grip. The Greek commentator might react with similar surprise at the simplicity of the argument, though she would not be able to base her criticism on practical examples from Greek jurisprudence on search and seizure; as previously demonstrated, there is hardly ever exclusion of such evidence in Greece.[109] Locating the logical weaknesses in the argument of the Court of Appeal, Birch restates it as a claim that 'the officers could have come by the evidence by following the Code, and were thus not presenting evidence obtained by impropriety which they could not have got through fair means'.[110] This appears to be a more tenable position, particularly from the viewpoint of a discretion that requires giving consideration to all the circumstances surrounding the obtaining of the evidence. There is, nonetheless, no denying the antipathy towards exclusion here. This is reinforced by the Court's observation that 'the fact that there have been breaches [of the Code of Practice], however many and however culpable, is not itself definitive of the judge's duty to exercise his discretion'.[111] Even within a discretionary framework, one would reasonably expect courts to recognise that the fact that a significant number of breaches may have been committed

[106] *R v Stewart* [1995] *Criminal Law Review* 500.
[107] ibid 501. See also Mirfield, *Improperly Obtained Evidence* (1997) 211.
[108] *R v Leatham* (1861) 8 Cox CC 498, 501.
[109] See ch 2.
[110] *R v Stewart* [1995] *Criminal Law Review* 500, 501.
[111] ibid 500.

would weigh heavily in favour of exclusion, especially if the breaches were deemed to be particularly culpable.

The Court of Appeal showed signs of a willingness to introduce exceptions to this wide admissibility position in *R v Sanghera*,[112] even if only in obiter dicta. The Court distinguished between situations where 'a serious breakdown in the proper procedures has taken place in the whole of the prosecution process', where 'the courts may well take the view that the nature of the breakdown is so significant that it would not be appropriate to allow the evidence to be admitted',[113] 'situations lower down the scale' where breaches might be 'significant but not serious' and which would be open to evaluation by the judge 'looking at all the circumstances',[114] and finally situations where breaches might be 'venial or technical', where 'the court will almost inevitably come to the conclusion that there has been no injustice or unfairness involved and will exercise its discretion in favour of allowing the evidence to be given'.[115] It might have seemed conceivable at the time that these distinctions could create new opportunities for the application of section 78(1), particularly at an era where procedural breaches would be more frequently associated with violations of the ECHR.[116] But *Sanghera's* distinctions failed to gain any momentum in section 78(1) jurisprudence, and the case itself seems to have been widely ignored in the relevant scholarly debates since then.

R (Cook) v Serious Organised Crime Agency (SOCA) provides another illustration of judicial endorsement of the ability to use evidence obtained through unlawful search and seizure. The search warrants there had been 'incorrectly drafted' and not properly executed',[117] as a result of which the High Court ordered SOCA to return the unlawfully seized documents to the defendants. But the High Court refused, at the same time, to order SOCA to destroy the copies of the seized documents that it had made, which were eventually adduced as evidence in court. Leveson LJ pointed to *Sang* and the many cases that followed, to provide a quick reminder that 'the deployment of unlawfully obtained evidence is not necessarily and inevitably prohibited irrespective of the circumstances',[118] with Ouseley J adding that this was 'well recognized at common law'.[119] In an analysis

[112] *R v Sanghera* [2001] 1 Cr App R 299.

[113] ibid 304–05.

[114] ibid 305.

[115] ibid.

[116] See generally A L-T Choo and S Nash, 'Evidence Law in England and Wales: the Impact of the Human Rights Act 1998' (2003) 7 *International Journal of Evidence & Proof* 31; P Roberts and J Hunter, 'Introduction – The Human Rights Revolution in Criminal Evidence and Procedure' in P Roberts and J Hunter (ed), *Criminal Evidence and Human Rights – Reimagining Common Law Procedural Traditions* (Hart, Oxford and Portland, 2012) 1.

[117] R Pattenden, 'Case Comment – Unlawfully Obtained Evidence – *R (Cook) v Serious Organised Crime Agency*' (2011) 15 *International Journal of Evidence & Proof* 82.

[118] *R (Cook) v Serious Organised Crime Agency* [2010] EWHC 2119 (Admin) [21].

[119] ibid [27].

of evidentiary remedies for improperly issued warrants, Sharpe observed in 2000 that a 'constitutional perspective [had not] yet been taken toward excluding real evidence' and that '[t]he reliability principle ha[d] been paramount and, illegality notwithstanding, such evidence had been admitted'.[120] Stone, writing in 2005, concluded from a comparison with pre-PACE case law that 'section 78, while introducing the potential for a more broadly based exclusionary rule than under the common law, did not in the area of entry, search and seizure produce any major change of approach'.[121] *Cook* demonstrates that these words have lost nothing of their relevance today.

Locating in the section 78(1) jurisprudence examples of cases diverging from this approach is not an easy task. *R (on the application of RSPCA) v Colchester Magistrates' Court* is a rare example of a lower court case where material evidence was excluded on the basis of a significant breach of the relevant Codes of Practice, and this despite the fact that the officers conducting the search had acted in good faith. '[G]ood faith is not enough to justify the non-exclusion of evidence', and '[a] breach which is significant is not made insignificant by good faith', observed the High Court when undertaking judicial review of the decision of the Magistrates' Court.[122] In exercising his discretion under section 78, the District Judge had stressed that to use the evidence would be to condone the relevant breaches.[123] *R v Veneroso*, a Crown Court judgment from 2002, provides another interesting demonstration.[124] Drugs were found in this case incident to an unlawful search of the house of the defendant. Finding that the search was in violation of Article 8 of the ECHR, the trial judge exercised the section 78(1) discretion to exclude the evidence, and this despite the fact that 'the police officers [had] acted at all times in good faith'. This unusual application of section 78(1) was underpinned by the idea that 'the public interest in bringing [the defendant] to trial for these offences did not outweigh the need to protect his rights under Article 8'.[125] For all its merit, from a normative point of view at least, this idea was 'difficult to reconcile' with English exclusionary jurisprudence. Ormerod was quick to point out that the use of 'incriminating evidence obtained from intrusions in breach of Article 8 ha[d] been endorsed by the House of Lords and the European Court of Human Rights'. In the context of exercising the discretion provided by section 78(1) the 'absence of bad faith', the 'reliability of the evidence' and the 'opportunity for the accused to challenge the incriminating evidence at trial' would go in favour of admitting the

[120] C Sharpe, *Search and Surveillance – The Movement from Evidence to Information* (Ashgate-Dartmouth, Aldershot, 2000) 67.

[121] R Stone, *The Law of Entry, Search and Seizure*, 4th edn (Oxford, Oxford University Press, 2005) 66.

[122] *R (on the application of RSPCA) v Colchester Magistrates' Court* [2015] EWHC 1418 (Admin) [36].

[123] ibid [18].

[124] *R v Veneroso* [2002] *Criminal Law Review* 306.

[125] ibid.

improperly obtained evidence, while the fact, in particular, that there was a breach of Article 8 would 'point to exclusion'.[126]

Choo draws a useful distinction here, between appellate review of the application of section 78(1) and the exercise of discretion contained therein by trial courts. He takes *Veneroso* as indicating that trial fairness is 'sufficiently nebulous to enable trial courts, if so minded, to achieve exclusion in a wider range of circumstances than might appear to be sanctioned by appellate decisions'.[127] This elastic concept is, in theory, susceptible of allowing more creative interpretations of section 78(1). The problem is we simply do not know the extent to which trial courts might be adopting such creative interpretations in practice, as trial level cases where evidence may have been excluded will normally not go to the Court of Appeal or be the subject of judicial review, and there is more generally limited access to trial court decisions addressing such issues.[128] What we do know is that appellate courts interpret trial fairness narrowly and readily confirm decisions to admit evidence obtained through unlawful searches. Not less worrying, from the point of view of preventing the use of unlawfully obtained evidence in court, is the fact that, in England and Wales, it is notoriously difficult for the defendant to prove that search and seizure has been unlawful. Public interest immunity 'will almost certainly be raised by the police to defeat any challenge to the sufficiency of information upon which the warrant was granted'.[129]

Though English and French historic resistance to excluding evidence obtained in violation of the right to privacy manifests itself par excellence in relation to search and seizure, the dearth of case law in this area, and limited academic attention it receives, means caution is required when extrapolating from search and seizure on the wider English and French evidentiary approaches to the use of evidence obtained in violation of the right to privacy. Jurisprudential analysis will therefore now be extended to the use of telephone intercepts and evidence obtained through the unauthorised bugging of premises and the use of other unlawful means of electronic surveillance. Much of this jurisprudence emphatically confirms that reliability and trial fairness considerations are central to the French and English *inclusionary* approaches to evidence procured through privacy violations. But, perhaps unexpectedly, there are signs too, in contemporary French jurisprudence, of a greater realisation of the need to avoid paying the right to privacy lip service. This is starting to generate sporadic yet noteworthy divergence between the English and French approaches to improperly obtained evidence.

[126] D Ormerod, 'Case Comment – Evidence: Entry on Premises to Ascertain Next of Kin – Drugs Found There – *R v Veneroso*' [2002] *Criminal Law Review* 306.

[127] A L-T Choo, *Evidence*, 4th edn (Oxford, Oxford University Press, 2015) 185.

[128] I am grateful to Andrew Choo for sharing his thoughts on this point.

[129] Sharpe, *Search and Surveillance* (2000) 65.

B. Telephone Intercepts and other Covert Electronic Recordings: Reliable Technological Evidence over Human Rights?

Unlike evidence of search and seizure, the use in court of telephone intercepts and covertly obtained recordings of private conversations has generated significant jurisprudence in England and France. Its analysis is key to comprehending the general principles, and specific applications, of the improperly obtained evidence regimes there. It will be useful to proceed to this analysis by separating unlawful telephone intercepts from other types of covert electronic recordings, and by paying particular attention to the bugging of police cells. This will more effectively bring to the fore the similarly narrow, reliability-centred, English and French approaches to discretionary exclusion, while leaving appropriate room to analyse the significance of emerging pockets of pro-human rights exclusionary jurisprudence more recently encountered in France.

i. A Blanket Rule of Inadmissibility for Intercept Evidence in the United Kingdom: But 'Business as Usual' for Section 78(1)

French and English law give diametrically opposite answers to the question of whether the use in court of intercepts of communications[130] – and not specifically the use of *unlawfully obtained* telephone intercepts – is permissible in law. France, like the United States and Greece, and the vast majority of modern legal systems, responds in the affirmative.[131] The United Kingdom, on the other hand, adopts the idiosyncratic position of a blanket rule of inadmissibility of *all* telephone intercepts,[132] which includes all those instances where no violation of the right to privacy has occurred and telephone taps have been lawfully authorised and carried out.[133] Section 56 of the Investigatory Powers Act 2016 prohibits

[130] In the United Kingdom, intelligence and law enforcement agencies can intercept all forms of electronic communications, telephone communications and communications by post. Sir J Chilcot, *Privy Council Review of Intercept as Evidence*, 30 January 2008, Cm 7324 [17].

[131] See generally D Giannoulopoulos and R Parizot, 'La preuve technologique des interceptions et surveillances' in G Giudicelli-Delage (ed), *Les transformations de l'administration de la preuve pénale: perspectives comparées* (Paris, Société de législation comparée, 2006) 245.

[132] See P Mirfield, 'Regulation of Investigatory Powers Act 2000: Part 2: Evidential Aspects' [2001] *Criminal Law Review* 91, 93.

[133] The intercept ban does not, however, apply to 'material intercepted in a foreign country under that country's law; to a telephone conversation recorded with the consent of one of the participants; or to a telephone conversation recorded by a hidden microphone not connected to the telephone. Intercept evidence can be adduced as evidence in all these cases. See Chilcot, *Privy Council Review* (2008) [22]. See also *R v Effik and another* [1995] 1 AC 309, where conversations on a cordless telephone, intercepted and taped by the police, were found to be admissible in evidence, on the basis that cordless telephone does not form part of the public telecommunications system (and only the interception of communications on public systems was regulated by the relevant Act).

the use of any evidence in court that discloses the contents of a warranted intercepted communication[134] and any evidence that tends to suggest that an interception may have occurred or is going to occur.[135] Section 17 incorporates an identical rule of inadmissibility enacted in 1984,[136] in the aftermath of *Malone v the United Kingdom*, where the UK regime of telephone interceptions was found by Strasbourg to be in breach of Article 8 of the Convention.[137] In other words, the legislator has, for more than 30 years now, deprived UK courts from the ability to draw upon potentially crucial and highly reliable evidence.

Perhaps we could speak of an English paradox here, considering, in particular, the necessity for the State to be able to undertake interceptions of telephone and electronic communications in the fight against terrorism and organised crime,[138] their 'widespread use […] as evidence across the world',[139] the paramount importance of relevance and reliability in the English Law of Evidence[140] and the correspondingly little attention given by English courts to the right to privacy in the context of evidence admissibility. In view of the above, it seems counterintuitive to exclude a whole range of inherently reliable evidence whose obtaining may clash with the right to privacy. But this would be to assume that the Investigatory Powers Act's blanket ban, and its predecessors, have been born out of a need to protect the right to privacy or that its existence deters British authorities from the systematic use of interception capabilities in the first place. Nothing could be further from the truth. The United Kingdom's emphasis on the electronic surveillance of private communications has come to the surface with dramatic force in the wake of the Snowden revelations about the United States National Security Agency's mass surveillance programme and the UK Government Communications Headquarters' (GCHQ) access to it,[141] notably revelations about the extent to which GCHQ operated its own bulk interception programme.[142] It is also openly

[134] Section 56(1)(a) Investigatory Powers Act 2016 came into force on 27th June 2018 replacing section 17(1)(a) Regulation of Investigatory Powers Act 2000.

[135] Section 56(1)(b) Investigatory Powers Act 2016 replacing section 17(1)(b) Regulation of Investigatory Powers Act 2000. On section 17's operation see generally D Corker, *Lawyers should be able to use spy material in court* (2018) *The Times*, September 12; D Ormerod and S McKay, 'Telephone Intercepts and Their Admissibility' [2004] *Criminal Law Review* 15; Uglow, *Evidence* (2006) 265–67; V Okechukwu Benjamin, 'Interception of Internet Communications and the Right to Privacy: An Evaluation of some Provisions of the Regulation of Investigatory Powers Act Against the Jurisprudence of the European Court of Human Rights' (2007) 6 *European Human Rights Law Review* 637; R Esen, 'Intercepting Communications "in Accordance with the Law"' [2012] *Journal of Criminal Law* 164.

[136] Section 9(1) Interceptions of Communications Act 1984.

[137] *Malone v United Kingdom* (1984) 7 EHRR 14.

[138] See *Klass and others v Germany* (1979–80) 2 EHRR 214.

[139] Chilcot (n 130) [3].

[140] Ormerod and McKay speak of a 'temptation […] to admit as much evidence as possible […] that would certainly square with the orthodox approach to relevant evidence in English law'. Ormerod and McKay, 'Telephone Intercepts' (2004) 38.

[141] On Snowden see generally the *Guardian*, which broke out the scandal, at www.theguardian.com/us-news/edward-snowden.

[142] Aspects of this programme were found to be in breach of Article 8 of the Convention, when the Investigatory Powers Tribunal ruled, for the first time in its short history, against the UK's intelligence

admitted that the interception of communications contributes to a large number of arrests.[143] As to the rationale underlying the ban on intercept evidence, the House of Lords has stated that it is the need 'to preserve the secrecy of the warrant system'.[144] Secrecy, not privacy, is the *raison d'être* of the ban.[145] The intercept ban merely sought to 'limit the use of material gathered from telephone intercepts to an "intelligence" rather than an "evidential" role'.[146] This is also illustrated by the Court of Appeal's admission that 'where secrecy [is] not required in the public interest' it will be in accordance with Article 8 of the Convention to admit 'all relevant and probative [telephone intercept] evidence' in order to 'assist in the apprehension and conviction of criminals and ensure that their trial was fair'.[147]

Telephone intercepts were indeed held to be admissible in those exceptional cases where the intercept ban did not apply and where the use of telephone intercepts therefore turned on the exercise of the wider discretion under section 78(1). In *R v Aujla*, intercept evidence had been obtained in the Netherlands, by the Dutch authorities, in accordance with national law, and was adduced against the defendants in the Crown Court proceedings in England. In reaching the conclusion that the ban on intercept evidence did not apply to material obtained by *foreign* phone tapping, the Court logically then went on to conclude that the evidence could not have been excluded under section 78(1) either, as there was 'no apparent breach of Article 8'.[148] Echoing conventional section 78(1) jurisprudence, the Court added that 'even if it were to emerge that there was some breach of Dutch law, and it could be said that there was some breach of Article 8, that would not necessarily result in the exclusion of this evidence as admissible evidence at the appellant's trial'.[149] An 'apparent breach' of Article 8 'is not a decisive factor' when exercising section 78(1)'s discretionary power, concluded the Court.[150] The ban on intercept evidence should therefore not be mistaken for a protection of the right to privacy.[151] Section 78(1) is construed no less narrowly here than in other fields already studied. Like evidence obtained through search and seizure,

agencies. See *Liberty and others v the Secretary of State for Foreign and Commonwealth and others* [2015] UKIPTrib 13 77-H. The European Court of Human Rights confirmed, in *Big Brother Watch and others v the United Kingdom* (Applications Nos 58170/13, 62322/14 and 24960/15, 13 September 2018), that the UK's bulk interception regime entailed a violation of Article 8 of the Convention.

[143] As well as 'recoveries of firearms, and seizures of drugs and cash', in the context, for instance, of investigations carried out by the Serious Organised Crime Agency. See Chilcot (n 130) [34].

[144] *Attorney-General's Reference (No 5 of 2002)* [2005] 1 AC 167, 184, *per* Lord Nicholls.

[145] See also Privy Counsellor Review Committee, *Anti-Terrorism, Crime and Security Act Review: Report*, 18 December 2003 [209], available at www.statewatch.org/news/2003/dec/atcsReport.pdf.

[146] Ormerod and McKay (n 135) 31.

[147] *R v P and others* [2002] 1 AC 146–47.

[148] *R v Aujla* [1998] 2 CrAppR 17, 23. For a recent manifestation, see *R v Knaggs* [2018] EWCA Crim 1863.

[149] ibid.

[150] ibid.

[151] As the House of Lords held in *R v Effik and another* [1995] 1 AC 309, 319, the Act was not 'designed nor does it purport to confer any general protection against eavesdropping or intrusion on the privacy of individuals'.

unlawfully obtained telephone taps – those not covered by the intercept blanket ban – are in principle admissible in court. In fact, the absence of a similar ban for a whole range of other, technologically advanced, surveillance capabilities – such as covert interceptions by means of a surveillance device, carried out in relation to anything taking place on residential premises or private vehicles – [152] has meant that electronic recordings obtained in such ways are unexceptionally adduced as evidence in court. The section 78(1) discretion is nowhere seen to have a weaker effect than in relation to evidence obtained via covert electronic surveillance, which provides further proof of English law's predisposition against excluding evidence for violations of the right to privacy. But before engaging with that jurisprudence, we must compare the English approach on the use of telephone intercepts with that adopted in France.

ii. Telephone Interceptions in France: Common Practice, Little Exclusion

Telephone interceptions (*écoutes télephoniques*) are commonly employed in France by the security services but also, unlike in the United Kingdom, by the police and investigating judges in the context of judicial investigations.[153] Pradel's account from 1992 points to 'hundreds of judicial telephone interceptions [taking place] at any given date' and explains that 'three thousand people were listened to every year' in operations undertaken by the security services.[154] The 2014 annual report of the independent commission charged with the authorisation and control of these 'security interceptions' (*interceptions de sécurité*) paints a picture of a historic 'love affair' with *les écoutes*, showing that around 6,000 of them are ordered every year,[155] a reality much better portrayed by Ministry of Justice statistics that demonstrate that the number of *judicial* telephone interceptions has skyrocketed in the last 15 years, raising, for instance, from 20,000 in 2006 to 35,000 in 2013.[156] There is no better proof of the pervasive influence of telephone interceptions in France than the alarming apathy demonstrated by the public in the face of the

[152] See Investigatory Powers Act 2016, Part II on 'Surveillance and Covert Human Intelligence Sources'.

[153] See generally E Tomlinson, 'Nonadversarial Justice: The French Experience' (1983) 42 *Maryland Law Review* 131, 177; C Guerrier, *Les écoutes téléphoniques* (Paris, CNRS Droit, 2000) 50.

[154] J Pradel, 'Un exemple de restauration de la légalité criminelle: le régime des interceptions de correspondances émises par la voie des télécommunications (commentaire de la loi nº 91-646 du 10 juillet 1991)' (1992) *Recueil Dalloz* 49.

[155] Interestingly, the report shows no increase in the number of interceptions authorised between 2006 and 2013, the years during which the Commission exercises this supervisory role and for which statistics are available, with the overall number (including applications for extension of existing interceptions) being slightly over 6,000. See Commission nationale de contrôle des interceptions de sécurité, 22e rapport d'activité, Années 2013–2014 (*La Documentation Française*, January 2015) 86.

[156] See C Guerrier, *Étude de droit comparé en matière d'organismes de contrôle pour les interceptions téléphoniques* (Paris, IDEFIS, January 2009); E Daoud and B Bouche, 'Interceptions judiciaires: "mais qui gardera les gardiens?"' (2014) *Actualité juridique pénal* 333, 334.

news that the investigating judge and prosecuting authorities had for more than a year been listening to the telephone conversations of the former French President, Nicolas Sarkozy, including, notably, private conversations that he was having with his lawyer in connection with various affairs that Sarkozy was being investigated about.[157]

Until the beginning of the 1990s, these practices were unregulated by statutory legislation and the CPP, and yet their evidential fruits, in the case of judicial interceptions, were admissible in evidence, with the courts resorting to a distinction between judicial telephone interceptions undertaken prior to bringing charges against the defendant, which were lawful, and post-charging interceptions, which were not.[158] Admission seemed warranted on the basis of a generic provision, article 81 of the CPP, which empowered the investigative judge to 'take all the investigative measures which he deem[ed] useful for establishing the truth'. This included telephone taps and other measures not specifically prescribed by provisions of the CPP.[159] Given this apparent inability to exercise a control of *legalité* to the admission of intercept evidence in court – since the *legalité* principle links the pronouncement of a nullity with violations of the CPP, and provisions specific to telephone taps did not exist in the latter – French courts resorted, during this time, to the alternative safeguard of a control of *loyauté*. Telephone intercepts could therefore not be used in court where the defendant had been tricked, deceived or in other way entrapped into having the intercepted telephone conversation.[160] Though symptomatic of an ability for exclusion on the basis of wider considerations relating to the integrity of the criminal justice system, the *loyauté* principle – seen as going no further than deception, trickery or entrapment – was at the same time unable to offer the wider protection of the right to privacy required under Article 8 of the ECHR. For purposes of illustration, we can look at a Cour de cassation decision from 1985, which held that:

> The interception of the telephone line attributed to a person suspected of an offence, which the investigating judge has regularly instructed the police to undertake, should constitute neither a reason for nullity of the procedural acts nor a violation of

[157] See, eg, J Parienté, M Vaudano and S Laurent, *Affaire des écoutes: ce qui est reproché à Nicolas Sarkozy*, Le Mondre.fr, 13 March 2014; E Delève, *Écoutes de Sarkozy: Les juges sont allés trop loin (bâtonnier), France Info*, 2 July 2014; E Fansten, *Écoutes de Sarkozy: un rapport accablant, Libération*, 22 September 2014.

[158] See, eg, *Crim* 12 June 1952, JCP 1952, II, 7241 note Bouchot; S 1954, 1, 69, note Legal; *Crim* 18 March 1955, JCP 1955, II, 8909, note Esmein; (1955) *Recueil Dalloz* 573, note Savatier. But see the *Tournet* case, which held that were lawful even telephone interceptions taking place after the defendant had been charged. See *Crim* 9 October 1980, *Bull crim* n 255, D 1981, 332, note Pradel; JCP 1981, II, 19578, note Di Marino. The controversy created as a result of this decision has led to the introduction of legislation regulating telephone interceptions to ensure conformity with the ECHR. See C Guerrier, *Les écoutes téléphoniques* (Paris, CNRS Droit, 2000) 30–34.

[159] See *Crim* 9 October 1980, *Bull crim* n 255, note Di Marino; *Crim* 15 May 1990, *Bull crim* n 193. See also *Kruslin v France* (1990) 12 EHRR 547, 555; *Crim* 26 November 1990, appeal n 90-84.594.

[160] See B Bouloc, 'Les abus en matière de procédure pénale' (1991) *Revue de sciences criminelle* 221, 238. See, eg, case law discussed in *Kruslin v France* (1990) 12 EHRR 547, 556.

> Article 8 of the European Convention [...] since this investigative measure was conducted without trickery and no stratagem was used and since it cannot be established that this measure compromised the rights of the defence.[161]

In 1989, a judgment of the plenary session of the Cour de cassation departed from this position, pronouncing the nullity of the telephone interception in question on the basis that it was not 'in accordance with the law', as a result of not being provided by a legislative text as dictated by Article 8 of the Convention.[162] France then felt the strong pull of Strasbourg, deriving from the seminal cases of *Huvig v France* and *Kruslin v France*, where the absence of a procedural framework specific to telephone interceptions was found to marry ill with Article 8, notably with regards to the 'foreseeability' of this investigative measure.[163] The Law of 10 July 1991 that was subsequently enacted and incorporated into articles 100 to 107 of the CPP, to regulate the interception of telephone correspondence, now forms the basis for the exclusion of improperly obtained intercepts in France,[164] at least in theory, as there is very little exclusion in practice. The discretion to pronounce nullities is exercised narrowly in this area, while a number of intercepts are disqualified as such and are therefore no longer susceptible to be subjected to the control of *legalité* through the pronouncement of nullity.

A few examples will suffice to illustrate the French inclusionary approach towards intercept evidence, which makes the English ban on intercept evidence all the more incomprehensible, viewed through Continental law lenses at least. We can observe, for instance, that even after the introduction of the CPP provisions on the interception of telephone correspondence, the exercise of the discretion to pronounce a nullity often did not go any further than a control of *loyauté*. Evidence was excluded only where there was a finding of trickery or deception.[165] Today, even where the focus is on *legalité* and breaches of the CPP provisions, the need to establish that the defendant has suffered prejudice as a result of the breach limits the scope for the pronouncement of nullity and the exclusion of illegally obtained intercepts. We can take the example of breaches of the provision that mandate that the prosecutor undertaking the telephone interception (*Procureur de la République*) informs 'without delay' the judge who issues the interception warrant (*Juge des libertés et de la detention*).[166] The Cour de cassation has rejected the notion that a breach could in itself lead to exclusion. In a case from 2007,

[161] *Crim* 23 July 1985, *Bull crim* n 275. See also *Crim* 15 March 1988, *Bull crim* n 128. See also J Pradel, 'Écoutes téléphoniques et Convention européenne des droits de l'homme (à propos de Cass Ass Plén, 24 nov 1989, *affaire Baribeau*, D 1990, 34)' (1990) *Recueil Dalloz* 16.

[162] *Crim*, Ass Plén, 24 November 1989, *Bull crim* n 440.

[163] *Huvig v France* (1990) 12 EHRR 528, 543–45 [29–35]; *Kruslin v France* (1990) 12 EHRR 547, 563–65 [30–36].

[164] Loi n 91-646 du 10 juillet 1991 relative au secret des correspondances émises par la voie des communications électroniques, JORF n 162 du 13 juillet 1991, 9167.

[165] See, eg, *Crim* 27 February 1996, *Bull crim* n 93; D 1996, 346, note Ch Guery.

[166] Art 706-95 para 3 CPP.

it reversed the decision of a lower judicial panel (*Chambre de l'instruction*) that had reached this conclusion. This was not a provision that had been set in the protection of the 'public interest', admitted the Court. There would be no nullity unless it could be demonstrated that 'the breach had as an effect to cause harm to the interests of the defendant'. As the defendant failed to 'demonstrate with precision the nature of such harm', the 'omission', from the part of the authorities, to act in accordance with the 'formal requirements of the law did not, in this case, cause harm to the interests' of the defendant. In fact, the Court took it upon itself to evaluate, *in concreto*, whether the defendant had suffered any prejudice. It concluded that no harm could be demonstrated in this case, since the deadlines set by the judicial warrant in question had been respected, only conversations related to the issues under investigation had been intercepted and the defendant had not in other ways contested the legality of the interceptions.[167] There was an identical outcome in a case where the judge issuing the interception warrant had been kept informed by the prosecutor about operational matters – such as in relation to the date when the interceptions had been initiated and the fact that they had allowed the prosecutor to bring charges – but had not received the written reports providing details about the content of the interceptions. The Court read down the provision as requiring only the former, which meant that the defendant had not suffered any prejudice.[168] Much less problematic was the admission of intercept evidence in a case where the written request from the prosecutor to the judge issuing the interception warrant was missing from the investigation file. The Cour de cassation found no prejudice in this case, given that the interception warrant had made specific reference to the written request, indirectly proving its existence.[169] Perhaps, drawing an analogy with the decision of the English Court of Appeal in *Sanghera*, one might be able to speak here of a 'venial or technical' breach, where the court will 'almost inevitably' admit the evidence.[170]

These narrow interpretations of the discretion to pronounce nullities go hand in hand with judicial interpretations that exclude the application of the provisions of the CPP to various types of interceptions, such as where a mechanical device to record a telephone conversation has not been used[171] or where the police intercept messages received in a pager.[172] As Molina puts it, we can regret here that the jurisprudence 'is once again tempted to disqualify certain interceptions, neutralising

[167] *Crim* 26 June 2007, *Bull crim* n 172, D 2007; (2008) *Revue de sciences criminelle* 362, obs Finielz.

[168] *Crim* 26 March 2008, F-P+F, n 07-88.281, *Actualités Dalloz*, comm S Lavric.

[169] *Crim* 5 March 2013, n 12-88.167, (2013) *Actualité juridique pénal* 479, 480.

[170] *R* v *Sanghera* [2001] 1 Cr App R 299.

[171] 'The written report containing remarks overheard by police officers during a telephone conversation taking place in their presence, where no trick or stratagem had been used' was therefore admissible. See *Crim* 18 May 1993, appeal n 93-80.550; *Crim* 2 April 1997, *Bull crim* n 131. See also Rapport de la Cour de cassation (Paris, La Documentation française, 1997) 311.

[172] Aix-en-Provence, 12 December 1996, JCP 1998, I, 22975, note Molina; *Crim* 14 April 1999, *Bull crim* n 82.

existing regulations, only in the interest of effectively suppressing crime'.[173] Equally worrying is the blanket admission of telephone correspondence intercepted by private parties, on the basis that their probative value can be determined through discussion in the adversarial context of the criminal trial and that no exclusionary safeguard is therefore required.[174] This reflects French law's permissive attitude to using evidence that has been obtained unlawfully by private parties and will be discussed in detail later. It suffices to note here that, in view of the unprecedented access of individuals to interception technology in recent years, including through now universally available 'smartphones', the position of French law seems substantially outdated. One final example relates to the need to demonstrate that a *personal* interest has been prejudiced for the defendant to be able to request that the telephone intercept be excluded.[175] In other words, there can be no exclusion where the telephone intercept has been obtained in violation of the rights of persons other than those of the defendant. This 'standing' requirement, to use the American term, has considerable capacity to restrict the exclusion of unlawfully obtained intercepts in France.

The above leave little doubt of a strong jurisprudential preference for the use of intercept evidence in court. There is no better illustration than Cour de cassation jurisprudence that, under particular circumstances, holds as admissible even interceptions where the lawyer of the defendant is involved as one of the parties in the conversation, notably where the telephone conversation is between the lawyer and a close relation of the defendant[176] or where the interception has the capacity to provide evidence of the participation of the lawyer in the offences that the defendant is suspected to have committed.[177] This is true even where the offence revealed by the interception is different to the offence that has led to the authorisation of the interception in the first place.[178] The extent of the problem has come to light with the *écoutes de Sarkozy* affair.[179] Such was the potential impact of the intercepted conversations between Sarkozy and his lawyer in this case that the Court of appeal of Paris, in taking a highly unusual procedural step, decided

[173] E Molina, *La liberté de la preuve des infractions en droit français contemporain* (Aix-en-Provence, Presses Universitaires d'Aix-Marseille, 2001) 404.

[174] *Crim* 12 September 2000, *Bull crim* n 265. See also Porteron (n 84) 145.

[175] *Crim* 10 March 1993, *Bull crim* n 106.

[176] *Crim* 10 May 1994, *Bull crim* n 180. The exception to this rule is where the lawyer is also representing the close relation of the defendant. See *Crim* 18 January 2006, *Bull crim* n 22; (2006) *Revue de sciences criminelle* 413, obs Buisson.

[177] See, eg, *Crim* 14 November 2001, *Bull crim* n 238.

[178] See, eg, *Crim* 1 October 2003, *Bull crim* 177. See generally T Halmenschlager, 'Du problème politique et juridique de la légalité des écoutes dites fortuites', *Dalloz actualité*, 25 March 2014. A representative of the Paris Bar Association explained that lawyers' communications today are never quite out of reach for judicial authorities and there is a risk of 'destroying' legal professional privilege. V Nioré, 'Le secret professionnel de l'avocat à l'épreuve de l'interception et de la captation de données informatiques à distance: un secret en lambeaux?' (2013) *Dalloz avocats* 92. See also C Porteron, 'Le secret professionnel de l'avocat' (2009) *Actualité juridique pénal* 158.

[179] See F Rome, Éditorial – Les indignés, *Recueil Dalloz*, 20 March 2014.

to suspend the legal proceedings against Sarkozy until the court could decide whether the intercepts should be admissible in evidence or not.[180]

iii. Surreptitiously Obtained Recordings of Private Conversations: A French Carte Blanche to Use by Private Parties

A fundamental institutional difference between English and French criminal procedure that significantly affects the law on the use of improperly obtained evidence is the participation of private parties in the criminal process. In contrast to common law, victims of crime and other private parties with interests in the prosecution of related criminal offences are routinely represented in French criminal trials as *parties civiles* and play an active role in the administration of the process, including, importantly, through submitting criminal evidence for examination in court.[181] Against this backdrop, it is easy to appreciate why the Cour de cassation's carte blanche to the use in court of recordings of private conversations surreptitiously obtained by private parties merits special attention.

The French Criminal Code (*Code pénal*) punishes the act of secretly recording a conversation with a person that does not consent to it,[182] and yet evidence obtained through the commission of this offence is always admissible in court. As Judge Marsat put it:

> [T]he act of concealing a tape recorder with the objective of recording a conversation to establish that an offence has been committed does not give rise to pronouncing a nullity of the procedure and is not considered an interception of communications, a stratagem or a violation of the right to privacy.[183]

This is the result of long-standing Cour de cassation jurisprudence that evidence obtained by private parties should not be excluded for the sole reason of having been unlawfully obtained, since judges in criminal courts have as their only mission to evaluate the probative value of such evidence, after first subjecting it to discussion in the adversarial context of the trial.[184] The supreme jurisdiction of

[180] See C Piquet, *Affaire des écoutes: pourquoi l'enquête visant Sarkozy a été suspendue*, LeFigaro.fr, 24 September 2014, available at http://www.lefigaro.fr/actualite-france/2014/09/24/01016-20140924 ARTFIG00159-affaire-des-ecoutes-pourquoi-l-enquete-visant-sarkozy-a-ete-suspendue.php.

[181] See ch 2 in relation to Greece.

[182] Art 226-1 CP.

[183] C Marsat, 'La flagrance, la liberté et la loyauté de la preuve', *Droit pénal*, October 1999, 6.

[184] See *Crim* 28 April 1987, *Bull crim* n 173; *Crim* 11 February 1992, *Bull crim* n 66; *Crim* 23 July 1992, *Bull crim* n 274; *Crim* 15 June 1993, *Bull crim* n 210; *Crim* 6 April 1994, *Bull crim* n 136; *Crim* 11 June 2002, *Bull crim* n 131; *Crim* 27 January 2010, *Bull crim* 16. However, evidence obtained by private parties will be excluded where it will be demonstrated that their actions have been prompted by the police or the prosecution authority. See *Crim* 28 October 1991, *Bull crim* n 381; *Crim* 11 May 2006, *Revue de sciences criminelle* 2006, 848, note R Finielz. Where a police officer has surreptitiously recorded a conversation with a suspect, the recording cannot be used in court. See *Crim* 16 December 1997, *Bull crim* n 427. *Cf Crim* 19 January 1999, *Bull Crim* n 9.

France adopts here a minimalist approach to regulating the fairness of the criminal process, partly based on the positivist premise that 'no provision of the *Code de procedure pénale* prohibits bringing evidence in court that can be used to support the criminal charges'[185] – a view that curiously disregards the CPP provisions on nullity – and partly based on a construction of the role of private parties as substantially different from that of the police or the prosecution authority, even where their actions may not differ in practice in relation to providing judges with crucial evidence sustaining the criminal charges. According to this construction, the acts of private parties only contribute evidence for the consideration of the triers of fact and cannot be equated to procedural acts subject to the pronouncement of nullities.[186] But as Garé illustrates, 'it is difficult to see how this free discussion [in court] can make the illegality originating from the obtaining of the evidence disappear'.[187] What underpins these justifications is a solemn attachment to the iconic Continental law principle of free proof and truth discovery orientation of the criminal process,[188] unadulterated from 'infectious' interactions with the fast-emerging constitutionalisation of criminal procedure[189] and no doubt facilitated by constitutional rights' continued lack of penetration in areas where state actors are not involved. Also deriving from the above is the oxymoronic position of private parties having free rein to adduce illegally obtained evidence in court, even if their actions are nowhere in criminal procedure subject to regulation and despite the fact that they can make no claim to possessing the expertise or independence required to provide a priori assurances about the quality of criminal evidence obtained.[190] Criminal procedure strictly regulates, on the other hand, the actions of the police, the investigating judge and prosecuting officials, restricting the admissibility of criminal evidence precisely where the actors of the criminal process possess these values par excellence. The Cour de cassation's unyielding acceptance of evidence unlawfully obtained by private parties likewise fails to take note of the risk that the police might coalesce with private parties

[185] See Rapport de la Cour de cassation (Paris, La Documentation française, 1992) 422.

[186] See, eg, *Crim* 28 April 1987, *Bull crim* n 173. See Conchon (n 66) 75–77.

[187] T Garé, 'L'admission de la preuve illégale: la Chambre criminelle persiste et signe' (2000) *Recueil Dalloz* 391, 394. Reliance on discussion in the adversarial context of the criminal trial as an effective safeguard limiting the risk of improperly obtained evidence adduced by private parties prejudicing the rights of the defence and the integrity of the criminal process is reminiscent of the approach adopted by the ECtHR on the exclusion of improperly obtained evidence. As will be argued later on, to consider this an effective safeguard is to read too much into adversarialism.

[188] Free proof (*liberté de la preuve*) underpins judicial tolerance towards private parties, notes Finielz, a prosecutor at the Cour de cassation. R Finielz, 'Loyauté et liberté de preuves' (2007) *Revue de sciences criminellle* 331.

[189] See, eg, DM Amann, 'Harmonic Convergence? Constitutional Criminal Procedure in an International Context' (2000) 75 *Indiana Law Journal* 809, 823; B de Lamy, 'De la loyauté en procédure pénale' (2006) 99.

[190] Rassat notes that 'there is, in reality, no serious guarantee about the quality, the exact location of discovery or even the consistency of what is adduced by private parties as evidence'. ML Rassat, *Manuel de procédure pénale* (Paris, Presses Universitaires de France, 2002) 99.

to ensure the obtaining of criminal evidence where legislation and procedural regulation might be obstructing the police from obtaining the evidence in the first place.[191] It also fails to consider that private actors may nowadays possess sophisticated means of discovery of evidence, and that professional interests may be at stake, where private detectives are acting on behalf of private parties. The actions of private parties may therefore in no way differ from those of the police or prosecuting officials.

That the narrow focus of the Cour de cassation jurisprudence on the use of evidence obtained by private parties in criminal cases warrants critique is also revealed if one takes as a comparative point of reference the Court's jurisprudence on civil cases, which categorically rejects the use of evidence surreptitiously recorded by private parties. In 2011, this constant jurisprudence was extended to anti-trust litigation, in a seminal case where the Cour de cassation twice reversed a decision of the Court of Appeal of Paris.[192] The Court had upheld the use of telephone conversations which had been secretly intercepted by a private party and were implicating two major international companies in breaches of anti-trust legislation. In a plenary session of its chambers, the Cour de cassation solemnly confirmed that the *principe de loyauté* should be strictly applied in civil matters, to prohibit private parties from producing unlawfully intercepted evidence in civil proceedings. But as far as criminal law proceedings were concerned, the Court emphasised that freedom of proof reigned supreme, before providing strong confirmation of the continued operation of its jurisprudence that permits private parties to adduce improperly obtained evidence in criminal proceedings. Surprisingly, the Court did not subject the 'free proof' rhetoric to a more detailed examination under the prism of the *loyauté* principle that it now universally applies to civil cases, and did not reflect on the extent to which the evidential contributions of private parties to the outcome of criminal cases truly differ from those of the police. As a result, it missed a good opportunity to bridge the conceptual gap that is currently separating its civil and criminal jurisprudence, and consequently to inject more coherence into the position that it takes on the use of improperly obtained evidence by private parties.

[191] The Cour de cassation was confronted with police coalescence with private parties aimed at obtaining criminal evidence in a 2016 case. The private parties had unlawfully intercepted private communications with persons who were blackmailing them, while police officers were monitoring the venue of the rendezvous, obtained the recordings afterwards directly from the private parties, transcribed the recordings in an official report and stayed in regular contact with the private parties and other relevant judicial authorities until taking the decision to arrest the suspects. The Court found that the participation of the public authorities involved in the unlawful production of the intercept evidence by the private parties had breached the right to fair trial and the *principe de loyauté*, and overturned, on those grounds, the decision of the lower judicial chamber. *Crim* 20 September 2016, *Bull crim* n 244.

[192] Cass (Assemblée plénière) n 587, 7 January 2011 (appeal n 09-14.316 and 09-14.667).

iv. Using Surreptitiously Obtained Recordings of Private (Non-Telephone) Conversations: The UK Judiciary's Unwavering Seal of Approval

When trying to locate the contemporary English approach to the exclusion of evidence obtained in violation of the right to privacy, one need not look further than *R v Khan (Sultan)*.[193] So unreservedly has the Court of Appeal applied this seminal decision of the House of Lords that it is difficult to imagine English law on improperly obtained evidence without it. Its principles seem to be set in stone, and so is English law's preference for allowing the use of criminal evidence in court in the face of privacy violations.

In *Khan* the police had attached a listening device to a residential property without the knowledge of the owner. By means of that device, they obtained a tape recording of a conversation between the owner and Khan who visited the property. The recording clearly showed that Khan was a party to the importation of prohibited drugs to the UK. Khan contested the admissibility of the tape at his trial, on the basis that the attachment of the listening device had involved a civil trespass and had occasioned some damage to the property, and the police had no statutory authority to install listening devices on private property. Khan also contended that even if the tape were a priori admissible, the judge should exercise his discretion under section 78(1) to exclude it, and that admission of the tape would breach Article 8 of the ECHR. But the trial judge declined to rule the evidence inadmissible. The defendant pleaded guilty and was sentenced, the Court of Appeal dismissed his appeal, and the case reached the House of Lords which held that:

> Under English law, there was in general nothing unlawful about a breach of privacy and the common law rule that evidence obtained by the police by improper or unfair means was admissible in a criminal trial, notwithstanding that it was obtained improperly or even unlawfully, applied to evidence obtained by the use of surveillance devices which invaded a person's privacy.[194]

The evidence was admissible, as dictated by '*R v Sang* and the many decisions which ha[d] followed it',[195] explained Lord Nolan, giving the opinion of the Court.[196] The pervasive influence of the common law *in*clusionary jurisprudence is crystal clear here. The introduction of the section 78(1) discretion had made little difference in practice.[197] A breach of Article 8 of the ECHR was, at best, 'a matter which [might] be relevant to the exercise of the s 78 power', noted Lord

[193] *R v Khan (Sultan)* [1997] AC 558.

[194] ibid.

[195] ibid.

[196] That *Sang* should remain the position of principle under English law was also underlined in the opinions of Lord Browne-Wilkinson (ibid 291) and Lord Slynn of Hadley (ibid 293).

[197] As Tapper explained, the result in *Khan* accorded 'with the trend of much previous English case law'. C Tapper, 'Overhearing and Oversight' (1996–1997) 1 *International Journal of Evidence & Proof* 162, 167.

Nolan, 'a consideration which [might] be taken into account for what it is worth'.[198] The significance of the breach would 'normally be determined not so much by its apparent unlawfulness or irregularity, as upon its effect, taken as a whole, upon the fairness or unfairness of the proceedings'.[199] In this case, the trial judge was right to hold that the effect of the breach of Article 8 was not such as to require the exclusion of evidence, said the House of Lords.[200] Lord Nolan 'confessed' that he had reached this conclusion 'with relief', as 'it would be a strange reflection on [English] law if a man who ha[d] admitted his participation in the illegal importation of a large quantity of heroin should have his conviction set aside on the grounds that his privacy ha[d] been invaded'.[201] One would struggle to find a more stark demonstration of a pragmatic approach to the use of evidence in the face of privacy violations, prioritising convicting the guilty over rights or judicial integrity considerations.[202] Now, *Khan* was decided prior to the incorporation of the ECHR into UK law,[203] so one might highlight, from a positive angle, that the House of Lords accepted that Convention breaches were pertinent to the applications of section 78(1).[204] The subsequent failure, however, to give Article 8 violations any effect in practice, even after the Human Rights Act 1998 came into effect, leaves no doubt about epistemic considerations taking absolute priority in this case. Writing in 1998, Ashworth noted that *Khan's* effect was 'to assign relatively weak significance to the right to privacy'.[205] With the benefit of hindsight, it will be argued below that, in reality, *Khan's* effect was to assign this fundamental right virtually no significance at all. Mirfield explained *Khan* by noting that the nineteenth century inclusionary approach encapsulated in *Leatham* 'continue[d] to exercise its grip upon the appellate judicial mentality' at the time.[206] Post-*Khan* jurisprudence ensured that, in relation to violations of the right to privacy at least, the same inclusionary mentality remained in full force in the twenty-first century.

R v Chalkley is a case in point. The prosecution had adduced highly incriminating evidence of covertly recorded conversations between the defendants, which had been obtained by installing a listening device in Chalkley's home. In applying

[198] ibid 301.

[199] ibid.

[200] ibid 302.

[201] ibid.

[202] As Choo notes, 'considerations of integrity were not uppermost in the minds of the Law Lords in *R v Khan*'. A L-T Choo, 'The Legal Aspects of Undercover Police Operations in England and Wales' (1998) 2 *International Journal of Police Science and Management* 144.

[203] Roberts' and Zuckerman's observation that, '[p]rior to the advent of the Human Rights Act the attitude of the English courts towards the ECHR was at best lukewarm' and that '[s]ome senior judges made no secret of their impatience with arguments founded on breaches of Convention rights' is most relevant here. P Roberts and A Zuckerman, *Criminal Evidence*, 2nd edn (Oxford, Oxford University Press, 2010) 201.

[204] See generally Mirfield (n 1) 316.

[205] A Ashworth, 'Should the Police Be Allowed to Use Deceptive Practices' (1998) 114 *Law Quarterly Review* 108, 132.

[206] Mirfield, 'Regulation of Investigatory Powers Act 2000' (2001) 101.

Sang, the Court accepted that there was 'no discretion to exclude evidence unless its quality was or might have been affected by the way in which it was obtained'.[207] It noted more specifically that:

> [T]here was no dispute as to [the] authenticity, content or effect [of the evidence]; it was relevant, highly probative … and otherwise admissible; it did not result from incitement, entrapment or inducement or any other conduct of that sort; and none of the unlawful conduct of which complaint [was] made affect[ed] the quality of the evidence.[208]

The Court of Appeal therefore upheld the conviction. 'The commitment to a reliability principle in both cases', as the sole basis for the exclusion of improperly obtained evidence, was 'abundantly clear'.[209] This very 'narrow' approach, which is 'contrary to the plain meaning of the words of section 78(1)'[210] and treats breaches of the fundamental right to privacy as of secondary importance, quickly became symptomatic of the exercise of the section 78 discretion where covertly recorded conversations were being adduced as evidence.[211] But English law goes even further in promoting reliability as the guiding principle for exclusion. Breaches of the right to privacy do not trigger exclusion even where they go hand in hand with breaches of the right to silence and the privilege against self-incrimination, for instance where the police have surreptitiously recorded the conversations of suspects detained at the police station.

R v Bailey, a pre-*Khan* authority, set the tone for appellate court jurisprudence upholding the use of suspects' conversations covertly recorded in police cells.

[207] *R v Chalkley and another* [1998] QB 848, 875.

[208] ibid 876.

[209] S Nash and A L-T Choo, 'What's the Matter with section 78?' [1999] *Criminal Law Review* 929, 936.

[210] ibid 935.

[211] See, eg, *R v Wright* [2001] EWCA Crim 1934, where the Court of Appeal upheld the convictions of the defendants in a case where the prosecution had adduced 'the evidence of admissions made by the appellants to their fellow conspirator … over the telephone and in a hotel room where the conversations were audio and video recorded'; *R v Bailey and others*, 165 *Justice of the Peace* 235, where police officers concealed tape recorders at the flat of one of the defendants and recorded various conversations, and the Court of Appeal found there had been no unfairness even if the trial judge had found that prior authorisation had not been sought and there was a breach of Art 8 of the ECHR; *R v GS* [2005] EWCA Crim 887, where the appellant sought access to material that had led to the authorisation of intrusive surveillance during which evidence of incriminating covertly recorded conversations was obtained, and where the Court found that the lawfulness of the authorisation 'did not necessarily have an effect on any decision as to admissibility under s. 78'; *R v Redmond* [2006] EWCA Crim 1744, where, again in relation to covertly recorded conversations, the Court of Appeal held, in upholding the conviction of the defendant, that 'even if evidence probative of guilt had been obtained unlawfully, such evidence was not automatically rendered inadmissible and nor was it automatically the case that it would be unfair for that evidence to be considered by a jury'; *R v Khachik and others* [2006] EWCA Crim 1272 [45], where the Court of Appeal found that the admission in evidence of a probe, which had been unlawfully installed in a car and had picked up all conversations within the car, could not possibly be seen as unfair, as 'there was no challenge to the integrity of the material produced by reason of the probe'. See also Colvin, who notes, from a wider theoretical perspective, that the argument for exclusion rightly fails in such cases, as 'persons who commit or plan crimes cannot legitimately expect the police to eschew all forms of covert activity or deception in the search for evidence' and 'using covert activity or deception is neither necessarily nor characteristically unfair'. E Colvin, 'Fairness and Equality in the Criminal Process' (2006) 6 *Oxford University Commonwealth Law Journal* 1, 21.

The secretly taped conversations had been obtained after the defendants had exercised their right to silence in interview, and the police had played a trick upon them to allay any suspicion about their being put together into the same cell.[212] In placing emphasis on the 'very serious crime' in question (a robbery), and the absence of oppression or any suggestion that the confessions were other than wholly reliable, the Court found it 'hardly surprising that the trial judge [had] exercised his undoubted discretion' to admit the evidence.[213] Identical outcomes were reached in a range of cases where suspects had been secretly filmed or their conversations had been secretly recorded at the police station. Consistently with the House of Lords' section 78(1) jurisprudence established in *Khan*, the Court of Appeal elevated 'the right to fair hearing' as the sole test of admissibility, finding that contraventions of Article 8 of the Convention did not interfere with the fairness of the proceedings.[214] Non-compliance with the right to privacy did not therefore prohibit the use of secretly obtained tape-recordings in court.[215] Trial judges were required to take infringements of Article 8 into account, but these needed to be balanced with the gravity of the offences in question, the safety of the public and the need to protect law and order. Article 8 breaches gave way to the protection of these values, and secretly recorded evidence was generally deemed to be admissible.[216]

The Court of Appeal provided fresh confirmation of this thesis in two cases that were decided in 2013 within a few months from each other. In *R v Plunkett*, the defendants' incriminating statements were secretly recorded when on three occasions they were being transported in a police van from prison to a police station.[217] In *R v Khan (Imran)*, the conversations that the two defendants had in a police van were similarly covertly recorded, in the course of their transport from police custody to the magistrates' court.[218] In both cases the recordings

[212] *R v Bailey and another* [1993] 3 All ER 513, 516.

[213] ibid 524. In doing so, the Court confirmed a long line of authorities preceding section 78(1): *R v Mills, R v Rose* [1962] 3 All ER 298, [1962] 1 WLR 1152, where a constable had tape recorded the defendants' conversations from a neighbouring empty cell; *R v Buchan* [1964] 1 All ER 502, where the suspect was making incriminating statements in the belief that nothing was being written down, while another officer was making a contemporaneous record in the room next door; *R v Stewart* [1970] 1 All ER 689, where a constable had dressed to look like a fellow prisoner and noted down an incriminating conversation from an adjoining cell. The Court paid particular attention to *R v Ali (Shaukat)*, where the police had covertly recorded a conversation between the defendant and his family at a police station, and that after having first brought charges against the defendant. Despite recognising the trickery involved in *Ali (Shaukat)*, the Court was satisfied with the finding there that there was 'a very broad discretion under s 78' to admit evidence, even when obtained under such circumstances. It subsequently saw 'no reason to decry the police's conduct' in *Bailey* 'nor to doubt the essential fairness of th[e] evidence having been held admissible'. *R v Ali (Shaukat)* (1991) Times, 19 February.

[214] *R v Loveridge* [2001] 2 Cr App R 29 [33]. The Court explained that it had given 'full weight to the breach of the Convention' and was satisfied that this had 'not interfere[d] with the fairness of the hearing'.

[215] See *R v Mason* [2002] EWCA 385.

[216] ibid.

[217] *R v Plunkett* [2013] EWCA Crim 261, [2013] 2 Cr App R 2.

[218] *R v Khan (Imran)* [2013] EWCA Crim 2230.

were admitted in evidence. The Court of Appeal found that there was no breach of the right to privacy in *Plunkett*, but concluded that the use of the surreptitiously obtained recordings would have been the right outcome even if there had been such a breach. In *Khan (Imran)*, the Court found a breach of Article 8 of the ECHR, but concluded that the secretly obtained recordings had been rightly adduced as evidence. In both cases, the Court argued that there was no misrepresentation, entrapment or trickery, and no oppression or coercion. No lies had been used to obtain the admissions, and the defendants were simply afforded the opportunity to talk to each other.[219] Equal emphasis was placed on the seriousness of the crimes the defendants were on trial for; an aggravated burglary involving a 'terrifying attack' on the victims in *Plunkett*,[220] an 'attempted murder' in the course of a 'contract killing' that had not worked in *Khan (Imran)*.[221] In both cases breaches of Article 8 were seen as trivial compared to the 'immense seriousness'[222] of the crimes in question. In addition, nothing in these breaches had stopped the defendants from challenging the evidence. As the Court explained specifically in *Khan (Imran)*, the Article 8 breaches did not have any effect on the fairness of the trial, and it was 'fairness of the criminal trial process overall that [was] now the touchstone of the law in this area'.[223] This was the legacy of *Khan (Sultan)* and the European Court of Human Rights decision in that case, which had separated the question of breaches of Article 8 from questions relating to breaches of the right to fair trial and had cemented prior Strasbourg jurisprudence consistently holding 'that issues of admissibility of evidence obtained unlawfully [were] for the national courts to decide based on principles of fairness'.[224]

Plunkett particularly demonstrates why the consequences of the narrow exercise of the section 78 discretion in the light of *Khan (Sultan)* can be a cause for concern. The defendants there had not had an opportunity to privately consult with a solicitor before talking to the police, though Code of Practice C and section 58 PACE 1984 specifically provide for this right. As Andrew Roberts points out, the effect of permitting the evidential use of admissions obtained as a result of this breach is to undermine these significant safeguards of the right to legal advice.[225] It is precisely in relation to such cases, where breaches of the right to privacy might coincide with breaches of the right to silence or the right to legal advice, that English law can gain an insight of recent developments in Cour de cassation jurisprudence.

[219] ibid [55].

[220] *R v Plunkett* [2013] EWCA Crim 261 [39].

[221] *R v Khan (Imran)* [2013] EWCA Crim 2230 [56].

[222] *R v Plunkett* [2013] EWCA Crim 261 [58].

[223] *R v Khan (Imran)* [2013] EWCA Crim 2230 [55].

[224] ibid [41], citing *Khan v United Kingdom* (2001) 31 EHRR 45.

[225] A Roberts, 'Case Comment – *R. v Plunkett (Daniel)*: evidence – admissibility – suspects' conversations in police van covertly recorded' [2013] *Criminal Law Review* 766, 769. See also D Carney, 'Covert surveillance of suspects in police vehicle' (2013) *Police Journal* 340, 344.

III. Evidence Obtained Through the Bugging of Police Cells: French Lessons for England and Wales?

The bugging of police cells and the covert recording of conversations of suspects detained at the police station for the purposes of interrogation (*garde à vue*) was originally perceived as a lawful practice by the Cour de cassation, mainly on the premise that no provision of the CPP prohibited it.[226] Legislation introduced in 2004 provided for the bugging of premises in organised crime investigations[227] and since then compliance with the relevant framework, which revolves around judicial authorisation of the practice, has also become the key criterion for judging the legality of adducing in court evidence obtained through the bugging of police cells.[228] This was a positive development, as judicial authorisation could go some way towards safeguarding against arbitrary aspects of this practice.[229] But a recent decision of the Cour de cassation demonstrates that French law is now going further than a simple examination of the legality of the practice (*principe de légalité*), to embrace alignment with the wider normative standards deriving from the *loyauté* principle. This makes the French example particularly pertinent to the exclusion of evidence obtained through the bugging of police cells in England and Wales, as the section 78(1) discretion likewise encompasses (or, interpreted widely, should ideally encompass) consistency with the normative standards inherent in the 'fairness enquiries' that the judge must undertake when exercising the discretion.

We can direct our attention to the decision of 7 January 2014.[230] Upon a request by the police investigating a suspected armed robbery in this case, the

[226] See, eg, *Crim* 17 March 1992 (n 91-86.888 inédit). See also J Pradel, 'Le parloir n'a plus de secret pour le juge d'instruction en matière de criminalité organisée' (2006) *Recueil Dalloz* 1504. Supervision exercised by the Investigating Judge was seen as another basis for the legality of the practice. See G Accomado and C Guéry, 'La sonorisation: un mode légal de preuve' (2002) *Recueil Dalloz* 2001. It was also being argued that the practice was consistent with the ECHR, on the basis that penitentiary personnel had the right to interfere with conversations of detained persons. See D Mayer, 'Y-a-t-il une place pour l'hypnose en procédure pénale?' (2001) *Recueil Dalloz* 1340.

[227] See art 707-96 CPP, introduced with Loi n 2004-204 du 9 mars 2004 portant adaptation de la justice aux évolutions de la criminalité.

[228] See *Crim* 1 March 2005, cited by J Pradel, 'Le parloir n'a plus de secret' (2006) 1504. The conversations of the suspect with family members during their visit to the police station were adduced as evidence in court. The Cour de cassation found that the relevant legislative provisions had been respected and upheld the decision to admit the incriminating conversations in this case. In a case from 2006 the Cour de cassation upheld the decision to admit conversations of the suspect captured by the bugging of the police cell in which he was being detained. The main justification for that were that the operation had been ordered, and supervised, by the Investigating Judge, for a short period of time and for the purposes of investigating a serious crime. See *Crim* 1 March 2006, Juris-Data n 2006-032780; (2007) *Revue de sciences criminelle* 611, obs J Buisson. See also S Guinchard and J Buisson, *Procédure pénale*, 4th edn (Paris, Lexis-Nexis Litec, 2008) 938.

[229] See, eg, a case from 2008, where the highest jurisdiction reversed a decision of a Judicial Chamber which had admitted intercepted conversations in the face of a defective authorisation of the Investigating Judge entrusted with overseeing the operation. *Crim* 13 February 2008, n 07-87.458.

[230] *Crim* 7 January 2014, *Bull crim* 2014 n 1.

Investigating Judge had authorised the bugging of the police station cells where the two suspects would be detained following their arrest. The suspects were placed in adjacent cells, from which they communicated with each other during break times from the interrogation. During these communications one of the suspects made incriminating statements, and was then charged and remanded in custody. He then submitted a request to the chambre de l'instruction at the Court of Appeal in Versailles (the judicial chamber overseeing the investigation) for the suppression of the surreptitious recordings. In line with Cour de cassation precedent, the chambre de l'instruction rejected the application, on the basis that the bugging of the police cells had been in accordance with the relevant provisions of the CPP. The Court added that the police had not detained the suspects with the objective to intercept their conversations, that the right to silence applied only during the interrogation and not during break times and that the right to privacy did not apply at all in custodial interrogations of the suspect. More importantly, the Court equated the legality principle with the *loyauté* principle, holding that since the conversations had been recorded in conformity with the Code, they could not be seen as having been obtained in an unfair or improper way.[231]

In reversing the decision of the chambre de l'instruction, the Cour de cassation rejected this narrow understanding of the *loyauté* principle. The Court accepted that there had been judicial authorisation in accordance with the provisions of the law. But the combination of the *garde à vue* measure and the bugging of the police cells had led the suspect to incriminate himself, and was therefore an unfair or improper practice that rendered invalid the a priori lawful procedural acts. As Vergès notes, the suspects' conversations were recorded during breaks from the interrogation, when the suspects would have every right to believe that their conversations were private and that no recording could take place.[232] Vlamynck rightly intimates that the police cannot notify the suspects of their right to silence, on the one hand, and secretly intercept their conversations, on the other.[233] In surreptitiously recording these conversations, the police had breached the rules relating to the *garde à vue* with the direct aim to deceive the defendants.[234] The Cour de cassation referred the case back to another chamber, the chambre de l'instruction at the Court of Appeal in Paris. When this refused to follow the High jurisdiction's lead and validated the use of the surreptitiously recorded evidence, the case went back to the Cour de cassation. In its 6 March 2015 plenary judgment, the latter categorically declared that the stratagem employed by the police and the investigating judge had breached 'the right to a fair trial, the right to silence and the right against self-incrimination as well as the *loyauté* principle'.[235]

[231] See commentaire in (2014) *Revue de sciences criminelle* 130, 131–32.

[232] Vergès, 'Loyauté et licéité' (2014) 407, 409.

[233] H Vlamynck, 'Droit de ne pas s'auto-incriminer et loyauté de la preuve' (2014) *Actualité juridique pénal* 194.

[234] Vergès (n 25) 407, 409.

[235] *Crim* 6 March 2015, *Bull crim* 2. When discussing the decision in its annual report, however, the Court explained that it did not rule out surreptitious recordings at the police station. It was rather the

The decision could be read as signalling the beginning of a wider evolution of Cour de cassation jurisprudence on the exclusion of improperly obtained evidence, which could provide a useful contrast to English appellate courts' narrow interpretations of section 78 in cases relating to violations of the right to privacy. For the time being, however, both English and French appellate courts generally remain reluctant to overturn lower court decisions admitting evidence obtained through privacy violations. Of more immediate relevance to English law are the lessons that derive from the Cour de cassation jurisprudence on the specific issue of the exclusion of evidence obtained through the bugging of police cells. English commentators have already pointed out the risk of indirectly undermining significant custodial interrogation rights by allowing the use of evidence obtained through this practice.[236] Safeguarding custodial interrogation rights, the right against self-incrimination in particular, provided the main impetus for the Cour de cassation jurisprudence. France had just introduced a major reform of custodial legal assistance, which aimed to reinforce the right against self-incrimination.[237] The 2014 and 2015 decisions on the bugging of police cells was the by-product of that reform. The Cour de cassation could not allow the 'new' rights applying at the custodial interrogation stage – a duty to notify the suspect of his or her right to silence and the right to be assisted by a lawyer during interrogation – to be undermined by allowing the police to secretly record the conversations of the suspect during rest breaks. In admitting such evidence, English courts, on the other hand, place emphasis on the strength and reliability of the intercepted communications, and the seriousness of the crimes involved. Such factors have not stopped the Cour de cassation from opting for exclusion. In the January 2014 case, there was no doubt about the credibility of the intercepted communications and the offence in question was exceptionally serious. It is also interesting to correlate the influence of Strasbourg case law[238] in this jurisprudential twist in France with the influence that the same case law might have the capacity to exercise in England and Wales. It was the seminal decision of the ECtHR in *Salduz v Turkey* and post *Salduz* decisions that sparked the reform of custodial interrogation in France and generated the 'police cell' jurisprudence there. There is no reason why the same ECtHR case law could not generate a similar jurisprudential U-turn in England and Wales.

The January 2014 decision offers English observers a view from abroad that might also encourage them to take a fresh look at related developments in the area of abuse of process. The decision of the Court of Appeal in *R v Grant* that

stratagem employed by the police that had triggered the strict application of the *loyauté* principle in this case. Cour de cassation, *Rapport 2015 de la Cour de cassation* (La Documentation française, 2016).

[236] See, eg, Roberts, 'Case Comment – *R. v Plunkett (Daniel)*' (2013) 769.

[237] Loi n 2011-392 du 14 avril 2011 relative à la garde à vue. See ch 4.

[238] *Salduz v Turkey* (2008) 49 EHRR 421. See ch 5 in detail. See generally J Hodgson, 'The French Prosecutor in Question' (2010) 67 *Washington & Lee Law Review* 1361; J Alix, 'Les droits de la défense au cours de l'enquête de police après la réforme de la garde à vue: état de lieux et perspectives' (2011) *Recueil Dalloz* 1699; A Dorange and S Field, 'Reforming Defence Rights in French Police Custody: A Coming Together in Europe?' (2012) 16 *International Journal of Evidence and Proof* 153.

proceedings should have been stayed as an abuse of process – in a case where the police had placed covert listening devices in a police yard and audio-recorded communications between the defendant and his solicitor during a break from police questioning, in breach of legal professional privilege – is capable of encouraging a bolder approach to excluding secretly recorded communications between suspects at the police station.[239] Perhaps looking at *Grant* in combination with the Cour de cassation's January 2014 decision could add new relevance to taking a more stringent approach to excluding evidence obtained by the bugging of police premises.[240]

IV. Concluding Thoughts

The study of discretionary exclusion in France and England and Wales provides a strong contrast to exclusionary rules for privacy violations in Greece and the United States. Even where the latter are not strictly applied, they remain automatic in nature and have the capacity to generate exclusion in a much broader range of circumstances than their counterparts in England and France. And yet, one might have expected that the wide discretionary remedies adopted there would have enabled courts to take a more robust approach to excluding improperly obtained evidence. The open-ended concept of 'fairness' that defines section 78 in England and Wales, and the equally ambiguous notions of 'procedural harm' or '*loyauté*' that are at the centre of procedural nullities in France, would seem capable of giving English and French courts an 'all encompassing' discretion.[241]

Jurisprudential analysis demonstrates, however, that courts in England and France construe 'fairness' and '*loyauté*' respectively in a way that fails to give due weight to rights considerations. The focus on reliability and the need to pursue

[239] It must be noted that the Court of Appeal held that the proceedings would have to be stayed even if it had found no unfairness to the defendant in this case. Though the surreptitiously obtained recordings had not revealed any information of potential value to the prosecution, the deliberate interference with legal professional privilege 'seriously undermine[d] the rule of law and justifie[d] a stay on grounds of abuse of process, notwithstanding the absence of prejudice'. *R v Grant* [2005] EWCA Crim 1089 [57], (2005) 9 *International Journal of Evidence & Proof* 300. See also Choo, *Abuse of Process* (2008) 127–28.

[240] *cf*, however, *Warren and others v Attorney General for Jersey* [2012] 1 AC 22, 35, where the Privy Council opined that the decision in *R v Grant* was wrong. Even if the Court agreed that a breach of legal professional privilege could be 'a serious affront to the integrity of the justice system', and could therefore lead to a stay of the proceedings, this was not necessarily the case where 'the misconduct [had] caused no prejudice to the accused' and 'had no influence on the proceedings at all'.

[241] See D Ormerod, 'ECHR and the Exclusion of Evidence: Trial Remedies for Article 8 Breaches?' [2003] *Criminal Law Review* 61, 76. Dennis stressed that the concept of 'fairness' was 'wide enough' to account for exclusionary outcomes resting on very different rationales, while Ormerod and Birch have gone so far as to note that the 'unconstrained breadth of the [section 78] discretion which provides the courts with such flexibility and prompts their unquestioning approval raises serious problems'. Dennis, *The Law of Evidence* (2013) 319; Ormerod and Birch, 'The Evolution of the Discretionary Exclusion of Evidence' (2004) 785.

accurate fact-finding is made particularly explicit in English appellate court jurisprudence.[242] 'Fairness' is widely recognised as the key benchmark for exclusion there,[243] but it is fairness to the prosecution as much as to the defendant,[244] and it is hardly ever seen as an obstacle to the admission of cogent incriminating evidence, especially if the accused has had the opportunity to challenge the evidence at trial.[245] French appellate courts exercise their discretion equally narrowly, failing to read into violations of the right to privacy any prejudicial effect upon the interests of the defendant.[246] Where evidence is adduced by private parties, French courts do not challenge admissibility at all, irrespective of whether a privacy violation has occurred. A first paradox that becomes apparent from the above lies in the fact that the judiciary in both England and France have been equally invested with significant discretionary powers to exclude improperly obtained evidence, and, in relation to privacy violations at least, they have taken a 'hands-off' approach in both countries.[247] The second paradox merits equal attention. Given the

[242] See generally Spencer, 'Bugging and Burglary by the Police' (1997) 6; Choo and Nash, 'What's the Matter with Section 78?' (1999) 933; S Uglow, 'The Human Rights Act 1998: Part 4: Covert Surveillance and the European Convention on Human Rights' [1999] *Criminal Law Review* 287, 293; B Fitzpatrick and N Taylor, 'Human Rights and the Discretionary Exclusion of Evidence' (2001) 65 *Journal of Criminal Law* 349, 358; P Mirfield, 'Regulation of Investigatory Powers Act 2000' (2001) 101; *R* v *Cook* [1995] 1 Cr App R 318; *R* v *Chalkley* [1998] 2 All ER 155, 180; *AG's Reference (No 3 of 1999)* [2001] 1 All ER 577; *R* v *Sanghera* [2001] 1 Cr App R 299.

[243] *R v Khan (Imran)* [2013] EWCA Crim 2230 [55].

[244] *R v Sanghera* [2001] 1 Cr App R 299, 305.

[245] One might read into the English appellate courts' heavy reliance on 'fairness' a tendency to avoid the opportunity to develop the rules of evidence, 'by taking refuge in the vagaries of general terminology, and discretion […]'. Tapper draws this conclusion from a review of Court of Appeal jurisprudence on bad character evidence, including in relation to the application of section 78 PACE 1984 in its modified form in section 101(3) Criminal Justice Act 2003 in this domain. C Tapper, 'The Law of Evidence and the Rule of Law' (2009) 68 *Cambridge Law Journal* 67, 88. Tapper points to an additional problem with giving the concept of 'fairness of the proceedings' a central role in decisions relating to evidence admissibility. He notes that, as a 'backward looking concept', fairness 'may well be appropriate at the appellate stage', but is of 'little use to trial judges', since 'it is very hard to see how such a concept can be applied to the admissibility of a piece of evidence which *ex hypothesi* has to be adduced before the proceedings have terminated, and so in advance of any definitive categorisation of them as fair or unfair'. Tapper, ibid 73. Shortly before section 78 came into force, Zuckerman correctly predicted that 'the record of English judiciary [was leaving] little hope that this jurisdiction [would] be exercised to advantage'. His prediction that, because of its generality, section 78 would be used as 'an excuse for achieving whatever result [would be] wanted without rigorous justification', also proved accurate. A Zuckerman, 'Illegally Obtained Evidence – Discretion as a Guardian of Legitimacy' [1987] *Current Legal Problems* 55, 60.

[246] See generally G Clément, 'De la règle, pas de nullité sans grief, en droit judiciaire privé et en procédure pénale' (1984) *Revue de sciences criminelle* 433, 440; J-C Soyer, *Droit pénal et procédure pénale* (Paris, LGDJ, 1994) 351; Brouillaud, 'Les nullités de procédure' (1996) 100; P Hennion-Jacquet, 'Les nullités de l'enquête et de l'instruction. Un exemple du déclin de la légalité criminelle' (2003) *RPDP* 7; P Hennion-Jacquet, 'L'encadrement relatif de la liberté de la preuve par la Convention européenne des droits de l'homme' (2005) *Recueil Dalloz* 2575.

[247] Choo makes this observation in relation to English law. See A L-T Choo, *Comments on the Auld Report* (on file with author). See also R Glover and P Murphy, *Murphy on Evidence*, 13th edn (Oxford, Oxford University Press, 2013) 66.

unstructured nature of the discretionary powers afforded the English and French judiciaries in this domain, it would have perhaps been counterintuitive to expect their exclusionary jurisprudence to present high levels of coherence. And yet, this jurisprudence is surprisingly coherent, as appellate courts in both countries have essentially narrowed down the discretion to exclude improperly obtained evidence to a reliability test. In doing so, they have de facto turned a regime of exclusionary discretion to a virtually 'inclusionary' one.[248]

Of course, the lack of empirical data as to the exercise of discretionary exclusion at trial and pre-trial level in England or France should give us pause before attempting to draw any wider conclusions as to the extent of exclusion in practice, at least until future empirical research might finesse the hypothesis that the English and French judiciaries are in principle unwilling to exclude. It might indeed be tempting to assume that English and French courts exercise their discretion creatively at trial level (and at pre-trial judicial chamber level, as far as France is concerned), and that they do give human rights violations sufficient weight in the balancing exercise that they are seemingly undertaking when exercising discretion. There are sporadic case reports and some empirical evidence that suggests the possibility of this happening.[249] On the other hand, there is a risk of reading too much into such evidence, against the backdrop of court of appeal and 'supreme' court jurisprudence that in practice deals with violations of the right to privacy as a peripheral issue.

With this caveat in mind, it is also instructive to reflect on the alleged complexity, growth and controversial nature of the law in this area. Roberts and Zuckerman, for instance, point out that 'section 78's exclusionary empire is constantly being expanded', that section 78 is a 'free floating', 'all-purpose remedy', that its 'jurisprudence is growing at a fantastic rate' and that the provision 'plays a pivotal role in allowing the courts to address rights violations – the more so when the rights in question enjoy the elevated constitutional status of "human rights"'.[250] Ormerod

[248] See L Heffernan, 'The Fourth Amendment's Exclusionary Rule: Blurring the Line Between Rule and Exception' (2011) 9 *International Commentary on Evidence* 2, article 3. It must be noted here that the judiciaries in England and Wales and France would possibly strongly disagree with the idea that they have propounded a principle of non-exclusion (I am grateful to Andrew Choo for discussion on this point). The section 78 discretion in England and Wales or the need to determine substantial breaches and establish a prejudicial effect on a case-by-case approach in France are constant points of reference in the relevant jurisprudence anyway. It is nonetheless difficult to see how it could be maintained that discretion is not exercised in a way that pays lip service to privacy violations.

[249] See, eg, *R v Veneroso* (2002) *Criminal Law Review* 306. See also the only empirical survey generally known in this area, undertaken in England and Wales more than 20 years ago. M Hunter, 'Judicial Discretion: Section 78 in Practice' [1994] *Criminal Law Review* 558, 561. The survey suggested that the 'Court of Appeal seemed to use the reliability principle far more frequently than the Crown Court and that Crown Court rulings […] seemed to favour the protective rationale'. This would indicate an approach in Crown Courts much more favourable to the defendant than that which derives from examination of appellate court jurisprudence. However, the survey barely touched upon examples of evidence obtained through unlawful police searches, telephone intercepts or the bugging of premises.

[250] Roberts and Zuckerman (2010) 198.

and Birch have similarly seen section 78 as 'providing the judiciary with a very broad canvas on which to work'.[251] When looking at the exercise of section 78 discretion across the evidentiary spectrum, there is evidence to support this positive and optimistic view.[252] But when one takes a closer look, section 78's ability to act as the all-purpose exclusionary remedy for human rights violations that some perceive it to be quickly begins to fade. In a similar vein, it might be argued that an account of section 78 jurisprudence as 'complex' and 'controversial',[253] and a jurisprudence that is in a state of confusion,[254] is accurate only when the observer takes into account its inconsistent application in relation to different types of improperly obtained evidence[255] and inconsistencies in relation to how other procedural remedies are applied.[256] But when examined from the angle of privacy violations only, section 78's operation can be seen as surprisingly uncontroversial and simplistic. Reliability weighs heavily in favour of admission, and that is that. We might follow the same line of thought in relation to French law, where procedural nullities appear to be highly complex when seen as a whole, yet are applied in a rather straightforward inclusionary direction when it comes to privacy violations. On reflection, the contextual analysis undertaken in this chapter brings to the surface a highly homogenous, inclusionary, approach that might have otherwise remained hidden from public view.

It is opportune to link the above with preceding analysis of the American and Hellenic exclusionary rules for privacy violations. Chapter two placed emphasis on the demise of the exclusionary rule of *Mapp v Ohio*. This development was contrasted with the enhancement of the protective scope of the constitutional exclusionary rule in Greece (the 'tax and corruption offences' exception notwithstanding). This external view of the exclusionary rule confirmed what American commentators are observing from within their legal system, namely the progressive undermining of the American exclusionary rule as a mechanism for the protection of the Fourth Amendment. Compared with the narrowly applied exclusionary discretions in England and France, on the other hand, the American exclusionary rule can still be seen as providing strong levels of protection, even when one takes into consideration all the qualifications that currently apply to the original *Mapp* jurisprudence. The American exclusionary rule's logic remains

[251] Ormerod and Birch, 'Discretionary Exclusion of Evidence' (2004) 777.

[252] This is mainly due to the exercise of section 78 discretion in relation to confessional evidence. See ch 4.

[253] Dennis (n 54) 303.

[254] Colvin, 'Fairness and Equality in the Criminal Process' (2006) 8.

[255] By taking examples of breaches relating to different types of evidence – such as confessions, identification evidence and evidence obtained in violation of the right to privacy – Glover and Murphy conclude that the case law does 'not present any consistent picture of the circumstances under which the s. 78 power is to be exercised'. Glover and Murphy, *Murphy on Evidence* (2013) 65.

[256] Choo regards this 'a highly controversial area of the law', noting inconsistencies between section 78 and the more drastic remedy of a stay of the proceedings. A L-T Choo, Comments on the Auld Report (on file with author).

automatic, and this is not even to mention the statutory exclusionary rule for illegal wiretaps or the exclusionary rules that apply under State Constitutions, which provide more stringent protection than *Mapp*. Now, foreign commentators often dismiss the American exclusionary rule as an effective safeguard of the right to privacy, and one might query whether this is simply because they are versed in American scholarship highly critical of modern Supreme Court jurisprudence. In other words, foreign commentators may be internalising an American understanding of the rule that may not accurately reflect its remaining strengths as a constitutional safeguard from a comparative perspective. Such strengths emerge, however, from comparisons with countries that adopt discretionary exclusion. The theory of 'simultaneous contrasts', that we can borrow from colour theory, is pertinent here. Just as juxtaposing colour opposites, when these are contiguous, leads to mutual enhancement of colour intensity, so too the contrast between the opposite exclusionary systems becomes more intense when they are placed against each other.[257]

This, of course, is not to say that American observers are wrong to centre their attention on what modern Supreme Court case law has done to *Mapp*, but it is still worth asking whether an external view might help put this modern evolution of the rule into perspective. Here there are possible lessons for both the supporters and critics of the rule. The former might take satisfaction from the fact that, for all its weaknesses, *Mapp* – compared to the discretionary regimes of France and England and Wales for instance – still provides stringent protection (where exceptions do not apply). Contrasted with the principled approach of the Greek constitutional exclusionary rule, *Mapp* seemed to rest on a more empirical foundation. But in light of the pragmatic approach taken by the judiciaries in England and France – starting with the historic reluctance to recognise any exclusionary rule for improperly obtained evidence and moving to narrowly exercising their discretionary powers today – *Mapp* may in comparison still be seen as taking a principled approach. Of course, the comparative argument cuts both ways. The critics of the rule might point out that advanced legal systems, such as those of England and France, routinely admit evidence obtained in violation of the right to privacy and are yet not necessarily brought into disrepute. This observation might provide ammunition to renewed calls for the Supreme Court to strike the rule down and bring the United States in line with the more pragmatic approaches that foreign legal systems adopt.[258]

Conversely, analyses of the American and Hellenic exclusionary rules can work as a magnifying glass bringing into focus the English and French exclusionary

[257] See generally PD Owen, 'Painting', Encyclopaedia Britannica, www.britannica.com/art/painting#ref364642

[258] It may be useful to remind here that in *Wolf v Colorado* the Supreme Court drew support from the English admissibility position under the common law for the abandoning of the strict exclusionary rule that had been adopted with *Weeks v United States*. See ch 3.

regimes' continued inability to place due weight to violations of the right to privacy. The Cour de cassation's jurisprudence on the bugging of police station premises constitutes an important exception. The Cour de cassation's stringent exclusionary position on this point may present particular interest for observers in Greece and the United States, especially since it marks the unexpected evolution from an inclusionary position to a strict exclusionary one. The fine distinctions drawn up by American and Hellenic jurisprudence, as to the conditions that activate the operation of the exclusionary rule, might also suggest the need for the English and French judiciaries to bring more precision to their vague discretionary powers. Starting a transition to a structured discretion[259] or even introducing a presumption of exclusion for specified rights[260] may be alternatives worth exploring. It is worth adding that it is counterintuitive that fine distinctions – such as in relation to good faith, standing or violations by private parties – have been developed in the context of narrowly defined exclusionary rules rather than vague discretionary powers giving judges room for manoeuvre.

At a macro-comparison level, the remarkable convergence identified between the English and French discretionary systems, both in terms of historic development and contemporary applications, allows us again to question the importance of the divide between the adversarial and inquisitorial legal cultures as to the exclusion of improperly obtained evidence. As methodically discussed in this chapter, England and France have historically shared the same reservations towards excluding evidence obtained in violation of the right to privacy. In fact, France now seems to be taking a more robust approach to excluding such evidence, at least in areas where the right to privacy coincides with the right to legal assistance, and this despite having strong roots in the inquisitorial legal culture. The identification of some engagement with the improperly obtained evidence debate since at least the end of the nineteenth century in France likewise allows us to question the other conventional view, namely that the improperly obtained evidence doctrine is idiosyncratic of adversarial criminal procedure[261] and that it has, for

[259] For proposals that would take English law in this direction see Ormerod and Birch (n 48) 786–87; M Wasik, T Gibbons and M Redmayne, *Criminal Justice: Text and Materials* (London and New York, Longman, 1999) 450. See also Mirfield's analysis of *Khan (Sultan)* and his effort to identify the factors that may be relevant to the exercise of discretion. Mirfield (n 1) 212–13.

[260] See Ormerod, 'ECHR and the Exclusion of Evidence' (2003) 78–80. Choo and Nash have advocated the adoption of a strong presumption for specified rights, which 'should be able to be rebutted only by compelling considerations in favour of the evidence being admitted'. Choo and Nash, 'Evidence Law in England and Wales' (2003) 49. Choo and Nash have also more generally called for an urgent rationalisation and reform of the law. See generally Choo, Comments on the Auld Report (on file with author); S Nash, Comments on the Auld Report (on file with author).

[261] Jackson point to this 'fault line between the procedural traditions', 'the fact that adversarial systems are [commonly considered] able to accommodate the exclusion of evidence … more easily than inquisitorial systems which have a stronger commitment to the ideal of free proof'. J Jackson, 'Cultural Barriers on the Road to Providing Suspects with Access to a Lawyer' in R Colson and S Field, *EU Criminal Justice and the Challenges of Diversity – Legal Cultures in the Area of Freedom, Security and Justice* (Cambridge, Cambridge University Press, 2016) 181, 187.

the most part, migrated to Europe from the United States. The two examples from inquisitorial criminal procedure examined so far – those of Greece and France – strongly point to indigenous attitudes as a source for the development of the improperly obtained evidence doctrine there.

The comparison of the converging discretionary French and English solutions with their automatic counterparts in the United States and Greece can also support an argument from the contrary as to the forces that shape convergence across legal traditions in this domain. Following the line of argument developed in chapter two – that the constitutionalisation of criminal procedure has the capacity to generate cross-cultural, rights-centred, exclusionary rule convergence – the point can be made that the absence of constitutionalisation in French and English criminal procedure may explain local judicial aversion to the rights thesis. The absence from the French constitution of a charter of fundamental rights regulating aspects of criminal procedure or the fact that Britain's unwritten constitution finds its limit in parliamentary sovereignty[262] can perhaps provide quick explanations about the underlying forces that resist the emergence of a constitutional criminal procedure, and constitutional exclusionary rules, akin to those observed in legal systems where Bill of Rights reign supreme. Put simply, English and French criminal procedure are not exposed to constitutional rights influences similar to those traversing American and Greek criminal procedure. Violations of constitutional rights are therefore not perceived, perhaps quite naturally, as having the same detrimental effect in the former as they do in the latter. The international human rights influences coming from Strasbourg, to which English and French criminal procedure are, of course, not immune, are a separate issue, and we will be evaluating their impact in the following chapter.

We can also correlate the absence of a constitutionalisation of criminal procedure with an overpowering 'law and order' culture, as opposed to rights-centred, approaches to excluding improperly obtained evidence. As far as French and English criminal procedure are concerned, there is strong evidence of attachment to a law and order, securitarian, culture,[263] symptomatic of Packer's 'crime control'

[262] See, eg, X Deligianni-Dimitrakou, *Introduction to comparative law* (Athens-Salonica, Sakkoulas, 1997) 87 (in Greek); M Delmas-Marty, 'Introduction' in M Delmas-Marty and C Lucas de Leyssac, *Libertés et droits fondamentaux: introduction, textes et commentaires*, 2nd edn (Paris, Seuil, 2002) 9, 11; A Garapon and I Papadopoulos, *Juger en Amérique et en France* (Paris, Odile-Jacob, 2003) 48; K Martin-Chenut and F De Melo e Silva, 'La constitutionnalisation/ conventionnalisation du droit de la preuve' in Giudicelli-Delage (dir), *Transformations de la preuve pénale* (2006) 31, 44.

[263] See generally K Stenson, 'Making Sense of Crime Control' in K Stenson and D Cowell (ed), *The Politics of Crime Control* (London, SAGE, 1991) 1; D Downes and R Morgan, 'The Skeletons in the Cupboard: the Politics of Law and Order at the Turn of the Millenium' in M Maguire, R Morgan and R Reiner (ed), *The Oxford Handbook of Criminology*, 3rd edn (Oxford, Oxford University Press, 2002); T Newburn and R Reiner, 'From PC Dixon to Dixon PLC: Policing and Policing Powers since 1954' [2004] *Criminal Law Review* 601; F Saint-Pierre, 'Les droits de la défense dans la loi Perben II' in Journées d'études Dalloz, *Le nouveau procès pénal après la loi Perben II* (Paris, Dalloz, 2004) 429; F Saint-Pierre, 'Le véritable enjeu des contrôles juridictionnels de la légalité des procédures pénales: la "sûreté" des justiciables' *Actualité juridique pénal* 2005 177; A Ashworth, 'Four Threats to the Presumption of

model,[264] and it is not outlandish to perceive this as symmetrical to adopting evidentiary approaches that favour the public interest over individual rights.

The link between procedural legal tradition and the adoption of particular exclusionary attitudes will be further explored in chapters four and five, in view of an emerging consensus on the exclusion of improperly obtained confessions, as a result, among other things, of international human rights influences shaping domestic criminal justice attitudes.

Innocence' (2006) 10 *International Journal of Evidence & Proof* 241; JP Jean, 'Politique criminelle et nouvelle économie du système pénal' (2006) *Actualité juridique pénal* 473; F Chopin, 'Vers un nouveau modèle de justice pénale' in *Mélanges offerts à Raymond Gassin – Sciences pénales et sciences criminologiques* (Aix-Marseille, Presses universitaires d'AixMarseille III, 2007) 135; M Delmas-Marty, 'Le paradigme de la guerre contre le crime: légitimer l'inhumain' (2007) *Revue de sciences criminelle* 461; R Reiner, *Law and Order – An Honest Citizen's Guide to Crime and Control* (Cambridge, Polity Press, 2007); P Robert, 'Ordre, insécurité, liberté: les incertitudes de la procédure pénale' in Cour de cassation, *La procédure pénale en quête de cohérence* (Paris, Dalloz, 2007) 37, 40; G Wenzelburger, 'Parties, Institutions and the Politics of Law and Order: How Political Institutions and Partisan Ideologies Shape Law-and-Order Spending in Twenty Western Industrialized Countries' (2015) 45 *British Journal of Political Science* 664; G Wenzelburger and H Staff, 'The "Third Way" and the Politics of Law and Order: Explaining Differences in Law and Order Policies between Blair's New Labour and Schröder's SPD' (2017) 56 *European Journal of Political Research* 553.

[264] H Packer, *The Limits of the Criminal Sanction* (California, Stanford University Press, 1965).

4

Improperly Obtained Confessional Evidence: Converging Rights-Based Approaches

Chapters two and three brought to light two opposing approaches towards the administration of improperly obtained evidence. They serve to draw a significant contrast between exclusionary rules and exclusionary discretion, and set apart a principled, rights-centred, view of procedural fairness from a more pragmatic view that draws on epistemic considerations and prioritises free proof. When moving from such abstract conceptualisations to more contextual interpretations – and away from the ends of the exclusionary spectrum – different iterations of these contrasting approaches immediately surface. The contextual study undertaken in the preceding chapters thus helped us mark the difference between strict and elastic rules, widely construed and narrowly interpreted discretions or opting for the protective and judicial integrity principles as opposed to a deterrent or reliability-centred logic. These iterations, however, simply brought precision to the nature of existing divergence. They did not divert from it. They rather highlight the existing divide at the comparative law level as regards conceptualising the impact of privacy violations upon the fairness of the proceedings. Put simply, they indicate that there is currently considerable difference of opinion as to whether the use of evidence obtained in violation of the right to privacy affects the right to fair trial, and whether evidence should be excluded to remedy such violations, deter similar violations in the future or protect the integrity of the proceedings.

This chapter will now move the discussion to improperly obtained confessional evidence. It will demonstrate that England and Wales, France, Greece and the United States find much more common ground in this area, irrespective of the judicial remedy adopted (exclusionary rules, procedural nullities or judicial discretion) and irrespective of how far they go in requiring the exclusion of improperly obtained confessional evidence. England and Wales and France take a far stricter view of procedural violations at the police station than they do with regards to privacy violations – France much more than England and Wales – and this brings them much closer to the automatic, bright-line rule, exclusionary approach adopted by the United States and Greece across the board. This does not change the fact that there is still much that keeps these systems apart, including as a result of transformations within the automatic exclusionary systems themselves.

The gradual minimisation of the protective scope of the *Miranda* exclusionary rule in the United States is a well-known theme in exclusionary rule scholarship for that matter. Still, in contrast to the divergent views that these systems take on evidence obtained in violation of the right to privacy, in relation to improperly obtained confessional evidence we can observe significant rapprochement as a result of a growing realisation of the importance of custodial interrogation rights and the risks inherent in the use of potentially unreliable evidence.

A preliminary observation must be added. By revealing a difference of opinion as to evidence obtained in breach of the right to privacy that has English and French law, on the one side, and Greek and United States law, on the other, chapters two and three directed attention to surprising convergence between two pairs of Anglo-American and Continental law systems as well as divergence between legal systems within the same legal culture. The United States and Greece perceive the improperly obtained evidence enigma in nearly identical ways, placing the emphasis on mandatory exclusion and constitutional rights protection, even if there is substantial differentiation in how strictly they apply their exclusionary rules in practice and even if this differentiation is partly due to subscribing to different exclusionary rationales. Similar observations have been made in relation to the converging solutions adopted by England and Wales and France. In other words, chapters two and three bring to light converging procedural solutions that go beyond the Anglo-American and Continental law divide. In highlighting an existing rapprochement and emerging consensus on improperly obtained confessional evidence across the Anglo-American and Continental legal cultures, chapter four will make an emphatic statement about the same.

This chapter will also relocate the focus of explanation from reliable evidence obtained via privacy violations to unreliable and intangible evidence, 'fragile evidence'[1] that historically generates miscarriages of justice.[2] 'Confession evidence is inherently dangerous';[3] police violence, deception, the intrinsically coercive nature of custodial interrogation or suspects' psychological vulnerabilities during custody and interrogation are some of the key factors that explain why.[4] These place emphasis on regulating custodial interrogation and empowering suspects

[1] P Conte and P Maistre du Chambon, *Procédure pénale*, 4th edn (Paris, Armand Colin, 2002) 37.

[2] See I Dennis, 'Miscarriages of Justice and the Law of Confessions: Evidentiary Issues and Solutions' [1993] *Public Law* 291. See also F Belloni and J Hodgson, *Criminal Injustice – An Evaluation of the Criminal Justice Process in Britain* (London, Macmillan Press, 2000) 51–63.

[3] *DPP (at the suit of Walsh) v Cash* [2007] IEHC 108 [32].

[4] See generally G Gudjonsson, 'Unreliable Confessions and Miscarriages of Justice in Britain' (2002) 4 *International Journal of Police Science & Management* 332; G Gudjonsson, *The Psychology of Interrogations and Confessions*, Wiley Series in Psychology of Crime, Policing and Law (New Jersey, Wiley, 2003); S Kassin and G Gudjonsson, 'The Psychology of Confessions: A Review of the Literature and Issues' (2004) 5 *Psychological Science in the Public Interest* 33. See also K Roach, 'Unreliable Evidence and Wrongful Convictions: The Case for Excluding Tainted Identification Evidence and Jailhouse and Coerced Confessions' (2007) 52 *Criminal Law Quarterly* 210; M Kassin, S Drizin, T Grisso, G Gudjonsson, R Leo and A Redlich, 'Police-Induced Confessions: Risk Factors and Recommendations' (2010) 34 *Law and Human Behaviour* 3.

through attribution of appropriate procedural rights capable, in theory, to counter the police station's intimidating atmosphere.[5] The key question then becomes what should happen when the suspect has not been afforded these rights or where he has been subjected to forces that can overpower a suspect's will regardless. In answering this question, we must not lose sight of the fact that, despite the rise and rise of scientific evidence,[6] the mythical status of confessional evidence as *regina probationis* continues unabated. It is still seen as the 'evidence par excellence',[7] and we go so far as acknowledge a so called 'religion of the confession, often a pretext for detaining the suspect at the police station, remanding him in custody and eliminating the lawyer [from the police station] for as long as possible',[8] so that we can increase the chances of proving the guilt of the individual at our disposal.[9] This chapter will now address these issues from the vantage point of French, English, United States and Greek law.

I. The Modern Metamorphoses of the French *Nullités* of the *Garde À Vue*: The Road to Automatic Nullities

French law provides a perfect illustration of a shifting ideology on the exclusion of confessional evidence as a means to protect the fair trial rights that apply at the police interrogation phase, the French *garde à vue*.[10] This is the result of modern Cour de cassation jurisprudence which no longer requires establishing that the defendant has suffered a procedural 'harm' as a result of the improper obtaining of evidence. The link between the breach and prejudicial effect is rather automatic. Violations of fair trial rights applying to custodial interrogation lead to pronouncements of nullity. Courts have no leeway to ignore the procedural taint. The relevant procedural act is invalidated, and where confessional evidence has been obtained,

[5] For a critique of custodial interrogation rights' power to diminish the police station's intimidating atmosphere, see L Laudan, *Truth, Error and Criminal Law: An Essay in Legal Epistemology* (Cambridge, Cambridge University Press, 2006) 176.

[6] See generally P Roberts, *Expert Evidence and Scientific Proof in Criminal Trials* (London, Routledge, 2014). See also J Singer, K Miller and M Adya, 'The Impact of DNA and Other Technology on the Criminal Justice System: Improvements and Complications' (2007) 17 *Albany Law Journal of Science & Technology* 87; L Meintjes-Van der Walt, 'Tracing Trends: The Impact of Science and Technology on the Law of Criminal Evidence and Procedure' (2011) *South African Law Journal* 147.

[7] C Perelman, 'La preuve en droit, essai de synthèse' in C Perelman and P Foriers, *La preuve en droit* (Brussels, Bruylant, 1981) 358.

[8] J Robert, Intervention in conference on 'force ou faiblesse de la constitutionnalisation du droit pénal' in Cour de cassation, *La procédure pénale en quête de cohérence* (Paris, Dalloz, 2007) 103, 107. See also P Maistre du Chambon, 'Propos critiques et désabusés sur une réforme mort-née de la procédure pénale' in Mélanges en l'honneur de J Larguier (Fontaine, PUG, 1993) 191.

[9] M Bennilouche, 'Les objectifs du procès pénal' in G Giudicelli-Delage (ed), *Les transformations de l'administration de la preuve pénale: perspectives comparées* (Paris, Société de législation compare, 2006) 19, 21.

[10] The *garde à vue* can be translated as a coercive measure allowing for the detention and questioning of suspected offenders by the police. See art 62-2 CPP (France).

it cannot be used in court, even though it is important to keep in mind that 'exclusion' in France often means that the relevant investigative or judicial authority will repeat the 'invalidated' procedural act, this time by making sure that the rights of the defendant are respected.[11]

We must emphasise that nullities applying to the *garde à vue* were historically regarded 'private interest'-based, discretionary nullities (*nullités d'intérêt privé*), and that the Cour de cassation had in general little sympathy for triggering nullities for violations occurring at this stage of the criminal process.[12] Until around the beginning of the 1990s, the highest jurisdiction in France was systematically rejecting nullity applications for breaches of *garde à vue* rules. Its jurisprudence on this matter was 'nearly non-existent'.[13] The Court required from the interested party to demonstrate that the procedural breach had fundamentally affected the search for truth.[14] Violations of suspects' rights would not in themselves trigger the pronouncement of nullity. Bouloc put it quite bluntly, that 'the *garde à vue* jurisprudence was a disappointment',[15] whilst the 1990 edition of one of the classical texts of French criminal procedure astoundingly declared that 'in reality, there are no nullities in the *garde à vue*. It is as if the "real" procedure does not start until after the defendant has been charged with the offence'.[16]

We can take the example of a case where the suspect had not been given the required rest time during an interrogation. The Cour de cassation decided to reject a nullity application in that case after drawing on the report provided by the psychiatrist who had examined the suspect 27 hours into the interrogation. This report established that, at the time of examination, the suspect was not exhibiting any signs of exhaustion, which meant that the procedural violation had not in any way prejudiced the suspect. The Court took a pragmatic view of the effect of the procedural breach in question, in accordance with the article 802 CPP requirement for a finding of procedural harm. A commentary in the *Recueil Dalloz* noted:

> [I]n order to legitimise the use of [self-incriminating] statements made during the *garde à vue*, judges refer to different facts ... the [suspect's] refusal to be examined by a lawyer, the existence of a negative medical report or a detailed statement by the suspect when [after the *garde à vue*] he appears before the investigating judge ... or the fact that the relevant prosecutor has been supervising the *garde à vue*.[17]

[11] See ch 1.

[12] M Guerrin, *Les irrégularités de procédure sanctionnées par la nullité dans la phase préalable au jugement pénal*, PhD thesis, Université Strasbourg III – Robert Schuman (1999) 61.

[13] Rapport de la Cour de cassation (Paris, La documentation française, 1998) 340.

[14] See *Crim* 17 March 1960, JCP 1960, II, 11641, note Chambon; 10 October 1968, *Bull crim* n 252; 17 April 1980, JCP 1981, II, 19632; 21 October 1980, (1981) *Recueil Dalloz* 104, note Mayer; 11 June 1985, *Bull crim* 226; 22 December 1987, (1989) *Recueil Dalloz* 323, note Julien-Laferrière; *Crim* 26 Feburary 1991, *Bull crim* n 97, (1992) *Recueil Dalloz* 99. See also H Matsopoulou, *Les enquêtes de police*, Bibliothèque des sciences criminelles (Paris, LGDJ, 1996) 702.

[15] B Bouloc, 'Les abus en matière de procédure pénale' (1991) *Revue de sciences criminelle* 221, 223.

[16] J Pradel, *Procédure pénale*, 5th edn (Paris, Cujas, 1990) n 317. See also M Gendrel, 'Garde à vue et droit de l'individu. La défense doit-elle commencer dans les locaux de gendarmerie ou de police ?', *Ed Techniques, Droit pénal*, March 1992, 1.

[17] *Crim* 26 February 1991, (1992) *Recueil Dalloz* 99.

The demands of article 802 continue to be of relevance in some cases today. There is no nullity, for instance, where the police notify the suspect of his rights but fail to draft the relevant report. The Court finds no nullity where the suspect has gone on to exercise his rights despite the lack of notification.[18] Or in relation to the right to interpretation, the Court concentrates on whether the suspect has been de facto prejudiced by the undertaking of the act in French. The Court has found that a suspect of Tunisian nationality, for instance, was not prejudiced by the notification of his rights in French. He had been residing in France for 14 years and had himself admitted that he had understood the notification in French when asked later in the presence of an Arabic interpreter.[19] The same solution was given in a case where the suspect was notified of his rights by an interpreter, but was not given a letter of rights in his own language.[20]

However, since the beginning of the 1990s, we observe a rapid metamorphosis of the nullities of the *garde à vue*. The Cour de cassation is starting to set aside the need to establish a prejudicial effect, transforming the private interest, non-automatic, nullities of the *garde à vue* into public interest ones.[21] Interestingly, this transformative jurisprudence marks the passage from an understanding of suspects' rights as reflecting solely the individual interests of those involved to an understanding of suspects' rights as an integral part of a democratic criminal process which we must safeguard at all costs.[22] Bouloc's analysis on this point gives us an insight of the uncertainty surrounding this jurisprudential development, as to the normative foundations that supported it. He takes as his point of departure that rules applying at the *garde à vue* qualify as fundamental principles of criminal procedure, but still inquires whether it is normatively correct to consider that their breach should indeed lead to public interest nullities. He takes the suspect's ability to waive custodial interrogation rights as pinpointing the private interest nature of such rights; no court or other public authority can *ex officio* trigger the application of such rights, he correctly notes. But he ultimately accepts that violations of suspects' rights constitute 'gross procedural irregularities', which put 'in danger the rights of the person who is detained at the police station', and it is therefore legitimate to presume the prejudicial effect of such violations.[23] This means that the court is no longer required to undertake a case-by-case analysis to

[18] *Crim* 6 December 1995, *Bull crim* n 369; *Crim* 19 December 2000, *Droit pénal*, April 2001, 25.

[19] *Crim* 11 Feburary 1998, *Bull crim* n 55. The civil chamber of the Cour de cassation reached the same outcome in a case where it had emerged that, in the absence of the interpreter, the suspect had communicated with the police officers in French, even if the relevant report noted that the suspect had difficulties in expressing himself correctly. Civ 2e, 10 October 2002, *Bull civ* II, n 215.

[20] *Crim* 7 February 2017, n 16-85187.

[21] See JP Delage, 'La sanction des nullités de la garde à vue: de la sanction juridictionnelle à la sanction parquetière' (2006) *Archives de politique criminelle* 137; Dumont, Juris-Classeur Procédure pénale, art 802, n 35.

[22] A Decocq, J Montrevil and J Buisson, *Le droit de la police* (Paris, Litec, 1998) 818.

[23] B Bouloc, 'Observations sur les nullités en matière de procédure pénale' in Mélanges offerts à Pierre Couvrat, *La sanction du droit* (Paris, PUF, 2001) 417, 422.

establish the prejudicial effect of *garde à vue* breaches. The prejudicial effect necessarily follows from the procedural violation.[24] Pronouncement of the nullity is automatic. Article 802, this 'escape route for so many improper procedural acts',[25] takes no effect. Courts routinely declare in such cases that the procedural breach 'necessarily harms the interests of the person concerned' (*atteinte nécessaire aux intérêts de la personne concernée*), though they remain cryptic about the normative justifications for this transition to automatic nullities.

We see applications of this jurisprudence in connection with three key *garde à vue* safeguards: those concerning time limits for the *garde à vue*,[26] notifying the suspect of his rights[27] and notifying the prosecutor with responsibility of supervising the *garde à vue* – the *Procureur de la République* – from the moment this measure has been triggered,[28] even if this rights-based approach to nullities extends to other aspects of the *garde à vue*.[29]

For the purposes of illustration on violations of time limits, we can take what seems to be a quite far-reaching application, a case where the suspect was originally interviewed for nine hours in 1989, and then for 43 hours and 30 minutes in 1995, taking the overall duration above the 48-hour limit and leading the Cour de cassation to reject the use of the confessional evidence in question.[30]

The same solution is given where the police do not immediately inform the *Procureur* that a suspect has been placed under a *garde à vue*, so that he can exercise his judicial supervision role.[31] Any unjustified delay in exercising this duty 'intrinsically harms the interests of the person placed under a *garde à vue* without this person needing to demonstrate any prejudice'.[32] In a case from 2016, a delay of 45 minutes provided the basis for an automatic nullity, even if the suspect had been arrested at his home and the prosecutor was notified shortly after the suspect was taken to the police station to be interrogated.[33] Even in a case where the suspect was taken to the police station late at night, and a contact

[24] See M Guerrin, 'Les changements opérés par la loi relative à la présomption d'innocence sur les nullités de procédure dans la phase préalable au jugement pénal' (2000) *Revue de sciences criminelle* 757; D Karsenty, 'L'article 63-1 du Code de procédure pénale dans la jurisprudence récente de la chambre criminelle' (2000) *Droit pénal*, 6 June, 4, 6.

[25] J Pradel, 'Nullité d'une procédure pour défaut d'enregistrement de l'interrogatoire d'un mineur en garde à vue' (2007) *Recueil Dalloz* 2141.

[26] Art 63 CPP (France).

[27] Art 63-1 CPP (France).

[28] Art 63 CPP (France).

[29] See eg Cour de cassation case law which mandates nullity of the *garde à vue* where a doctor has found that the suspect is not in a state to be detained and questioned by the police. *Crim* 27 October 2009, n 09-82.505.

[30] *Crim* 13 February 1996, (1996) *Recueil Dalloz* 258.

[31] See generally B Cotte, discours de rentrée du TGI de Paris, *Gazzette du Palais*, 1 May 1993, 42.

[32] *Crim* 14 Feburary 2001, *Droit pénal*, January 2002, 23. See also *Crim* 24 November 1998, *Bull crim* n 314; *Procédures*, May 1999, n 138. See also *Crim* 29 Feburary 2000, *Bull crim* n 93; *Droit pénal*, June 2000, n 80; (2000) 3 *Poiniki Dikeosini* 861, note D Giannoulopoulos (in Greek); *Crim* 13 December 2006, *Bull crim* n 312; *Crim* 20 March 2007, *Bull crim* n 85.

[33] *Crim* 24 May 2016, *Bull crim* n 155.

number for the *Procureur* had mistakenly not been made available, the Cour de cassation found that the delay had necessarily harmed the interests of the suspect. The Court recognises an exception where there exists an insurmountable obstacle (*impossibilité insurmontable*) to notifying the *Procureur*, but lacking a contact number and failing to reach one at 10 o'clock in the night did not qualify as such.[34]

The supreme French jurisdiction takes an equally strict approach where interrogating officers fail to notify the suspect of his rights. A delay of one and a half hours, for instance, is seen as having an automatic prejudicial effect.[35] A delay of 30 minutes had the same effect in a case where the suspect was apprehended in his house but was not notified of his rights until arrival at the police station.[36] More tellingly, the Cour de cassation finds a nullity even where it can be demonstrated that the suspect has gone on to exercise his rights.[37] Similarly, a notification of rights at the beginning of the *garde à vue* cannot remedy the absence of notification at the time of extending the *garde à vue* beyond the initial 24-hour limit. Notifying the suspect of his rights is 'a condition for their effective exercise', held the Cour de cassation in this case.[38] To take another example, upon arrival at the police station, the lawyer is entitled to consult the official report of the notification of rights along with other key documentation such as reports made of any interviews that may have taken place up to that point. Violations of these rules necessarily affect the rights of the defendant, held the Cour de cassation in a 2015 judgment.[39]

These are some of the most emphatic illustrations yet that, in the area of custodial interrogation, the Court has abandoned the pragmatic – *in concreto* – logic that it traditionally applies in other areas of pre-trial investigation, notably in relation to evidence obtained through unlawful police searches and electronic interceptions of private communications. Save for the insurmountable circumstances exception

[34] *Crim* 2 February 2005, *Bull crim* n 40; (2005) *Actualité Juridique pénal* 162, obs Roussel. See also *Crim* 29 February 2000, (2000) *Recueil Dalloz* 108; 10 May 2001, *Bull Crim* n 119; 3 September 2003, appeal n 02-85-697, Légifrance; A Pitoun, 'Appréciation judiciaire *a minima* d'un contrôle d'identité et de l'information d'un placement en garde à vue incident', (2004) *Actualité juridique pénal* 160; *Crim* 19 February 2004, *Bull civ* II, n 70; *Crim* 12 April 2005, *Bull crim* n 125.

[35] *Crim* 29 April 1998, *Bull crim* n 145; *Procédures*, December 1998, n 264. The same solution was adopted in a case where the notification took place 1 hour and 55 minutes after the beginning of the *garde à vue*. See *Crim* 6 December 2000, *Droit pénal*, March 2001, 21. See also *Crim* 30 April 1996, *Bull crim* n 182; 3 December 1996, n J 96-84.503; *Crim* 11 October 2000, *Bull crim* n 296; *Crim* 31 May 2007, appeal no 07-80.928, Juris-Data no 2007-039748; *Crim* 24 June 2009, *Bull crim* n 136.

[36] *Crim* 24 May 2016, *Bull crim* n 155.

[37] *Crim* 14 December 1999, *Bull crim* n 302; *Procédures*, March 2000, n 39; 10 May 2000, *Bull crim* n 182.

[38] *Crim* 1 December 2015, *Bull crim* 270. It is worth noting that the Court reached this decision even if the lawyer of the suspect was present during the interrogation and made no observations at the time the 24-hour extension was decided, and even if the police had given the suspect a 'letter of rights' at the beginning of the *garde à vue*. The Court explained that the 'letter of rights' could not remedy the police officers' omission to read the suspect her rights.

[39] *Crim* 17 November 2015, *Bull crim* 255.

that applies to notifying the suspect of his rights,[40] there is in the area 'an absolute presumption of prejudicial effect'[41] upon the interests of the defendant; 'an automatic nullity founded on an absolute presumption of a prejudicial effect upon the rights of the defendant',[42] which strongly echoes the Cour de cassation's increasing enthusiasm for remedying through nullity rights violations at the *garde à vue*.[43]

This gradual jurisprudential metamorphosis of the *nullités* of the *garde à vue* in France reached a kind of apotheosis with seminal Cour de cassation jurisprudence on the right to custodial legal assistance. Following on the path of the European Court of Human Rights (ECtHR) momentous decision in *Salduz v Turkey*,[44] which has read into the right to fair trial the right to consult a lawyer and have a lawyer present during custodial interrogation, the Cour de cassation consistently drove the point home that failing to provide the suspect with the right to legal assistance would necessarily affect the fairness of the proceedings. In October 2010, a few months prior to the enactment of legislation in France that gave effect to the *Salduz* case law, a plenary session of the Cour de cassation unequivocally held that for the requirements of article 6 of the Convention to be satisfied, the suspect must not be questioned in the absence of his lawyer,[45] that he must be informed of the right to silence and be assisted by a lawyer from the beginning of the *garde à vue*, unless there are compelling reasons to restrict the right or the suspect has

[40] Exceptional circumstances can relate to elements intrinsic to the person who is detained at the police station, or to temporal elements and elements external to that person. The Cour de cassation has confirmed such exceptional circumstances where the suspect was in a state of drunkenness, where there was a manifestation at the police station obstructing the presentation of the suspect to the interrogating officer (*Crim* 10 April 1996, (1996) *Gazette du Palais*, 2.136; (1996) *Procédures*, comm 229, obs Buisson) or where an interpreter could not be made immediately available to the suspect (*Crim* 26 May 1999, (2001) *Recueil Dalloz*, 519). See, for example, *Crim* 3 April 1995, *Bull crim* n 140, where the suspect was read his rights eight hours after the beginning of the *garde à vue*. The Court reasoned that the suspect was in a state of drunkenness which would not have allowed him to understand the effect of the rights that would be notified to him. Even if he did, he would not have been in a position to exercise them effectively. But it must be noted that this exception is applied quite rarely.

[41] *Crim* 26 May 1999, ibid. See D Karsenty, 'L'article 63-1 du Code de procédure pénale dans la jurisprudence récente de la Chambre criminelle', *Droit pénal*, June 2000, chr n 21, 4.

[42] *Crim* 3 April 2007, *Bull crim* n 104, note J Pradel, 'Nullité d'une procédure pour défaut d'enregistrement de l'interrogatoire d'un mineur en garde à vue' (2007) *Recueil Dalloz* 2141. In this case, the Cour de cassation found a nullity in a case where the interrogation of a minor had not been audio-visually recorded, due to a technical mistake.

[43] M Guerrin, *Les irrégularités de procédure sanctionnées par la nullité dans la phase préalable au jugement pénal*, PhD thesis, Université Strasbourg III – Robert Schuman (1999) 70. *Cf* Cour de cassation judgment of 27 May 2015, where the Court reverted to the *in concreto* logic, rejecting the nullity application on the basis that a failure to notify the suspect of the specific location of the offence in question had not had a prejudicial effect upon his rights. *Crim* 27 May 2015, *Bull crim* 126. A commentator at Dalloz observed that this notification does not concern a procedural right – such as the notification of the right to legal assistance, the right to silence and the other rights applying at the *garde à vue* – but a substantive point. This means that violation of the duty to make this notification does not have a (presumed) immediate and direct effect upon the rights of the defendant, and it therefore makes sense to establish whether the rights of the defendant have indeed been prejudiced on a case-by-case basis. C Benelli-de Bénazé, 'Garde à vue: conséquences de l'omission de la notification du lieu de l'infraction', *Dalloz actualité* 15 June 2015.

[44] *Salduz v Turkey* (2008) EHRR 421.

[45] *Crim* 19 October 2010, *Bull crim* n 163.

unequivocally waived his right,[46] and, finally, that the right to access to a lawyer cannot be restricted solely on the basis of the nature of the offence concerned.[47] Then in January 2011, the supreme jurisdiction specifically declared that confessional evidence obtained in the course of the *garde à vue*, without the suspect benefiting from effective legal assistance, was inadmissible in trial.[48] The final steps in this revolutionary Cour de cassation jurisprudence were first taken with four decisions published on 15 April 2011, only a day after the enactment of the *Salduz* legislation in France. The Court, again in a plenary session, gave the new rights immediate effect, leaving courts no room to manoeuvre away from the duty to find a nullity where the right to legal assistance had not been respected.[49] In the last major episode of the *Salduz* implementation saga, the Cour de cassation gave the right to legal assistance jurisprudence full retroactive effect. On May 31, it found violations of the right to a fair trial in four cases where suspects had been subjected to custodial interrogation prior to the coming into effect of the rules adopted by the *assemblée plenière* on April 15. The suspects had neither been notified of their right to remain silent nor been assisted by a lawyer from the beginning of the *garde à vue*.[50] The Court found a nullity in all four cases. This was a remarkable development, since thousands of *garde à vue* measures could subsequently be retroactively invalidated.[51] At a normative level, the focus on the *Salduz* jurisprudence has also helped more clearly identify adherence to the right to fair trial as the normative basis for the relevant procedural nullities in France, though Cour de cassation jurisprudence remains obscure as to what particular aspects of trial fairness would be engaged if *garde à vue* breaches were not followed by automatic nullity.

Since the above epoch-making decisions, the Cour de cassation has time and again confirmed its new-found faith in applying a rights-based approach to *garde à vue* violations, for instance where the police have not contacted the lawyer

[46] *Crim* 19 October 2010, *Bull crim* n 164; *Crim* 17 January 2012, *Bull crim* n 15. See also *Crim* 10 September 2014, *Bull crim* n 185, where the Cour de cassation overturned the decision of the Court of Appeal of Dijon which had convicted the defendants by relying on self-incriminating evidence obtained in the absence of a notification of the right to silence and in the absence of a lawyer.

[47] *Crim* 19 October 2010, *Bull crim* n 165.

[48] *Crim* 4 January 2011, n 10-85.520, (2011) *Recueil Dalloz* 242, obs M. Léna; *Crim* 18 January 2011, n 10-83.750, (2011) *Recueil Dalloz* 381. See also *Crim* 16 February 2011, n 10-82.865, *Recueil Dalloz* 953.

[49] *Crim* 15 April 2011, 4 judgments (n P 10-17.049, F 10-30.313, J 10-30.316 and D 10-30.242), (2011) *Recueil Dalloz*, 1080; (2011) *Recueil Dalloz* 1128, interview G Roujou de Boubée; (2011) *JCP*, n 17, 483, S Détraz.

[50] *Crim* 31 May 2011, n 11-81.412, 10-88.809, 10-80.034 and 10-88.293, (2011) *Recueil Dalloz* 1563. With a December 2011 decision, the Court specified that non-notification of the right to silence further aggravated the prejudicial effect caused by the breach of the right to legal assistance. *Crim* 11 December 2011, *Bull crim* 256.

[51] See, eg, *Crim* 16 December 2015, *Bull crim* n 307, where the Cour de cassation quashed a conviction on the basis that the decision of the mixed tribunal had relied on a confession obtained in 2005 in the absence of a lawyer and with no notification of the right to silence. See also J Pradel, 'Procédure pénale: septembre 2010 – août 2011' (2011) *Recueil Dalloz* 2231; J Alix, 'Les droits de la défense au cours de l'enquête de police après la réforme de la garde à vue: état de lieux et perspectives' (2011) *Recueil Dalloz* 1699.

designated by the suspect.[52] The Court also routinely applies a sort of 'fruit of the poisonous tree' rule to invalidate procedural acts linked with the unlawful obtaining of the evidence,[53] where it can be established that a *garde à vue* violation is directly linked to subsequent procedural acts.[54] To be sure, there are other Cour de cassation decisions that demonstrate that its approach on this topic is far from settled,[55] but the post-*Salduz* transformation of nullities for violations of suspects' rights must be recognised as nothing short of a revolution in French criminal procedure.

II. Automatic Nullities for Violations of Suspects' Rights in Greece

Chapter two provided a detailed account of the strict exclusionary rules applying to privacy violations in Greece. Chapter four will reveal a similarly robust approach to confessional evidence obtained in violation of custodial interrogation rights there. It will demonstrate that Greece consistently adopts a rights-based approach to improperly obtained evidence, irrespective of the type of evidence in question and the nature of the constitutional right that has been breached in the process. Unlike its 'exclusionary rule'-centred approach to privacy violations, however, Greece regulates the administration of improperly obtained confessional evidence through procedural nullities. From this angle, we will be able to identify important similarities with the evolving rights-based procedural nullity approach adopted in recent years in France, at a normative and methodological level. The converging French and Greek approaches will then offer a useful comparative vista for the study of the exclusion of improperly obtained confessional evidence in England and Wales and the United States.

[52] *Crim* 21 October 2015, *Bull crim* 229.

[53] Art 174 CPP (France).

[54] To pronounce a nullity the court must find that the unlawful procedural act has provided 'necessary support' (*support nécessaire*) to a subsequent act. See, eg, *Crim* 16 June 2015, *Bull crim* n 149, where the illegal obtaining of self-incriminating statements at the *garde à vue* also tainted the subsequent Investigating Judge proceedings. For examples where the Court did *not* establish a direct link between the violation at the *garde à vue* and subsequent procedural acts see *Crim* 12 April 2005, *Bull crim* n 125; *Crim* 26 March 2008, *Bull crim* n 76, (2008) *Revue de sciences criminelle* 926, obs Finielz.

[55] Article 63-4-1 CPP (France), for instance, gives lawyers limited access to the investigation dossier. The Cour de cassation refused to find a nullity in a case where the suspect was requesting full access. In the same case, the Court found that the notification of the right to silence at the *garde à vue* had cured a lack of notification of the same right when the suspect appeared before the investigating judge. See *Crim* 14 April 2015, *Bull crim* 83. More controversially, with a decision of 12 February 2014, the Court rejected a nullity application in a case where the suspect had not been notified of the right to silence and had not been questioned in the absence of a lawyer, simply on the grounds that the lower judicial chamber had not exclusively, or even essentially, relied on the incriminating statements when referring the defendant to trial, and that the defendant would still be able to challenge the probative value of the evidence during the adversarial trial. *Crim* 12 February 2014, *Bull crim* n 41.

By way of introduction, it is worthwhile outlining the principles underlying the operation of procedural nullities in Greek law. The Code of Penal Procedure (CPP) distinguishes between 'relative' and 'absolute' nullities. 'Relative' nullities are those that the legislator has specifically written into provisions of the Code,[56] which can be triggered only by the party concerned – the party whose right has been violated or who has suffered some other procedural 'harm', not a third party or the court *ex officio* – subject to the party concerned having not waived the right to apply for a nullity or provoked the procedural irregularity in the first place.[57] These nullities are cured (or 'purged') when the pre-trial process moves beyond a certain point, which means parties cannot raise them any longer.[58] Much more central to our inquiries are 'absolute' nullities. These are general clauses that describe a range of procedural irregularities that can affect the integrity of the proceedings ('public order') and the rights of the defendant.[59] They are triggered *ex officio*, and can be raised by the parties until committal to trial has become irreversible,[60] whereas if the illegality takes place during the trial, they can be invoked at any time, even at the Court of cassation, the Arios Pagos.[61]

Article 171 para 1(a)–(c) of the CPP provides that absolute nullities are triggered when there has been a violation of provisions that relate to jurisdictional issues, the initiation of criminal prosecution as well as suspending charges where the time limits for prosecution have been exceeded, but for the purposes of the study of improperly obtained confessional evidence it is article 171 para (d) that we need to concentrate upon. This states that there is nullity when there has been a violation of any of the provisions of the Code that determine: 'the participation, representation and defence of the accused and the exercise of the rights that are provided to him, in the circumstances, and under the conditions, imposed by law'.

In other words, where a court establishes a procedural breach that relates to the exercise of defence rights, it is required to find a nullity. The procedural breach is presumed to have a prejudicial effect upon the interests of the defendant. The nullity is automatic, and so is the exclusion of evidence obtained through the tainted act.[62]

[56] Art 170 CPP (Greece).

[57] Art 173, para 3 CPP (Greece).

[58] Art 173, para 1 CPP (Greece).

[59] A Papadamakis, *Penal procedure: theory, practice, jurisprudence* (Athens-Thessaloniki, Sakkoulas eds, 2002) 210 (in Greek).

[60] Art 173, para 2 CPP (Greece).

[61] Art 171 CPP (Greece).

[62] See generally D Dzioras, *The system of Hellenic criminal procedure*, Tome I (Athens, 1973) 435 (in Greek); G Barbaretos, *Code of penal procedure*, 6th edn (Athens, Sakkoulas, 1982) 567 (in Greek); P Kaisaris, *Code of penal procedure*, tome III, articles 127–179 (Athens-Komotini, Sakkoulas, 1984) (in Greek); X Dedes, *Criminal procedure*, 9th edn (Athens-Komotini, AN Sakkoulas, 1989) 216 (in Greek); A Karras, 'Procedural sanctions for violations of defendants' rights' in Hellenic Association of Criminal Law, *Defendants' Rights in the Criminal Process in General* (Athens, PN Sakkoulas, 1989) 103.

Defence rights in Greece take their source in the Constitution – the right to the protection of human dignity[63] and the right to a judicial process[64] in particular – and Article 6 of the European Convention on Human Rights (ECHR), which translate into specific guarantees in the CPP. Following a radical legislative reform in 1996, which for the first time provided suspects at the police station with access to legal assistance and other key defence rights,[65] suspects now have the right to be assisted by a lawyer,[66] and communicate freely with her,[67] when questioned by the police and in other pre-trial examinations, including the examination by the Investigating Judge. The lawyer can ask questions and make observations, which have to be noted in the relevant report,[68] and has the right to access the investigation dossier in its entirety.[69] The police must notify the suspect about the right to legal assistance, legal aid, the right to be notified about the charges, the right to translation and interpretation and the right to silence.[70] Since these provisions all relate to the exercise of the rights of the defence any violations must be remedied through the pronouncement of an absolute nullity, without the need to establish that the suspect has suffered specific prejudicial harm. The Code in fact specifically mandates that interviews that are conducted in violation of the aforementioned rights of the suspect, and in violation of the duty to notify the suspect of these rights, are 'null and void' and are 'not taken into consideration' by the court,[71] and that they should be removed from the investigation dossier.[72]

The rule that requires removal of the tainted interviews from the investigation dossier can be found in the provisions that regulate the preliminary judicial inquiries that precede the initiation of criminal proceedings in relation to more serious offences. Since these inquiries take place at a very early stage of the proceedings,

[63] Art 2, para 1 Constitution (Greece).

[64] Art 20, para 1 Constitution (Greece). See generally A Karras, *The 'judicial process' principle in the criminal process*, Poinika 29 (Athens-Komotini, Sakkoulas, 1989) (in Greek).

[65] Law 2018/1996 reforming provisions of the Penal Code, the Code of Penal Procedure, the Code for the Treatment of Detained Persons and other provisions. See ΦΕΚ Α' 104, 4 June 1996. The 1996 legislation was of paramount importance for the protection of suspects' rights, by bringing into the police station the fair trial guarantees that were previously only applying to interrogations by the Investigating Judge. The legislation aimed to put an end to the controversial police practice whereby suspects were examined as 'witnesses' to avoid giving effect to legal assistance rights to which they would otherwise be entitled. See notably N Androulakis, 'Concerning the problem of confessions obtained in police interrogations' (1974) 22 *Nomiko Bima* 1345 (in Greek). See also Arios Pagos 129/2006, Poinika Chronika 2006, 712, which was highly critical of the pre-1996 'unacceptable regime of violating the rights of defendants in custodial interrogation', highlighting how it 'sustained abusive practices offensive to human dignity' and how it generated negative attitudes towards the police.

[66] Article 100, para 1 CPP (Greece).

[67] Article 100, para 4 CPP (Greece).

[68] See N Androulakis, *Fundamental notions of the criminal process*, 2nd edn (Athens-Komotini, AN Sakkoulas, 1994) 273 (in Greek).

[69] Art 101 CPP (Greece).

[70] Art 99A CPP (Greece) introduced with Law of 11 February 2014 implementing Directive 2010/64/EU on the right to translation and interpretation and Directive 2012/13/EU on the right to information in criminal proceedings. The right to silence is protected by art 273 para 2 CPP (Greece).

[71] Art 105 CPP (Greece).

[72] Art 105 CPP (Greece) refers to art 31, para 2 CPP (Greece) in that respect.

the persons involved are not immediately given the status of the defendant, and defence rights are not immediately triggered. This means that the persons involved may be questioned in the absence of a lawyer, as if they had the status of a witness. To eliminate the risk of these persons incriminating themselves, the CPP specifically instructs that records of preliminary inquiry interviews, conducted in the absence of a lawyer, 'cannot be part of the investigation dossier'.[73] In other words, if charges are eventually brought against these persons, any self-incriminatory statements made in the absence of a lawyer are excluded from the consideration of the court. This is an absolute exclusionary rule, as Karras points out, in response to an Arios Pagos decision that upheld the conviction of the defendant on the basis that the lower court did not rely, in the end, on the self-incriminating statements which had been unlawfully retained in the investigation dossier. Karras convincingly argues that the legislator introduced this exclusionary rule to eliminate the risk that judges would obtain knowledge of the tainted information, to ensure they are in no way influenced by it in the exercise of their fact-finding function.[74] From this point of view, it is indeed irrelevant whether the court relied on the tainted self-incriminating statements or not. What matters is that it has been exposed to the tainted evidence.

The exclusion of confessional evidence obtained in the absence of a lawyer or in breach of other key custodial interrogation rights was settled with two seminal judgments of the plenary session of the Arios Pagos. In the first one, in 1999, the Court categorically declared that violations of defence rights should lead to absolute nullities, and that self-incriminating statements obtained through these acts should be removed from the investigation dossier.[75] A second plenary judgment in 2004 concerned a murder charge. The judicial chamber decision that had committed the defendant to trial took into consideration self-incriminating statements that he had made when examined by the police in the absence of his lawyer, and without benefitting from any of the other legal assistance rights that should apply at the police interrogation stage. More specifically, the committal decision pointed out serious inconsistencies between the defendant's statements to the Investigating Judge, made in the presence of his lawyer, and earlier self-incriminating statements made to the police at the preliminary inquiry stage, in the absence of a lawyer. Arios Pagos declared that the use of the self-incriminating statements had generated an 'absolute' nullity, as a result of a violation of 'the right to silence and right against self-incrimination, as a specific expression of the right to fair trial'.[76] In relation to cases where the suspect is questioned as a witness without benefitting from the exercise of his defence rights, the Court noted more particularly

[73] Art 31, para 2 CPP (Greece).

[74] A Karras, *Penal procedure law*, 4th edn (Athens, Nomiki Bibliothiki, 2011) 266 (in Greek).

[75] Arios Pagos (plenary session) 2/1999, 49 Poinika Chronika 811. See also Arios Pagos 129/2006, 56 Poinika Chronika 712.

[76] Arios Pagos 1/2004, Poinikos Logos 2004, 523, Poinika Chronika 2005, 113. The plenary session reversed the decision of a chamber of the Arios Pagos, which had found no nullity in this case. See Arios Pagos 92/2004, Poiniki Dikeosini 2004, 403, Poinikos Logos 2004, 130.

that the evidential use of any self-incriminating statements must be equated with compelling the defendant to confess. The Court underlined how the right against self-incrimination was firmly grounded in international human rights law, the ECHR and the International Covenant on Civil and Political Rights more specifically, leaving lower courts no room to doubt its application in future exclusionary cases.[77]

In view of the above, it is instructive to observe that the gradual recognition of progressive defence rights at the police station, in both Greece and France, went hand in hand with the recognition of an automatic exclusionary approach in this area, which takes the right to fair trial, and the privilege against self-incrimination, as its normative foundation. It is now interesting to correlate the exclusionary developments in these two Continental jurisdictions with the continued minimisation of the protective scope of the renowned *Miranda* exclusionary rule in the United States. Like *Mapp v Ohio, Miranda v Arizona* captured the imagination of American procedural scholars like few other Supreme Court judgments, while also attracting great attention from comparative law observers. There are significant lessons to learn in Europe from the *Miranda* exclusionary rule saga, especially if the ECtHR goes on to renege on its *Salduz* and post-*Salduz* exclusionary promises, as its *Ibrahim* jurisprudence suggests;[78] a reversal of the *Salduz* jurisprudence would have strong echoes of modern US Supreme Court case law backtracking on the original *Miranda* understanding to substantially weaken the effect of its exclusionary rule. Conversely, current developments in Europe will offer a timely comparative point of reference for continuing debates across the Atlantic, particularly if we place the emphasis on the dramatic impact that the *Salduz* jurisprudence has had, since its inception, upon regimes of custodial interrogation rights in Europe.

III. *Miranda v Arizona*: The Exclusionary Rule in Fast Decline (but Exclusion is Still Automatic)

There are few cases as ingrained in American legal, political and popular culture as *Miranda v Arizona*.[79] Analysis of the life of this legendary case – from the original judgment of the Warren Court up to contemporary applications that have brought

[77] See also Arios Pagos 129/2006, Poinika Chronika 2006, 712.

[78] See ch 5.

[79] *Miranda v Arizona* 384 US 436 (1966). As the Supreme Court noted in *Dickerson v United* States, 530 US 428, 430 (2000), 'Miranda has become embedded in routine police practice to the point where the warnings have become part of our national culture'. It is also estimated that 80% of the United States population at large are familiar with the *Miranda warnings*. See S Walker, *Taming the System: The Control of Discretion in Criminal Justice 1950–1990* (Oxford, Oxford University Press, 2000) 51 cited by C Slobogin, 'An Empirically Based Comparison of American and European Regulatory Approaches to Police Investigation' (2001) 22 *Michigan Journal of International Law* 423. Similarly, in a 1989 American Bar Association poll of its members, '*Miranda* came in fourth place as a milestone of American legal

its strict exclusionary rule close to a flatline – raises complex issues of constitutional interpretation that we will be examining in detail in this chapter.

A. *Miranda's* Original Understanding

Miranda took issue with the practice of 'incommunicado interrogation', which was 'at odds with one of [the] Nation's most cherished principles – that the individual may not be compelled to incriminate himself'.[80] The incommunicado interrogation environment was created 'for no purpose other than to subjugate the individual to the will of the examiner', carrying 'its own badge of intimidation'.[81] The Court recognised that examples of 'physical brutality – beating, hanging, whipping',[82] the infamous 'third degree', were 'undoubtedly the exception' at the time of *Miranda*. The Court's logic moved beyond physical intimidation, taking as its point of departure that '[e]ven without employing brutality, the "third degree" or [...] specific stratagems [...], the very fact of custodial interrogation exacts a heavy toll on individual liberty, and trades on the weakness of individuals',[83] and that incommunicado detention may not be 'physical intimidation, but it is equally destructive of human dignity'.[84]

The Court then took the leap that led to the establishment of the *Miranda* exclusionary rule. It concluded that custodial interrogation was 'inherently coercive';[85] that 'without proper safeguards, the process of in-custody interrogation of persons suspected or accused of crime contains inherently compelling pressures which work to undermine the individual's will to resist and to compel him to speak where he would not otherwise do so freely'.[86]

The Court did away with the case-by-case approach previously adopted under the 'due process voluntariness totality of the circumstances test',[87] which was recognising that an interrogation could be compulsive, depending on the circumstances, and moved to a presumption that custodial interrogations are inherently compulsive. It followed from this that '[u]nless adequate protective devices are employed to dispel the compulsion inherent in custodial surroundings, no statement obtained from the defendant can truly be the product of his free choice'.[88] The Court then went on to define what protective devices should be employed to

history'. See J Grano, 'Introduction – The Changed and Changing World of Constitutional Criminal Procedure: The Contribution of the Department of Justice's Office of Legal Policy' (1988–1989) 22 *University of Michigan Journal of Law Reform* 395, 400.

[80] *Miranda v Arizona*, 384 US 436, 457–58 (1966).

[81] ibid 157.

[82] ibid 446.

[83] ibid 455.

[84] ibid 157.

[85] ibid 533.

[86] ibid 467.

[87] See below text to fn 206.

[88] *Miranda v Arizona*, 384 US 436, 458 (1966).

dispel the compulsion inherent in custodial interrogations, bringing into life the – mythical – '*Miranda* warnings' (or '*Miranda* rights') and the exclusionary rule that is triggered where these have been breached. The Court explained that:

> [W]hen an individual is taken into custody or otherwise deprived of his freedom by the authorities in any significant way and is subjected to questioning [...] [h]e must be warned prior to any questioning that he has the right to remain silent, that anything he says can be used against him in a court of law, that he has the right to the presence of an attorney, and that, if he cannot afford an attorney one will be appointed for him prior to any questioning if he so desires. Opportunity to exercise these rights must be afforded to him throughout the interrogation. After such warnings have been given, and such opportunity afforded him, the individual may knowingly and intelligently waive these rights and agree to answer questions or make a statement. But unless and until such warnings and waiver are demonstrated by the prosecution at trial, no evidence obtained as a result of interrogation can be used against him.[89]

The Court also explained that if the suspect:

> indicates in any manner and at any stage of the process that he wishes to consult with an attorney before speaking, there can be no questioning. Likewise, if the individual is alone and indicates in any manner that he does not wish to be interrogated, the police may not question him. The mere fact that he may have answered some questions or volunteered some statements on his own does not deprive him of the right to refrain from answering any further inquiries until he has consulted with an attorney and thereafter consents to be questioned.[90]

Miranda's original understanding, as encapsulated in the above, represented a radical departure from previous practice.[91] It treated the privilege against self-incrimination as absolute[92] and sent a strong message that the Supreme Court was determined to put an end to police lawlessness in this critical area of pre-trial criminal proceedings. Rooting *Miranda* and its procedures in the Fifth Amendment would allow it to do the double-duty of preserving the privilege through the application of bright-line rules while also preventing officers from obtaining statements involuntarily. *Miranda* became in this way a symbol of the due process revolution initiated by the Warren Court in the 1960s.[93] *Mapp v Ohio* was

[89] ibid 478–79.

[90] ibid 444–45.

[91] Even though, if compared to the rule which had been introduced by *Escobedo v Illinois*, 378 US 478 (1964), two years earlier *Miranda* could be seen as 'something of a compromise'. In the light of *Escobedo*, some commentators feared that *Miranda* would go so far as prohibit all interrogations without counsel, whilst after *Miranda* 'interrogations still could continue, though within set procedures that would protect Fifth amendment rights'. See, in detail, C Weisselberg, 'Saving Miranda' (1998) 84 *Cornell Law Review* 109, 121. See also Barrett Lain, who argues that, compared to *Escobedo, Miranda* was 'a comparatively weak decision'. C Barrett Lain, 'Countermajoritarian Hero or Zero? Rethinking the Warren Court's Role in the Criminal Procedure Revolution' (2004) 152 *University of Pennsylvania Law Review* 1409.

[92] G Caplan, 'Questioning Miranda' (1985) 38 *Vanderbilt Law Review* 1417, 1447.

[93] See K Roach, 'Dialogue or Defiance – Legislative Reversals of Supreme Court Decisions in Canada and the United States' (2006) 4 *International Journal of Constitutional Law* 347, 350. See also C Bradley, *The Failure of the Criminal Procedure Revolution* (Philadephia, University of Pennsylvania Press, 1993).

the other. But as with *Mapp*, so, too, with *Miranda*, Supreme Court attack upon Supreme Court attack, since Earl Warren's golden era of constitutional criminal procedure, led to a dilution of the rule's original understanding and deprived the Fifth Amendment exclusionary rule of much of its (original) substance.

B. 'Falling out of Favour': Narrowing the Scope for the Exercise of *Miranda* Rights

The story of *Miranda's* fall from favour with the Supreme Court starts with the Burger Court 'constru[ing] the key terms "custody" and "custodial interrogation" rather narrowly.'[94] *Miranda* held that the Miranda rights – and synonymous exclusionary rule – are triggered only 'after a person has been taken into custody or otherwise deprived of his freedom of action in any significant way'[95] and 'questioning [has been] initiated by law enforcement officers'.[96] In *Beckwith v United States*, the Supreme Court interpreted this to mean that there was no duty to warn a suspect of his *Miranda rights* when the interview has taken place in his private home, even where the suspect was the focus of the relevant investigation.[97] The Court came to this conclusion even if it accepted that 'noncustodial interrogation might possibly in some situations, by virtue of some special circumstances, be characterized as one where the behavior of … law enforcement officials was such as to overbear petitioner's will to resist and bring about confessions not freely self-determined'.[98] The suspect in this case was questioned about his tax returns. Justice Brennan argued that '[i]nterrogation under conditions that have the practical consequence of compelling the taxpayer to make disclosures, and interrogation in "custody" having the same consequence [were, in his view] peas from the same pod'.[99] His, however, was a lonely voice in this 7:1 case. The Burger Court had no appetite for extending *Miranda's* scope to situations outside the police station. In the same vein, Burger Court jurisprudence established that *Miranda* warnings did not apply where the suspect had voluntarily come to the police station for questioning and was informed that he was not under arrest,[100] where there has been no formal arrest or restraint on freedom of movement of the degree associated with formal arrest,[101] or where there was no express questioning of the suspect.[102] The Supreme Court under Justice William Rehnquist went even further, holding that

[94] Y Kamisar, 'On the Fortieth Anniversary of the Miranda Case: Why We Needed It, How We Got It – And What Happened to It' (2007–2008) 5 *Ohio State Journal of Criminal Law* 163, 180.

[95] *Miranda v Arizona*, 384 US 436, 444 (1966).

[96] ibid.

[97] *Beckwith v United* States, 425 US 341 (1976).

[98] ibid 348.

[99] ibid 350.

[100] *Oregon v Mathiason*, 429 US 492 (1977); *California v Beheler*, 463 US 1121 (1983).

[101] *Minnesota v Murphy*, 465 US 420 (1984).

[102] *Rhode Island v Innis*, 446 US 291 (1980).

the warnings did not apply where incriminating statements had been obtained after the police placed an undercover agent in a jail cellblock with the suspect.[103]

Far more devastating, for *Miranda's* original understanding, was the effect of Supreme Court jurisprudence that 'lowered the bar to finding waivers of rights and, at the same time, established quite demanding requirements for invocations'.[104] *Miranda* had set a high threshold on waivers, by requiring that these be made 'voluntarily, knowingly and intelligently'.[105] But the Supreme Court adopted narrow interpretations of these requirements since then. It accepted, for instance, that 'a defendant's ignorance of the full consequences of his decisions does not vitiate their voluntariness',[106] and that trickery from the part of the interrogators did not necessarily invalidate a suspect's waiver.[107] It also accepted that an explicit waiver was not "invariably necessary", and an implicit waiver could therefore, depending of the circumstances, suffice.[108] *Moran v Burbine* is one of the high-water marks of this jurisprudence.[109] The police in this case had deceived the suspect's attorney by giving her false information about whether her client would be questioned, and they deceived the suspect himself by failing to inform him of his attorney's communications and efforts to represent him. The Supreme Court still held that keeping this information from the suspect had not vitiated his waiver.[110] In interpreting *Miranda's* waiver requirements in this way, the majority opinion had 'trampled on well-established legal principles and flouted the spirit of [the United States] accusatorial system of justice', pointed out Justice Brennan in his dissent.[111]

[103] *Illinois v Perkins*, 496 US 292 (1990).

[104] C Weisselberg, 'Exporting and Importing *Miranda*' (2017) 97 *Boston University Law Review* 1235, 1248.

[105] *Miranda v Arizona*, 384 US 436, 444 (1966). See generally R Leo and W White, 'Adapting to *Miranda*: Modern Interrogators' Strategies for Dealing with the Obstacles Posed by *Miranda*' (1999–2000) 84 *Minnesota Law Review* 397.

[106] *Connecticut v Barrett*, 479 US 523 (1987).

[107] In *Colorado v Spring*, 479 US 564, 580–82 (1987), the law enforcement officials had kept silent about the true subject matter of the interrogation. In his dissent, Justice Marshall noted that a 'psychological ploy' with 'coercive aspects' had been used by the interrogating officers, and that their 'preconceived plan' was 'to obtain a waiver from [the defendant] with reference to a particular federal offense and then ask about a separate, unrelated state offense'. The Supreme Court permitted more generally the use of trickery when questioning suspects. See eg *Oregon v Mathiason*, 429 US 492 (1977); *Frazier v Cupp*, 394 US 731 (1969) and *Moran v Burbine*, 475 US 412 (1986).

[108] *North Carolina v Butler*, 441 US 369 (1979). The suspect had refused to sign the waiver form, and had said nothing when advised of his right to the assistance of a lawyer. He was given an 'Advice of Rights' form, and was told that agents wanted to speak to him. He replied that he would talk to them, but was 'not signing any form'. His indication that he was willing to answer questions was taken to be an implicit waiver.

[109] According to *Miranda*, 'a heavy burden rest[ed] on the government to demonstrate that the defendant knowingly and intelligently waived his privilege against self-incrimination and his right to retained or appointed counsel'. *Miranda v Arizona*, 384 US 436, 475 (1966). But in *Colorado v Connelly*, 479 US 157, 168 (1986), the Supreme Court held that this 'heavy burden' was not more than the burden to establish waiver by the preponderance of the evidence.

[110] *Moran v Burbine*, 475 US 412 (1986).

[111] ibid 468.

Now, while the Supreme Court was making findings of waivers easier to establish, it was simultaneously making it more difficult for the suspect to invoke his rights.[112] In *Berghuis v Thompkins*, the most important *Miranda* judgment of recent times,[113] these two jurisprudential strands came together, striking a double blow at *Miranda*. In *Davis v United States* the Supreme Court had found that invocation of the right to counsel required 'at a minimum, some statement that [could] reasonably be construed to be an expression of a desire for the assistance of an attorney'.[114] Failing this, questioning could continue.[115] The Supreme Court applied *Davis* to the situation in *Thompkins*, which raised the issue of whether an ambiguous invocation of the right to silence was possible (an issue the Court's jurisprudence had not clarified before). The suspect had remained silent throughout his interrogation, until two hours and 45 minutes into it, when he finally chose to speak to the police, making self-incriminating statements. The Supreme Court found that there was no reason to adopt different standards for invocation of the right to counsel and invocation of the right to silence, and so *Davies* applied; the suspect had not made an unambiguous invocation of his right to silence. The fact that he had remained silent for two hours and 45 minutes was not enough to persuade the Supreme Court that he had '"invoked his privilege" by not saying anything for a sufficient period of time'.[116] It followed from this that the police did not have a duty to stop the interrogation[117] and incriminating statements had been lawfully obtained and then admitted in court. After *Thompkins*, therefore, anything short of a direct statement from the suspect that he wants to remain silent or does not want to talk to the police will not trigger *Miranda* rights.[118]

In *Thompkins* the Supreme Court accepted not only that the suspect needs to explicitly invoke his right to silence for *Miranda rights* to come into effect, but

[112] Even where the suspect had invoked his *Miranda* right to counsel, the Supreme Court introduced exceptions to the *Edwards v Arizona* rule, which does not allow the interrogation to continue 'until counsel has been made available to him, unless the accused has himself initiated further communication, exchanges, or conversations with the police'. *Edwards v Arizona*, 451 US 477 (1981). In *Oregon v Bradshaw*, 462 US 1039, 1055–56 (1983), the Supreme Court read the 'initiation' requirement very broadly, in a way that 'flie[d] in the face of the basic purpose of the *Miranda* safeguards' and so did not stop the authorities from capitalising on the inherent compulsion of the custodial setting. Similarly, in *Michigan v Moseley*, 423 US 96, 102 (1975), the Supreme Court found that incriminating statements were admissible, where the suspect had originally exercised his 'right to cut off questioning' by exercising the right to silence, but later made incriminating statements after a fresh set of warnings had been given.

[113] *Berghuis v Thompkins*, 560 US 370 (2010). Weisselberg, 'Exporting and Importing *Miranda*' (2017) 1248.

[114] *Davis v United States*, 512 US 452, 459 (1994), citing *McNeil v Wisconsin*, 501 US 171, 178 (1991).

[115] ibid. Questioning could continue where the suspect's statement was 'ambiguous or equivocal'. A statement would be ambiguous or equivocal 'in that a reasonable officer in light of the circumstances would have understood only that the suspect *might* be invoking the right to counsel'.

[116] *Berghuis v Thompkins*, 560 US 370 (2010).

[117] As per *Edwards v Arizona*, 451 US 477 (1981).

[118] It must be added that 'unambiguous' had already 'proven to be a difficult standard for suspects to meet'. J Hammack, 'Turning Miranda Right Side Up: Post Waiver Invocations and the Need to Update the Miranda Warnings' (2011) 87 *Notre Dame Law Review* 421, 432.

also that an 'implicit waiver' of the 'right to remain silent' is sufficient to admit the suspect's statement into evidence,[119] holding that 'the defendant's silence, coupled with an understanding of his rights and a course of conduct indicating waiver' would amount to such an implicit waiver.[120]

Justice Sotomayor's dissent, with whom Justices Stevens, Ginsburg and Breyer joined, provided scathing criticism of this logic:

> The Court concludes today that a criminal suspect waives his right to remain silent if, after sitting tacit and uncommunicative through nearly three hours of police interrogation, he utters a few one-word responses. The Court also concludes that a suspect who wishes to guard his right to remain silent against such a finding of "waiver" must, counterintuitively, speak – and must do so with sufficient precision to satisfy a clear-statement rule that construes ambiguity in favor of the police. Both propositions mark a substantial retreat from the protection against compelled self-incrimination that *Miranda* v. *Arizona*, 384 U.S. 436 (1966), has long provided during custodial interrogation.

Yale Kamisar, the 'father of *Miranda*',[121] pointed out the paradox in the position adopted by the Supreme Court, by noting that '*Thompkins requires a suspect to prove* that he invoked his right to remain silent *instead of requiring the prosecution to prove* that the suspect waived that right'.[122] Such a reversal of the burden of proof that had been defined by *Miranda* clearly demonstrates that *Thompkins* could not be viewed as 'simply another instance of chipping away at *Miranda*',[123] as some commentators had suggested, but 'a case where the Court fired point-blank at *Miranda*'.[124]

To put this in context, we must also take into consideration that a valid waiver of *Miranda* rights means that any incriminating statements the suspect makes thereafter are presumed to have been made voluntarily, and courts will therefore be very reluctant to examine the voluntariness of these statements by applying the 'totality of circumstances' test.[125] Coupled with the fact that a clear majority of suspects in the United States are waiving their rights,[126] it seems that *Miranda*

[119] As per *North Carolina v Butler*, 441 US 369, 376 (1979).

[120] ibid 373.

[121] J Vile and D Hudson (ed), *Encyclopedia of the Fourth Amendment, Volume 1* (London, Sage, 2013) 371.

[122] Y Kamisar, 'The Rise, Decline and Fall (?) of *Miranda*' (2012) 87 *Washington Law Review* 965, 1019.

[123] ibid.

[124] ibid.

[125] See generally M Godsey, 'Rethinking the Involuntary Confession Rule: Toward a Workable Test for Identifying Compelled Self-Incrimination' (2005) 93 *California Law Review* 466, 513; S White, 'Miranda's Failure to Restrain Pernicious Interrogation Practices' (2001) 99 *Michigan Law Review* 1211, 1217–221. See also W White, 'What Is an Involuntary Confession Now?' (1998) 50 *Rutgers Law Review* 2001, 2014-020; R Leo, S Drizin, P Neufeld, B Hall and A Vatner, 'Bringing Reliability Back In: False Confessions and Legal Safeguards in the Twenty-First Century' [2006] *Wisconsin Law Review* 480, 498. Leo et al argue that 'trial judges almost always declare a confession voluntary if the *Miranda* procedures appear to have been properly followed'.

[126] Cassel and Hayman's survey in the 1990s found that 84% of suspects were waiving their rights, with only 7% asking for an attorney and 5% invoking their right to silence. The survey was, however,

is, in most police interrogation cases, deprived of protective effect upon suspects' rights. To speak like Richard Leo, *Miranda* has, because of the above, 'become a "manageable annoyance" – the anti-climax of custodial questioning – to American police that once waived does not affect the subsequent interrogation because it does not prohibit any post-waiver interrogation techniques, and suspects rarely invoke their rights following the warnings'.[127]

The Supreme Court's assault on *Miranda* has not, however, been limited to interpreting the original jurisprudence in a way that avoids the triggering of *Miranda rights* in practice. It rather extended to introducing exceptions to *Miranda's* exclusionary rule and its constitutional rationale.

C. 'Falling out of Favour': Introducing Exceptions to *Miranda's* Exclusionary Rule

The first direct attack at *Miranda's* exclusionary rule occurred shortly after Warren Burger succeeded Earl Warren as Chief Justice at the Supreme Court. In *Harris v New York*, the Supreme Court introduced the impeachment exception, which allows statements that are inadmissible in the prosecution's case in chief – because of violations of *Miranda rights* – to 'be used for impeachment purposes to attack the credibility of defendant's trial testimony'.[128] Warren Burger wrote the opinion of the Court, which rested on the premise that evidence obtained in violation of *Miranda rights* was not a violation of the privilege against self-incrimination per se. The Court locked the rationale for *Miranda's* exclusionary rule exclusively in its 'deterrent effect on proscribed police conduct', then went on to argue that assuming that the exclusionary rule had such an effect in practice, 'sufficient deterrence flows when the evidence in question is made unavailable to the prosecution in its case in chief'.[129] Put differently, the Court found that there would be no added deterrence benefit from stopping the prosecution from using self-incriminating statements obtained in violation of *Miranda* where these are used simply to attack the credibility of the defendant. The dissenters' criticism was twofold. First, the privilege against self-incrimination protected suspects from incriminating themselves 'in *any* manner', as settled in *Miranda*,[130] and this 'dispose[d] of any distinction between statements used on direct as opposed to cross-examination'.[131] Equally

based on a very small sample (129 suspects) taken from just one county (Salt Lake County, Utah, a large urban area). See P Cassel and B Hayman, 'Police Interrogation in the 1990s: An Empirical Study of the Effects of *Miranda*' (1996) 43 *UCLA Law Review* 839. See also GC Thomas III, 'Stories About *Miranda*' (2004) 102 *Michigan Law Review* 1959, who calculated the waiver rate at 68 per cent.

[127] R Leo, *Police Interrogation and American Justice* (Cambridge, Massachusetts, Harvard University Press, 2008) 124.

[128] *Harris v New York*, 401 US 222 (1971). See also *Oregon v Hass*, 420 US 714 (1975).

[129] ibid 225.

[130] *Miranda v Arizona*, 384 US 476, 477.

[131] *Harris v New York*, 401 US 231 (1971).

importantly, deterrence was 'only part of the larger objective of safeguarding the integrity of our adversary system',[132] stressed Justice Brennan; 'it is monstrous that courts should aid or abet the law-breaking police officer', he concluded.[133] In turning away from the constitutional basis for exclusion and towards deterrence as the exclusive rationale, *Harris* 'began the radical reformulation of *Miranda's* logic and the transformation of its rule of inadmissibility from a constitutional right into a mere exclusionary rule'.[134] It also created a substantial incentive for police officers to bypass *Miranda* rights in practice, with a view to either introducing un-Mirandised self-incriminating statements through the back door, as an impeachment device, or stopping the defendant from taking the stand altogether, 'virtually a no-lose situation for the police'.[135] The Supreme Court later acknowledged this risk in *Oregon v Hass*,[136] yet dismissed it as 'speculative possibility', noting that the balance had been struck in *Harris* and the Court was not disposed to change it.[137]

The Burger Court's growing antipathy towards *Miranda* was laid bare in *Michigan v Tucker*, a 'fruit of the poisonous tree' case, which allowed the use of testimony that had only been found as a result of self-incriminating statements obtained in violation of *Miranda*.[138] The procedural safeguards recognised by *Miranda* 'were not themselves rights protected by the Constitution', said the Court, 'but were, instead, measures to insure that the right against compulsory self-incrimination was protected'.[139] On that basis, the incomplete notification of the *Miranda rights* in *Tucker* was held not to violate the privilege. It had rather 'departed only from the prophylactic standards' laid down by *Miranda* 'to safeguard that privilege'.[140] *Miranda's* exclusionary rule was 'a judicially-devised dictate – not part of the Fifth Amendment's core protection'.[141] Exclusion for breach of the *Miranda* safeguards was not a constitutional right.

Tucker's undermining of *Miranda's* constitutional foundations created the conditions for a full-frontal assault in *New York v Quarles*,[142] where the Court

[132] ibid.

[133] ibid 232.

[134] J Tomkovicz, *Constitutional Exclusion* (Oxford, Oxford University Press, 2011) 149. See also C Weisselberg, 'Saving *Miranda*' (1998) 84 *Cornell Law Review* 109, 127.

[135] G Stone, 'The Miranda Doctrine in the Burger Court' (1977) *Supreme Court Review* 99, 112. Kamisar agrees with this point. Kamisar, 'Rise, Decline and Fall' (2012) 982.

[136] 'The officer may be said to have little to lose and perhaps something to gain by way of possibly uncovering impeachment material'. *Oregon v Hass*, 420 US 714, 723 (1975).

[137] ibid. See also Weisselberg, 'Saving *Miranda*' (n 134) 128.

[138] *Michigan v Tucker*, 417 US 433 (1974). *Oregon v Elstad*, 470 US 298 (1985) similarly made it clear that 'the *Miranda* presumption does not require that fruits of otherwise voluntary statements be discarded as inherently tainted' (470 US 298, 307). The suspect had made an incriminating statement without having been given the *Miranda* warnings. He was then advised of his *Miranda* rights at the police station, waived them and signed a written confession. The trial court excluded the first statement, but admitted the written confession. The Court held that 'though *Miranda* requires that the unwarned admission must be suppressed, the admissibility of any subsequent statement should turn in these circumstances solely on whether it is knowingly and voluntarily made' (470 US 298, 309).

[139] ibid 444.

[140] ibid 446.

[141] Tomkovicz, *Constitutional Exclusion* (2011) 113.

[142] *New York v Quarles*, 467 US 649 (1984).

created a 'public safety' exception to *Miranda*. This allows for the use of un-*Mirandised* statements in the prosecution's case in chief, when these have been obtained in exigent situations in which police officers ask questions by a concern for the public safety. The Court found that in this case there was an immediate necessity to ascertain the whereabouts of a gun discarded by the suspect, which the police believed posed a danger to public safety, as an accomplice might make use of it or it might later come into the possession of a customer or employee. In devising this exception, the Court relied on *Tucker's* finding that the *Miranda* warnings played the instrumental role of prophylaxis of the Fifth Amendment privilege against self-incrimination, but were not themselves constitutional rights.[143] The application of the exclusionary rule therefore depended on a cost benefit analysis, and the Court came to the conclusion that the need to protect the 'public safety' in situations like this outweighed the need for the prophylactic rule.[144] *Miranda* immediately became vulnerable to future attempts to weaken its effect.

In *Dickerson v United States*,[145] the Court of Appeals for the Fourth Circuit 'went for the kill', finding that, because exclusion for violations of *Miranda rights* was not a constitutional right, the Court could substitute other effective remedies for it. The Fourth Circuit applied 18 USC § 3501, a statute that had been enacted two years after *Miranda*, but that had not been applied in practice since then, due to *Miranda's* insurmountable constitutional obstacle.[146] With 18 USC § 3501 the admissibility of self-incriminating statements turned solely on whether they had been made voluntarily. The Fourth Circuit's decision created for the Supreme Court a real dilemma. It was faced with a choice between confirming that *Miranda's* exclusionary rule was a constitutional right – in which case it would also have to revisit its post-*Miranda* jurisprudence negating the exclusionary rule's constitutional basis – or the Fourth Circuit was correct, exclusion was not a constitutional right and 18 USC § 3501's voluntariness test could substitute for it.[147] There was hope, in other words, in both the anti- and pro-*Miranda* doctrinal camps, that the Supreme Court would take the opportunity to provide some clarity, after a long period of muddying the waters with a jurisprudence that was progressively chipping away the rule's original understanding while still proclaiming its adherence to its core tenets. But the Court failed terribly in that. On the one hand, it held that '*Miranda* [had] announced a constitutional rule that Congress may not supersede legislatively'.[148] This was a victory for *Miranda*. The rule was safe. 'The Court had an epiphany', as Thomas III and Leo graphically put it.[149] *Miranda* survived to

[143] ibid 654.

[144] ibid 657.

[145] *Dickerson v United States*, 530 US 428 (2000).

[146] See P Brooks, *Troubling Confessions: Speaking Guilt in Law and Literature* (Chicago, Chicago University Press, 2000) 33.

[147] See generally C Bateman, '*Dickerson v. United States*: *Miranda* is Deemed a Constitutional Rule, but Does it Really Matter ?' (2002) 55 *Arkansas Law Review* 177.

[148] *Dickerson v United States*, 530 US 428, 444 (2000).

[149] GC Thomas III and R Leo, *Confessions of Guilt – From Torture to Miranda and Beyond* (Oxford, Oxford University Press, 2012) 188.

live another day. On the other hand, the Court not only did not overrule its post-*Miranda* jurisprudence, it went so far as underline that its 'subsequent cases' had 'reduced the impact of the *Miranda* rule on legitimate law enforcement'.[150] The rule continued to be in force, but it was a rule considerably weakened by the exceptions and limitations that the Burger and Rehnquist Courts had created over the years. *Dickerson* had, quite paradoxically, left them intact.

The Court's logic left academic commentators in disbelief. A 'terribly disappointing' case,[151] reacted Klein, while Dripps stoically observed that the decision was a reminder that the Supreme Court can practically do what it likes, as it either had to 'repudiate the prophylactic-rule cases, or offer some ingenious reconciliation of the two lines of precedent', and it simply did neither.[152] Giving a more moderate response, Tomkovicz spoke of an 'ambiguous, even cryptic' ruling, which provided 'reason to believe that *Miranda's* exclusionary rule could be poised for a renaissance'.[153] He was right not to dismiss *Dickerson's* strong symbolism. We should not forget that *Dickerson* saved *Miranda* at a time when everyone thought it was dead in the water, while the opinion of the Court was written by Chief Justice Rehquist, a renowned opponent of the rule. 'Reaffirm[ing] the vitality of *Miranda*, albeit not in the most resounding terms, [was] of considerable significance', commented Mirfield on this side of the Atlantic.[154]

Dickerson's recognition of *Miranda's* constitutional character proved to be empty rhetoric though. The Court quickly reverted to its 'prophylactic'-orientated jurisprudence four years later, in *United States v Patane*, which recognised that *Miranda* did not require the exclusion of any derivative evidence, 'signal[ing] a return of the grudging attitude toward *Miranda* suppression and a determination to severely curtail its impact'.[155] Then *Thompkins*, discussed above, put the final, until now, nail in *Miranda's* coffin. *Thompkins* must be seen in the wider context of what Ronald Dworkin described in 2007 as the emerging 'right wing', 'unbreakable phalanx' at the Supreme Court, which was 'bent on remaking constitutional law by overruling, most often by stealth, the central constitutional doctrines that generations of past justices, conservatives as well as liberal, had constructed'.[156] The Court took, with it, one more step towards overruling *Miranda*, without conceding that it was doing so. If, on other hand, we were to assess the *Miranda* jurisprudence in isolation of the Supreme Court's continuous movement to the right, the following two explanations could perhaps be advanced about the reasons leading the Court

[150] *Dickerson v United States*, 530 US 428, 443 (2000).

[151] S Klein, '*Miranda's* Exceptions in a Post-*Dickerson* World' (2001) 91 *The Journal of Criminal Law & Criminology* 567, 568.

[152] DA Dripps, 'Constitutional Theory for Criminal Procedure: *Dickerson, Miranda*, and the Continuing Quest for Broad-But-Shallow' (2001) 43 *William and Mary Law Review* 1, 33.

[153] Tomkovicz (n 134) 118.

[154] P Mirfield, 'Miranda Exclusionary Rule Re-affirmed: *US v Dickerson*' (2001) 5 *International Journal of Evidence & Proof* 61.

[155] Tomkovicz (n 134) 120.

[156] R Dworkin, *The Supreme Court Phalanx, The New York Review of Books*, 27 September 2007.

to prioritise the ability to obtain statements over the need to provide full protection to the privilege against self-incrimination, as per *Miranda's* original understanding. Firstly, the Court no longer seems to believe that a violation of Miranda leads to compelled self-incrimination or an involuntary statement, and so it has progressively become comfortable with the use of coercive tactics by the police so long as there is no physical force or an express threat or promise. Secondly, we must look at *Miranda's* architecture, which makes invocation of *Miranda* rights an all-or-nothing proposition. That is, when a suspect invokes his *Miranda* rights, questioning must cease. There is no middle ground, in contrast with most European countries, where questioning will continue with counsel present (though, in many Continental countries, counsel will be present and limited to a passive role). The risk that the defendant will use *Miranda's* 'nuclear option' may therefore be making the Supreme Court loath to have the *Miranda* rights exercised except in the clearest and smallest possible set of cases.[157]

IV. Confessional Evidence, Reliability and Suspects' Rights: A Mixed Picture in the UK

Despite variations, American, French and Greek law are aligned as far as the use of mandatory exclusion as the appropriate response to violations of custodial interrogation rights is concerned. English law, on the other hand, remains engrained in the discretionary logic of section 78 of the Police and Criminal Evidence Act (PACE) 1984, and so it is a different beast entirely, as far as the procedural mechanism upon which exclusion operates is concerned. We still find in English law a longstanding concern for the protection of suspects' rights, notably through providing effective guarantees for the right to custodial legal assistance and – to a lesser degree – the right to silence. This concern has historically been translated into the courts exhibiting considerable willingness to exercise the section 78 discretion to exclude confessional evidence when the rights of the suspect have been breached, which can be contrasted with the passive approach that they routinely take towards the exercise of the same discretion in relation to evidence obtained in violation of the right to privacy. If one takes into consideration that English law also adopts a rule of mandatory exclusion for confessions obtained by oppression or in circumstances which could render the confession unreliable, then a mixed picture emerges, but it is one that is consistent with analysis in previous sections in this chapter, highlighting Anglo-American and Continental law rapprochement around the importance of effectively safeguarding custodial interrogation rights and excluding inherently unreliable evidence obtained in breach of these rights, particularly in contrast to exclusionary attitudes relating to tangible, inherently reliable, evidence obtained in violation of the right to privacy.

[157] I am grateful to Charles Weisselberg for discussion on these points (notes on file with author).

A. Exercising the Section 78 Discretion to Exclude Evidence Obtained in Violation of Suspects' Rights

Having previously looked at the historic background and modern applications of the section 78 discretion, in the context of the exclusion of evidence obtained in violation of the right to privacy,[158] it is now instructive to concentrate on the rich, but highly inconsistent, section 78 jurisprudence for confessional evidence obtained in violation of custodial interrogation rights, most notably the right to silence, the right to be assisted by a lawyer and have a lawyer present during interrogation, the right to have an appropriate adult present when a young person is questioned by the police and the right to a contemporaneous record, including audio-visual recording, of police questioning.[159]

Unlike the United States, where the duty of the police to issue the *Miranda* warnings is established in (the synonymous) case law, police officers in the UK must act in accordance with the provisions of PACE 1984, notably Code C of the Act which provides a list of requirements for the detention, treatment and questioning of suspects in police custody. Section 10 regulates when a caution must be given, and the terms in which it must be given, requiring the police to notify the suspect of the right to silence, but also of the power of the Court to draw adverse inferences if the suspect does 'not mention when questioned something which [he] later rel[ies] on in Court'.[160] The question therefore arises whether an omission from the part of the police to make these notifications should lead to the exclusion of any self-incriminating statements made by the suspect, and it is important to note from the outset that, compared to analysis of French, Greek and United States law, the position of English law is much more nuanced. Courts exercise their discretion to exclude improperly obtained confessional evidence based on a contextual analysis of whether the procedural violation in question would have an adverse effect on the fairness of the proceedings, relying *not* on a structured discretion that could operate upon a pre-determined set of factors – provided by legislation or judicial precedent – but rather a case-by-case approach which gives them significant leeway.

With reference to the duty to notify the suspect of his right to silence English courts have in this way paid particular attention to the question of whether breaches of the Code are "substantial". Non-notification after a long break in questioning would generate such a substantial breach for instance.[161] Non-notification

[158] See ch 4.

[159] These rights are enshrined in different provisions of the Police and Criminal Evidence Act (PACE) 1984 and its Code of Practice C for the detention, treatment and questioning of persons by Police Officers.

[160] Section 10, Code C PACE 1984.

[161] This is a violation of section 10.8 of Code of Practice C. See *R v Miller* [1998] Crim LR 209, 210, where the suspect had originally been notified of his rights, but the Court of Appeal underlined the importance of a new notification observing that 'in the anxiety of being arrested and questioned by

is 'in most circumstances bound to be significant',[162] with a 'deliberate' or 'flagrant' breach increasing the likelihood that the courts will make such a finding,[163] but exclusion is by no means a given and breaches of the Code do not in themselves require exclusion.[164] Ex post facto analysis by appellate courts on how (a hypothetical) notification of the right *would have* changed the outcome – inquiring, more specifically, whether notification would have enabled the suspect to exercise his right to silence – is often a key factor in determining whether non-notification should be seen as a substantial breach requiring exclusion.[165] It is not difficult to imagine that American exclusionary rule experts reading these lines may have shivers down the spine. The English Court of Appeal's logic would have no evidentiary consequences attaching to a failure to read the suspect his *Miranda rights* so long as the trial court could, somehow – hypothetically – establish that the suspect would *not* have exercised his *Miranda* rights even if notification had ensued. French and Greek commentators would also find this practice at odds with indigenous exclusionary rules. We have seen, for instance, how the Cour de cassation's new automatic nullities apply with particular force to non-notification of rights.

The English Court of Appeal's ex post facto analysis logic – which could perhaps be summarised as the court making an (informed, at best) guess about whether the presence of a lawyer would have stopped the suspect from making self-incriminatory statements – also applies to excluding confessional evidence obtained in violation of the right to custodial legal assistance. We can take the example of *Samuel*,[166] where the suspect denied his complicity in the offence four times, before eventually making self-incriminatory statements. But at the Court of Appeal, his lawyer gave evidence that he would have advised his client to remain silent had he been present. Or we can revisit *Walsh*,[167] where the suspect was denied the right to consult with his lawyer, and confessed, but quickly exercised his right to silence upon finally meeting with the lawyer. The Court of Appeal concluded in both cases that the suspects would not have spoken to the police if

those in authority it was possible to forget the rights of which the person had been earlier informed'. See also *R v Bryce* (1992) 95 Cr App R 320.

[162] *R v Pall* [1992] Crim LR 126, 127; *R v Keenan* (1990) 2 QB 54.

[163] *R v Sparks* [1991] Crim LR 128, 129.

[164] *R v Gill* [2003] 4 All ER 681.

[165] ibid. At [73] the Court of Appeal found that 'the judge was entitled to conclude, as in effect he did, that the presence of an appropriate adult would have made no difference'; the Court subsequently held that self-incriminating statements had therefore been properly adduced despite the absence and dismissed the appeal. See also *R v Sanusi* [1992] Crim LR 43. The suspect was originally not notified of his right to silence. The Court concluded that 'had [the suspect] been told earlier [of his rights] he would have declined to answer any questions'. It did so based on its observations that when the suspect was eventually informed of his rights, he asked for a solicitor and refused to answer further questions. In other words, the Court based its exclusionary finding on the assumption that 'had [the suspect] been told earlier [of his rights] he would have declined to answer any questions', which meant that non-notification had in effect deprived him of the opportunity to exercise his rights.

[166] *R v Samuel* [1988] 1 QB 615, 630.

[167] *R v Walsh* (1990) 91 Cr App R 161. See also *R v Parris* (1989) Cr App R 68, 72; *R v McGovern* (1991) 92 Cr App R 229, 234.

they had been given access – as PACE and Code of Practice C required – to their lawyers, and concluded that the evidence should therefore not have been admitted. The Court asked these 'what if' questions, and went on to deduce the answers to them from observations about how the key players – the suspects and their lawyers – acted at later stages of the process.

Using the same deductive apparatus, however, it reached the opposite conclusions in cases where it formed the view that the presence of the lawyer would *not* have influenced the behaviour of the suspect. We can see an illustration of this in two cases where the Court found that the suspects already knew their rights, and so the presence of the lawyer would have added nothing to knowledge they already possessed.[168] In one of these cases, the Court took into consideration the fact that the suspect had given a few 'no comment' answers, which indicated in itself a familiarity with the right to silence.[169] There is a real paradox here, in that knowing your rights places you at a disadvantage as to exercising them in practice.

The Court of Appeal's creative efforts to grapple with the discretionary logic's inherent complexities should not go unnoticed, and we should not forget that this, to some extent, is not a problem of its own making; the Pythic text of section 78 was the legislator's 'gift'. There is, however, much to be said about the deductive fallacies of the ex post facto rationalisation upon it rests. Setting aside for a moment the variability of the conditions that may affect the suspect's conduct, and the number of players – notably the solicitor and police officers involved – whose sheer presence may exercise an influence upon the nature of these conditions, there is also the fundamental problem of perceiving custodial legal assistance as an one-dimensional phenomenon, where the presence of a lawyer *only* or *exclusively* serves to impart on the suspect *knowledge* of his rights rather than provide guidance or assistance in the effective exercise of these rights. Hodgson was right to point out early in the development of the section 78 jurisprudence that if simple knowledge were enough, then the lawyer's presence when the suspect is questioned by the police would be redundant.[170] This is all the more the case after the introduction in 1994 of the power to draw adverse inferences when the suspect has exercised the right to silence.[171] Suspects knowing their rights is one thing, being able to exercise them effectively, particularly when there is the risk of significant adverse inferences being drawn against them, is quite another. Focus on knowledge alone also disregards the ability of the lawyer to provide psychological support to the suspect who is faced with the pressures inherent in custodial interrogation,[172]

[168] *R v Alladice* (1988) 87 Cr App R 380, 387; *R v Dunford* (1990) 91 Cr App R 150. See also *R v Oliphant* [1992] Crim LR 40.

[169] *R v Dunford*, ibid.

[170] J Hodgson, 'Tipping the Scales of Justice: The Suspect's Right to Legal Advice' [1992] *Criminal Law Review* 854.

[171] Criminal Justice and Public Order Act 1984, sections 34–39.

[172] I have recently chaired a Q & A panel following a screening of 'The Lost Honour of Christopher Jefferies'. The film tells the story of the subject in the title, a retired schoolteacher who had been wrongly accused of murdering Joanna Yeates, in a 'trial by media' that became one of the catalysts of the Leveson

which counter-balances, to some degree, the police officers' dominant presence and helps orientate the process towards better 'equality of arms'. The lawyer truly has a 'unique role' to play in custodial interrogation, as the 'watchdog of procedural regularity'.[173] It is equally important that the lawyer who attended the police station can provide a counterpoint to accounts offered by the police about what happened at the police station.[174]

Perhaps no one has encapsulated the lawyer's multi-dimensional role at the police station better than the European Court of Human Rights in *Dayanan v Turkey*, where the Court held that:

> the fairness of proceedings requires that an accused be able to obtain the whole range of services specifically associated with legal assistance. In this regard, counsel has to be able to secure without restriction the fundamental aspects of that person's defence: discussion of the case, organisation of the defence, collection of evidence favourable to the accused, preparation for questioning, support of an accused in distress and checking of the conditions of detention.[175]

In other words, *Dayanan* found that the right to legal assistance was going beyond the mere right to legal advice during police interrogation to cover other aspects of the lawyer's role during the entire interrogation phase.[176] In the same vein, the Court found a breach of article 6 in *Aras v Turkey (no 2)*, in a case where the suspect's lawyer had been 'allowed to enter the hearing room during the questioning' of the suspect, but 'this was a passive presence without any possibility at all to intervene to ensure respect for the applicant's rights'.[177] In view of these progressive fair trial-based accounts offered by Strasbourg, on the active and wide-ranging role that the lawyer should claim in custodial interrogation, it is difficult to escape the conclusion that the knowledge-only focused approach taken by UK courts in the context of section 78 is not going very far in providing the ex post facto protection required.

There are other interesting demonstrations of how the discretionary logic and hypothetical reasoning of the Court of Appeal are conducive to significant

Inquiry into press ethics. There is a moment in the film where the solicitor tells Jefferies, in the course of his long interrogation, that he would not be leaving the police station without him. I asked Jefferies about this in the Q & A. His response was that that moment alone had allowed him to get through the ordeal of being interrogated for an offence he had not committed. See Knowing our Rights, *Human rights and abuse of power by the press*, available at www.knowing-our-rights.com/human-rights-abuse-power-press.

[173] *Dvorski v Croatia* (2016) 63 EHRR 7, concurring opinion of Judges Kalaydjieva, Pinto de Albuquerque and Turković [OII-20].

[174] See *R v Walsh* [1989] Crim LR 822, 824, note Di Birch; M Doherty, 'Judicial Discretion: Victimising the Villains?' (1999) 3 *International Journal of Evidence & Proof* 44, 51.

[175] *Dayanan v Turkey*, Application No 7377/03, Merits and Just Satisfaction, 13 October 2009 [32].

[176] See JD Jackson, 'Responses to *Salduz*: Procedural Tradition, Change and the Need for Effective Defence' (2016) 97 *Modern Law Review* 987, 1008, who distinguishes between 'the protective role that the lawyer can play in ensuring that detained persons are not coerced into making confessions' and the 'representational role that is required in advising on the complexities of the case against the accused and gathering and using evidence'.

[177] *Aras v Turkey (no 2)*, Application No 15065/07, Merits and Just Satisfaction, 18 November 2014 [40].

variability of section 78 outcomes. The absence of an appropriate adult, when a young person is questioned by the police, will, in some cases, be taken to automatically lead to exclusion for instance.[178] But the Court of Appeal has made it clear, on the other hand, that the fact that there has been:

> a breach of the Codes of Conduct does not in itself mean that the evidence must be excluded. The learned judge must [...] decide specifically whether the admission of the evidence would have such an adverse effect on the fairness of the proceedings that the court ought not to admit it.[179]

In evaluating the potential for adverse effect the Court of Appeal again often grounds its pronouncements on second-guessing whether the suspect would have made the self-incriminatory statements regardless,[180] while also placing some emphasis on the nature of the procedural rights that have been violated. The more serious – substantial – breaches are contrasted with technical breaches.[181] The former are often taken as indicators of the need to exclude[182] while the latter's effect on the fairness of the proceedings is dismissed as insignificant.[183] The above also apply to breaches of the provisions that relate to contemporaneous interview records, a final case in point.[184]

In comparison to the automatic exclusion approach adopted in the United States, France and Greece, the position taken in English law remains nuanced, with courts retaining wide discretionary powers to admit self-incriminating evidence even where it has been obtained in violation of procedural safeguards that apply to police questioning. This should not take our attention away from the fact that, in comparison to how reluctant English courts are to exclude evidence obtained

[178] *R v Fogah* [1989] Crim LR 141. The suspect was a 16-year-old juvenile who confessed to being involved in a robbery after having been asked 16 questions during arrest in the street, without an appropriate adult being present. The Crown Court quickly concluded that the whole interview should have been excluded, as 'an appropriate adult who was designed to protect the defendant's interests was not present'.

[179] *R v Weekes* (1993) 97 Cr App R 222, 227.

[180] *R v Aspinall* [1999] 2 Cr App R 115.

[181] See, eg, *R v Keenan* (1990) 2 QB 54; *R v Okafor* [1994] Cr App R 97, 103.

[182] See *R v Absolam* (1989) 88 Cr App R 332, where the Court of Appeal opined, *per curiam*, that 'if the judge had concluded that there had been significant and substantial breaches of the Codes he would probably have excluded D's answers'. The editors of Archbold draw from this case the principle that 'the breach must be significant and substantial, and the more so, the more likely the judge is to exclude the evidence'. See Archbold, *Criminal Pleading Evidence and Practice* (London, Sweet & Maxwell-Thomson Reuters, 2017) [15-13]. Choo similarly argues that 'a "significant and substantial" breach of the rules will weigh heavily in favour of exclusion'. A L-T Choo, *Evidence*, 4th edn (Oxford, Oxford University Press, 2015) 101. See also CPS's legal guidance to Crown Prosecutors which explains that '[t]he Court will look for a significant and substantial breach before going on to consider whether or not to exclude evidence obtained as a result of the breach'. See CPS, *Confessions, Unfairly Obtained Evidence and Breaches of PACE*, available at https://www.cps.gov.uk/legal-guidance/confessions-unfairly-obtained-evidence-and-breaches-pace.

[183] See, eg, *R v Mathews, Dennison and Voss* (1990) 91 Cr App R 43, 45; *R v Park* (1994) 99 Cr App R 270, 277.

[184] See, eg, *R v Delaney* (1989) 88 Cr App R 338; *R v Dunn* (1990) 91 Cr App R 237; *R v Langiert* [1991] Crim LR 777. See sections 11.7–11.14 Code C PACE 1984.

in violation of the right to privacy, they take a favourable approach to excluding self-incriminating evidence. The parallel existence of a rule of mandatory exclusion for self-incriminating statements rendered unreliable in consequence of the methods used by the police to obtain them reinforces this point.

B. A Categorical Exclusionary Rule for Unreliable Evidence

We have previously seen how the common law had, already from the eighteenth century, adopted an automatic exclusionary rule for involuntary confessions.[185] Section 76(2) of the Police and Criminal Evidence Act 1984 continued with this tradition. It provides that:

> (2) If, in any proceedings where the prosecution proposes to give in evidence a confession made by an accused person, it is represented to the court that the confession was or may have been obtained—
>
> (a) by oppression of the person who made it; or
>
> (b) in consequence of anything said or done which was likely, in the circumstances existing at the time, to render unreliable any confession which might be made by him in consequence thereof,
>
> the court shall not allow the confession to be given in evidence against him except in so far as the prosecution proves to the court beyond reasonable doubt that the confession (notwithstanding that it may be true) was not obtained as aforesaid.

This novel exclusionary rule was the intellectual product of the work of the Criminal Law Revision Committee of 1972 and the Royal Commission on Criminal Procedure of 1981, which agreed that English law needed to signal its aversion for confessions obtained by oppression by instituting an automatic exclusionary rule.[186] 'The rule against admitting a confession which was not made voluntarily was based not only upon its potential unreliability', explained the House of Lords, 'but also upon the principle that a man cannot be compelled to incriminate himself and upon the importance attached in a civilised society to proper behaviour by the police towards those in their custody'.[187] We can trace an ambition here to rest section 76 upon a broad exclusionary rationale that goes beyond epistemic considerations related to reliability.

The material scope of the rule is equally broad to the rationale that underpins it, extending beyond evidence obtained by oppression to include confessional evidence 'obtained by any behaviour whatsoever which tends to make

[185] See *Ibrahim v The King* [1914] AC 599; *R v Harz* [1967] 1 AC 760; *Lam-Chi Ming v The Queen* [1991] 2 AC 212 cited by Lord Bingham of Cornhill in *A and others v Secretary of State for the Home Department (No 2)* [2006] 2 AC 221, 248. See also ch 4.

[186] See J Doak and C McGourlay, *Criminal Evidence in Context* (Exeter, Law Matters Publishing, 2005) 245.

[187] *R v Mushtaq* [2005] 1 WLR 1513, 1530, citing Lord Griffiths giving the opinion of the Privy Council in *Lam Chi-ming v The Queen* [1991] 2 AC 212, 220.

[the evidence] less reliable',[188] for example where there have been 'threats to withhold bail, charge more serious offences, or switch attention to the suspect's family members if he fails to co-operate; and promises of immediate release, reduced charges, or a lighter sentence in exchange for a confession'.[189]

Section 76(8) defines that 'oppression' 'includes torture, inhuman or degrading treatment, and the use or threat of violence (whether or not amounting to torture)'. Court of Appeal jurisprudence brought further precision to the concept, explaining in *R v Fulling* that:

> 'oppression' in section 76(2)(a) should be given its ordinary dictionary meaning. The Oxford English Dictionary as its third definition of the word runs as follows: 'Exercise of authority or power in a burdensome, harsh, or wrongful manner; unjust or cruel treatment of subjects, inferiors, etc.; the imposition of unreasonable or unjust burdens.' One of the quotations given under that paragraph runs as follows: 'There is not a word in our language which expresses more detestable wickedness than oppression.'[190]

As Choo observes, the Court of Appeal has interpreted the word oppression to mean 'fairly harsh treatment of the confessor' and so 'it is only in rare cases that the prosecution would be unable to prove that a confession was *not* obtained by oppression'.[191] Indeed, to exclude confessional evidence on the basis of oppression a high threshold must be crossed. A police officer being rude and discourteous to the suspect, and becoming impatient and irritated when questioning him, did not fulfil this requirement, found the Court of Appeal in *R v Emmerson*, even if the police officer had 'raised his voice and used some bad language' and 'was saying in effect that it was plain that the appellant had committed the offences and why was he wasting their time'.[192] In *R v Paris, Abdullahi and Miller* on the other hand, the Court of Appeal decision that brought to light the miscarriage of justice in the notorious 'Cardiff Three' case, the Lord Justices perceived the police behaviour as outrageous, even if they established that it did not involve physical violence.[193] The police in this case had aggressively interrogated one of the suspects, Miller, 'for some 13 hours', over five days. There were 19 tapes of the recordings, and Miller

[188] J Pradel, *Droit pénal comparé* (Paris, Dalloz, 1995) 422.

[189] P Roberts and A Zuckerman, *Criminal Evidence*, 2nd edn (Oxford, Oxford University Press, 2010) 532.

[190] *R v Fulling* [1987] QB 426, 432. But see Roberts and Zuckerman, *Criminal Evidence* (2010) 530, who argue that 'equating oppression with "detestable wickedness" surely goes too far' and who pinpoint alternative definitions in the Oxford English Dictionary that would be 'more appropriate' but have been 'ignored by the Court', such as 'the feeling of being oppressed or weighed down; bodily or mental uneasiness or distress'. See also the definition adopted by the Court of Appeal in *R v Prager* [1972] 1 WLR 260, 266, cited by Lord Carswell in the decision of the House of Lords in *R v Mushtaq* [2005] 1 WLR 1513,1536, according to which oppression is 'questioning which by its nature, duration or other circumstances (including the fact of custody) excites hopes (such as the hope of release) or fears, or so affects the mind of the subject that his will crumbles and he speaks when otherwise he would have stayed silent'. This interpretation of oppression is wide enough to include both components of section 76(2) – in sections 76(2)(a) and 76(2)(b) – and not just 'oppression' per se as defined in section 76(2)(a).

[191] Choo, *Evidence* (2015) 96; A L-T Choo, *The Privilege Against Self-Incrimination and Criminal Justice* (Oxford, Hart Publishing, 2013) 83.

[192] *R v Geoffrey Emmerson* (1991) 92 Cr App R 284.

[193] *R v Paris, Abdullahi and Miller* (1993) 97 Cr App R 99.

denied both participation and presence at the scene on tapes 1 to 7, beginning to accept that he was present in tapes 8 and 9. The suspect 'denied involvement well over 300 times', before being finally persuaded to make three admissions. But the trial Court admitted the self-incriminating statements, even if it was also presented with evidence that the suspect 'was on the borderline of mental handicap with an IQ of 75, a mental age of 11 and a reading age of eight'.[194] Lord Taylor, the Lord Chief Justice at the time, who gave the opinion of the Court, noted that, on hearing tape 7 in particular,

> each member of this Court was horrified. Miller was bullied and hectored. The officers … were not questioning him so much as shouting at him what they wanted him to say. Short of physical violence, it is hard to conceive of a more hostile and intimidating approach by officers to a suspect.[195]

The second prong of this mandatory exclusionary rule – section 76(2)(b) – allows English courts to extend their inquiries beyond oppression to much less straightforward cases, where it can be established that the confession was obtained in consequence of anything said or done which was likely, in the circumstances existing at the time, to render unreliable any confession which might be made by the person who confesses, even in cases where there has been no impropriety on the part of the questioner.[196] The Court does not concern itself with whether the confessional evidence in question was indeed rendered unreliable. It rather asks the hypothetical question of whether the confession was obtained in conditions that were, in general, conducive to unreliability.[197] If it answers this question in the affirmative the confession must be excluded 'notwithstanding that it may be true'.[198] In other words, section 76(2) institutes a categorical exclusionary rule based on the normative premise of 'promoting the reliability of confession evidence on aggregate and over time' rather than make its operation dependent upon 'case-specific inquiries and *ad hoc* exceptions'.[199] In this way, section 76(2) allows English courts to cast a wide net to prevent the admission of improperly obtained confessional evidence in court. Personal characteristics of the defendant that make him or her more susceptible to be influenced by something said or done – such as young age, being mentally handicapped or his or her naivety – will be taken into consideration, and a confession may be excluded even where the pressure or influence to make the confession did not originate from a police officer[200] or where the suspect

[194] ibid 105.

[195] ibid 103. In a report published in *The Guardian* at the time of the hearing at the Court of Appeal, Miller's counsel, Michael Mansfield QC, was quoted as stating that 'the officers [had] bullied his client… in order to mentally strip him down'. See 'Cardiff murder appeal man "beaten over head" verbally', *The Guardian*, 10 December 1992, available at www.theguardian.com/uk/1992/dec/10/cardiff-three-wales.

[196] See, eg, *R v Walker* [1998] Crim LR 211.

[197] R Munday, *Evidence*, 8th edn (Oxford, Oxford University Press, 2015) 430.

[198] Final clause of section 76(2).

[199] Roberts and Zuckerman, *Criminal Evidence* (n 189) 531.

[200] See eg *R v Harvey* [1988] Crim LR 241, where the defendant was a woman of low normal intelligence and was suffering from a psychopathic disorder. Psychiatric evidence raised the possibility that the defendant might have been prompted to make a confession on hearing her lover confess in

confesses in consequence of 'innocent representations and other conduct [which] may be such as to be likely to render a confession unreliable'.[201]

It must be noted, on the other hand, that the provision does not go so far as allow for influences due to an internal condition – for example, the suspect's own state of mind – to be conceived as something said or done that was likely to render the confession unreliable. This means that an addict who confesses as a result of withdrawal symptoms will not be able to rely upon section 76(2)(b).[202] Similarly, the exclusionary rule will not be triggered where the factor that influences the suspect has originated from himself or herself, such as in a case where the suspect instructed his solicitor to inquire with the police to see whether an arrangement could be made about his relatives who were also in custody.[203]

In view of the above, there appears to be considerable merit in the operation in English law of a categorical exclusionary rule that concentrates specifically on averting the use of potentially unreliable evidence, in present and future cases, and that aims to give effect to the privilege against self-incrimination and maintaining custodial interrogation methods appropriate for a civilised society at the same time. If we also take into account that this exclusionary rule operates in parallel with the discretionary exclusionary test for confessional evidence obtained in violation of suspects' rights (under section 78 PACE 1984) and that there are strong elements of exclusion in the latter – for example where there are significant and substantial breaches of the Codes of Practice and these procedural breaches had a material effect upon the way the suspect exercised his rights – then it can be easily concluded that English law provides a strong impetus, at least in theory, for the exclusion of improperly obtained confessional evidence. The extent to which

order to protect her. The trial court excluded the evidence based on the psychiatric evidence. The case provides a good example of how section 76(2)(b) has considerably extended the scope of exclusion of involuntary statements compared to the previous test under the common law, as this, per *Ibrahim v R* [1914] AC 599, would require the incentive to confess to proceed from a 'person in authority' and to be 'an inducement, in the technical sense of something which "excited fear of prejudice or hope of advantage', as noted in the case comment in the *Criminal Law Review*, ibid. See similarly *R v Barry* (1992) 95 Cr App R 384, where the police had told the suspect that 'it would be most beneficial' to his case if he assisted the police in recovering evidence (the property that the defendant was suspected of having stolen). The trial judge admitted the confessional evidence, then the Court of Appeal concluded that he 'had approached section 76(2) … with a narrow, contractual analysis, whereas a broad approach was required'. In *R v Dhorajiwala (Bhavna)* [2010] 2 Cr App R 21, the Court of Appeal, held, obiter dicta, that 'D's evidence … that she had been prevented from leaving the interview room; she had not been allowed access to legal advice, she was threatened that the consequence of what she was alleged to have done was prison and the interview was conducted in a threatening manner' could have raised a reasonable argument for exclusion on either limb of section 76(2).

[201] *JA v The Queen* [2010] EWCA Crim 1506.

[202] *R v Goldenberg* (1989) 88 Cr App R 285. In *R v De Silva (Marc Anthony)* [2003] 2 Cr App R 5, the defendant had been induced by the officers to incriminate himself on the basis that he would receive a reduced sentence. The Court of Appeal concluded that it was fundamentally, inherently unfair to admit the evidence, 'notwithstanding that the officers had acted in good faith, had not used coercion or bullying, had not falsely misled D and had provided legal advice to D'. This suggests how far-reaching the application of section 76(2) can be (even if in this case the Court of Appeal upheld the conviction of the defendant notwithstanding the wrongful admission, on the basis that the case against D was overwhelming).

[203] *R v Wahab* [2003] 1 Cr App R 15.

this theoretical impetus transforms into exclusion in practice is a different matter. The variability of outcomes inherent in the discretionary test of section 78 leads to a blurred view of the law in action.

We must also not overlook scholarly accounts that minimise the significance of the application of the exclusionary rule of section 76(2) in practice, in view of the intricate relationship with discretionary exclusion under section 78. Fenwick offers a pessimistic view. Confessional evidence is rarely excluded through section 76(2), she argues, literally because judges strongly wish to safeguard their discretionary power to determine the admissibility of such evidence.[204]

Considered in the round, English law on the exclusion of improperly obtained confessional evidence can lead to intriguing comparative law inquiries. It offers an illustration of a novel exclusionary system that brings together a mandatory exclusionary rule with a test of discretionary exclusion, even with the caveat that the operation of the one – the discretionary test – seemingly undermines the operation of the other. It also offers a view of an exclusionary solution focused on preventing the use of unreliable evidence, thus exposing significant gaps in other Anglo-American and Continental legal systems which, in modern times, have shifted their attention to indirect ways of achieving this aim, notably by attaching an exclusionary remedy to violations of relevant procedural rights. French and Greek law are a case in point, where despite the rise of automatic procedural nullities for breaches of suspects' rights, there are no exclusionary devices allowing for the independent investigation of the quality of the confessional evidence in question.[205] This means that, if the courts there satisfy themselves that the relevant provisions affording the suspect specific custodial interrogation rights – such as the right to silence or the right to legal advice – have been respected, they will not be required to undertake a separate inquiry about whether the confession has nonetheless been obtained in a way which was likely to render it unreliable.

[204] H Fenwick, *Civil Liberties and Human Rights* (London-Sydney, Cavendish Publishing, 2002) 880. See also M Delmas-Marty, 'Necessity, legitimacy and feasibility of the Corpus Juris' in M Delmas-Marty and JAE Vervaele, *The Implementation of the Corpus Juris in the Member States*, vol I (Antwerpen, Groningen, Oxford, Intersentia, 2000) 27. Choo alludes to the same fact when he notes that '[s]ection 78 is of very considerable practical importance in the context of the possible exclusion of confession evidence, possibly more than section 76(2) itself'. Choo, *Privilege Against Self-Incrimination* (2013) 83. Grevling argues too that '[i]t is evident that many cases which could have fallen to be decided under section 76 are instead being considered by the courts under section 78(1)' and this is why 'the jurisprudence on section 76 remains surprisingly underdeveloped given the difficulties of interpreting it'. K Grevling, 'Fairness and the Exclusion of Evidence Under Section 78(1) of the Police and Criminal Evidence Act' (1997) 113 *Law Quarterly Review* 667, 667–68.

[205] Weigend makes the wider observation, with respect to the German criminal process, that 'a lack of reliability certainly is not a legitimate ground for excluding evidence', as, in the absence of a lay jury and as a result of systemic confidence in the ability of professional judges to assess the reliability and persuasiveness of the evidence, there is a 'tendency to let everything come in'. T Weigend, 'Throw It All Out? Judicial Discretion in Dealing with Procedural Faults' in M Caianiello and J Hodgson, *Discretionary Criminal Justice in a Comparative Context* (North Carolina, Carolina Academic Press, 2015) 185, 189.

It is even more opportune to juxtapose section 76(2) with the exclusion of improperly obtained confessions in US law where a voluntariness test, which paid attention to considerations similar to those that inform the application of the exclusionary rule under section 76(2), has historically played an important role in the development of the exclusionary rule there and remains in force today, even if there is little scope for its application in practice. Discussion of American law in this chapter has so far focused on the *Miranda* exclusionary rule, but it is now appropriate to remind the reader that *Miranda* was designed as a replacement for the case-by-case approach that was previously adopted under this voluntariness test, which came to be known as the 'due process voluntariness totality of the circumstances test'. Exclusion under this test has always depended (and still depends) on the circumstances of each particular case. An involuntary confession can be excluded where it can be demonstrated that it was not 'the product of [the suspect's] free and rational choice'[206] and 'his will was simply overborne'.[207]

Brown v Mississippi was the history-changing judgment in which the Supreme Court concluded for the first time that the Constitution, through the Fourteenth Amendment, barred the use of coerced confessions in the States.[208] The Court was so repelled by the use of torture in this case that it drew an analogy with 'the chief inequity, the crowning infamy, of the Star Chamber and the Inquisition, and other similar institutions'.[209] The widespread use of torture during this period – known as the 'third degree' or, when viewed from outside the United States, 'the American method'[210] – led the Supreme Court to focus its inquiries on sheer reliability issues in a first phase of development for the voluntariness test.[211] But with time, coercive techniques employed by the police became more subtle, and more difficult to identify,[212] and so the Supreme Court abstracted the locus of explanation for the exclusion of confessional evidence from pure reliability issues and relocated it in a wider concept of fairness. In *Lisenba v California* it held that:

> The aim of the requirement of due process is not to exclude presumptively false evidence, but to prevent fundamental unfairness in the use of evidence, whether true or false … As applied to a criminal trial, denial of due process is the failure to observe

[206] *Greenwald v Wisconsin*, 390 US 519, 521 (1968).

[207] *Mincey v Arizona*, 437 US 385 (1978).

[208] *Brown v Mississippi*, 297 US 278 (1936).

[209] ibid 287, citing *Fisher v State*, 145 Miss 116, 134, 110 So 361, 365.

[210] Thomas III and Leo, *Confessions of Guilt* (2012) 112.

[211] See eg *Chambers v State of Florida* 390 US 227 (1940), where the Court characterised the evidence in question as 'confessions of murder procured by repeated inquisitions of prisoners without friends or counselors present, and under circumstances calculated to inspire terror'. For five days, the suspects were subjected to interrogations culminating in an all-night examination, and over this period 'they steadily refused to confess, and disclaimed any guilt'. Torture was part of 'tyrannical governments' and 'secret inquisitorial processes', opined the Supreme Court. See also W Ritz, 'Twenty-Five Years of State Criminal Confession Cases in the U.S. Supreme Court' (1962) 19 *Washington and Lee Law Review* 35, 43; *Ward v Texas* 316 US 547 (1942).

[212] See generally D Huitema, 'Miranda: Legitimate Response to Contingent Requirements of the Fifth Amendment' (2000) 18 *Yale Law & Policy Review* 261, 282.

> that fundamental fairness essential to the very concept of justice. In order to declare a denial of it, we must find that the absence of that fairness fatally infected the trial; the acts complained of must be of such quality as necessarily prevents a fair trial. Such unfairness exists when a coerced confession is used as a means of obtaining a verdict of guilty.[213]

In deciding whether the admission of improperly obtained confessional evidence would prevent a fair trial courts are therefore required to undertake a complex balancing exercise, assessing the effect of both the personal characteristics of the suspect and the circumstances relevant to the questioning. Put differently, courts determine admissibility on grounds of fairness by undertaking an evaluation of 'the subjective capacity of the suspect to resist police pressure', on the one hand, *and* 'the objective tendency of the police methods to cause a typical suspect to confess', on the other.[214] Personal characteristics include the age of the suspect,[215] the fact that the suspect was suffering from physical injury or emotional stress, or that he was under the influence of alcohol or drugs[216] and these can be opposed to the suspect being of 'high intelligence, maturity and extensive experience with law enforcement'.[217] Circumstances relating to police questioning that the Supreme Court has objectively assessed as leading a typical suspect to confess include the use of torture,[218] threatening the suspect with the use of force,[219] suggestive questioning combined with threats and promises, by a supposedly friendly person who is brought into the interrogation ('false friend' method),[220] holding the interview away of the police station without advice of counsel, friends or family,[221] not notifying suspects of their right to silence and depriving them of access to legal assistance,[222] or holding suspects incommunicado without access to legal assistance, with very little food or other support.[223]

[213] *Lisenba v California*, 314 US 219, 236–37 (1941).

[214] D Dripps, 'Constitutional Theory for Criminal Procedure: Dickerson, Miranda, and the Continuing Quest For Broad – But Shallow' (2001) 34 *William & Mary Law Review* 1, 9. It is worth noting that the subjective and objective elements need to coincide. As the Supreme Court held in *Colorado v Connelly*, 479 US 157 (1986) '[c]oercive police activity is a necessary predicate to finding that a confession is not "voluntary" within the meaning of the Due Process Clause … While a defendant's mental condition may be a "significant" factor in the "voluntariness" calculus, this does not justify a conclusion that his mental condition, by itself and apart from its relation to official coercion, should ever dispose of the inquiry into constitutional "voluntariness"'.

[215] *Cf Haley v Ohio*, 332 US 596 (1948), where the suspect was 15 years old and *Crooker v California*, 357 US 433 (1958), where the suspect was a mature person of 31 years of age.

[216] See W LaFave, J Israel and N King, *Criminal Procedure*, Hornbook Series (St Paul, Minnessota, West Group, 2000) 316.

[217] Tomkovicz (n 134) 87.

[218] *Williams v New York*, 341 US 97 (1951).

[219] See *Payne v Arkansas* 356 US 560 (1958); *Rogers v Richmond* 365 US 534 (1961); *Lynumn v Illinois* 372 US 528 (1963).

[220] *Leyra v Denno*, 347 US 556 (1954). In this case a psychologist pretending to act as a 'doctor' was brought into questioning, supposedly to give the suspect medical relief.

[221] *Fikes v Alabama*, 352 US 191 (1957).

[222] *Haynes v Washington*, 373 US 503 (1963); *Davis v North Carolina*, 384 US 737 (1966).

[223] *Payne v Arkansas*, 356 US 560 (1958).

There are clear parallels with section 76(2) here, which equally operates by reference to external pressures and influences, and the characteristics of the suspect that affect his susceptibility to make self-incriminating statements in consequence of such external factors, with both the English and American systems also recognising that internal conditions alone are not likely to generate unfairness or render a confession unreliable.[224] Viewing the totality of circumstances test through English law lenses, American commentators may therefore be prepared to question the limited role that modern US Supreme Court jurisprudence affords voluntariness inquiries in the post-*Miranda* world. Section 76(2) may help them stand on its head the assumption that where law enforcement authorities have abided by *Miranda's* requirements, there is no scope to evaluate whether self-incriminating statements have been obtained involuntarily, and whether their admission would deny the defendant a fair trial. This assumption is firmly grounded on US Supreme Court jurisprudence. In *Berkemer v McCarty* the Court makes the point succinctly, leaving little room for doubt:

> We do not suggest that compliance with *Miranda* conclusively establishes the voluntariness of a subsequent confession. But cases in which a defendant can make a colorable argument that a self-incriminating statement was 'compelled' despite the fact that the law enforcement authorities adhered to the dictates of *Miranda* are rare.[225]

Weisselberg echoes these concerns. '[T]he voluntariness doctrine theoretically exists alongside *Miranda*', he notes, but *Miranda* 'has practically displaced voluntariness determinations'.[226] He takes Justice Souter's opinion in *Missouri v Seibert* as a good illustration of this point: 'giving the warnings and getting a waiver has generally produced a virtual ticket of admissibility; maintaining that a statement is involuntary even though given after warnings and voluntary waiver of rights requires unusual stamina, and litigation over voluntariness tends to end with the finding of a valid waiver'.[227]

Against this backdrop, section 76(2) may be able to offer an intriguing comparative law perspective to American commentators. Exclusionary questions relating to compliance with *Miranda*-like safeguards in English law – covered mainly under section 78 PACE 1984 – are independent of reliability considerations central to the exclusionary rule under section 76(2). A finding of admissibility under the former does not necessarily bar the Court from excluding evidence that was likely to have been rendered unreliable under the latter. English law genuinely operates a dual

[224] We must not overlook, however, that section 76(2) goes further than the 'totality of circumstances test' in allowing for exclusion even where the source of the influence has not been an official party. The United States Supreme Court explained in *Colorado v Connelly* that even 'the most outrageous behavior by a private party seeking to secure evidence against a defendant does not make that evidence inadmissible under the Due Process Clause', citing *Walter v United States*, 447 US 649, 656 (1980); *Coolidge v New Hampshire*, 403 US 443, 487–488 (1971); *Burdeau v McDowell*, 256 US 465 (1921).

[225] *Berkemer v McCarty*, 468 US 420, 433 (1984).

[226] C Weisselberg, 'Mourning *Miranda*' (2008) 96 *California Law Review* 1519, 1596.

[227] ibid 1597. *Missouri v Seibert*, 542 US 600, 608–09 (2004).

test for the admissibility of improperly obtained confessions. The United States might want to take a closer look at this practice. The need to do so is reinforced by modern critiques of *Miranda* which bring to light the full force of contemporary US Supreme Court jurisprudence that has weakened the effect of *Miranda's* exclusionary rule. Thomas III and Leo make this point well:

> The *Miranda* warning and waiver ritual … makes almost no difference in American police interrogation because virtually all suspects waive (or are legally constructed to have waived) their *Miranda* rights, and almost no confession is ever excluded from evidence at trial because of a *Miranda* violation. For the large universe of suspects who waive their rights, the *Miranda* 'revolution' did not protect them from police interrogation. Instead, *Miranda* has effectively deprived those suspects of the voluntariness flourish that the FDR Court created from the due process clause. Thus, odd though it may sound, and as totally weird as it would have sounded to the nine members of the *Miranda* Court, a case can be made that suspects as a whole are worse off now when they get to court than before *Miranda* was decided.[228]

In other words, Supreme Court jurisprudence first uprooted the voluntariness test from the centre of the exclusionary system, then minimised the effect of *Miranda* exclusionary safeguards themselves. This had as a result that defendants are today often faced with the 'double whammy' of effectively not being able to rely on *Miranda's* protections, in all these cases where they are taken to have waived their rights, and not being able to rely on the due process voluntariness test either, once they have been read – and taken to have waived – their *Miranda* rights. Hence the paradox of suspects arguably being in a worse position now than before *Miranda*, at least as far as evidentiary exclusion is concerned;[229] in the past they could have the admissibility of their confessions tested on the basis of the voluntariness test.

Faced with these inherent contradictions in contemporary applications of *Miranda*, even commentators friendly to its legendary exclusionary rule are beginning to contemplate the prospect that abolishing *Miranda's* warning and waiver requirements might actually 'do some good': 'At a minimum, it could clear the way for full assessments of voluntariness … and could promote candid discussions of police practice and [the privilege against self-incrimination]'.[230] In offering a comparative vista of a system where such assessments of voluntariness to some degree co-exist with exclusion based on breaches of *Miranda*-like procedural guarantees, English law can perhaps demonstrate that there might be a better way.

[228] Thomas III and Leo (n 149) 208. See also Weisselberg, 'Exporting and Importing *Miranda*' (n 113) 1236, who explains that 'when used as directed, *Miranda* now functions mostly as a "safe harbor" for police. If officers comply with its formalisms and obtain a statement, law enforcement can typically avoid a more searching inquiry into the voluntariness of the statement, and there is rarely a barrier to admissibility'.

[229] Thomas III and Leo (n 149) 208. It is indeed a different matter 'whether suspects are also worse off in the police interrogation room'. Ibid.

[230] Weisselberg, 'Mourning *Miranda*' (2008) 1597.

V. Concluding Thoughts

As we continue to delve into the exclusionary rules for improperly obtained confessional evidence in four Anglo-American and Continental legal systems, fascinating transmutations, ongoing controversies and the potential for close interaction between these legal systems begin to reveal themselves, and we identify an emerging rapprochement on the importance of custodial interrogation rights and the risks inherent in the use of potentially unreliable evidence,[231] particularly when we contrast these developments with significant divergence over exclusionary rules for evidence obtained in violation of the right to privacy. In France, we observe a radical transition from private interest, non-automatic, nullities, based on ad hoc findings of procedural harm, which are rarely established in practice, to procedural nullities that are automatically triggered by violations of rights of the suspect. We see that Greece regulates the police interrogation stage with similar rigour, applying automatic nullities to violations of defence rights, in line with the rigorous exclusionary standards applying to violations of the right to privacy in the country. It is equally noteworthy that in both countries an understanding of suspects' rights not just as reflections of individual interest, but also as values whose protection serves the public interest, as integral elements of the rule of law and a democratic criminal process, is gaining momentum.

Continuing on this comparative law track, we note how United States Supreme Court jurisprudence has dramatically minimised the effect of *Miranda rights*, by narrowing their scope and introducing a number of exceptions to the exclusionary rule. But we can't fail to notice, on the other hand, that American commentators have been predicting the death of *Miranda* for many years now,[232] and that *Miranda's* automatic logic has nonetheless survived unscathed, at least where *Miranda rights* apply and exceptions to the exclusionary rule aren't. Furthermore, in the eyes of foreign observers, accustomed to far less stringent domestic approaches to custodial interrogation rights, *Miranda* can also be said to retain much of its original appeal, as a quite idiosyncratic categorical exclusionary rule that puts constitutional rights first and reliability or the public interest in the conviction of the guilty second. This is the level of protection that exclusionary rules in France and Greece emulate, even if their development has not necessarily been influenced by American standards. The American, French and Greek exclusionary rules have had different starting points, and are perhaps moving, at

[231] See also A Soo, '(Effective) Remedies for a Violation of the Right to Counsel during Criminal Proceedings in the European Union: An Empirical Study' (2018) 14 *Utrecht Law Review* 18, 29, who concludes, on the basis of empirical findings, that self-incriminating statements obtained in violation of the right to custodial legal assistance would be excluded from criminal trials in 23 out of the 28 member states of the European Union.

[232] See, eg, BJ Gilday, 'The Exclusionary Rule: Down and Almost Out' (1977) 4 *Northern Kentucky Law Review* 1; A Garcia, 'Is *Miranda* Dead, Was It Overruled, or Is It Irrelevant' (1998) 10 *St Thomas Law Review* 461; GC Thomas III, 'The End of the Road for *Miranda v Arizona*? On the History and Future of Rules for Police Interrogation' (2000) 37 *American Criminal Law Review* 1; Kamisar (n 122) 965.

different speeds, towards different destinations, but they can now be seen as meeting at the same crossroads, where there is a common understanding around the need for violations of suspects' rights to not go unchecked and around the role of exclusionary rules in ensuring that this happens.

English law takes a different path to protecting these rights, opting for discretionary exclusion. But this is a discretion that courts seem to be more prepared to exercise, vis-à-vis discretionary exclusion for violations of the right to privacy. Significant and substantial breaches, and bad faith from the part of the police, are factors English courts take into account, even if they are not determinative of the outcome of the exercise of discretion per se and much depends on the circumstances of the case. More importantly, discretionary exclusion for breaches of suspects' rights goes hand in hand with a strict exclusionary rule applying to confessions obtained by oppression and confessions obtained in circumstances which were likely to render them unreliable. In this respect, English law goes further than American, Greek and French law in providing protection against the use of unreliable confessional evidence, even if it does not take an equally categorical approach to excluding evidence where custodial interrogation rights have not been respected.

Significant though these domestic law developments are in themselves, they should not be seen in isolation. We will therefore now begin to describe the tectonic shifts that we are simultaneously witnessing in European Court of Human Rights (ECtHR) jurisprudence and EU legislation in relation to custodial interrogation rights and the judicial remedies applying to their violations. These shifts can substantially influence – and be substantially influenced by – developments in the national legal systems, as far as European countries are concerned, and they are pertinent to legal systems outside Europe as well, notably the United States, where it will naturally be interesting to connect *Miranda's* erosion with modern ECHR jurisprudence, which gave birth to a *Miranda*-like rights-based exclusionary rule (but then went on to attack the basic premise upon which the exclusionary rule had been founded) and EU legislation that seeks to solidify the effect of *Miranda*-like rights.

5

Confessional Evidence and European Court of Human Rights Jurisprudence: Building Rights-based Consensus or Backtracking on Rights Protection?

Chapter four traced significant movement towards a common understanding in Anglo-American and Continental law around the need to take rights seriously when adducing self-incriminating evidence in criminal proceedings. Chapter five will now bring to light that these merging approaches at the comparative law level coincide with seminal jurisprudential developments at the regional human rights level, with the European Court of Human Rights (ECtHR) reading into the right to legal assistance an automatic exclusionary rule for improperly obtained self-incriminatory statements. The *Salduz v Turkey* jurisprudence[1] signals for the first time a potential departure from the Court's longstanding position that the admissibility of evidence is primarily a matter for regulation under national law,[2] which has tremendous scope to accelerate the rapprochement across national jurisdictions around the exclusion of confessional evidence obtained in violation of the right to fair trial.

This is all the more so since the same ECtHR jurisprudence has in recent years fuelled a suspects' rights revolution in Europe, within contracting parties[3] but also

[1] *Salduz v Turkey* (2008) EHRR 421.

[2] See generally *Schenk v Switzerland* (Application No 10862/84, 12 July 1988) [46].

[3] See generally J Alix, 'Les droits de la défense au cours de l'enquête de police après la réforme de la garde à vue: état de lieux et perspectives' (2011) *Recueil Dalloz* 1699; J Blackstock, E Cape, J Hodgson, A Ogorodova and T Spronken, *Inside Police Custody: An Empirical Account of Suspects' Rights in Four Jurisdictions* (Cambridge, Intersentia, 2014); J Chalmers and F Leverick, '"Substantial and Radical Change": A New Dawn for Scottish Criminal Procedure?' (2012) 75 *Modern Law Review* 837; A Dorange and S Field, 'Reforming Defence Rights in French Police Custody: A Coming Together in Europe?' (2012) 16 *International Journal of Evidence & Proof* 153; D Giannoulopoulos, 'Custodial Legal Assistance and Notification of the Right to Silence in France: Legal Cosmopolitanism and Local Resistance' (2013) 24 *Criminal Law Forum* 291; D Giannoulopoulos, '"North of the Border and Across the Channel": Custodial Legal Assistance Reforms in Scotland and France' [2013] *Criminal Law Review* 369; D Giannoulopoulos, 'Strasbourg Jurisprudence, Law Reform and Comparative Law: A Tale of the Right to Custodial Legal Assistance in Five Countries' (2016) 16 *Human Rights Law Review* 103; J Hodgson, 'Safeguarding Suspects' Rights in Europe: A Comparative Perspective' (2011) 14 *New Criminal Law Review* 611; JF Renucci, 'L'avocat et la garde à vue: exigences européennes et réalités nationales' (2009) *Recueil Dalloz* 2897; Sénat de Belgique, Commission de la Justice, Rapport 'Les suites de l'arrêt Salduz', 2 March 2011.

at the transnational level. A host of procedural EU directives have followed the lead of the ECtHR, creating common minimum standards across EU member states to ensure that basic pre-trial rights of suspects are protected sufficiently.[4] This unique combination of uniform procedural standards being introduced at a fast pace in police station procedures across Europe, and an emerging interventionist approach by Strasbourg on evidential matters, creates outstanding momentum for the existing rapprochement between national jurisdictions on the exclusion of confessional evidence to crystallise into a wider consensus.

This would be all well and good, had it not been for the Grand Chamber judgment in *Ibrahim v UK*,[5] which has now put the longevity of the *Salduz* jurisprudence into doubt, by reversing its key tenet that the interrogation of the suspect in the absence of a lawyer will irretrievably prejudice the rights of the suspect and result in a violation of the right to fair trial. *Ibrahim* instead requires courts to assess the overall fairness of the trial, which means that self-incriminating evidence obtained in the absence of a lawyer can eventually be admitted in trial where other procedural safeguards applied. *Ibrahim* can considerably slow down, if not bring to an end, the *Salduz*-generated trend in domestic law towards automatic exclusion of self-incriminating evidence obtained in violation of the right to custodial legal assistance. Comparative analysis is most timely here, including, arguably, as a factor that the Strasbourg Court must take into consideration when determining the future directions of this crucial jurisprudence. As this chapter will demonstrate, a potential departure from *Salduz* – such as the one implicitly attempted in *Ibrahim* – must be assessed in the context of the fundamental reforms *Salduz* itself has already generated across Europe, both in terms of enhancing safeguards giving effect to the right to legal assistance as well as introducing an exclusionary remedy for violations of the latter, but also in the context of the emergence of a common understanding in Anglo-American and Continental law, as illustrated in chapter four, that respect of custodial interrogation rights is a precondition for the use of confessional evidence in criminal trials. *Ibrahim's* 'unfortunate' timing must also be assessed against the backdrop of the growing influence of the relevant EU directives, and we must ask the pressing question of how the EU's move towards uniform procedural rights can possibly be reconciled with the ECtHR's backtracking on the judicial remedies that should apply to violations of these rights. This will also be a question about 'leading and following', when Strasbourg and the EU

[4] See generally M Jimeno-Bulmes, 'The EU Roadmap for Strengthening Procedural Rights of Suspected or Accused Persons in Criminal Proceedings' (2009) *Eucrim* 157; J Blackstock, 'Procedural Rights in the European Union: a Road Well Travelled?' (2012) 2 *European Criminal Law Review* 23; C Morgan, 'Where Are We Now with EU Procedural Rights?' (2012) 4 *European Human Rights Law Review* 428; I Anagnostopoulos, 'The Right of Access to a Lawyer in Europe: A Long Road Ahead?' (2014) 4 *European Criminal Law Review* 3; Ed Cape and J Hodgson, 'The Right to Access to a Lawyer at Police Stations – Making the European Union Directive Work in Practice' (2014) 5 *New Journal of European Criminal Law* 4; I Anagnostopoulos, 'Defendants' Rights in the European Union – The Directives 2010/64/EU and 2012/13/EU' (Athens, PN Sakkoulas, 2017) (in Greek).

[5] *Ibrahim and others v the United Kingdom*, nos 50541/08, 50571/08, 50573/08 and 40351/09, 13 September 2016.

institutions are dancing together; who is doing the leading and who is doing the following? If Strasbourg has taken the first steps with *Salduz* and its progeny, and the EU followed with the directives, it may now be the latter's turn to show the way.

I. The European Court of Human Rights' *Miranda* Moment: The *Salduz* Jurisprudence

Until the seminal judgment of the Grand Chamber of the European Court of Human Rights (ECtHR) in *Salduz v Turkey*,[6] the Court was accepting that pre-trial violations, such as violations of the right to custodial legal assistance, were not in themselves leading to violations of the right to fair trial under Article 6 of the European Convention on Human Rights (ECHR). In assessing trial fairness, the Court was having regard to the totality of the proceedings.[7] The use of self-incriminating statements obtained during police questioning in the absence of a lawyer did not ipso facto constitute a violation of the right to fair trial where, for example, there was other evidence to support the convictions.[8] The Court was not subscribing to a 'rights theory' which would require automatic exclusion of the evidence in question in order to vindicate the Convention rights breached.[9] Any fair trial shortcomings at the pre-trial stage could be cured by the provision of legal assistance and the exercise of other procedural guarantees at later stages of the criminal process,[10] and violations of substantive rights did 'not give rise *per se* to the obligation to exclude the evidence thereby obtained'.[11] The Court, importantly, had long resisted reading any rules on the admissibility of evidence into Article 6, considering this 'primarily a matter for regulation under national law'.[12]

The ECtHR made a historic U-turn in *Salduz*. The suspect was a minor of 17 years of age who had been interrogated at an anti-terrorism branch of the Turkish police in the absence of a lawyer, making several admissions about his involvement in the suspected offences. The case was first examined by a Chamber

[6] *Salduz v Turkey* (2008) EHRR 421.

[7] See, eg, *Imbrioscia v Switzerland*, 24 November 1993, Series A no 275; *John Murray v the United Kingdom*, 8 February 1996, *Reports of Judgments and Decisions* 1996-I; *Averill v the United Kingdom*, no 36408/97, ECHR 2000-VI; *Magee v the United Kingdom*, no 28135/95, ECHR 2000-VI; and *Brennan v the United Kingdom*, no 39846/98, ECHR 2001-X.

[8] See, eg, a series of ECtHR cases relied upon by the Turkish Government in the *Salduz* case: *Saraç v Turkey*, no 35841/97, 2 September 2004; *Yurtsever v Turkey*, no 42086/02, 31 August 2006; *Uçma v Turkey*, no 15071/03, 3 October 2006; *Yavuz and Others v Turkey*, no 38827/02, 21 November 2006; and *Yıldız v Turkey*, nos 3543/03 and 3557/03, 5 December 2006.

[9] See ch 6. See also JD Jackson and SJ Summers, *The Internationalisation of Criminal Evidence – Beyond the Common Law and Civil Law Traditions* (Cambridge, Cambridge University Press, 2012) 194.

[10] See generally A Flynn, J Hodgson, J McCulloch and B Naylor, 'Legal Aid and Access to Legal Representation: Redefining the Right to a Fair Trial' (2016) 40 *Melbourne Law Review* 207, 232.

[11] V Costa Ramos, 'The Rights of the Defence According to the ECtHR – An Illustration in the Light of *A.T. v. Luxembourg* and the Right to Legal Assistance' (2016) 7 *New Journal of European Criminal Law* 397, 410.

[12] *Schenk v Switzerland* (1991) 13 EHRR 242.

of the ECtHR which found no violation of the right to fair trial, on the basis that the applicant had had legal representation during the trial and appeal proceedings, his statement was not the sole basis for conviction, the applicant had had the opportunity of challenging the prosecution's allegations and the Turkish Court that convicted the applicant had had regard to the circumstances of his arrest as well as other evidence that demonstrated his guilt.[13] This finding was in line with the pre-*Salduz* approach of assessing fairness with regard to the entirety of the proceedings.[14]

But the Grand Chamber reversed the Chamber judgment and set a new standard for establishing whether violations of the right to access to a lawyer and related interrogation rights – and the use of confessional evidence obtained as a result of such violations – also amounted to violations of the right to fair trial enshrined in Article 6 of the Convention. It placed emphasis on the suspect's vulnerable position at the investigation stage, noting that 'in most cases, this particular vulnerability can only be properly compensated for by the assistance of a lawyer'[15] and that 'early access to a lawyer is part of the procedural safeguards to which the Court will have particular regard when examining whether a procedure has extinguished the very essence of the privilege against self-incrimination'.[16] The Court then concluded that Article 6(1) of the Convention requires that 'as a rule, access to a lawyer should be provided as from the first interrogation of a suspect by the police, unless it is demonstrated in the light of the particular circumstances of each case that there are compelling reasons to restrict this right'.[17] The Grand Chamber moved from this point to conclude that, '[t]he rights of the defence will in principle be irretrievably prejudiced when incriminating statements made during police interrogation without access to a lawyer are used for a conviction'.[18]

In doing so, it construed an absolute, rights-based, categorical exclusionary rule for confessional evidence obtained during custodial interrogation without access to a lawyer. Article 6 of the ECHR barred the admission of such evidence in Court, since use of the evidence would in principle irretrievably prejudice the right to fair trial. The exclusionary rule was based on 'a purely automatic application of the requirement of legal assistance under Article 6, para 3(c), without it being deemed necessary to show that the lack of such assistance had a prejudicial effect, even speculatively, on the fairness of the applicant's trial'.[19] The assistance provided subsequently by a lawyer or the adversarial nature of the ensuing proceedings could not cure the defects occurring during police custody.[20] The Court left no doubt about how far-reaching the newly introduced exclusionary

[13] *Salduz v Turkey* (2008) EHRR 421 [46].
[14] ibid [48].
[15] ibid [54].
[16] ibid.
[17] ibid [55].
[18] ibid.
[19] *Aras v Turkey (no 2)*, no 15065/07, 18 November 2014, dissenting opinion of Judge Spano [2].
[20] ibid [58].

rule was, explaining that the 'appropriate form of redress' for violations of Article 6 like the ones committed in this case would be to ensure that 'the applicant, as far as possible, is put in the position in which he would have been had this provision not been disregarded'.[21] This aspect of the decision was of 'the utmost importance', noted in their joint concurring opinion Judges Rozakis, Spielmann, Ziemele and Lazarova Trajkovska.[22] '[W]herever possible, the Court should seek to restore the *status quo ante*',[23] they concluded, resting the *Salduz* exclusionary rule on a solid, normative, rights-centred rationale.

Salduz quickly generated a strong line of Chamber judgments that put flesh on the bones of this revolutionary jurisprudence. Weeks only after *Salduz* was decided, the ECtHR decided *Panovits v Cyprus*,[24] where neither the applicant, who was a minor of 17 years of age, nor his father, who was accompanying him at the police station, were adequately informed of the suspect's right to legal representation, and the suspect was interrogated in the absence of a lawyer. The Court held that the authorities had a 'positive obligation to furnish the applicant with the necessary information enabling him to access legal representation', and that they had instead adopted a 'passive approach'.[25] They had notified him of his right to silence, but 'it was unlikely that a mere caution … would be enough to enable him to sufficiently comprehend the nature of his rights' to seek and obtain legal representation,[26] and the suspect had not waived his right to receive legal representation 'in an explicit and unequivocal manner'.[27] The Court repeated the key *Salduz* tenet that 'Article 6 requires that the accused be given the benefit of the assistance of a lawyer already at the initial stages of police interrogation',[28] and stressed that the right against self-incrimination 'presuppose[d] that the prosecution' did not 'resort to evidence obtained through methods of coercion or oppression in defiance of the will of the accused'.[29] The Court then concluded that there had been a violation of Article 6 'on account of the lack of legal assistance'[30] and subsequently on account 'of the use in trial of the applicant's confession' which had been obtained in violation of that right.[31] It was clear that the Court was no longer looking at the overall fairness of the proceedings.[32] Judge Erotocritou's dissenting opinion insisted on

[21] ibid [72].
[22] ibid, joint concurring opinion, Judges Rozakis, Spielmann, Ziemele and Lazarova Trajkovska [4].
[23] ibid [8].
[24] *Panovits v Cyprus*, no 4268/04, 11 December 2008.
[25] ibid [72].
[26] ibid [74].
[27] ibid [73].
[28] ibid [66].
[29] ibid.
[30] ibid [77].
[31] ibid [86].
[32] See also *Pavlenko v Russia*, no 42371/02, 1 April 2010, where, 'having found that the pre-trial restriction on the applicant's right to counsel had no justification', the Court held that it 'did 'not need to consider further what effect the restriction had on the overall fairness of the criminal proceedings against the applicant'. See similarly *Pakshayev v Russia*, no 1377/04, 13 March 2014, where the suspect's right of access to a lawyer was restricted during the first hours of police custody and he did

the application of the 'overall fairness' of the proceedings test, describing in detail the guarantees that, in his view, mitigated the effect of the alleged violations of Article 6.[33] He complained also that the ECtHR 'should refrain from acting as an appellate court by re-examining the admissibility of the confessions'.[34] His reaction is a good indication of Strasbourg's mindset on evidence admissibility until *Salduz* was decided, and of the impact that the Court's new, groundbreaking, strict exclusionary rule was having from the outset.

The Court brought more precision on the substantive aspects of *Salduz* in *Dayanan v Turkey*, where it explained that a suspect should be assisted by a lawyer 'as soon as he or she is taken into custody … and not only while being questioned'.[35] As explained before, *Dayanan* provided a bold vision of the role of the lawyer prior to and during police interrogation, in finding that the right to legal assistance goes beyond the mere right to legal advice during police interrogation to cover other aspects of the lawyer's role during the entire interrogation phase.[36] *Dayanan*, and the more recent case of *Aras v Turkey*,[37] bring to light the Court's desire to transform the lawyer's presence into a substantive guarantee, ensuring that *Salduz*-generated reforms will not be cosmetic. They are both underpinned by the logic that the presence of a lawyer at the police interrogation stage does not suffice in itself to secure the rights of the suspect.[38] Coupled with the categorical exclusionary rule constructed in *Salduz*, this imaginative broadening of the angle of vision of the Court, concerning the substantive aspects of the right to custodial legal assistance, offers new vistas of possibility for the effective implementation of the right to fair trial in the police interrogation stage.

Taking another important step in the direction of safeguarding the application of the right to legal assistance in practice, the Court found in *Pishchalnikov v Russia* that a suspect 'who had expressed his desire to participate in investigative steps only through counsel, should not be subject to further interrogation by the

not have the benefit of legal assistance when he made his confession to the police. The Court found that 'irrespective of whether the applicant had the opportunity to challenge the evidence against him before the courts, the absence of a lawyer while he was in police custody irretrievably affected his defence rights'. ibid [31].

[33] *Panovits v Cyprus*, no 4268/04, 11 December 2008, dissenting opinion, Judge Erotocritou [3]. The Judge observed that '[t]he applicant, less than 24 hours after his arrest, had the services of a lawyer who represented him at the remand proceedings the very next day. Within one week he appointed a second lawyer and, throughout the one and a half years the trial lasted, he was at all times legally represented and had the opportunity to test all the evidence adduced'.

[34] ibid [7].

[35] *Dayanan v Turkey*, no 7377/03, 13 Oct 2009 [32].

[36] For a discussion of the distinction between the right to legal advice and the right to legal assistance, see F Leverick, 'The Right to Legal Assistance During Detention' (2011) 15 *Edinburgh Law Review* 352, 354.

[37] *Aras v Turkey (no 2)*, Application No 15065/07, Merits and Just Satisfaction, 18 November 2014 [40].

[38] The Court concluded in *Aras (no 2)* that 'the mere presence of the [suspect's] lawyer in the hearing room cannot be considered to have been sufficient by Convention standards'. ibid [40].

authorities until counsel has been made available to him'.[39] In *Brusco v France*, the Court found a violation of Article 6 in a case where the suspect had not been notified of his right to silence and had not been assisted by a lawyer until 20 hours of interrogation had passed, explaining that, in line with *Salduz* and *Dayanan*, the suspect 'has the right to be assisted by a lawyer from the beginning of [the detention] as well as during questioning, and this is a fortiori the case when he has not been informed by the authorities of his right to silence'.[40] In *Navone and Others v Monaco* the Court removed any remaining doubts on the issue of the lawyer's presence during police interrogation,[41] noting that it had on many occasions already specified that the right to legal assistance during police detention should be particularly understood as assistance 'during questioning'.[42] It also underlined that the right to access to a lawyer and the right to silence were distinct custodial interrogation rights, and that a potential waiver of the one did not necessarily mean that the suspect had also waived the other.[43] The Court struck there another blow to the 'overall fairness' of the proceedings test, finding that the violation of Article 6 was complete, as a result of the breach of the right to access to a lawyer, even if the suspect had exercised his right to silence in this case and even if he had had the opportunity to contest the use of the confessional evidence in subsequent proceedings.[44] In *AT v Luxembourg*, the Court clarified that the lawyer's presence during questioning will not suffice for the right to fair trial to be respected, and that national legislation must also provide for private consultation with a lawyer prior to the beginning of the interrogation.[45] 'The lawyer must be able to provide effective and practical assistance, not just abstract backing via his presence, during the first interrogation by the investigating judge',[46] further explained the Court, also noting 'the importance of consultations between the lawyer and his client upstream of the first interrogation by the investigating judge',[47] as this provided an 'opportunity for holding crucial exchanges, if only for the lawyer to remind his client of his relevant rights'.[48]

Equally worthy of note is the Court's jurisprudence on waivers. *Zachar and Čierny v Slovakia* provides a key illustration. The Court reiterated there that waivers 'must be established in an unequivocal manner and must be attended

[39] *Pishchalnikov v Russia*, no 7025/04, 24 September 2009 [79].

[40] *Brusco v France*, no 1466/07 19 October 2010 [45]. See also JF Renucci, 'Garde à vue et CEDH: la France condamnée à Strasbourg' (2010) *Recueil Dalloz* 2950.

[41] The issue was still being hotly debated in certain European countries, eg in the Netherlands. See generally Giannoulopoulos, 'Strasbourg Jurisprudence' (2016) 114.

[42] *Navone and Others v Monaco*, nos 62880/11, 62892/11 and 62899/11, 24 Oct 2013 [79]. The Court cited the examples of *Karabil v Turkey*, no 5256/02, 16 June 2009 [44]; *Ümit Aydin v Turkey*, no 33735/02, 5 January 2010 [47]; and *Boz v Turkey*, no 2039/04, 9 February 2010 [34].

[43] ibid [74].

[44] ibid [84].

[45] *AT v Luxembourg*, no 30460/13, 9 April 2015 [87].

[46] ibid.

[47] ibid [86].

[48] ibid.

by minimum safeguards commensurate with the waiver's importance', and that 'before an accused can be said to have implicitly, through his conduct, waived an important right under Article 6, it must be shown that he could reasonably have foreseen the consequences of his conduct'.[49] In finding that the waiver in this case had not been attended by the minimum safeguards required,[50] the Court specifically paid attention to the fact that the suspects had been notified of their rights 'via the first pages of [...] pre-printed [police questioning] forms' – which were 'informing the applicants, without providing any commentary or further explanation, that they had the right to remain silent and the right to choose a lawyer' – and the fact, conversely, that 'no individualised advice about their situation and rights was provided to the applicants'.[51]

Taken together, *Salduz* and its progeny now mandate that suspects should be notified of their right to silence and afforded the right to legal assistance as soon as they are taken into custody. They should be more specifically afforded the right to consult with a lawyer prior to interrogation and have a lawyer present – and be actively assisted by him or her – during interrogation. Where there have been breaches of these fundamental rights, any self-incriminating statements will be automatically excluded, without consideration of the 'overall fairness' of the proceedings, as their use causes irretrievable prejudice upon the right to fair trial.

Salduz was the ECtHR's big *Miranda* moment.[52] Both judgments symbolise a turning point in the jurisprudence of the two Courts in the area of custodial interrogation rights. *Miranda* still reverberates in police stations across the United States, becoming an integral part of the cultural fabric of police interrogation there, despite post-*Miranda* jurisprudence limiting the exclusionary rule's protective effect. Some 50 years later, we are witnessing *Salduz* and its progeny having a similar effect in Europe, more so within the European Union (EU), where the radical developments that we have observed at the ECtHR have also given rise to groundbreaking EU Directives creating common minimum procedural standards across member states for the protection of suspects' rights. These developments at the national, regional and transnational law level tell a story of fast accelerating rapprochement around the need to guarantee suspects' rights and the exclusion of self-incriminating evidence obtained in violation of these rights.

[49] *Zachar and Čierny v Slovakia*, nos 29376/12 and 29384/12, 21 July 2015 [60], citing *Aleksandr Zaichenko v Russia*, no 39660/02, 18 February 2010 [40] with further references.

[50] *Zachar and Čierny v Slovakia*, nos 29376/12 and 29384/12, 21 July 2015 [74].

[51] ibid [70].

[52] For insightful comparisons see T Van de Laar and RL de Graaf, '*Salduz* and *Miranda*: Is the US Supreme Court Pointing the Way? [2011] *European Human Rights Law Review* 304; C Weisselberg, 'Exporting and Importing *Miranda*' (2017) 97 *Boston University Law Review* 1235.

II. From *Salduz's* Exclusionary Rule to Common Custodial Interrogation Rights in Europe (Passing by the EU Procedural Rights Directives)

Salduz triggered pioneering reforms of the right to access to a lawyer in custodial interrogations in European countries which, for varying historical, political, cultural and institutional reasons, had long resisted legislative change in this area. Scotland, France, Belgium, the Netherlands, and Ireland provide key illustrations. I have explored these in detail in other work,[53] so only the highlights will be mentioned below. To start with Scotland, the UK Supreme Court's decision in *Cadder v HM Advocate*[54] that the Scottish regime of custodial interrogation was wanting vis-à-vis *Salduz* led the UK Government to rush through emergency legislation which recognised suspects' right to have a private consultation with a solicitor before any questioning begins and at any other time during such questioning.[55] In Belgium, the Government enacted legislation in August 2011 that provides the right to consult confidentially with a lawyer from the beginning of the interrogation and prior to the first questioning by the police[56] as well as the right to be assisted by a lawyer during questioning.[57] *Salduz* 'served as the detonator' for this radical development,[58] as also evidenced by the fact that the legislation introducing these guarantees is widely known as the '*Salduz* legislation'.[59] In France, where many attempts at legislative reform since at least the beginning of the 1990s had failed to change the status quo,[60] *Salduz* triggered legislation which recognised for the first time the right of suspects to be assisted by a lawyer *during* questioning.[61] Various decisions of the Cour de cassation had already begun to reverse trial court judgments where evidence obtained in the absence of legal counsel or in violation of the right to silence had been admitted, thus giving

[53] See Giannoulopoulos, 'Custodial Legal Assistance' (2013) 291; Giannoulopoulos, '"North of the Border"' (2013) 369; Giannoulopoulos, 'Strasbourg Jurisprudence' (2016) 103. See also Hodgson, 'Safeguarding Suspects' Rights' (2011) 662; Dorange and Field, 'Reforming Defence Rights' (2012) 153; JD Jackson and SJ Summers, 'Confrontation with Strasbourg: UK and Swiss Approaches to Criminal Evidence' (2013) *Criminal Law Review* 114; JD Jackson, 'Responses to *Salduz*: Procedural Tradition, Change and the Need for Effective Defence' (2016) 97 *Modern Law Review* 987.

[54] *Cadder v HM Advocate* [2010] UKSC 43, 2010 SLT 1125.

[55] Criminal Procedure (Scotland) Act 1995 s 15A (3), as inserted by Criminal Procedure (Legal Assistance, Detention and Appeals) (Scotland) Act 2010, s 1(4).

[56] Art 4 of the Law of 13 August 2011 adding art 2bis, para 1 to the Law of 20 July 1990.

[57] Art 4 of the Law of 13 August 2011 adding art 2bis, para 2 to the Law of 20 July 1990.

[58] Circulaire n 8/2011 du Collège des procureurs généraux près les Cours d'appel, 23 November 2011, at 16.

[59] See, eg, Service de la politique criminelle, Évaluation de la 'loi Salduz', available at www.dsb-spc.be/web/index.php?option=com_content&task=view&id=152.

[60] See eg Loi n 93-1013 du 24 août 1993 modifiant la loi n 93-2 du 4 janvier 1993 portant réforme de la procédure pénale; and Loi n 2000-516 du 15 juin 2000 renforçant la protection de la présomption d'innocence et les droits des victimes.

[61] Loi n 2011-392 du 14 avril 2011 relative à la garde à vue.

immediate effect to *Salduz's* categorical exclusionary rule.[62] Reform took much longer in the Netherlands, and there was significant resistance, but on 22 December 2015, the Supreme Court finally recognised that, as of 1 March 2016, all suspects should have the right to be assisted by a lawyer when questioned by the police,[63] opening the way for the enactment of the relevant legislation.[64] The December 2015 judgment also directly addressed the issue of the exclusionary rule, finding that violations of the right to consultation will, as a rule, lead to the exclusion of any statement obtained thereby. Ireland took similarly long to make the adjustments required by Strasbourg, but *Salduz* and other international jurisprudence eventually drove the Supreme Court to prohibit any questioning prior to the arrival of the lawyer,[65] though it must be noted that the shift to allowing suspects to have a lawyer present during questioning has proven less straightforward.[66]

Viewed together, these modern transformations of custodial legal assistance in Europe provide ample demonstration of the ECtHR's drastic influence on national legal systems,[67] and confirm Strasbourg's power to effect reform in areas where the balance of local powers – political, professional or institutional – may have long deprived the national legal system from the capacity to venture forward in imaginative bold ways. *Salduz* represents 'a triumph of "cosmopolitan" jurisprudence which is encouraging national courts to engage in transnational judicial dialogue that reaches out beyond their domestic legal cultures and traditions'.[68] But it also exposes how often legal cosmopolitanism is faced with local resistance, and how challenging it can become to negotiate the two.[69] As we saw above, different European legal systems responded to the *Salduz* jurisprudence in diverging ways. Scotland, France and Belgium swiftly introduced legislation to grant suspects the right to legal counsel during police interrogation, whilst in the Netherlands the right was enacted into legislation only after

[62] See *Crim* 19 October 2010, *Bull crim* 163; *Crim* 19 October 2010, *Bull crim* 164; Crim 19 October 2010, *Bull crim* 165; Crim 4 January 2011, n 10-85.520, (2011) *Recueil Dalloz* 242, obs Léna; *Crim* 18 January 2011, n 10-83.750, (2011) *Recueil Dalloz* 381; I 16 February 2011, n 10-82.865, (2011) *Recueil Dalloz* 953; *Crim* 15 April 2011, 4 judgments (n P 10-17.049, F 10-30.313, J 10-30.316 and D 10-30.242), (2011) *Recueil Dalloz* 1080; (2011) *Recueil Dalloz* 1128, interview Roujou de Boubée; *Jurisclasseur pénal* 2011, 17, 483, Détraz. See generally Giannoulopoulos, 'Custodial Legal Assistance' (n 3) 314–16.

[63] HR 22 December 2015, ECLI:NL:HR:2015:3608, r.o. 6.3 and 6.4.3, NJ 2016/52 m.nt. AH Klip.

[64] For the official implementation act which introduces the right, amending the Dutch Code of Penal Procedure see Staatsblad (2016) 475.

[65] *DPP v Gormley; DPP v White* [2014] IESC 17.

[66] See *DPP v Boyle* [2017] IESC 1.

[67] See E Cape, Z Namoradje, R Smith and T Spronken, *Effective Criminal Defence in Europe* (Antwerp, Intersentia, 2011); Hodgson (n 3) 662.

[68] Jackson, 'Responses to *Salduz*' (2016) 988.

[69] I have used *Salduz* as a platform for the study of how legal cosmopolitanism can generate local resistance, and how to negotiate the two, in Giannoulopoulos, 'Custodial Legal Assistance' (n 3). See also R Montana, 'Procedural Tradition in the Italian Criminal Justice System – The Semi-Adversarial Reform in 1989 and the Inquisitorial Cultural Resistance to Adversarial Principles' (2016) 20 *International Journal of Evidence & Proof* 289.

many years of disagreement at the Supreme Court and in domestic criminal procedure scholarship. To take the example of a country not mentioned above, it likewise took Malta more than eight years to 'acknowledge that automatic restrictions of the right to access to a lawyer in the pre-trial stage amount to a violation of the right to a fair trial',[70] and this only after the European Court of Human Rights found, in *Mario Borg v Malta*,[71] that domestic custodial interrogation practice was in violation of Article 6 of the Convention for 'continuously ignoring the principles developed in its jurisprudence'.[72] In Ireland, less than three years after implicitly recognising that suspects had the right to be assisted by counsel when questioned by the police, the Irish Supreme Court made an unexpected U-turn, holding that *Salduz* did not provide for the right to have a lawyer present during questioning.[73] Similar back-and-forths can be identified in other Council of Europe contracting parties. For example, French and Belgian law and the Dutch draft bill restricted lawyers to a passive role during that phase of the process, whilst Scotland did not define the lawyer's role in legislation. In a similar vein, national laws differ in the time an interrogation can be delayed for until the suspect's lawyer's arrival or in the duration and frequency of private consultations with a lawyer.[74] These variations show that the process of ECtHR-generated reform in national jurisdictions is far more complex than first acquaintance might suggest. Not every country discussed above has responded to *Salduz* with the same urgency or enthusiasm, and reform of aspects of the right to custodial legal assistance is still pending in some of them.[75] There is no doubt that the Court has a unique ability to instil positive change in domestic law, but its 'cosmopolitan influences for reform are [often] mediated by competing judicial and legislative agendas, local resistance and a variety of other political, institutional and economic factors'.[76] But all this does not change the fact that the ECtHR is leading the way in a Europe-wide 'revolution' of fair trial rights, and that its *Salduz* jurisprudence has set the foundations for a plethora of national reforms that – it is reasonable to assume – would not have occurred otherwise.[77] By relying on an assessment of the overall fairness

[70] A Spitieri, *The right to access to a lawyer in Malta: a few steps forward, a few steps back*, 21 December 2016, Fair Trials blog, available at www.fairtrials.org/the-right-to-access-to-a-lawyer-in-malta-a-few-steps-forward-a-few-steps-back.

[71] *Mario Borg v Malta*, n 37537/13, 12 January 2016.

[72] Spitieri, 'Malta' (2016).

[73] See D Robinson, *Access to a lawyer: is Ireland turning back the clock?*, Fair Trials blog, 13 February 2017, available at www.fairtrials.org/access-to-a-lawyer-is-ireland-turning-back-the-clock.

[74] See generally Giannoulopoulos, 'Strasbourg Jurisprudence' (n 3) 116–20.

[75] ibid 121–25.

[76] ibid 104.

[77] The contextual study of post-*Salduz* reform of custodial interrogation in France provides a useful prism for exploration on this point. For many years there was in the country 'undoubtedly an awareness that the *garde à vue* was falling short of European and international standards giving custodial interrogation an adversarial character. The willingness to bring the *garde à vue* into line with such standards was apparently missing. This changed only when the ECtHR proceeded to outright rejection of certain inquisitorial traits of custodial interrogation'. Giannoulopoulos, 'Custodial Legal Assistance' (n 3) 309–10.

of the proceedings, where the right to custodial legal assistance was treated as one only of many factors which could potentially lead to a violation of Article 6, the ECtHR jurisprudence that preceded *Salduz* was limited, by definition, in its ability to lead contracting parties to recognise that the right to legal assistance was an integral part of Article 6. Only when the Court mandated 'access to a lawyer as a rule', and established irretrievable prejudice as the consequence of the evidentiary use of breaches of this rule, have these leading-edge national reforms of custodial interrogation rights become possible. *Salduz,* in other words, created momentum in domestic jurisdictions for the reform of custodial interrogation rights and, in some cases, the introduction of automatic exclusionary rules for their violations. We must now link Strasbourg's impact on domestic jurisdictions with equally significant developments at the level of EU legislation.

To begin with, we can take note of the 2009 Roadmap of procedural rights which set out a gradual approach towards establishing a full catalogue of procedural guarantees for suspects across the EU.[78] The Roadmap was the culmination of a process that had begun many years earlier, with a European Commission Proposal for a Council Framework Decision on certain procedural rights.[79] Strong opposition from some Member States had originally derailed the process,[80] but *Salduz* breathed new life into the idea of harmonising suspects' rights across Europe and got the process back on the rails,[81] in the context of the Stockholm programme this time, which placed special emphasis on the idea of 'a Europe built on fundamental rights' as one of its basic tenets.[82] Applying the Roadmap, and building on fair trial rights laid down in the Charter of Fundamental Rights, the EU adopted, within a few years only, far-reaching Directives on the rights to interpretation and translation (2010),[83] information (2012),[84] and access to a lawyer in criminal proceedings (2013),[85] which also paved the way for a second generation of EU Directives on procedural safeguards – all legislated in 2016 – affording

[78] Resolution of the Council of 30 November 2009 on a Roadmap for strengthening procedural rights of suspected persons in criminal proceedings, 2009/C 295/01.

[79] Proposal for Council Framework Decision on certain procedural rights in criminal proceedings throughout the European Union, 28 April 2004, COM (2004) 328.

[80] T Spronken, 'EU Policy to Guarantee Procedural Rights in Criminal Proceedings: an Analysis of the First Steps and a Plea for a Holistic Approach' (2011) *European Criminal Law Review* 212, 217.

[81] J Hodgson, 'Safeguarding Suspects' Rights in Europe: A Comparative Perspective' (2011) 14 *New Criminal Law Review* 611, 656.

[82] Council of Europe, The Stockholm Programme – An Open and Secure Europe Serving and Protecting the Citizens, 2 December 2009, 17024/09. For a review of developments in EU law leading to the provision of common procedural rights see generally A Ryan, *Towards a System of European Criminal Justice – The Problem of Admissibility of Evidence* (London and New York, Routledge, 2014) 35–46.

[83] Directive 2010/64/EU of the European Parliament and of the Council of 20 October 2010 on the right to interpretation and translation in criminal proceedings, 26 October 2010, L280/1.

[84] Directive 2012/13/EU of the European Parliament and of the Council of 22 May 2012 on the right to information in criminal proceedings, 1 June 2012, L142/1.

[85] Directive 2013/48/EU of the European Parliament and of the Council of 22 October 2013 on the right of access to a lawyer in criminal proceedings and in European arrest warrant proceedings, and on the right to have a third party informed upon deprivation of liberty and to communicate with third persons and with consular authorities while deprived of liberty, 6 November 2013, L294/1.

protection to children suspected or accused in criminal proceedings,[86] the presumption of innocence[87] and the right to legal aid.[88] These Directives signal 'a fundamental shift in the focus of European criminal law, from a system privileging inter-state judicial and police cooperation to a system where the protection of the fundamental rights of the affected individuals should be fully ensured'.[89] Their ramifications for regulating custodial interrogation in Europe, in parallel with the strong influences coming from Strasbourg, cannot be overemphasised.

We can take the Directive on the right of access to a lawyer as an example. It recognises the right of suspects to have access to a lawyer 'without undue delay', and, in any case, 'before they are questioned by the police or by another law enforcement or judicial authority',[90] as well as 'the right to meet in private and communicate with the lawyer representing them, including prior to questioning',[91] whilst it imposes upon Member States to respect the confidentiality of these communications.[92] It also extends the application of the right to access to a lawyer outside the police station, to other investigative or evidence-gathering acts:[93] identity parades, confrontations and reconstructions of the scene of a crime.[94] More importantly, the Directive removes any doubt about whether the right to legal assistance, as encapsulated in *Salduz*, extends to having a lawyer present when questioned by the police, as the Directive instructs Member States to ensure that suspects 'have the right for their lawyer to be present and participate effectively when questioned'.[95] Depending on how broadly the requirement for 'effective participation' is interpreted by the Court of Justice of the European Union (CJEU) in the future, or by the ECtHR itself the next time the Court takes the opportunity to draw on the EU Directive when applying *Salduz*,[96] there is

[86] Directive (EU) 2016/800 of the European Parliament and of the Council of 11 May 2016 on procedural safeguards for children who are suspects or accused persons in criminal proceedings, 21 May 2016, L132/1.

[87] Directive (EU) 2016/343 of the European Parliament and of the Council of 9 March 2016 on the strengthening of certain aspects of the presumption of innocence and of the right to be present at the trial in criminal proceedings, 11 March 2016, L65/1.

[88] Directive (EU) 2016/1919 of the European Parliament and of the Council of 26 October 2016 on legal aid for suspects and accused persons in criminal proceedings and for requested persons in European arrest warrant proceedings, 4 November 2016, L297/1.

[89] V Mitsilegas, 'The Future of European Criminal Justice', paper prepared for the Commission Expert Group on EU Criminal Law Policy, 12 March 2014. See also T Konstadinides and N O'Meara, 'Rebalancing Judicial Protection in Criminal Matters after Lisbon and Stockholm' in C Murphy and D Acosta Arcarazo (eds), *EU Security and Justice Law: After Lisbon and Stockholm* (Oxford, Hart Publishing, 2014) 77.

[90] Art 3, para 2 Directive 2013/48/EU.

[91] ibid, Art 3, para 3.

[92] ibid, Art 4.

[93] ibid, Art 3, para 2(b).

[94] ibid, Art 3, para 2(c).

[95] ibid, Art 3, para 3(b).

[96] To provide two recent illustrations, in *AT v Luxembourg* Application No 30460/13, Merits and Just Satisfaction, 9 April 2015 [87], the ECtHR drew, for the first time, on the Directive on the right of access to a lawyer, when reaching the important conclusion that the lawyer's presence during questioning will not suffice for the right to fair trial to be respected, and that national legislation must also provide for

potential here for these radical reforms of suspects' rights to drastically impact custodial interrogation in practice.[97]

However, a key element in the equation is missing. The Directive on the right to access to a lawyer defers to 'national rules and systems on the admissibility of evidence' in the assessment of whether the use of statements made by suspects in breach of their right to a lawyer has violated Article 6 of the Convention.[98] In other words, the Directive has shied away from introducing an exclusionary rule for violations of these rights, preferring not to disturb the status quo in certain Member States. This puts the Directive at a 'regrettably weak' position, offering 'no sufficient protection against the use of evidence acquired in breach of the right of access to a lawyer', notes Anagnostopoulos, who also touches upon the normative considerations which would underpin a categorical exclusionary rule. Failure to have one in place risks undermining the right to fair trial, opens the door to miscarriages of justice and makes it difficult to 'dissuade police and prosecuting authorities from applying abusive practices and systematically violating suspects' rights', he points out.[99]

This worrying gap can perhaps be explained by reference to the 'varying rules of procedure and evidence' of EU Member States,[100] which 'are in general the result of each national legal tradition'[101] and admittedly make it difficult for the exclusionary 'remedy to be required system wide'.[102] But this explanation is also somewhat misleading. The entire *Salduz* jurisprudence is advancing, with force, a

private consultation with a lawyer prior to the beginning of the interrogation. In *Zachar and Čierny v Slovakia* Applications Nos 29376/12 and 29384/12, Merits and Just Satisfaction, 21 July 2015, the Court relied on the Directive on the right of access to a lawyer and the Directive 2012/13/EU on the right to information in criminal proceedings [2012] OJ L 142/1, when finding that a waiver of the right to custodial legal assistance had not been effective.

[97] As Tinsley explains, the right to 'effective participation' is one of the key aspects that the Directive does not define with precision. *Right of Access to a Lawyer Directive*, Fair Trials practitioner training on the Roadmap Directives, Athens, 4–6 March 2016. It is entirely possible therefore that the CJEU could interpret this requirement broadly.

[98] Art 3, para 2 Directive 2013/48/EU.

[99] Anagnostopoulos, 'The Right of Access to a Lawyer in Europe' (2014) 16–17. See also Caianello, who is critical of the 'excessive interpretative space' that the judicial remedy lacuna in the directive leaves to national jurisdictions, creating the risk that 'a violation of the rights recognised by the directive could run either completely unpunished, or have very mild consequences (for example on the evaluation of the evidence)'. M Caianello, 'Procedural Sanctions in the EU Framework: Toward a Harmless Error Doctrine and Practice?' in M Caianello and J Hodgson, *Discretionary Criminal Justice in a Comparative Context* (North Carolina, Carolina Academic Press, 2015) 207, 213.

[100] Weisselberg, 'Exporting and Importing *Miranda*' (2017) 1272.

[101] M Caianello, 'To Sanction (or not to Sanction) Procedural Flaws at EU level? A Step Forward in the Creation of an EU Criminal Process' (2014) 22 *European Journal of Crime, Criminal Law and Criminal Justice* 317.

[102] Weisselberg (n 52) 1272. Jackson and Summers offer a similar explanation when attempting to interpret the hesitancy of the ECtHR to regulate the admissibility of criminal evidence (pre-*Salduz*, as far as violations of Art 6 are concerned). This might be the 'result of awareness of the differences between the various jurisdictions in the regulation of criminal evidence', they explain, noting that 'there can be little doubt that there are substantial variations both within and between the various European legal systems' in this area. Jackson and Summers, *The Internationalisation of Criminal Evidence* (2012) 152.

common exclusionary position irrespective of variations of rules of evidence and procedure across the Council of Europe, and the same is true with regards to the substantive guarantees that the Roadmap Directives are requiring Member States to implement throughout the EU. It is equally worthwhile to note that the Commission's proposal for the Directive originally provided for a categorical exclusionary rule, which was inspired by *Salduz* and was based on a rights-centred *status quo ante* rationale,[103] but the rule was dropped by the Council. In view of the above, one may think, at the risk of oversimplification, that it is not necessarily the variation of rules of evidence and procedure that put the breaks on efforts to add an exclusionary rule to the Directive, but perhaps, in some cases, concern that serious evidentiary consequences would attach to violations of the substantive guarantees introduced with these Directives. Experience with the law in action across the EU suggests that there is often a willingness to write procedural rights into legislation, but little enthusiasm for applying them rigorously in practice. Adding a strict exclusionary rule to the Directives was perhaps out of tune with the culture, in some Member States, of paying lip service to fair trial guarantees.[104]

To end on a more optimistic note on the point of remedies, we should not overlook that Recitals in the Directive still specify that Member States should 'put in place adequate and effective remedies', and that 'regard should be had to the case-law of the European Court of Human Rights', particularly *Salduz's* irretrievable prejudice rule.[105] This is another reminder of the crucial interactions between the ECtHR's *Salduz* case law and the EU Directives, and of the many interlinks between the jurisprudence of the two international courts responsible for their implementation, the ECtHR and the CJEU.

It is now safe to conclude that, whatever the gaps in the Roadmap Directives[106] or implementation of *Salduz* in national jurisdictions, Continental Europe is making a momentous turn towards the injection of adversarial guarantees into pre-trial proceedings. This historic transformation of a core element of inquisitorial criminal procedure cannot go unnoticed, not least by commentators from across the Atlantic. Weisselberg, a prolific *Miranda* scholar, notes in this regard that, '[w]hile the *Salduz* doctrine is still developing, and not all of the Directives have

[103] European Commission, Impact assessment accompanying the Proposal for a Directive on the right of access to a lawyer in criminal proceedings and on the right to communicate upon arrest, 8 June 2011, SEC (2011) 686, 18. See also Anagnostopoulos, 'The Right of Access to a Lawyer in Europe' (n 4) 15.

[104] For a contextual study of such a complacent approach to the enforcement of suspects' rights in Europe see D Giannoulopoulos, '"Falling on Deaf Ears": Looking for the *Salduz* Jurisprudence in Greece' in JD Jackson and SJ Summers (eds), *Obstacles to Fairness in Criminal Proceedings: Individual Rights and Institutional Forms* (Oxford, Hart Publishing, 2018) 155.

[105] Recitals 49–50 Directive 2013/48/EU.

[106] For a substantial critique of the EU Procedural Directives see D Sayers, 'Protecting Fair Trial Rights in Criminal Cases in the European Union' (2014) 14 *Human Rights Law Review* 733. Sayers argues that the piecemeal approach taken with the Directives, as a result of politically driven incrementalism, has led to incoherent solutions and a potential 'race to the bottom' with the ECtHR, whose jurisprudence provides a higher level of protection compared to the Directives. See similarly Caianello, 'To Sanction (or Not to Sanction) Procedural Flaws at EU level?' (2014) 317.

yet been implemented, they appear in theory to provide more robust protection for suspects than *Miranda*, particularly with respect to noncustodial questioning, the content of warnings, waiver, and invocation'.[107]

This observation is indicative of the depth and breadth of the *Salduz* jurisprudence and the 'Roadmap Directives', and the fast pace at which many European countries have moved from keeping lawyers away from the police station to assigning them – in theory at least – a key role in custodial interrogation. If we also take into account that, under the same cosmopolitan influences, European countries have begun to endorse categorical exclusionary rules applying to violations of the right to legal assistance, then the full extent of the ongoing transformation of Continental police interrogation is revealed.

This remarkable legacy is nevertheless now openly threatened by a radical change of mood within the ECtHR towards *Salduz's* exclusionary rule.

III. Throwing *Salduz* 'Off the Rails'?

Decided nearly eight years after *Salduz*, in the context of the fight against terrorism in the United Kingdom – in close connection with the London 7/7 attacks – the pivotal decision by the Grand Chamber in *Ibrahim and others v the United Kingdom*[108] threatens to throw off the rails the *Salduz*-instigated revolution of suspects' rights in Europe. The decision reverses *Salduz's* key tenet, the categorical exclusionary rule applying to the use of incriminating statements made during police interrogation without access to a lawyer, and reverts to determining whether the admission of incriminating statements violates Article 6 of the Convention based on the overall fairness of the proceedings.

A. *Ibrahim v the United Kingdom* Reverses *Salduz's* Exclusionary Rule

The *Ibrahim case* related to the failed terrorist attacks in London on 21 July 2005, which took place two weeks after the devastating 7/7 bombings. The first three applicants in this case (Muktar Said Ibrahim, Ramzi Mohamed and Yassin Omar) detonated four bombs which failed to explode, on three underground trains and a bus in central London on 21 July, while a fifth bomb was discovered undetonated in a London park two days later. The fourth applicant, Ismail Abdurahman, gave shelter to a fourth person involved in the attacks, Hussain Osman, who was not a party in the Strasbourg proceedings. After the arrest of the first three suspects,

[107] Weisselberg (n 52) 1258.

[108] *Ibrahim and others v the United Kingdom*, nos 50541/08, 50571/08, 50573/08 and 40351/09, 13 September 2016 (hereinafter mentioned as *Ibrahim* case).

the police conducted 'safety interviews' with them; these are interviews that are conducted in exigent circumstances, to avert harm to the public, for example by preventing a new terrorist attack. The police have the discretion to delay providing suspects with access to legal advice, which is indeed what happened in this case.[109] The police failed, however, to issue the suspects with the correct caution. The suspects were told that the court could draw adverse inferences from their silence, though this is not allowed in 'safety interviews', on account of suspects not having the opportunity to consult with a lawyer. The suspects did not make any incriminating statements, but then claimed in court that the bombs had merely been intended as an elaborate hoax as a protest against the war in Iraq and had been constructed with flaws to ensure they would not detonate. The prosecution then relied on their answers in their safety interviews to undermine their defence.[110] In relation to the fourth applicant, police officers began interviewing him as a witness, but an hour into questioning they considered that the suspect was risking incriminating himself and should therefore be cautioned and informed of his right to legal advice. They decided to seek instructions from senior officers, but were asked to continue to interview the suspect as a witness. The suspect then made several self-incriminating statements, qualified by the fact that he had come to give shelter to Hussain Osman as a result of a chance encounter, had not taken part in any plan to assist him and had only let Osman stay at his home because he had been afraid after the latter's revelations that he had taken part in the failed attacks on 21 July.[111]

In relation to the first three applicants, the Court found no violation of article 6, despite accepting that there had been a delay in affording them access to legal advice and despite the admission at trial of statements made in the absence of legal advice, considering that the proceedings as a whole were fair.[112] The Court held that there were compelling reasons to restrict the suspects' right to legal advice temporarily.[113] This satisfied the first stage of the *Salduz* test, explained the Court, adding that, in the second stage, it had to evaluate whether the overall fairness of the proceedings had nonetheless remained intact.[114] It is in elaborating upon this second stage that the Grand Chamber reconceptualised *Salduz*, in a way that shows striking indifference to its original understanding. The approach taken in *Salduz* did not support the argument that there was an intention to lay down a bright-line rule, observed the Court.[115] To support this thesis, the Court relied on a literal interpretation of the crucial excerpt from *Salduz* that '[t]he rights

[109] ibid [23]. This is in accordance with the provisions of the Terrorism Act 2000, Sch 8, para 8.

[110] For the details surrounding the arrests and interviews of the first three applicants see ibid [20]–[57].

[111] For the details relating to the questioning of the fourth applicant see ibid [137]–[152].

[112] *Ibrahim* case [294].

[113] ibid [279].

[114] ibid.

[115] ibid [260].

of the defence will *in principle* be irretrievably prejudiced'[116] when incriminating statements acquired in violation of the right to legal assistance are used for a conviction.[117] According to the Court, the use of the words 'in principle' indicated that 'the rule while strict, was not absolute'.[118] The Court then made cursory references to comparative law examples and the EU Directive on the right of access to a lawyer. It admitted that 'the approach in the United States [was] a strict one', but seemed to pay more attention to the fact that the EU Directive did *not* contain an exclusionary rule.[119] This was followed by a puzzling, Pythic, observation about the laws of the Contracting Parties in the Council of Europe, which simply drew on some 'information available to the Court'.[120] These laws showed 'a diversity of practice', explained the Court, 'with some favouring automatic exclusion and others preferring to allow judicial discretion'.[121] Canada and the international criminal tribunals were mentioned too, with the Court highlighting that evidence obtained in violation of the privilege against self-incrimination 'may be admissible at trial'.[122]

Based on the above, the Court concluded that it was 'necessary to view the proceedings as a whole'.[123] Where compelling reasons to deprive suspects of access to the right to a lawyer are established, 'a holistic assessment of the entirety of the proceedings must be conducted'.[124] Where no compelling reasons have been established, the Court must apply 'a very strict scrutiny to its fairness assessment', with 'the onus being on the Government to demonstrate convincingly why, exceptionally and in the specific circumstances of the case, the overall fairness of the trial was not irretrievably prejudiced by the restriction on access to legal advice'.[125] The Grand Chamber then drafted a 'non-exhaustive list of factors' that 'should, where appropriate, be taken into account' when examining the proceedings as a whole, including whether the applicant was particularly vulnerable, whether an exclusionary rule applied at trial and the applicant had the opportunity to challenge the authenticity of the evidence and oppose its use, the quality of the evidence, the nature of the violation, whether a statement was promptly retracted or modified, whether the evidence in question formed an integral or significant part of the probative evidence upon which the conviction was based, the strength of the other evidence in the case, whether guilt was assessed by professional judges or lay jurors, the weight of the public interest and other relevant procedural safeguards afforded by domestic law and practice.[126]

[116] *Salduz v Turkey* (2008) EHRR 421 [55], with emphasis added.
[117] *Ibrahim* case [260].
[118] ibid.
[119] ibid [261].
[120] ibid [228].
[121] ibid [261].
[122] ibid.
[123] ibid [262].
[124] ibid [264].
[125] ibid [265].
[126] ibid [274].

It is useful to look at how these factors were applied in *Ibrahim*. In relation to the first three applicants, the Court noted that there was a legal framework which allowed for the restriction of access to legal advice, and the police had strictly adhered to it.[127] The applicants had an opportunity to challenge the use of evidence in a 'trial within a trial' (*voir dire*) as well as during the trial and before the Court of Appeal.[128] The quality of the evidence had not been affected by the unlawful obtaining,[129] and the evidence was not 'marginal or unimportant' to the central issue in the trial.[130] There was 'damning',[131] 'overwhelming'[132] scientific evidence that the applicants had constructed the bomb as well as other extensive evidence linking them to the failed attacks,[133] and the evidence had been described in detail by the trial judge in his summing up.[134] Finally and perhaps more importantly, there was a strong public interest in investigating and punishing these 'indiscriminate terrorist attacks' which 'by their very nature, intended to strike fear into the hearts of innocent civilians, to cause chaos and panic and to disrupt the proper functioning of everyday life'.[135]

Now, in the face of such an abhorrent attempted terrorist attack, not many will disagree with the outcome of the exercise of this balancing test, not least those who happened to live in London at the time of the 7/7 bombings and 21/7 attack or those who have in recent times experienced similar horrors in the United Kingdom. But it is worrying and oxymoronic, on the other hand, that a balancing test which seeks to assure that fundamental Convention rights have not been violated – whatever the merit of the balancing test, and regardless of whether it was legitimate for the Grand Chamber to substitute it for *Salduz's* exclusionary rule, issues that I will be discussing shortly – focuses predominantly on the public interest and epistemic considerations, while paying little attention to rights-based factors.[136]

The application of the balancing test led to a different outcome in the case of the fourth applicant. The absence of compelling reasons for depriving the suspect of the right to access to a lawyer there meant that the burden of proof had shifted to the Government,[137] which, as noted above, would have to satisfy a 'very strict scrutiny' to the overall fairness of the proceedings test.[138] In undertaking this test, the Grand Chamber took into account that there was no basis in domestic law

[127] ibid [280].
[128] ibid [282]–[284].
[129] ibid [285].
[130] ibid [288].
[131] ibid.
[132] ibid [289].
[133] ibid [290]–[291].
[134] ibid [292].
[135] ibid [293].
[136] For a critique of the Court's 'endorsement of public interest balancing' in *Ibrahim* see R Goss, 'Out of Many, One? Strasbourg's *Ibrahim* Decision on Article 6' (2017) 80 *Modern Law Review* 1137, 1147.
[137] *Ibrahim* case [301].
[138] ibid [265].

for continuing to question the suspect as a witness, and that he had subsequently not been notified of his procedural rights, including his right to silence.[139] It also weighed heavily in the assessment of the Court that the trial court did not hear evidence from the senior police officer who had authorised the continuation of the witness interview,[140] and the evidence had formed 'an important part of the prosecution case'.[141] In assessing the public interest considerations, the Court seemed to suggest that the fourth applicant's offence could possibly be distinguished from those of the first three applicants, though it clarified that 'the threat posed by terrorism can only be neutralised by the effective investigation, prosecution and punishment of all those involved in terrorism'.[142] Without elaborating any further on the assumingly crucial public interest point, the Court concluded that, considering the 'high threshold' which applied where there had been no compelling reasons and 'the cumulative effect of the procedural shortcomings', the Government had failed to demonstrate that the overall fairness of the trial had not been irretrievably prejudiced in this case.[143] The ability of the Court to apply the overall fairness test in a way that can provide protection to the right to fair trial is evident in the above. We should not forget that this case related to an extremely serious incident threatening the public order, in the immediate aftermath of the worst terrorist attack in the recent history of the United Kingdom, and yet the Court upheld the right to fair trial for the fourth applicant.

However, what is also evident in the above is that the new balancing test offers little certainty in safeguarding the right to fair trial, as the outcomes of the exercise of discretion it affords the Court can vary greatly depending on the circumstances.[144] It speaks volumes that the joint partly dissenting opinion of Judges Hajiyev, Yudkivska, Lemmens, Mahoney, Silvis and O'Leary found that *there were* compelling reasons to deprive temporarily the fourth applicant of the right to access to a lawyer (satisfying the first stage of the *Salduz* test), and the evidence had not denied the applicant of his right to fair trial (satisfying the second test of the *Salduz* test as construed by *Ibrahim*). Strong public interest reasons underpinned this outcome, they explained. The case related to matters that 'directly involve[d] the human rights of many other people than the four applicants',[145] noted the opinion, and the Court was required to balance 'the right

[139] ibid [303].
[140] ibid [304].
[141] ibid [307].
[142] ibid [311].
[143] ibid [311].
[144] The 'overall fairness' test 'threaten[ed] to subordinate the fundamental guarantee to legal assistance of one's own choosing to other interests that have less, if any, significance in terms of the Convention', warned Judges Kalaydjieva, Pinto de Albuquerque and Turković in their concurring opinion in *Dvorski v Croatia* (2016) 63 EHRR 7 [OII-18]. The balancing test 'is too malleable an approach' and '[t]here is a potential danger that [it] will give rise to excessive discretion in the manner in which breaches of basic procedural rights, such as the right to a lawyer of one's own choice, are weighed against other procedural interests', they added. ibid [OII-20].
[145] ibid, joint partly dissenting opinion of Judges Hajiyev, Yudkivska, Lemmens, Mahoney, Silvis and O'Leary [2].

to fair trial … with the right to life and bodily security of the persons affected by the alleged criminal conduct'.[146] Furthermore, the suspect had been afforded sufficient counter-balancing safeguards. His statement had not been obtained by coercion or compulsion, was not objected to by him as being untrue and was never retracted. There was other strong incriminating evidence and any violations of the relevant Codes of Practice had been weighed in the balance by the UK courts, and careful directions were given.[147] In other words, six out of the 17 judges in the Grand Chamber applied the overall fairness test factors very differently to those supporting the majority opinion, reaching the opposed conclusion that trial fairness had *not* been compromised.

B. Three Critiques of *Ibrahim*

Three main critiques of *Ibrahim* derive, in my view, from the above. The first critique draws on the majority's interpretation of the original *Salduz* jurisprudence. The second relates to the Court's comparative law methodology. The third, partly empirical and partly normative, supports a claim for distinguishing *Ibrahim* in future cases as fact-specific and reverting to *Salduz's* original understanding. The joint partly dissenting, partly concurring opinion of Judges Sajó and Laffranque captures many of the key aspects of these critiques.

i. Incorrect Interpretation of the 'Irretrievable Prejudice' Rule and De Facto *Departure from* Salduz *Case Law*

The first critique can be put bluntly, in the words of Sajó and Laffranque. The majority's literal interpretation of *Salduz*, as a case which has introduced a rule which 'while strict, was not absolute',[148] is 'not correct'.[149] The majority opinion understood 'in principle' as meaning 'subject to exception', but this interpretation is 'contrary to the standard use of the expression in the Court's case law, and it is contrary to the meaning given in standard dictionaries'.[150] Moreover, the renewed emphasis on the 'overall fairness' test[151] 'misconstrues the letter and spirit of the *Salduz* test and related case law, and the national and EU understanding

[146] ibid.

[147] ibid [37].

[148] ibid [260].

[149] ibid, joint partly dissenting, partly concurring opinion of Judges Sajó and Laffranque [7].

[150] ibid. Sajó and Laffranque cite from the Oxford Dictionary of English here: '"In principle" – as a general idea or plan, although the details are not yet established …'. They explain that no other meaning is given by the dictionary and that 'the opposite is "in practice"'. Standard French dictionaries give the same meaning to the term 'en principe', used in the French version of the judgment. The online version of the Collins French to English dictionary defines the term as meaning 'as a rule' (*habituellement*) and 'in theory' (*théoriquement*).

[151] *Ibrahim* case [257].

developed in response to *Salduz*'.[152] *Salduz* had identified 'irretrievable prejudice' from a violation of the right to access to a lawyer as 'an absolute rule, and not as a rule with exceptions', concluded Sajó and Laffranque, adding, emphatically, that they '[could not] see how irretrievable prejudice [could] be remedied without the exclusionary rule'.[153] Section 1 above argued the same point. It discussed *Salduz* and its progeny in detail, to conclude that there was no doubt that the Grand Chamber in *Salduz* had construed an absolute, categorical exclusionary rule for incriminating statements obtained during custodial interrogation without access to a lawyer, on grounds that use of the incriminating statements for a conviction would in principle irretrievably prejudice the right to fair trial. Discussion there also brought to light that everyone in the Court was understanding *Salduz* as introducing a strict, bright-line rule of exclusion.

Perhaps one of the most detailed descriptions of the categorical exclusionary rule introduced with *Salduz* is provided by the concurring opinion of Judges Kalaydjieva, Pinto de Albuquerque and Turković, in the 2015 case of *Dvorski v Croatia*.[154] The Judges took as their starting point that '[i]n criminal procedure, there are some procedural rights so basic to a fair trial that their infringement can never be viewed as fair. The infringement of these rights results in a structural error, which affects the framework within which the trial proceeds'.[155]

The opinion drew on US Supreme Court jurisprudence on this point to explain that such structural errors necessarily impact upon the right to fair trial,[156] as was also evident in the ECtHR's jurisprudence on Article 3 and real evidence obtained by torture.[157] The concurring opinion then explained:

> As the Court underlined in *Salduz*, the evidence obtained during the investigation stage determines the framework within which the offence charged will be considered at the trial, and therefore any such procedural errors committed during this stage will necessarily have an impact on the fairness of the proceedings. Since the 'exclusionary rule' has been established for the protection of the privilege against self-incrimination, the use of evidence collected in breach of this basic privilege will always render a trial unfair, irrespective of any other circumstances of the case. Thus, the Court found in *Salduz* that any conviction based on an admission or statement given in violation of the right of access to a lawyer constituted a violation of the general right to a fair trial

[152] ibid, joint partly dissenting, partly concurring opinion of Judges Sajó and Laffranque [8].

[153] ibid. Judge Serghides makes a similar claim in his partly dissenting opinion in *Simeonovi v Bulgaria*, Application no 21980/04, 12 May 2017). He argues that according to *Salduz* 'an overall assessment is required only when there are compelling reasons for the restriction' of access to a lawyer (para 7 of his partly dissenting opinion), and that, in imposing an overall fairness test even where there are no compelling reasons, the Grand Chamber in *Ibrahim* had 'overlooked … the literal meaning' of specific words in key parts of the *Salduz* judgment. ibid [17].

[154] *Dvorski v Croatia* (2016) 63 EHRR 7.

[155] ibid [OII-16].

[156] The violation of these fundamental rights could never be treated as a 'harmless error', pointed out the opinion, citing *Chapman v California*, 386 US 18 (1967) and *Arizona v Fulminante*, 499 US 279, 309–10 (1991). ibid [OII-16].

[157] ibid [OII-17], citing *Jalloh v Germany* (2007) 44 EHRR 32 [99] and [105]; *Harutyunyan v Armenia* (2009) 49 EHRR 9 [63]; *Gäfgen v Germany* (2011) 52 EHRR 1 [176].

> guaranteed under Article 6(1) of the Convention. In other words, *Salduz* introduced *an automatic exclusionary rule for self-incriminatory statements obtained without a lawyer being present during questioning* when there were no compelling reasons for denying access to a lawyer (that is, in situations of unjustified denial of access to a lawyer).[158]

The opinion subsequently concluded that '[i]f a tainted self-incriminatory statement is not excluded prior to trial, such an error in itself should be seen as a violation of the Convention without there being any need to assess the overall fairness of the proceedings',[159] and '[i]f that tainted evidence comes to the knowledge of the judges sitting in the case, the conviction should automatically be quashed', as '[n]o other legal remedy could rectify such errors and ultimately ensure the fundamental right to a fair trial'.[160] The opinion leaves no doubt about the normative, rights-centred rationale upon which the exclusionary rule rested. The fact that the Court in *Ibrahim* has chosen to ignore all this is troubling.

> The above reinforce Sajó's and Laffranque's critique that the Court in *Ibrahim* fail[ed] to adhere to the guarantees of Article 6 as interpreted in its own well-established case law, and without expressly stating it, *de facto* depart[ed] from that earlier well-established case law, which has been widely applied by national courts. This [was] most disappointing.[161]

The second critique follows from the first. In misinterpreting, and then departing de facto from, its *Salduz* case law, the Grand Chamber failed to pay attention to how national courts were applying this case law. The Grand Chamber also relied on a rudimentary comparative survey of the practice of contracting parties to reach the conclusion that there was no consensus around a bright-line exclusionary rule. I will claim that both shortcomings blurred the Court's vision on this crucial matter.

ii. The Court's Flawed Comparative Law Methodology

The Court's agnosticism of the applications of its own jurisprudence in Council of Europe countries is striking. The otherwise extremely comprehensive, 87-page long, majority opinion devotes three sentences altogether to discussion of the law in domestic jurisdictions.[162] No reference is made to the extensive reforms of custodial legal assistance generated by *Salduz* and the law in action in contracting

[158] ibid, with emphasis added and citations removed.

[159] ibid [OII-18].

[160] ibid.

[161] *Ibrahim* case, partly concurring opinion of Judges Sajó and Laffranque [2]. Speaking extra-judicially about *Ibrahim*, Judge Laffranque noted that *Salduz* was 'an extremely important milestone' which had already been accepted in contracting parties, and the Court was not very honest in *Ibrahim*, as it did not explain that it was departing from *Salduz*. J Laffranque, Keynote speech, Fair Trials Legal Experts Advisory Panel (LEAP), Annual conference, Athens, 3–4 March 2017 (contemporaneous notes on file with author).

[162] *Ibrahim* case [228].

parties (which, as I will explain later, can provide empirical support for reverting to *Salduz's* original exclusionary rule), nor to domestic court jurisprudence recognising that an exclusionary rule is inherent in this jurisprudence.

My discussion of these developments, earlier in this chapter, led to the claim, firstly, that *Salduz* had created unique momentum in contracting parties for radical reforms of custodial interrogation rights and, secondly, that it had led, in some cases, to the introduction of automatic exclusionary rules for violations of these rights. Scotland, France, Belgium, the Netherlands, Ireland and Malta were analysed as examples of the former, while the latter was illustrated by selective reference to the jurisprudence of the French Cour de cassation and the Dutch Supreme Court. *Salduz* led these Courts to break existing barriers in their local 'inquisitorial' culture, and overcome local resistance, to recognise exclusion as the inevitable consequence of the 'irretrievable prejudice' caused upon the right to fair trial by the admission of self-incriminating statements acquired in breach of the right to legal assistance.

But it is the decision of the UK Supreme Court (UKSCt) in *Cadder v HM Advocate* that drives the 'blurred vision' point home.[163] In applying the *Salduz* ruling in relation to Scotland, the Court took note of custodial legal assistance reforms that *Salduz* had ignited in 'the majority of those member states which prior to *Salduz* did not afford a right to legal representation at interview (Belgium, France, the Netherlands and Ireland) [which were] now recognising that their legal systems [were], in this respect, inadequate'.[164] Even more pertinent to *Ibrahim* was *Cadder's* understanding that '*Salduz* [had] given rise to a clear and constant jurisprudence', as *Salduz* had been 'followed repeatedly in subsequent cases',[165] and that 'the Strasbourg court [had] shown by its consistent line of case law since *Salduz* that the Grand Chamber's [irretrievable prejudice] finding [was] now firmly established in its jurisprudence'.[166] It must be added that the UKSCt left no doubt about how the irretrievable prejudice rule should be applied. 'The consequence of *Salduz* is that, as a general rule, such evidence is inadmissible', it unequivocally concluded.[167] *Cadder* provides an equally enlightening history of ECHR guarantees leading to *Salduz*, where it identifies the 'entirety of the proceedings' as the pre-existing test that the Grand Chamber in *Salduz* 'was determined to tighten up'.[168]

[163] *Cadder v HM Advocate* [2010] UKSC 43, 2010 SLT 1125. See generally Giannoulopoulos, '"North of the Border"' (n 3) 369. See also P Ferguson, 'The Right of Access to a Lawyer' (2009) *Scots Law Times* 107; 'Case Comment: *Cadder v HM Advocate*' (2010) *Scottish Criminal Law* 1265; P Ferguson, 'Repercussions of the *Cadder* Case: The ECHR's Fair Trial Provisions and Scottish Criminal Procedure' [2011] *Criminal Law Review* 743; J McCluskey, 'Supreme Error' (2011) 15 *Edinburgh Law Review* 276; RM White and PR Ferguson, 'Sins of the Father? The "Sons of *Cadder*"' (2012) *Criminal Law Review* 357; and PR Ferguson and FE Raitt, 'A Clear and Coherent Package of Reforms? The Scottish Government Consultation Paper on the Carloway Report' (2012) *Criminal Law Review* 909. See also Ferguson's and White's brief rejoinder to Giannoulopoulos, '"North of the Border"' (n 3).

[164] *Cadder v HM Advocate* [2010] UKSC 43 [49].

[165] ibid [47].

[166] ibid [48].

[167] ibid [55].

[168] ibid [33].

The ECtHR indeed tightened up its approach by mandating the presence of a lawyer – and the irretrievable prejudice rule that was attached to it – as necessary to ensure respect of the privilege against self-incrimination, pointed out the UKSCt.[169]

Cadder's analysis of how the privilege against self-incrimination was applied in *Salduz* gives further cause for reflection on *Ibrahim*. We have seen that the majority opinion in *Ibrahim* accepted that one of the factors that the Court should take into consideration when assessing the overall fairness of the proceedings was 'other relevant procedural safeguards afforded by domestic law and practice'.[170] Interestingly, the UKSCt was confronted with the similar argument in *Cadder* that the privilege against *compelled* self-incrimination would be protected notwithstanding that the right to access to lawyer would not be provided, 'if other safeguards to secure a fair trial … [were] in place'.[171] Safeguards otherwise available in Scottish criminal procedure included the right to intimation of detention to a solicitor, the fact that no questioning is allowed after caution and charge or the audio and video recording of the interview in serious cases.[172] But for the Supreme Court, the argument did not hold water. The Court recognised that if access to legal assistance, as understood in *Salduz*, was about protecting the right against *compelled* self-incrimination, then 'it might have been thought that the use of techniques such as tape-recording would meet the need to monitor the need for fairness', but since *Salduz's* emphasis was on the right against self-incrimination, then there was no possibility of resorting to such analysis.[173] 'The guarantees otherwise available [were] entirely commendable',[174] but, at the same time, 'beside the point'.[175] Put simply, *Cadder* read *Salduz* as establishing an exclusionary rule that went beyond protecting against 'the risk of ill-treatment or other forms of physical or psychological pressure as a means of coercing the detainee to incriminate himself'[176] to provide wider protection of the right against self-incrimination, by placing '[t]he emphasis throughout … on the presence of a lawyer as necessary to ensure respect for the right of the detainee not to incriminate himself'.[177] In *Ibrahim* the Court moved away from *Salduz's* wider understanding of the privilege against self-incrimination, since it is now possible for self-incriminating statements obtained with no access to a lawyer to be admitted in trial and the right to fair trial to remain intact, precisely on account of safeguards otherwise available. It is therefore unfortunate that the Court did not draw on *Cadder's* interpretation of *Salduz's* original understanding on the privilege against self-incrimination

[169] ibid [35].
[170] *Ibrahim* case [274].
[171] The argument had originally been developed in *HM Advocate v McLean* [2009] HCJAC 97, 2010 SLT 73 [31].
[172] ibid [27].
[173] *Cadder v HM Advocate* [2010] UKSC 43 [34].
[174] ibid [50].
[175] ibid [66].
[176] ibid [34].
[177] ibid [35].

(not *compelled* self-incrimination) as the rationale for the exclusionary rule it had introduced.

It is equally striking that the Court failed to take any note of *Cadder's* (and therefore *Salduz's*) impact on the English law for the exclusion of improperly obtained confessional evidence, the domestic law, in other words, in line with which the Court needed to decide the applicant's case. Dennis described this impact succinctly:

> Lord Hope's analysis [in *Cadder*] of the art.6 implications of a failure to provide access to legal advice before a police interview has a clear impact on English law. It must now be the case that where a suspect makes a confession after requesting legal advice, but failing to obtain it, the fair trial jurisprudence as interpreted in *Cadder* will require the judge to exclude the confession under s.78 of PACE except in the most compelling circumstances. The message for any police officer tempted to use ploys to discourage requests or delay consultations until after the interview is unmistakable.[178]

Choo subscribes to this reasoning too, concluding that 'automatic exclusion … would seem to be required' where the suspect has been deprived of access to a lawyer in the absence of 'compelling reasons'.[179] Put simply, these are examples of Evidence scholars in the UK unmistakably reading *Salduz* as requiring the exclusion of evidence obtained in violation of the right to legal assistance. But *Ibrahim* paid no attention to this and focused only on the exercise of the section 78 discretion by the trial judge, to reach the opposite conclusion in this instance. As a result of *Ibrahim*, Strasbourg now practically asks UK domestic courts to disregard previous national interpretations that were in line with *Salduz*, including of course the seminal *Cadder* jurisprudence that applied these standards to Scotland (and caused furore there about external interference with the national legal system), and to adopt the *Ibrahim* interpretation that goes against *Salduz's* letter and spirit.

The Grand Chamber's failure to engage with the jurisprudence of the domestic courts was unfortunately matched by 'a surprisingly laconic description of the practice of the member States'[180] that leaves much to be desired. The majority opinion simply referred to 'information available to the Court'[181] indicating the absence of consensus on a mandatory exclusionary rule for evidence obtained in violation of the right to legal assistance. Here one is left unsure about the research methods used, and the quality of the information produced. The Court seems to take the information at face value regardless. Its reliance upon a quantitative analysis as the sole criterion for analysis of whether there is consensus gives the

[178] I Dennis, 'Editorial – Legal Advice in Police Stations: 25 Years on' [2011] *Criminal Law Review* 1.

[179] A L-T Choo, *The Privilege Against Self-Incrimination and Criminal Justice* (Oxford, Hart Publishing, 2013) 89.

[180] *Ibrahim* case, partly concurring opinion of Judges Sajó and Laffranque [17].

[181] *Ibrahim* case [228].

Court a myopic view. By concentrating on (assumed) plain numbers, it remains oblivious to reforms that *Salduz* has already triggered in Europe and considerable rapprochement that it has set in motion.

It is intriguing too that the partly dissenting, partly concurring opinion of Judges Sajó and Laffranque reaches in fact the opposite conclusion as to the state of law in domestic jurisdictions. In expressing their disagreement with the Court's empirical observations they note that:

> The fact is that the overwhelming majority of the member States have codified a mandatory exclusion rule, or have binding case-law which mandates the application of exclusionary rules for *Salduz*-type incriminations which cause irretrievable prejudice, if for example the accused makes such a request. In some countries the violation of the right to silence is the basis of the exclusionary rule, in others it is the lack of access to a lawyer.[182]

Without any access to the comparative law information that the majority opinion or Sajó's and Laffranque's opinion drew upon, it is difficult to assess the empirical merits of their claims. But we can observe that Sajó's and Laffranque's opinion succeeds where the majority opinion fails, in that it identifies a strong trend towards recognising and implementing the exclusionary rule in Europe.[183] Empirical observations in chapter four support their conclusion, which, it is submitted here, is potentially more useful than a simple numerical survey of countries adopting one or the other position. It is intuitive to suggest that, even in the absence of an existing consensus, the Court should take caution not to disrupt domestic trends potentially leading to such consensus, all the more so when it is the Court's jurisprudence that has sparked this trend in the first place.

Here we can pause for a moment of reflection on the complexities of legal cosmopolitanism and the need to use the comparative law method as a compass when negotiating the unchartered waters of the new international legal order, where international and transnational law influences are shaping national legal systems in ways that are so dynamic as to call into question the 'capacities, competencies and legitimation claims of the nation state itself'.[184] In undertaking contextual studies of the ECHR-inspired national reforms of the right to legal assistance (and local resistance to them), I have consistently called for a renewed emphasis on comparative law and comparative legal studies, with a view to

[182] *Ibrahim* case, partly concurring opinion of Judges Sajó and Laffranque [17]. In support of their findings, see also A Soo, '(Effective) Remedies for a Violation of the Right to Counsel during Criminal Proceedings in the European Union: An Empirical Study' (2018) 14 *Utrecht Law Review* 18, 29.

[183] *Ibrahim* case, partly concurring opinion of Judges Sajó and Laffranque [17], fn 9.

[184] A Crawford (ed), *International and Comparative Criminal Justice and Urban Governance: Convergence and Divergence in Global, National and Local Settings* (Cambridge, Cambridge University Press, 2011) 1. See also J McLean, 'From Empire to Globalization: The New Zealand Experience' (2004) 11 *Indiana Journal of Global Legal Studies* 161 (2004); J Habermas, *The Divided West* (Cambridge, Polity, 2006) 176; D Held, *Cosmopolitanism: Ideals and Realities* (Cambridge, Polity, 2010) ch 3.

generating genuine interest from within national legal systems for the solutions adopted in foreign legal cultures and international legal orders, as a means to bypass divergence through synthesis and hybridisation or, conversely, as a means to explain the raison d'être of local variations as a path to safeguarding national solutions where required.[185] In the same work, I have stressed, however, the need for the ECtHR to view the reception of its jurisprudence from within the domestic jurisdictions it seeks to influence, thinking in terms of contracting party-centred explanations of acceptance of (or resistance to) this jurisprudence, which can help the Court identify the indigenous forces shaping national responses to its case law.[186] This is a fortiori the case where the Court hands down innovative judgments on controversial areas of criminal justice, where a common European position may have not yet fully crystallised and where a positive reception from relevant domestic jurisdictions or local resistance can make all the difference between successful implementation or obstructing acceptance of the Court's positions.

In *Ibrahim* the Grand Chamber was right to seek to obtain a view of the practice of contracting parties, but, by the same token, its (failed) attempt did more harm than good due to its methodological shortcomings. In the end, the echoes of *Salduz's* dramatic impact in many European countries have never been heard in Strasbourg. Perhaps the question that arises is whether the Court has the resources – human, economic, and in terms of 'know-how' – to do better than that, especially in major Grand Chamber judgments which set the tone for the protection of human rights across Europe and – sometimes – even beyond.[187] National Supreme Courts also have considerable scope to influence this process, by developing comparative lateral thinking, in undertaking these inquiries long before a case has left the shores of the national jurisdiction to travel to Strasbourg.[188] We should also not lose sight of the fact that there is an obvious opportunity here for relevant academic scholarship to fill the gap, and that this, more generally, may be the time for a rejuvenated comparative law, and legal cosmopolitan thinking, to act as a medium for the effective implementation of human rights, in Europe and beyond.

I close the parenthesis and move to the third, and final, critique, which is closely connected with the first two.

[185] Giannoulopoulos, 'Custodial Legal Assistance' (n 3) 329.

[186] Giannoulopoulos, 'Strasbourg Jurisprudence' (n 3) 103; Giannoulopoulos, '"Falling on Deaf Ears"' (2018) 155. See also discussion of the 'contracting party-based' explanation in Jackson (n 53) 1005.

[187] See, eg, the Superior Courts Network (SCN) which 'was created by the ECHR to ensure the effective exchange of information, with the national superior courts, on Convention case law and related information', available at www.echr.coe.int/Pages/home.aspx?p=court/network&c. I am very thankful to Julia Laffranque, the Estonian Judge at the European Court of Human Rights, for discussion on this point.

[188] The decision of the Irish Supreme Court in *DPP v Gormley* is an excellent manifestation of such cosmopolitan legal thinking applied in practice. *DPP v Gormley; DPP v White* [2014] IESC 17 discussed in Giannoulopoulos, 'Strasbourg Jurisprudence' (n 3) 125–29. The same is true about the decision of the UK Supreme Court in *Cadder*.

iii. Empirical and Normative Support for Salduz's *Categorical Exclusionary Rule*

We must now view the developments in *Ibrahim* from an empirical and normative perspective. In seeking to identify an empirical foundation, we will reflect on what has *Salduz* meant for the reform of custodial legal assistance in Europe, and what would subsequently be the ramifications of watering down its key protection, before exploring the normative foundations for keeping in place its exclusionary rule.

Once again, we must take as our point of departure that *Salduz* instigated fundamental reforms of custodial legal assistance across Europe. It has helped shift countries that were immovable on this point for decades.[189] Under the pre-*Salduz* 'overall fairness' test these countries had refrained from injecting even elementary adversarial elements into the inquisitorially dominated pre-trial stage of police interrogation, and it is fair to assume that keeping lawyers outside of the police station would have remained 'business as usual', had it not been for *Salduz*. I have provided empirical support for the above claims, in the form of a contextual study of the legislative and jurisprudential developments giving *Salduz* effect in contracting parties.[190]

It is also instructive to bring into the equation Jackson's analysis according to which domestic jurisdictions were reluctant to adopt *Salduz's* principle where there was no 'clear and constant' jurisprudence for it.[191] He takes as an example the 'Sons of *Cadder*' cases,[192] where the UKSCt failed to extend the right to legal assistance to non-custodial questioning taking place outside the police station[193] and read the waiver requirement narrowly,[194] and this despite the fact that the Court had previously enthusiastically adopted the key tenets of *Salduz*. The UK courts' approach could be summed up as 'keep[ing] pace with the *Strasbourg* jurisprudence', but not going beyond it, explained Jackson,[195] pointing to the dictum 'no more, but certainly no less',[196] and its more Eurosceptic version: 'no less, but certainly no more'.[197]

In view of the above it is logical to predict that the departure from *Salduz's* bright-line rule original understanding – coupled with the inability to point towards a 'clear and constant' jurisprudence, given the variability of outcomes inherent in the 'overall fairness' test – will considerably slow down this process,

[189] See, eg, France in Giannoulopoulos, 'Custodial Legal Assistance' (n 3) 291.
[190] Giannoulopoulos (n 104).
[191] Jackson (n 53) 1009.
[192] See generally White and Ferguson, 'Sins of the Father?' (2012) 357.
[193] *Ambrose v Harris* [2011] 1 WLR 2435 *per* Lord Bingham.
[194] *McGowan v B* [2011] 1 WLR 3121 *per* Lord Brown.
[195] Jackson (n 53).
[196] *R (Ullah) v Special Adjudicator* [2004] 2 AC 323 [20].
[197] *R (Al-Skeini and others) v Secretary of State for Defence* [2008] 1 AC153 [106].

if it does not push the *Salduz* jurisprudence off the rails altogether. This observation resonates well with the partly dissenting opinion by Sajó and Laffranque:

> We regret that this judgment departs from the standards of a fair trial as determined in *Salduz*, under the guise of interpreting it. It diminishes the level of protection without good reason. It frustrates years of European efforts to provide a high level of protection to procedural rights. We cannot accept such backtracking.[198]

Why backtracking on years of – successful – European efforts to reform custodial interrogation rights would be strongly counterintuitive and counterproductive, and its timing highly unfortunate, is further illustrated if seen in parallel with the EU Directive on the right to access to a lawyer that now requires EU Member States to introduce legislation or take other concrete measures to effectively implement the right to custodial legal assistance, ironically *as prescribed in Salduz and its progeny*. Put differently, at a time when EU Member States are coming together in providing protections to the right to access to a lawyer, putting into effect the core *Salduz* jurisprudence, the ECtHR is reversing the engines that have quickly brought about much positive reform.

We must now go one step further and correlate the legislative reforms initiated by *Salduz* in national jurisdictions with the question of whether they have indeed allowed for the effective implementation of the right to legal assistance in practice. In fact, there is strong empirical evidence bringing to light a worrying discordance between the law in theory and the law in action. We can point to a study of four European jurisdictions – England and Wales, France, the Netherlands and Scotland – by Blackstock, Cape, Hodgson, Ogorodova and Spronken, which has revealed significant problems in the implementation of key post *Salduz* rights including the right to custodial legal assistance.[199] Or a recent empirical study by Vanderhallen, van Oosterhout, Panzavolta and de Vocht, on procedural safeguards for young suspects in five countries (Belgium, England and Wales, Italy, Poland and the Netherlands), which brought to light similar concerns about the effective exercise of suspects' rights.[200] We can likewise draw on similar studies in England and Wales which unearthed that a significant proportion of suspects do not exercise their right to access to a lawyer in reality;[201] a worrying observation, if one

[198] *Ibrahim* case, joint partly dissenting, partly concurring opinion of Judges Sajó and Laffranque [4].

[199] J Blackstock, E Cape, J Hodgson, A Ogorodova and T Spronken, *Inside Police Custody* (Cambridge, Intersentia, 2014) 426.

[200] M Vanderhallen, M van Oosterhout, M Panzavolta and D de Vocht, *Interrogating Young Suspects – Procedural Rights from an Empirical Perspective* (Cambridge, Intersentia, 2016).

[201] J Hodgson and L Bridges, 'Improving Custodial Legal Advice' [1995] *Criminal Law Review* 101, 102; R Pattenden and L Skinns, 'Choice, Privacy and Publicly Funded Legal Advice at Police Stations' (2010) 73 *Modern Law Review* 349, 352. See E Cape, 'The Rise (and Fall?) of a Criminal Defence Profession' [2004] *Criminal Law Review* 401, 414; L Bridges and E Cape, *CDS Direct: Flying in the Face of the Evidence* (London, Centre for Crime and Justice Studies, King's College, 2008); V Kemp and N Balmer, *Criminal Defence Services: User's Perspectives*, Research Paper No 21 (London: Legal Services Research Centre, 2008); I Dennis, 'Editorial – Legal Advice in Police Stations: 25 Years On' [2011] *Criminal Law Review* 1; P Pleasence, V Kemp and N Balmer, 'The Justice Lottery? Police Station Advice 25 years on from PACE' [2011] *Criminal Law Review* 6; A Edwards, 'Legal Aid, Sentencing and Punishment

considers that England and Wales has, in many ways, long been seen as leading the way in the effective delivery of custodial interrogation rights in Europe. Elsewhere, I have linked such evidence with a contextual study of the law in action in Greece as regards the right to custodial legal assistance, to conclude that:

> Following the formal incorporation of the *Salduz* jurisprudence in most European legal systems that were previously resisting giving suspects access to a lawyer, and in parallel with the ongoing process of the transposition of the EU Roadmap Directives, national legal systems and European institutions are next required to seek the logistical gateways to make these rights work in practice. The contextual study of custodial legal assistance in Greece demonstrates quite clearly that the procedural rights transformations happening now in Europe will be devoid of substance until and unless we begin to find ways to ensure that suspects are not prevented or discouraged from exercising these rights.[202]

Such level of discordance between the law in theory and the law in action exists in the face of the post-*Salduz* legislative and jurisprudential reforms that we have witnessed, which naturally highlights the need to link the newly introduced substantive guarantees with judicial remedies, if we start from the position that evidentiary exclusion can serve as a guarantee of procedural rights. We can, more specifically, theorise this in terms of a remedial theory that focuses on exclusion as a means to protect procedural rights,[203] or from the viewpoint of a judicial integrity rationale that aims to safeguard the moral legitimacy of the proceedings or, even, a deterrence rationale that focuses on deterring police officers from violating these rights in the future.[204] Chapter six will analytically discuss the normative foundations for exclusion, with a focus on a rights-centred rationale, but it is worth pointing out here that the partly dissenting opinion by Judges Sajó and Laffranque promotes at least two of the above rationales – the remedial theory and the deterrent rationale – as justifications for safeguarding *Salduz's* original understanding.[205] The above divide between the law in theory and the law as applied in practice in Council of Europe members, even in the post-*Salduz* era – and despite the significant advances in terms of substantive custodial legal assistance guarantees achieved with the latter – gives significant ammunition to Sajó's and Laffranque's defence of the 'quasi-exclusionary rule of *Salduz*', as a mechanism that is 'crucial for the effective protection of the right to fair trial' and can achieve 'police deterrence'.[206] Unless we have such exclusionary mechanisms in place,

of Offenders Act 2012 – the Financial Procedural and Practical Implications' [2012] *Criminal Law Review* 584; L Skinns, 'The Right to Legal Advice in the Police Station: Past, Present and Future' [2011] *Criminal Law Review* 19, 34.

[202] Giannoulopoulos (2018) 176.

[203] See A Ashworth, 'Excluding Evidence as Protecting Rights' [1977] *Criminal Law Review* 723.

[204] See generally P Roberts and A Zuckerman, *Criminal Evidence*, 2nd edn (Oxford, Oxford University Press, 2010) 179–91.

[205] *Ibrahim* case, partly concurring opinion of Judges Sajó and Laffranque [16].

[206] ibid. In relation to deterrence, the opinion explained that '[p]rudential considerations of police deterrence also militate in favour of the quasi-exclusionary rule of *Salduz*. If the investigative authorities know that certain practices which violate the accused's Article 6 § 3 rights may result in a mistrial,

Salduz's substantive guarantees risk to remain an empty promise, all the more so in terrorism cases where *Ibrahim's* impact is likely to be felt the most.[207]

Where does *Ibrahim* leave the law of improperly obtained confessional evidence in Europe? Arguably, in a perilous state. In replacing *Salduz's* categorical exclusionary rule with the overall fairness test, the Court will no longer be in the position to provide leadership, or guidance, in the effective implementation of the right to legal assistance.[208] Its multi-factor balancing test will be a case of 'everything is relevant, but nothing is decisive', potentially allowing complacent Council of Europe countries to continue with existing practice, whilst those who have been proactively incorporating the *Salduz* unequivocal jurisprudence could slow down the process, notably if they subscribe to the ideology of 'no less, but certainly no more' protection of human rights vis-à-vis the ECtHR's jurisprudence. Of course, much will depend on what is made of *Ibrahim* in future Grand Chamber judgments. The Court may distinguish *Ibrahim*, limiting its effect to terrorism cases, or it may come to realise its 'incorrect reading of *Salduz* by referring to two compulsory stages of the assessment, whereas *Salduz* clearly indicates that stage two is required only if there are compelling reasons for the restriction'.[209]

they will be reluctant to apply such practices. And, as mentioned in *Salduz*, early access to legal advice (counsel) is a fundamental safeguard against ill-treatment'.

[207] As Seet commented in relation to the Chamber judgment in *Ibrahim*, '[i]n allowing for the admission of the applicants' statements made without lawyers present (contrary to [*Salduz*]), the Strasbourg Court in *Ibrahim* has taken a worrying position in regard to the interrogation of terrorist suspects'. Seet explains that '[c]ounter-terrorism efforts should never compromise important procedural safeguards in the justice system, particularly in Europe today where the Paris and Copenhagen shootings in early 2015 and the return of radical jihadis from Syria have raised widespread fears of terrorist attacks'. M Seet, 'Case Comment – Suspected Terrorists and the Privilege against Self-Incrimination' (2015) 74 *Cambridge Law Journal* 208, 211. See also 'Case Comment – Terrorist Suspects' Procedural Rights' [2017] *European Human Rights Law Review* 75, 79 which notes that 'sensitive cases concerning terrorism are often domains in which human rights are most difficult to justify, but arguably the most vital to enforce', suggesting that the Court was not successful in balancing the competing interests at play in such cases.

[208] The Grand Chamber's judgment in *Simeonovi v Bulgaria*, no 21980/04, 12 May 2017, provides a fresh illustration of why this will be the case. Again, there was significant disagreement in the Court about the outcome of the 'overall fairness' test, as evidenced by a majority of twelve votes to five that there had been no violation of the Art 6, paras 1 and 3, in a case where significant violations of the right to legal assistance had been committed. The Court had also found no compelling reasons for restricting access to a lawyer, which meant, according to *Ibrahim*, that it needed to apply strict scrutiny to its fairness assessment, with the onus on the Government to demonstrate why the overall fairness had not been irretrievably prejudiced (*Ibrahim and others v the United Kingdom*, nos 50541/08, 50571/08, 50573/08 and 40351/09, 13 September 2016 [265]). Judges Sajó, Lazarova-Trajkovska and Vučinić, joined by Judge Turković, were very concerned about the outcome. They argued that 'the Court [had] not only turn[ed] a blind eye to practices that target the very core of the rights of the criminally accused, but also grant[ed] police officers and prosecutors broad opportunities for undocumented, unregulated abuse'. They concluded that '[u]nder the reasons of the majority, suspects can be detained, kept in isolation and potentially intimidated, provided that no written record of these events is left behind'. *Simeonovi v Bulgaria*, no 21980/04, 12 May 2017, partly dissenting opinion of Judges Sajó, Lazarova-Trajkovska and Vučinić, joined by Judge Turković.

[209] *Simeonovi v Bulgaria*, no 21980/04, 12 May 2017, partly dissenting opinion by Judge Serghides [19].

If this happens, then the Court will also need to distinguish between the position taken in *Salduz* and that endorsed in *Ibrahim*, and give good reasons for departing from the unanimous decision in *Salduz* to adopt the approach in *Ibrahim*.[210] To bring this line of argument closer to the comparative law claims I have made above, the Court, in such a case, should also take into consideration the *Salduz*-generated reforms within contracting parties, combined with their undisputed acceptance that *Salduz* had introduced a categorical exclusionary rule, but, perhaps more importantly, consider existing empirical observations about the law in action and think normatively about how to effectively safeguard the right to legal assistance in contracting parties in the future.

IV. Concluding Thoughts

The preceding analysis raises more questions than it answers. Perhaps the wider, more fundamental issue that we are faced with following this long review concerns the complexity of modern cosmopolitan legal thinking and its symbiosis with antagonistic local resistance forces inherent in national legal cultures. Reform was achieved by *Salduz* in many European countries in the face of local resistance. In other countries, right from the outset *Salduz* found favourable conditions to grow. *Salduz* did not come out of nowhere. It rather coincided with a fast-accelerating rapprochement within Anglo-American and Continental law around the need to safeguard the right to legal assistance, including through the exclusion of self-incriminating statements obtained in violation of this fundamental right. The legacy of *Miranda's* original understanding still lives on, both in the United States and Europe, even if the Supreme Court's continuous attacks at its core principles have taken away much of its force. In England, courts have traditionally been reluctant to promote rights over the conviction of the guilty when confronted with improperly obtained evidence, yet have begun to show good reflexes when it comes to excluding self-incriminating statements on account of rights-based claims (notably in comparison to privacy violations). At the same time, strong, liberal, rights-centred exclusionary rules begin to emerge where they are most unexpected, at the centre of the inquisitorial tradition, in the parent Continental legal system of France, for example, but also on the (geographical) fringes of Continental Europe; the strict exclusionary rule in Greece is a good example. All this is happening against the backdrop of the perennial conflict between rights and the public interest, which brings us back to the role of the European Court of Human Rights.

Ibrahim, the latest big episode in the *Salduz* evolving saga, leaves us perplexed and worried, and more so about the future direction of the Court than the direction of some specific jurisprudence. Writing in 2012 to offer analysis of the

[210] ibid [21].

ECtHR's case law on the exclusion of evidence obtained in violation of fundamental rights, Ashworth urged caution that the Court was starting to put pragmatism before principle. He pointed to inherent inconsistencies in the Court's jurisprudence relating to the admissibility of evidence obtained in violation of Article 3 and Article 6 of the Convention as well as the Court's inadequate reasoning on the relationship between violations of Article 8 and Article 6, and raised the alarm about the resurgence of 'public interest' arguments which the Court was not resting on some convincing rationale (or, in some cases, *any* rationale). 'A Court that should shine as a beacon in international human rights litigation has lost its way', he concluded.[211] *Ibrahim* exacerbates his well-founded criticism, particularly if one considers the troubling oxymoron at its heart; *Ibrahim* goes against existing efforts in contracting parties, and the European Union institutions, to guarantee the right to custodial legal assistance, both in theory and in practice, and does so on the basis of loosely defined public interest considerations and the resurfacing of a balancing test dominated by them.

Salduz was seemingly not in Ashworth's radar at the time of his 2012 article. It is fair to assume that reflection on this seminal case would have given him some hope. The Grand Chamber rested the exclusionary rule on a principled basis there, the cases that followed it had all expanded upon it and public interest considerations had all but disappeared from the relevant opinions. Even with no vision of *Salduz*, Ashworth found two reasons to be optimistic. He noted that '[t]he absence of any sustained attention to underlying principles is thrown into sharp relief when set against a quite sophisticated scholarly debate, focused on reliability, rights protection, deterrence and moral integrity as the four most prominent and elaborated rationales for excluding evidence'.[212]

He equally optimistically pointed towards dissenting voices in the Court which had made some progress in the above direction.[213] Discussion in the next chapter will gravitate around this scholarly debate and its attention to principle. Before that I want to conclude this chapter by underlying the significance of the dissenting voices in the Court, for their ability to put rights before pragmatism.

The three critiques of *Ibrahim* that were developed above draw considerably on the 'dissenting voices' of Judges Sajó and Laffranque in *Ibrahim*. Finding themselves in a small minority of just two did not stop them from developing a passionate defence of the core values central to the Convention. Speaking extra-judicially on *Ibrahim* a few months after the judgment, Judge Laffranque's attachment to these

[211] A Ashworth, 'The Exclusion of Evidence Obtained by Violating a Fundamental Right: Pragmatism Before Principle in the Strasbourg Jurisprudence' in P Roberts and J Hunter, *Criminal Evidence and Human Rights – Reimagining Common Law Procedural Traditions* (Oxford, Hart Publishing, 2012) 145, 160. See also Choo, *Privilege Against Self-Incrimination* (2013) 116–17, which has as a recurrent theme that 'the Strasbourg Court's jurisprudence [on the privilege against self-incrimination] lacks analytical rigour', and that determinations about the scope of the privilege are 'ultimately … all a matter of balancing'.

[212] Ashworth (ibid) 161.

[213] ibid.

values was clear for everyone to see, and so was her concern about the impact of the Grand Chamber judgment. We should not forget that our mission is to protect 'the fragile rule of law', she said. We must stick to protecting human rights in order to remain true to ourselves; the ECtHR 'must set the example' and confirm our 'common attachment to human rights values', she added.[214] Echoing Judge Laffranque's views, I will now move to elaborate on a rights-centred theory for the exclusion of improperly obtained evidence in the next chapter.

[214] J Laffranque, Keynote speech, Fair Trials Legal Experts Advisory Panel (LEAP), Annual conference, Athens, 3–4 March 2017 (contemporaneous notes on file with author).

6

Reinvigorating the Rights Thesis

Our comparative law vista has so far been constructed by observation of the four Anglo-American and Continental law pillars in this book. These observations give us a kaleidoscopic view of conflicting cultural, procedural and institutional values – within domestic systems, within legal cultures, across legal cultures – shaping exclusionary rules and discretionary exclusion. But at this point the book changes tack, and asks the normative questions of whether, why or when we *should be* excluding improperly obtained evidence.

The wider normative justifications are well rehearsed, particularly in Anglo-American scholarship on the topic, which captures them in the form of the reliability, deterrence, judicial integrity and protective rationales.[1] These abstract theorisations remain highly contested today, particularly those that situate the locus of explanation for excluding improperly obtained evidence on non-epistemic values, not least the protective principle or 'rights thesis'. This is often seen as presenting the gravest threat to the search for truth, as it explicitly puts rights protection first and public interest considerations second, and is grounded on a non-consequential logic which justifies exclusion even if 'no further contingent consequences such as deterrence of misconduct by

[1] See generally A Ashworth, 'Excluding Evidence as Protecting Rights' [1977] *Criminal Law Review* 723; Royal Commission on Criminal Procedure, *The Investigation and Prosecution of Criminal Offences in England and Wales, The Law and Procedure*, Cmnd 8092 (1981) [4.123]–[4.130]; I Dennis, 'Reconstructing the Law of Criminal Evidence' [1989] *Current Legal Problems* 21; Y Kamisar, 'Does (Did) (Should) the Exclusionary Rule Rest on a "Principled Basis" Rather Than an "Empirical Proposition"' (1983) 16 *Creighton Law Review* 565; A Zuckerman, 'Illegally Obtained Evidence – Discretion as a Guardian of Legitimacy' [1987] *Current Legal Problems* 55; W Stuntz, 'The American Exclusionary Rule and Defendants' Changing Rights' [1989] *Criminal Law Review* 117, 118–19; H Jackson, '*Arizona v Evans*: Expanding Exclusionary Rule Exceptions and Contracting Fourth Amendment Protections' (1996) 86 *The Journal of Criminal Law & Criminology* 1201, 1221–24; P Mirfield, *Silence, Confessions and Improperly Obtained Evidence*, Oxford Monographs on Criminal Law and Justice (Oxford, Clarendon Press, 1997) ch 2; J McEwan, *Evidence and the Adversarial Process – The Modern Law*, 2nd edn (Oxford, Hart Publishing, 1998) 211–21; D Ormerod and D Birch, 'The Evolution of the Discretionary Exclusion of Evidence' [2004] *Criminal Law Review* 767, 778–84; A Ashworth and M Redmayne, *The Criminal Process*, 4th edn (Oxford, Oxford University Press, 2010) 344–48; P Roberts and A Zuckerman, *Criminal Evidence*, 2nd edn (Oxford, Oxford University Press, 2010) 179–91; JD Jackson and SJ Summers, *The Internationalisation of Criminal Evidence – Beyond the Common Law and Civil Law Traditions* (Cambridge, Cambridge University Press, 2012) 153–58; A L-T Choo, *Evidence*, 4th edn (Oxford, Oxford University Press, 2015) 172.

investigatory agents' are produced.[2] This chapter revisits the rights thesis, to further strengthen the case, already developed in previous chapters, for legal systems across the Anglo-American and Continental law world to place renewed emphasis on rights protection when excluding improperly obtained evidence. The chapter also sets in motion synergies with theories of judicial integrity and the moral legitimacy of the verdict. These, it will be argued, are required to fill in the gaps that are left open by the rights thesis. First, however, there is a wider, more fundamental, question we must answer, on the relationship between the search for truth, free proof and the aims of the criminal process.

I. Improperly Obtained Evidence and the Aims of the Criminal Process

Free proof is proportional to the importance we give to the search for truth. The more we place the emphasis on the latter, the fewer the restrictions it would be logical to impose on the former, and so any treatise on the reasons justifying the exclusion of improperly obtained evidence presupposes a positive answer to the question of whether we can divert from the search for truth in the first place, without undermining fundamental aims of the criminal process. Of course, a significant part of the law of evidence and criminal procedure does nothing else than deal with restrictions on free proof,[3] which in itself proves the point that the search for truth is not absolute. However, truth-seeking values continue, in many cases, to act as trump cards that justify the use of improperly obtained evidence in practice. This leads us to undertake an analysis of the overarching principle of modern criminal procedure: the search for truth is a cardinal, but by no means the only, aim of the criminal process. If we accept this as true, then we may also accept that evidence can be excluded in line with other aims of the criminal process.

A. The Search for Truth as a Cardinal Aim of the Criminal Process, and the 'Reliability Principle'

We can begin by isolating the first element in this principle. The search for truth is a cardinal aim of the criminal process. It is 'the aim of all judicial operations', wrote Faustin Hélie in the nineteenth century;[4] 'the very first objective assigned

[2] P Chau, 'Excluding Integrity? Revisiting Non-Consequentialist Justifications for Excluding Improperly Obtained Evidence in Criminal Trials' in J Hunter, P Roberts, SNM Young and D Dixon, *The Integrity of the Criminal Process – From Theory Into Practice* (Oxford and Portland, Oregon, Hart Publishing, 2016) 267.

[3] See generally M Damaška, 'Free Proof and its Detractors' (1995) 43 *American Journal of Comparative Law* 343.

[4] Faustin Hélie, *Traité de l'instruction criminelle*, Vol 1 (Brussels, éd belge de Nupels, 1863) n 4, 2.

to criminal procedure', echoed in recent times a prosecutor at the French Cour de cassation.[5] We can think of the search for truth as the *condicio sine qua non* of the criminal process,[6] the medium without which it is impossible to apply substantive criminal law.[7] Under the strong influence of German law, Greek law – like French law – elevates these ideas to fundamental principles of criminal procedure,[8] and this seems to apply to the majority of Continental European countries too.[9] Theories of punishment likewise give truth discovery a central place. The search for truth is seen as indispensable to restoring social peace,[10] for instance, and integral to 'just deserts',[11] since it is only when the criminal process has been able to draw an accurate picture of the moral wrong that has been committed that punishment can be applied proportionately. In the common law tradition, Bentham's rationalist model of adjudication called attention to the search for truth under the concept of 'rectitude of decision making'.[12] An accurate verdict depends on the ability to apply the relevant legal provision to the facts of the case where we have established that they are true,[13] and this requires having the freedom to evaluate all relevant evidence subject to it being of sufficient credibility.[14]

The common law and civil law traditions understand the search for truth in quite distinct ways, of course.[15] We can contrast Continental law's search for an 'objective truth' with the common law's reliance on the most credible version of the

[5] D Commaret, 'La procédure pénale vue comme modèle éthique et déontologique des professions judiciaires' in Cour de cassation, *La procédure pénale en quête de cohérence* (Paris, Dalloz, 2007) 313, 318. See also M Benillouche, 'Les objectifs du procès pénal' in G Giudicelli-Delage (ed), *Les transformations de l'administration de la preuve pénale: perspectives comparées* (Paris, Société de législation comparée, 2006) 19, 30.

[6] A Kostaras, *The search for truth in the criminal process* (Athens, AN Sakkoulas, 1998) 15 (in Greek); T Weigend, 'Should We Search for the Truth, and Who Should Do It' (2011) 36 *North Carolina Journal of International Law & Commercial Regulation* 389.

[7] J Jackson, 'Managing Uncertainty and Finality: The Function of the Criminal Trial in Legal Inquiry' in A Duff, L Farmer, S Marshall and V Tadros, *The Trial on Trial – Volume One: Truth and Due Process* (Oxford, Hart Publishing, 2004) 121, 124; W Hassemer, 'Human Dignity in the Criminal Process: The Example of Truth-Finding' (2011) 44 *Israel Law Review* 185, 186.

[8] See generally A Karras, *Penal procedural law*, 2nd edn (Athens-Komotini, AN Sakkoulas, 1998) 49 (in Greek). See also C Bakas, *The preparatory phase of the criminal process*, Poinika n 50 (Athens-Komotini, AN Sakkoulas, 1995) 17 (in Greek). Article 244 of the German Code of Penal Procedure requires courts to 'ex officio extend the taking of evidence to all facts and means of evidence which are relevant to its decision', '[i]n order to establish the truth'. See M Bohlander, *Principles of German Criminal Procedure* (Oxford, Hart Publishing, 2012) 163.

[9] Jackson and Summers, *Internationalisation of Criminal Evidence* (2012) 69.

[10] See generally N Androulakis, *Fundamental notions of the criminal process*, 2nd edn (Athens-Komotini, AN Sakkoulas, 1994) 33 (in Greek).

[11] P Robinson and M Cahill, *Law Without Justice – Why Criminal Law Doesn't Give People What They Deserve* (Oxford, Oxford University Press, 2006) 16.

[12] See generally W Twining, *Rethinking Evidence* (Cambridge, Cambridge University Press, 1990) 72.

[13] Twining, *Theories of Evidence, Bentham and Wigmore* (London, Weidenfled and Nicholson, 1985) 14. The 'criminal trial is first and foremost an *epistemic* engine', notes Laudan, 'a tool for ferreting out the truth from what will often initially be a confusing array of clues and indicators'. L Laudan, *Truth, Error and Criminal Law – An Essay in Legal Epistemology* (Cambridge, Cambridge University Press, 2006) 2.

[14] I Dennis, *The Law of Evidence*, 5th edn (London, Sweet & Maxwell, 2013) 29.

[15] See ch 1.

truth,[16] or speak of epistemologically diverse understandings that opposing methodologies reveal.[17] But there is no denying that the two legal cultures 'endeavour to get to the truth, and that in that respect there is little to choose between them'.[18] Both legal cultures likewise subscribe to freedom of proof, as a precondition for establishing truth, but to varying degrees, partly as a result of different institutional arrangements. Whilst freedom of proof is of paramount importance in Continental legal systems,[19] in the Anglo-American world its effect is considerably diluted, as a result of the continued attachment to exclusionary rules. This remains true even if under the influence of the 'new Evidence scholarship', freedom of proof is obtaining more prominence today.[20]

In view of the above, the exclusion of evidence can, first of all, be justified on grounds of ensuring that the criminal trial will not be contaminated with unreliable evidence, the admission of which could lead fact-finders to erroneous verdicts. This theoretical justification for exclusion is encapsulated in the 'reliability principle' in Anglo-American law and its far less well-known equivalent in Continental law, an example of which we come across in German criminal procedural scholarship: the *Wahreintsfindung* principle.[21]

These theories draw on the idea that the use of unreliable evidence in criminal trials risks to irretrievably frustrate one of the fundamental aims of the criminal process, the search for truth. The court's attention is diverted away from the truth in the direction of an erroneous conclusion, which can lead to the acquittal of the guilty if not generate the wrongful conviction of an innocent defendant. It is not surprising then that the reliability principle is seen as rather uncontroversial,[22] at least within the Anglo-American culture. Continental law is equally averse

[16] J Hodgson, 'Conceptions of the Trial in Inquisitorial and Adversarial Procedure' in A Duff, L Farmer, S Marshall and V Tadros, *The Trial on Trial – Volume Two: Judgment and Calling to Account* (Oxford and Portland, Hart Publishing, 2006) 223, 225. See also C Safferling, *Towards an International Criminal Procedure* (Oxford, Oxford University Press, 2001) 18.

[17] Hodgson, 'Conceptions of the Trial' (ibid) 225.

[18] J McEwan, 'Ritual, Fairness and Truth: The Adversarial and Inquisitorial Models of Criminal Trial' in Duff et al, *The Trial on Trial – Volume One* (2004) 63.

[19] In France, for example, article 427 of the CPP specifically instructs that 'criminal offences can be established through any means of evidence'. Article 179 of the CPP in Greece provides that 'in the criminal process any means of evidence is permitted'. Criminal procedure in Portugal, Belgium, Italy, the Netherlands and Germany likewise embrace the free proof principle, either explicitly or implicitly. See J Pradel, 'Rapport général', RIDP 1992, n 63, 13, 18–19; A Karras, 'Free evaluation of proof and "Cassation Court" review' in Hellenic Association of Criminal Law (ΕΕΠΔ), *Evidence in the criminal process*, Proceedings of the 6th panhellenic conference (Athens, PN Sakkoulas, 1998) 9 (in Greek).

[20] W Twining, *Rethinking Evidence*, 2nd edn (Cambridge, Cambridge University Press, 2006) See also R Lempert, 'The New Evidence Scholarship: Analyzing the Process of Proof' (1986) 66 *Boston University Law Review* 439; J Jackson, 'Analysing the New Evidence Scholarship: Towards a New Conception of the Law of Evidence' (1996) 16 *Oxford Journal of Legal Studies* 309; P Roberts, 'Rethinking the Law of Evidence: A Twenty-First Century Agenda for Teaching and Research' (2002) 55 *Current Legal Problems* 297. Choo points to 'an increasing embracement of the concept of free proof' and a transition towards 'free(r) proof'. Choo, *Evidence* (2015) 16.

[21] See generally C Feldmann, Das Tonband als Beweismittel in Strafprozeß, NJW 1959, 1166, cited by C Naintos, *Evidential prohibitions in the criminal trial* (Athens-Salonica, Sakkoulas, 2010) 29 (in Greek).

[22] Ashworth and Redmayne, *The Criminal Process* (2010) 343.

to wrongful convictions and wrongful acquittals, but continues to have faith in professional fact-finders' ability to give appropriate weight, or entirely disregard, unreliable evidence. Chapter four exemplified this contrast, by pinpointing exclusionary rules specifically applicable to unreliable and involuntary confessions in the United States and England and Wales, with no equivalent in either France or Greece.[23] Taken at face value, the absence in Continental law of exclusionary rules for unreliable evidence may suggest that Continental legal systems place disproportionate emphasis on free proof, and that realignment with the search for truth may be required. But this would also be to disregard that, in the above jurisdictions, unreliable evidence is still excluded where it has been obtained in violation of specific procedural rights, which are themselves underpinned, partly at least, by reliability considerations. We should not, in any case, forget that many constitutional rights 'unquestionably serve epistemic ends'.[24]

We see here how the reliability principle is aligned with the search for truth, but this is not the end of the matter when discussing theoretical justifications for the exclusion of improperly obtained evidence consistently with the objectives of the criminal process, unless, of course, one adopts the position that the search of truth is the only objective of the criminal process.[25] Bentham and Wigmore have vigorously defended this thesis, and they are joined by contemporary scholars who subscribe to similar accounts of rationalisation of doctrine and practice, in claiming that there should be no exceptions to admitting relevant evidence unless the quality of the evidence has been affected.[26] But contemporary criminal procedure thinking otherwise adopts a broader vision of the criminal process, which endorses the protection of non-epistemic values antagonistic to the search for truth as an objective of the criminal process.

B. Beyond the Search for Truth: Human Rights, Judicial Integrity and the Moral Legitimacy of the Verdict

Continental law scholarship and jurisprudence have long exposed the rather circumscribed conceptualisation of the search for truth as the sole objective of the

[23] It would be interesting to consider what Bentham or Wigmore would make of this difference of approach. Though calling for the suppression of all technical exclusionary rules, they were taking as their starting point exclusionary rules for unreliable evidence, to ensure that the search for truth would not be put in jeopardy by reliance on untrustworthy evidence. See generally Wigmore, *Wigmore on Evidence*, 3rd edn, vol 8 (1940), s 2183, 5. See also A Zuckerman, *The Principles of Criminal Evidence* (Oxford, Clarendon Press, 1989) 342–43.

[24] Laudan, *Truth, Error and Criminal Law* (2006) 218.

[25] As Ho Hock Lai explains, 'if, as it is commonly accepted, the criminal trial is aimed at ascertaining the truth of a criminal charge, it is inherently problematic to prevent the prosecution from adducing relevant evidence on the ground of its unlawful provenance'. Ho Hock Lai, 'The Criminal Trial, the Rule of Law and the Exclusion of Unlawfully Obtained Evidence' (2016) 10 *Criminal Law and Philosophy* 109.

[26] See generally discussion in Twining, *Theories of Evidence* (1985); Ashworth, 'Excluding Evidence as Protecting Rights' (1977) 725; Mirfield, *Improperly Obtained Evidence* (1997) 9–10; Zuckerman, *The Principles of Criminal Evidence* (1989) 342–43 citing Wigmore, *Wigmore on Evidence* (1940) vol 8 5.

criminal process.[27] Pradel takes as his starting point that 'the search for truth is not the only value that the Law is interested in'.[28] Garraud put it more graphically, at the beginning of the nineteenth century even, observing that the search for truth should be taking place 'within Law and by Law' (*dans le droit et par le droit*).[29] Other contemporary scholars speak of the conflicting values that we should strive to balance – truth and efficiency on the one hand, the legitimacy of the verdict (*legitimité*), on the other[30] – which throw the entire law of evidence and criminal procedure into a sharply bipolar division.[31] At a more abstract level, Continental law recognises a moral imperative for the search for truth to be in line with the fundamental values of civilised countries.[32] In Germany, the principle of human dignity transforms this otherwise amorphous moral imperative into constitutional principle. Hassemer reads in it a duty to reconcile the search for truth with protecting human rights; human dignity is seen as 'a shield against an excessive search for the truth', a safeguard against unconstitutional invasions of privacy or treating the suspect as an object when he is questioned by the police.[33] The German Federal Court of Justice (Bundesgerichtshof) has famously declared that 'there is no principle in criminal procedural law from which it derives that truth can be searched at all costs',[34] concluding that exclusionary rules for improperly obtained evidence (*beweisverbote*) should therefore be seen as setting appropriate limits to truth discovery.[35] The Greek supreme court echoed the Bundesgerichtshof's words, as is often the case. 'Justice [as in 'the search for truth'] cannot be done at all costs', it held, in a seminal case setting robust constitutional standards for the exclusion of evidence obtained in violation of the right to privacy.[36]

Continental law scholarship takes a similar view of freedom of proof. Respect of positive law is seen as a frontier that freedom of proof, no matter how widely

See also A Skeen, 'The Admissibility of Improperly Obtained Evidence in Criminal Trials' (1988) 1 *South-African Journal of Criminal Justice* 389, 390.

[27] As Jackson and Summers note, the doctrine of free proof is 'less controversial and less absolute than its reputation would suggest'. Jackson and Summers (n 1) 69.

[28] J Pradel, *Procédure pénale*, 10th edn (Paris, Cujas, 2000) 302. See also M Benillouche, 'Les objectifs du procès pénal' in Giudicelli-Delage (ed), *Transformations de la preuve pénale* (2006) 19.

[29] R Garraud, *Traité théorique et pratique d'instruction criminelle et de procédure pénale*, vol 1 (Paris, Librairie du Recueil Sirey, 1907) 5.

[30] M Delmas-Marty, 'La preuve pénale' (1996) *Droits* 52; G Giudicelli-Delage, 'Conclusion' in Giudicelli-Delage (n 5) 327, 339.

[31] D Commaret, 'Les métamorphoses de la preuve' (2004) *Revue pénitentiaire et de droit pénal* 735, 741–42.

[32] G Stefani, G Levasseur and B Bouloc, *Procédure pénale*, Précis Dalloz, 17th edn (Paris, Dalloz, 2000) 2. See also J Gauthier, 'Quelques remarques sur la liberté des preuves et ses limites en droit pénal' (1990) 2 *Revue pénale suisse* 184; H Leclerc, 'La loi du 15 juin 2000 (Gaz. Pal, Bull. lég. 13 juillet, p. 263 et circ. P. 287) renforçant la présomption d'innocence et les droits des victimes', *Gazette du Palais*, 29–30 September 2000.

[33] Hassemer, 'Human Dignity in the Criminal Process' (2011) 187.

[34] BGHSt, vol 14, 365.

[35] E Beling, *Die Beweisverbote als Grenzen der Wahrheitserforschung im Strafprozeß*, cited by Karras, *Penal procedural law* (1998) 635. See also N Foster and S Sule, *German Legal System*, 3rd edn (Oxford, Oxford University Press, 2002) 357–58.

[36] Arios Pagos 1/2001, 42 Elliniki Dikaiosini 375.

understood, should not cross.[37] Buisson pinpoints important limitations which show that free proof is not the only major principle of criminal procedure in France.[38] Androulakis explains that only legally obtained proof comes within the dominion of free proof in Greece.[39] Freedom of proof would quickly produce a caricature of the criminal process otherwise, favouring an imbalance between the State which has the legal obligation to prove its case, *dans le droit et par le droit*, and the individual charged with an offence.[40] Perhaps no other evidentiary principle exemplifies the limitations to free proof better than the French *principe de loyauté*, at a theoretical level. This imposes a positive obligation upon courts and the police to search for evidence within the parameters set by ethical and legal standards pertaining to the obtaining of proof, with prohibitions on entrapment a characteristic example.[41]

Now if Continental law, with its historic search for truth instincts, explicitly recognises that human dignity, individual rights or the legitimacy of the verdict constitute substantial limitations to conceptualising the search for truth as the ubiquitous aim of the criminal process, it should be no surprise that the – historically more loosely connected with truth discovery – common law would do so too. Let us take Ashworth's and Redmayne's anti-consequentialist, rights-based, exegesis of the aims of the criminal process as the starting point. When pursuing the aims of accurate judgments, convicting the guilty and delivering retributive justice, respect for rights is 'essential', they note, 'a concomitant aim of the criminal process – not merely a side-constraint' on the search for truth.[42] The criminal process has the 'twin goals' of producing accurate fact determinations while ensuring that fundamental rights are respected in the process, they add,[43] before they proceed to undertake a critique of balancing theories that often sacrifice human rights in the alter of public safety. They warn that the metaphor of balancing can seduce us into thinking that proper consideration is given to competing values of the criminal process, while, in reality, it allows for rights (of a small minority) to be traded off against the interests of the majority, substituting rhetoric for principled argument and leaving the arbitrary exercise of state power to go unchecked.[44] Roberts' and Zuckerman's work notes the significance of similar moral imperatives in the criminal process, in line with Kantian ideals, as barriers to the search for truth; treating defendants humanely, as subjects who cannot be deprived of their inherent humanity even where they have violated the humanity of others, rather

[37] S Guinchard and J Buisson, *Procédure pénale* (Paris, Litec, 2000) 38; Beling, *Die Beweisverbote* cited by Karras (n 35) 690.

[38] J Buisson, 'La légalité dans l'administration de la preuve pénale' (1998) *Procédures* 3.

[39] N Androulakis, 'Regarding the problem of confessions obtained illegally during police interrogation' (1974) 22 *Nomiko Bima* 1345, 1352 (in Greek). See also Karras, *Penal procedural law* (2011) 689.

[40] P Bouzat, 'La loyauté dans la recherche des preuves' in *Recueil d'études en hommage à M Louis Hugueney* (Paris, Pédone, 1964) 155, 156.

[41] See, eg *Crim* 27 February 1996, *Bull crim* n 93.

[42] Ashworth and Redmayne (n 1) 48.

[43] ibid 51.

[44] ibid 41–47.

than as objects that can be disposed of.[45] Dennis reinforces this view, arguing, strongly, that the aims of the criminal process go beyond an instrumental 'search for truth' ethic. His preferred theoretical framework rests on the need to safeguard the moral legitimacy of the verdict through balancing competing considerations, yet he accepts that rights considerations can take priority in this process.[46]

This quick review has been limited to jurisprudential perspectives, leaving aside a plethora of examples from positive law. Still it sheds light on the fact that, in both Anglo-American and Continental law, the search for truth is not a meta-value but only one value among several,[47] and that individual rights can act as catalysts for seeking truth in line with respecting human dignity and the moral imperatives intrinsic to treating the defendant as a subject in the criminal process. As Giudicelli-Delage argues:

> The ultimate aim of any criminal process, in either Continental or Anglo-American law – and independently of possible differences of evidential technique between these systems – is the search for truth. However, this cannot be undertaken at any cost … the desire to search for the truth must be articulated together with the need to ensure respect of the rule of law (*légitimité*), which has been reinforced by the process of integrating human rights into positive law, as these place emphasis on respecting the rule of law.[48]

These theories align, in other words, the aims of the criminal process with a Dworkinian 'taking rights seriously' imperative or the idea that rights should trump the public interest[49] and be immune from balancing exercises that could lead to rights reduction where there might seem to exist a social cost in giving them effect.[50]

[45] Roberts and Zuckerman, *Criminal Evidence* (2010) 21; P Roberts, 'Theorising Procedural Tradition: Subjects, Objects and Values in Criminal Adjudication' in Duff et al, *The Trial on Trial – Volume Two* (2006) 37, 41. See also W LaFave, J Israel and N King, *Criminal Procedure*, Hornbook Series (Minnessota, West Group, 2000) 30 and 37. For Trechsel, 'the degree to which the defendant gets the feeling that he is being respected as a fellow human being' is encapsulated in the principle of fairness, and 'might well be the most important element in humane criminal proceedings'. S Trechsel, 'Why Must Trials Be Fair' (1997) 31 *Israeli Law Review* 94, 119.

[46] Dennis, *Evidence* (2013) 37–51. Dennis draws on Dworkin and Rawls to describe the foundation values for individual rights as a method for settling objectives and ordering priorities in the criminal process, and on Maher's depiction of the principle of fairness as a precondition for the respect of dignity and rights of individuals as an aim of the criminal process. See R Dworkin, *Taking Rights Seriously* (London, Duckworth, 1977); J Rawls, *A Theory of Justice*, rev edn (1999) 209–10; G Maher, 'Natural Justice as Fairness' in DN McCormick and PBH Birks (eds), *The Legal Mind: Essays for Tony Honore* (Oxford, Clarendon Press, 1985) 115.

[47] Kamisar, '"Principled Basis"' (1983) 621. See also Roberts who argues that though the centrality of epistemic considerations in criminal adjudication cannot be denied, 'they are neither the exclusive concern of criminal procedure nor its overriding preoccupation'. P Roberts, 'Normative Evolution in Evidentiary Exclusion: Coercion, Deception and the Right to a Fair Trial' in P Roberts and J Hunter (ed), *Criminal Evidence and Human Rights* (Oxford, Hart Publishing, 2012) 163, 165–66.

[48] G Giudicelli-Delage, 'Conclusion' in G Giudicelli-Delage (n 5) 339. See also T Bingham, *The Rule of Law* (London, Penguin Books, 2011).

[49] Dworkin, *Taking Rights Seriously* (1977).

[50] A Ashworth, *Human Rights, Serious Crime and Criminal Procedure*, The Hamlyn Lectures (London, Sweet & Maxwell, 2002) 74.

Alternative theories extend their reach beyond rights to more abstract, moral conceptualisations of the aims of the criminal process. Most notable amongst them are theories that focus on safeguarding judicial integrity and the moral legitimacy of the verdict. Zuckerman's pioneering work in this area rested on the 'special moral dimension' of the criminal trial. He argued that the trial is concerned with 'the determination of moral blame, as well as of legal liability', and the willingness of the public to accept verdicts therefore 'depends on the extent to which the public believes in the moral legitimacy of the system'.[51] But such public acceptance of the verdict was conditioned upon the criminal justice system setting the example and rejecting an 'ends justify the means' approach. The criminal justice system could not endorse the use of immoral – illegal, unconstitutional or unfair – methods and their fruits, on the one hand, and command respect for its determinations of the moral responsibility of the individuals entering the system, on the other. Such an oxymoron would necessarily have a detrimental effect upon the ability of the state to claim the moral authority required to justify convicting those breaching key societal norms.

Dennis has, in similar terms, famously construed a theory of the moral legitimacy of the verdict, where moral legitimacy is 'the ultimate goal' of adjudication, a means which 'allows competing claims in the law of evidence to be settled', either through the adoption of rules or through the exercise of judicial discretion.[52] On this account, 'apparently reliable evidence may need to be excluded' to ensure consistency with other fundamental values of the criminal process, such as substantive values, for example 'respect for human autonomy and dignity, security of person and property from unjustified interference, privacy and freedom from discrimination', or procedural values, such as 'the presumption of innocence, fair trial according to principles of natural justice, and probity on the part of state agencies entrusted with coercive powers'.[53]

More recently, Duff, Farmer, Marshall and Tadros have identified the primary function of the criminal trial as calling defendants to account for their conduct, which, concomitantly, empowers defendants to challenge the standing of parties in the criminal process, in other words the parties' ability to hold defendants to account. Finding the defendant guilty amounts to moral condemnation of the defendant's conduct according to this account, but this presupposes that 'the state,

[51] See A Zuckerman, 'Illegally Obtained Evidence' (1987) 55–56. See also Zuckerman (n 23); A Duff, *Trials and Punishments* (Cambridge, Cambridge University Press, 1986); A LT Choo, *Abuse of Process and Judicial Stays of Criminal Proceedings*, 2nd edn (Oxford, Oxford University Press, 2008) 12–17. Choo elaborated upon Zuckerman's thesis to argue that proceedings could be stayed where there was an abuse of process. For a similar view in French criminal procedure scholarship see S Guinchard and J Buisson, *Procédure pénale* (Paris, Litec, 2000) 2, who comment that 'a severe sentence will be far better understood and accepted where the procedure will have had no flaws, and will have respected the rights of [all parties]'.

[52] Dennis (n 14) 56. This thesis was originally developed in Dennis, 'Reconstructing' [1989] 21. See also J Jackson, 'Managing Uncertainty and Finality' in Duff et al (n 7) 129.

[53] ibid 55.

through the trial, has the moral standing to condemn the defendant'.[54] The integrity-based argument that is deduced from this line of thinking is that the state will lack the moral standing to hold the defendant to account when its organs have been complicit in the wrongdoing that has brought about the criminal trial in the first place. This version of integrity is different from those discussed previously, in that it does not – explicitly – require taking into consideration the potential impact on integrity that would derive from collapsing trials and 'letting the guilty go free'. Even here, however, there is implicit reference to public attitudes. The authors speak of 'the inevitable frustration that arises from the application of the integrity principle … when the defendant is seen to have escaped "through a legal loophole"', and they urge caution in not adopting an account of integrity that would be 'too broad or too liberal in its application'.[55]

In the preceding theorisations, there are echoes of Justice Brandeis' and Justice Holmes' dissenting opinions in the seminal *Olmstead v United States* case,[56] which are paradigmatic of conceiving judicial integrity as a barrier to the 'search discovery' and 'free proof' principles. The difference here is that integrity is not linked to the views of the public. Confronted with a majority opinion that had confirmed the constitutionality of the use of evidence obtained by the secret tapping of a telephone line, Brandeis responded that:

> Decency, security and liberty alike demand that government officials shall be subjected to the same rules of conduct that are commands to the citizen. In a government of laws, existence of the government will be imperiled if it fails to observe the law scrupulously. Our Government is the potent, the omnipresent teacher. For good or for ill, it teaches the whole people by its example. Crime is contagious. If the Government becomes a lawbreaker, it breeds contempt for law; it invites every man to become a law unto himself; it invites anarchy. To declare that, in the administration of the criminal law, the end justifies the means – to declare that the Government may commit crimes in order to secure the conviction of a private criminal – would bring terrible retribution. Against that pernicious doctrine this Court should resolutely set its face.[57]

Holmes described the importance of judicial integrity with equal force, noting that 'the government should not itself foster and pay for other crime, when they are the means by which the evidence is to be obtained'.[58] The idea at the heart of

[54] Duff et al, *The Trial on Trial – Volume Three: Towards a Normative Theory of the Criminal Trial* (Oxford, Hart Publishing, 2007) 225.

[55] ibid 241. A more promising approach, for legal systems intent to take the public interest into account, may be the one adopted by Canadian law, where it is the views of the 'reasonable person' that are taken to represent the views of the community, and this is only if the 'community's current mood is reasonable'. *R v Collins* [1987] 1 SCR 265 [32]–[33]. In Canadian law, the impact on integrity is also evaluated from the viewpoint of the 'long-term consequences of regular admission or exclusion' on the integrity of the criminal justice system, not on the basis of the community's 'transitory enthusiasms or emotional outbursts'. See A L-T Choo and S Nash, 'Improperly Obtained Evidence in the Commonwealth: Lessons for England and Wales?' (2007) 11 *International Journal of Evidence & Proof* 75, 95 quoting *R v Collins*, ibid [31] and [34].

[56] *Olmstead v United States*, 277 US 438 (1928).

[57] ibid 485.

[58] ibid 470.

the integrity principle was that it would be 'a less evil that some criminals should escape than that the Government should play an ignoble part'.[59]

Ho Hock Lai has recently reconceptualised judicial integrity as underpinning a theory of the criminal trial emphasising the rule of law.[60] The trial cannot play this role unless it prevents the executive 'from securing a guilty verdict through its own unlawful conduct'.[61] From this angle, the exclusion of improperly obtained evidence is 'mandated, rather than at odds with, the suggested purpose of a criminal trial'.[62] This rule of law-centred version of integrity resembles Brandeis' and Holmes' view, and diverges from those that take public confidence in the criminal justice into consideration, in that it is 'non-instrumental'. The fact that, by holding the executive to account, including through the exclusion of improperly obtained evidence, the Court may increase public confidence in the administration of criminal justice, is just the consequence of its choosing to act in this way and not the reason for it. The theory is normatively premised on the idea that the Court is constituted to uphold the rule of law.[63] Young offers an equally original, public law-centred, theory of integrity, which also takes abstract statements about 'moral legitimacy' or 'integrity' as its starting point, but 'goes further' than that, 'requiring a specific articulation of the public interests engaged in a particular case and a justification for why a particular interest is of such overriding character to justify … excluding material evidence'.[64]

Judicial integrity finds its equivalent in the *loyauté* principle of French law,[65] and the 'moral superiority of the state' doctrine in German law (*sittliche Überlegenheit*), which posits a moral duty for state judicial authorities to abstain from founding

[59] ibid. This theory was premised on accepting a unitary theory of the criminal process, whereby the criminal investigation and prosecution phases are strictly connected with the trial phase, and the acts of police officers and prosecutors engage the responsibility of the court. The Government as prosecutor and judge are indistinguishable, and so neither prosecutors nor judges should be permitted 'to have a hand in such dirty business'. See generally T Shrock and R Welsh, 'Up from Calandra: the Exclusionary Rule as a Constitutional Requirement' (1974) 9 *Minnsessota Law Review* 251; R Grant, 'The Exclusionary Rule and the Meaning of Separation of Powers' (1991) 14 *Harvard Journal of Law & Public Policy* 173. Duff, Farmer, Marshall and Tadros speak of 'integrity as integration', which means that the different phases of the criminal process do not stand in isolation. Duff et al, *The Trial on Trial – Volume Three* (2007) 226. *cf* JH Wigmore, 'Using Evidence Obtained by Illegal Search and Seizure' (1922) 8 ABAJ 479, for an account of the fragmentary thesis, according to which courts do not implicate themselves in unlawful or improper conduct undertaken by other agents of the criminal process where they admit (unlawfully obtained but) reliable evidence in accordance with their truth-seeking function. On this side of the Atlantic, see A Ashworth, 'Exploring the Integrity Principle in Evidence and Procedure' in P Mirfield and R Smith, *Essays for Colin Tapper* (London, Lexis-Nexis Butterworths, 2003) 107, 117, who is critical of the fragmentary thesis.

[60] Ho Hock Lai, 'The Criminal Trial' (2016) 109.

[61] ibid.

[62] ibid.

[63] ibid 127. See also E Sundby, 'Everyman's Exclusionary Rule: The Exclusionary Rule and the Rule of Law (or why Conservatives Should Embrace the Exclusionary Rule)' (2013) 10 *Ohio State Journal of Criminal Law* 393; J Iontcheva Turner, 'The Exclusionary Rule as a Symbol of the Rule of Law' (2014) 67 *SMU Law Review* 821.

[64] SNM Young, 'A Public Law Conception of Integrity in the Criminal Process' in Hunter et al, *Integrity* (2016) 46.

[65] See ch 3.

their decisions on violations of the law. The state will otherwise risk destroying the 'purity' of the criminal process. Judicial integrity, from this viewpoint, operates on the basis of a fixed, objective, moral imperative, not on a fluctuating 'public acceptance of the verdict' test which would also take into account competing considerations and allow for balancing.[66] To speak like Mirfield, this is a 'court-centred' type of integrity where the court applies 'its own standards of propriety and decency'.[67]

So far in this chapter, we have begun to unravel the intricate relationship between the search for truth, free proof and the aims of the criminal process. But to provide a compelling normative justification for excluding improperly obtained evidence, against the backdrop of this book's comparative law observations, we must dig deeper. So, it may emerge from the above that, for both Anglo-American and Continental law, the protection of individual or human rights is a legitimate constraint upon the search for truth, and a proportionate qualification to the free proof principle, but does this mean we should exclude evidence to protect rights, and, if yes, what sort of rights? Do these need to be entrenched in a constitutional charter or international human rights convention, and what should be our approach to more trivial breaches? Ultimately, why should we single out the protection of rights rather than take them as one element in a balancing exercise that brings rights and the public interest together, and allows us to assess the impact of the admissibility of tainted evidence upon the integrity of the criminal justice system, the moral legitimacy of the verdict or the rule of law?

II. 'Excluding Evidence as Protecting Rights' Revisited

In 1977, Andrew Ashworth's ingenious legal mind gave us the 'protective principle'[68] (or 'remedial rationale'),[69] one of the most innovative and enduring explanatory theories in Anglo-American law for the exclusion of improperly obtained evidence. Ashworth's thesis has been '[p]rofusely cited ever since', soon passing 'into the terminological canon of criminal procedure scholarship'.[70] Forty years later, the protective rationale continues to occupy a central place in the scholarship, attracting support and criticism in equal measure. In advancing a rights-centred thesis for the exclusion of improperly obtained evidence, this chapter will now seek to elaborate on the strengths of the rationale, whilst addressing the main concerns

[66] See generally Eb Schmidt, Lehrkommentar zur Strafprozeßordnung und zum Gerichtsverfassungsgesetz (Auflage, Göttingen, 1964); JD Osmer, Der Umfang des Beweisverwertungsverbotes nach § 136a StPO (Hamburg, 1966) 102, cited by Naintos, *Evidential Prohibitions* (n 21) 31.

[67] Mirfield (n 1) 24.

[68] Ashworth, 'Excluding Evidence as Protecting Rights' (1977) 723.

[69] Ashworth and Redmayne (n 1) 345.

[70] P Roberts, 'Excluding Evidence as Protecting Constitutional or Human Rights?' in L Zedner and JV Roberts, *Principles and Values in Criminal Law and Criminal Justice – Essays in Honour of Andrew Ashworth* (Oxford, Oxford University Press, 2012) 171.

of its critics and drawing a strong connection with the judicial integrity principle. The chapter will then discuss the protective rationale against the backdrop of the comparative law observations undertaken so far, before widening the angle of view and zooming in on other examples from Anglo-American and Continental law. From this analysis, the chapter will extrapolate the need to place new emphasis on the rights thesis, in both Anglo-American and Continental legal systems, regardless of the choice of the exclusionary mechanism (automatic or discretionary) or exclusionary rationale (or rationales) currently embraced.

Let us start by revisiting Ashworth's description of the core elements of the principle, in the 1977 article and more recent work. Succinctly put, the principle militates that improperly obtained evidence is excluded so that we can protect, vindicate and restore the rights of the defendant. In the words of Ashworth, the principle argues that 'an infringement of an individual's rights (in the broadest sense that he is denied something to which he is entitled or subjected to treatment which is improper) supplies a prima facie justification for the exclusion of evidence obtained as a result of that infringement'.[71] One of the principle's key strengths lies in the simplicity of its logic,[72] particularly when we understand an individual's rights as fundamental human rights entrenched in a national constitutional charter or international human rights instrument. To admit evidence obtained in violation of constitutional or human rights is to deny the individual the enjoyment of fundamental protections central to the criminal process. As Ashworth explains, more generally:

> If a legal system declares certain standards for the conduct of criminal investigation – whether they are enshrined in a constitution, detailed in a comprehensive code or scattered in various statutes and judicial precedents – then it can be argued that citizens have corresponding rights to be accorded certain facilities and not to be treated in certain ways. If the legal system is to respect those rights, then it is arguable that a suspect whose rights have been infringed should not thereby be placed at any disadvantage: by 'disadvantage' is meant … that evidence obtained by the investigators as a result of the infringement should not be used against the suspect. And the appropriate way of ensuring that the suspect does not suffer this disadvantage is for the court of trial to have the power to exclude evidence obtained by improper methods. The presentation of evidence in court may in this context be viewed as the natural conclusion of a criminal investigation and it is therefore fitting that the court should protect the defendant from disadvantages resulting from any infringement of his rights during that investigation.[73]

[71] Ashworth (n 1) 725.

[72] This is true even if several alternative interpretations are possible when one starts to delve into each of the elements of the above definition. With inimitable rigour, Roberts has conceived 243 alternative interpretations of the protective principle. Roberts, 'Excluding Evidence' (2012). His analysis brings to the fore the protective principle's 'deceptive simplicity', but the same can be said, indeed a fortiori, about the judicial integrity principle for instance, given the multiplicity of factors that must be taken into account in the process of evaluating the impact of the admission of the evidence upon the fuzzy, ill-defined concept of judicial integrity.

[73] Ashworth (n 1) 725.

In other words, by excluding the evidence, 'the courts seek to put the defendant back in the position he would have been in had his rights not been breached'.[74] They aim to restore the status quo ante.[75] They take away from the state an unfairly obtained advantage, in the form of evidence that its agents would not have been able to obtain in the first place, had they acted in conformity with relevant procedural standards and underpinning human rights norms.[76]

Now, because the principle's original focus covered a wide spectrum of violations, Ashworth's thesis conceded from the outset that the violation of a right did 'not necessarily lead to the view that *all* improperly obtained evidence should be peremptorily excluded', and he regarded an exclusionary discretion – rather than a strict exclusionary rule – as the procedural device most compatible with the prima facie justification for exclusion supplied by the principle.[77] But once the focus of attention narrowed and shifted towards violations relating to 'a constitutional or codified declaration of individual rights', the principle's 'sphere of operation' immediately became 'clearer'.[78] In more recent work elucidating the application of the principle to violations of human rights, and taking the example of rights enshrined in the ECHR, Ashworth argued, with Redmayne, that there was 'a good case for going further and applying a strict, remedial approach'.[79] This was an immediate reflection on the importance of the fundamental interests at stake, and 'the consequence of accepting that', to protect these interests, 'sometimes the State will not be able to pursue the greater good'. Exclusion was the price to pay for the protection of rights.[80]

The idea of excluding evidence to protect constitutional or human rights has steadily gained support in the scholarship. For instance, Ormerod suggested the adoption of a presumption of exclusion for Convention breaches, based on 'a robust and rights-centred approach' that would afford Convention rights special status, in contrast to evidence obtained by technical or trivial breaches which would still be admissible.[81] Choo situated his approach to excluding improperly

[74] Ashworth and Redmayne (n 1) 345.

[75] ibid. See also W Schroeder, 'Restoring the Status Quo Ante: The Fourth Amendment Exclusionary Rule as a Compensatory Device' (1983) 51 *George Washington Law Review* 633; P Stewart, 'The Road to *Mapp v Ohio* and Beyond: The Origins, Development and Future of the Exclusionary Rule in Search-and-Seizure Cases' (1983) 83 *Columbia Law Review* 1365, 1392; Australian Law Reform Commission, Evidence (Interim Report) [1985] ALRC 26 [959]; *Arizona v Evans* 115 S Ct 1185, 1195 (1995), per Justice Stevens (dissenting opinion); J Norton, 'The Exclusionary Rule Reconsidered: Restoring the Status Quo Ante' (1998) 33 *Wake Forest Law Review* 261.

[76] The courts subscribe, in this way, to the idea that judicial authorities must strive to restore injustice, as efficiently as they possibly can. See P Traest, 'The Putting into Perspective of the Exclusionary Rule: Some General Remarks and the Belgian Experience' in C Breur, M Kommer, J Nijboer, J Reijntjes, *New Trends in Criminal Investigation and Evidence*, vol 2 (Antwerpen – Groningen – Oxford, Intersentia, 2000) 649, 650. See also discussion in P Robinson and M Cahill, *Law Without Justice* (2006) 150–51.

[77] Ashworth (n 1) 725.

[78] ibid 726.

[79] Ashworth and Redmayne (n 1) 360.

[80] ibid 360–61.

[81] D Ormerod, 'ECHR and the Exclusion of Evidence: Trial Remedies for Article 8 Breaches?' [2003] Crim LR 61, 78. Ormerod's approach can be viewed as particularly bold, if it is taken into account

obtained evidence on a broader integrity principle, yet he argued that 'superimposed on such an approach' should be a rule that 'evidence should automatically be excluded' where it has been obtained in violation of Convention rights. Integrity requires that rights should be 'taken seriously', and Convention rights 'especially seriously', he explained,[82] while he too advocated a balancing test where there is no violation of a Convention right and the 'fruit [of the official illegality] is not rotten to the core'.[83] Like Ormerod and Choo, Roberts takes as his starting point the idea that we could 'designate a special class of rights' which 'should occupy an elevated role in the analysis'. Their 'elevated normative status', he notes, could allow one to start from the idea that breaches of these rights will 'always have material implications for the admissibility of evidence obtained through their violation'.[84] One could eventually conclude that such violation 'presumptively provides a reason for triggering evidentiary exclusion in appropriate cases'.[85] Roberts identified constitutional and human rights as a class of rights having a priori this elevated moral status, and saw in them 'promising opportunities for developing a rejuvenated and super-charged protective principle', though he also pointed out the risks inherent in grounding the exclusionary rule on cosmopolitan human rights norms that may have the capacity to impinge 'on cherished values embedded in national legal traditions'.[86] Jackson and Summers recognise the right to fair trial as an example of such a class of rights, though they then go on to claim that the justification for exclusion only arises where the violation has undermined defendants' 'procedural rights and their opportunity to present their case as they see fit in adversarial proceedings'.[87] The violation of the right to fair trial, and subsequently the requirement to exclude the evidence, does not derive from 'the substantive

that it was developed with reference to a qualified Convention right, Article 8 ECHR, not an absolute one, such as the right against torture. See also Ormerod and Birch, 'The Evolution of the Discretionary Exclusion of Evidence' (2004) 787. See also SC Thaman, 'Balancing Truth Against Human Rights: A Theory of Modern Exclusionary Rules' in SC Thaman (ed), *Exclusionary Rules in Comparative Law* (New York, Springer, 2013) 403, 408. Thaman argues that violations of fundamental or constitutional rights 'are so serious that they should trigger a very strong presumption of non-use of the evidence resulting therefrom'.

[82] Choo (n 1) 189. See also DV MacDougal, 'The Exclusionary Rule and Its Alternatives: Remedies for Constitutional Violations in Canada and the United States' (1985) 76 *Criminal Law & Criminology* 608, 618; MA Fairlie, '*Miranda* and its (More Rights-Protective) International Counterparts' (2013) 20 *University of California Davis Journal of International Law & Policy* 1, 45. Similarly to Choo, Fairlie situates automatic exclusion within a broader judicial integrity context. She does not call for the adoption of automatic exclusion, but points out that, with regards to self-incriminating statements obtained in violation of custodial interrogation rights, automatic exclusion would achieve the aim of ensuring the integrity of the proceedings.

[83] Choo (n 1) 191. Writing with Nash, Choo goes further to deduce – from the absolute prohibition of Article 3 ECHR to use any evidence obtained in consequence of that breach – a robust exclusionary rule for evidence obtained in contravention of *any* Convention right, on the basis that its use would constitute a breach of Article 6 ECHR. Choo and Nash, 'Improperly Obtained Evidence' (2007) 105.

[84] Roberts (n 70) 184.

[85] ibid.

[86] ibid 189.

[87] Jackson and Summers (n 1) 197.

violation per se', they argue.[88] To take a final example, Bloom and Dewey promote the unexceptional application of an exclusionary rule that vindicates personal rights on the simple basis that it is the strongest remedy available for constitutional violations and the idea that '[e]very right must have a remedy and a weakened remedy points to a weakened right'.[89]

This chapter, and book, take the protective principle's logic – as applied particularly to evidence obtained in violation of constitutional and international human rights – as the key normative foundation, when making the claim that Anglo-American and Continental legal systems should place renewed emphasis on rights protection when excluding improperly obtained (but ostensibly reliable) evidence. Building on the inherent strength of the scholarship discussed above, whilst addressing contemporary critiques of a rights-centred approach to exclusion, the chapter will sketch below why the principle provides the most convincing rationale for exclusion, from the viewpoint of ensuring that rights considerations are not overshadowed by reliability considerations.

For a start, we can examine the claim, in Ashworth's original thesis, that '[t]he most appropriate criterion for the admissibility of improperly obtained evidence is a qualified protective principle', which accepts the idea that there should be no exclusion where the defendant has 'suffered no disadvantage as a result of the breach'.[90] Here Ashworth's thesis adds an element of causation to the exclusionary equation. The court has to assess the impact of the violation upon the rights of the defendant, on an ad hoc basis, and, from this angle, the protective principle can be seen as more compatible with an exclusionary discretion. We must note, however, that Ashworth elaborated on the causation requirement against the backdrop of a wider discussion of the protective principle, not a close examination of its application to violations of constitutional or international human rights. He still recognised both the complexity of the ad hoc (and ex post facto) calculations required, when assessing whether enjoyment of the right would have prevented the state authorities from obtaining the evidence,[91] and the danger of developing a haphazard approach to excluding improperly obtained evidence.[92] Other contemporary approaches – discussed above – go a step further, endorsing the idea of automatic or presumptive exclusion for evidence obtained in violation of constitutional or human rights; the normative thesis underpinning these approaches must then be that defendants *necessarily* suffer a disadvantage as a result of breaches of their constitutional or human rights. For example, where the police conduct a search in violation of relevant constitutional guarantees, a suspect unavoidably suffers the disadvantage of arbitrary interference with his or

[88] ibid 195.

[89] RM Bloom and E Dewey, 'When Rights Become Empty Promises: Promoting an Exclusionary Rule that Vindicates Personal Rights' (2011) 46 *Irish Jurist* 38, 68.

[90] Ashworth (n 1) 729. See also Ashworth and Redmayne (n 1) 345.

[91] See Ashworth and Redmayne (ibid).

[92] Ashworth (n 1) 734.

her constitutional or human right to privacy. Where the police deny a suspect access to a lawyer, the suspect is necessarily deprived of her right to custodial legal assistance, a fundamental component of the right to fair trial. Or where the police fail to notify suspects of their custodial interrogation rights, suspects are inevitably put at a disadvantage. They necessarily suffer prejudice which is 'deduced from the importance of the provision that should have been given effect (and wasn't)'.[93] Legal systems seeking to prioritise rights protection could endorse this more robust version of the protective principle, as the basis of a categorical exclusionary rule for evidence obtained in violation of constitutional or human rights. Legal systems worried about the pendulum swinging too far towards the rights thesis might wish to opt for the qualified protective principle instead.

This takes us to the next step in the analysis. Ultimately, legal systems must ask themselves whether they are serious about protecting rights. Ashworth's overarching normative foundation for the protective principle was the simple idea that the 'recognition [of rights] without any protection would be a pretence'.[94] Taslitz puts it bluntly when he notes that 'a right without a remedy is no right at all, [and] when a court says otherwise it engages in an act of hypocrisy – doing one thing while saying another – and that has pernicious social consequences'.[95] A rule without a remedy changes its nature from 'an order which must be strictly obeyed, to a mere suggestion, a guideline'.[96] A legal system 'sincere in its wish … to inculcate respect for human rights in criminal investigations' will not omit remedies for violations of rights,[97] all the more so higher order violations of constitutional or human rights. The more abstract idea that justice cannot be done when duly instituted rules – procedural, in our case – are not applied in practice finds philosophical grounding in the work of Aristotle, Montesquieu, Beccaria and Immanuel Kant,[98] among others. It animates the liberal ideals that underpin

[93] JP Brouillaud, 'Les nullités de procédure: des procédures pénales et civiles comparées' (1996) *Recueil Dalloz*, Chr 99.

[94] ibid 735.

[95] AE Taslitz, 'Hypocrisy, Corruption, and Illegitimacy: Why Judicial Integrity Justifies the Exclusionary Rule' (2013) 10 *Ohio State Journal of Criminal Law* 419, 437.

[96] M Caianello, 'Procedural Sanctions in the EU Framework: Toward a Harmless Error Doctrine and Practice?' in M Caianello and J Hodgson, *Discretionary Criminal Justice in a Comparative Context* (Durham, North Carolina, Carolina Academic Press, 2015) 207, 208.

[97] S Farrar, 'Degrading Searches and Illegally Obtained Evidence in the Malaysian Criminal Justice System' in Roberts and Hunter, *Criminal Evidence* (2012) 113.

[98] Aristotle elaborated that there was fundamentally no difference between not applying existing law and not having a law in the first place: '*ουδέν διαφέρει η μη κείσθαι η μη χρήσθαι (νόμος)*'. Aristotle, *Rhetoric*, 1375b, 20 (Athens, Kaktos, 1995). For Montesquieu, the duty to apply 'the letter of the law' derived from the Constitution and the principles of Republican government, whereas for Beccaria the respect for (procedural) formalities was indispensable to administering justice. Montesquieu, *De l'esprit des lois* (Paris, Garnier-Flammarion, 1979) 203; Beccaria, *Des délits et des peines* (Paris, Flammarion, 1991) 164. Following Kant, Roberts and Zuckerman devised one of their five foundational principles of criminal evidence to be that justice can be pursued 'only through action which is itself just and otherwise in conformity with relevant ethical standards'. Roberts and Zuckerman (2010) 22. Constitutional and human rights bring precision to the ethical standards that apply in the criminal process.

declarations of fundamental human rights,[99] and, in recent times, is encapsulated in Dworkin's famous aphorism that '[i]f the Government does not take rights seriously, then it does not take law seriously either'.[100]

A major critique of such emphatic rights-centred conceptualisations of the exclusion of tainted evidence is that they fail to take into account the public interest, providing disproportionate, over-personalised remedies to breaches of individual rights and outbalancing the supreme good of convicting the guilty.[101] We can call this the 'epistemic costs' or 'lost evidence' (and 'lost convictions') critique. At its centre is the idea that, by depriving the court from accessing potentially reliable evidence demonstrating the guilt of the defendant, rights-centred exclusion obstructs the criminal trial's truth-seeking, epistemic function. But besides the fact – analytically explored earlier in the chapter – that truth-seeking can be outweighed by rights and integrity considerations, in this critique lies a second, equally puzzling, act of hypocrisy towards taking rights seriously in the criminal process. Any 'lost evidence' is not the result of the operation of the exclusionary rule, but of the substantive or procedural rights whose violation the rule may seek to remedy.[102] It is the rights, not the remedy, that block the use of the improperly obtained evidence. The police would not have obtained the evidence in the first place, if they had behaved in line with the defendant's rights. These substantive and procedural rights are the outcome of a long and often complex balancing exercise – undertaken by the constitutional legislator and courts – between individual interests and the protection of the public. Whatever rights the individual is afforded are the sum of a prior calculation which has already taken into account the interest of the public in the conviction of the guilty and the potential cost in 'lost evidence' and 'lost convictions'. Part of the total protection that the individual would have otherwise enjoyed has already been taken away. The recognition of a constitutional right has frozen 'in place a prior act of balancing'.[103] The constitutional legislator has 'conferred a higher status on one value relative to another', with the protection of a particular constitutional right taking priority over the search for truth. The exclusionary rule simply ensures that, once this has happened, the result of the

[99] As the preamble to the French Declaration of the Rights of Man and of the Citizen of 1789 posits, for instance, 'ignorance, oversight or indifference to human rights are the only reasons for the misfortunes of the public and the corruption of Governments'.

[100] Dworkin (n 46) 205. See also HLA Hart, *The Concept of Law*, 2nd edn (Oxford, Oxford University Press, 1997) 146.

[101] See Redmayne's review of Laudan, 'Truth, Error and Criminal Law' (2006) in M Redmayne, 'Review' (2008) 11 *New Criminal Law Review* 181, 184. See also discussion in Duff et al (n 54) 225, 231; MH Yeo, 'The Discretion to Exclude Illegally and Improperly Obtained Evidence: A Choice of Approaches' (1981–1982) 13 *Melbourne University Law Review* 31, 41; M Madden, 'A Model Rule for Excluding Improperly or Unconstitutionally Obtained Evidence' (2015) 33 *Berkeley Journal of International Law* 442, 456.

[102] See D Dripps, 'The "New" Exclusionary Rule Debate: From "Still Preoccupied with 1985" to "Virtual Deterrence"' (2010) 37 *Fordham Urban Law Journal* 743, 750.

[103] AS Sweet and J Matthews, 'Proportionality Balancing and Global Constitutionalism' (2008) 47 *Columbia Journal of Transnational Law* 72, 88–89. See also Karras (n 8) 640–41, discussed in D Giannoulopoulos, 'The Exclusion of Improperly Obtained Evidence in Greece: Putting Constitutional Rights First' (2007) 11 *International Journal of Evidence & Proof* 181, 186.

balancing exercise will be respected,[104] and there will be no double-weighting of the public interest in truth-discovery and the conviction of the guilty.[105] A potential second limb of the response to the 'epistemic costs' critique is that, if, at the end of the day, the public or the state are no longer satisfied with how the balance between individual rights and the public interest has been struck, they should be honest about it and pursue a renegotiation of the relevant substantive or procedural rights, within existing constitutional and international human rights law 'constraints', not attack the exclusionary rule that seeks to enforce these rights. To do otherwise is arguably to engage in a cynical exercise of paying lip service to constitutional or human rights, whilst undermining them in practice, by making their violations non-consequential and allowing the government to benefit from the fruits of such violations.[106]

We must add that the above critique is also underpinned by misconceptions about the relationship between individual rights and the public interest in truth-discovery. Ho Hock Lai rightly objects that 'society as a whole has an interest in the state adhering to due process and respecting the rights of fellow citizens who are under investigation',[107] and that '[i]t is distorting to frame the problem as one of "community needs versus individual rights"'.[108] From this angle, rights-centred exclusionary remedies do not just protect the individual concerned, but society as a whole, and the 'epistemic costs' rhetoric becomes obsolete. The 'cost–benefit' metaphor also loses its explanatory force if we take into account, firstly, that truth-seeking enjoys no entrenched constitutional right status, and therefore it cannot be put in the balance with defendants' rights once these have obtained such status.[109] Secondly, we must give regard to the fact that potential alternative sanctions would carry the same cost, if applied as effectively as rights-centred exclusion.[110]

[104] Ashworth (n 1) 733. See also G Kaminis, *Illegally obtained evidence and constitutional guarantees of human rights (The exclusion of evidence in criminal and civil proceedings)* (Athens-Komotini, AN Sakkoulas, 1998) 163–64 (in Greek).

[105] See also Kamisar (n 1) 600.

[106] As Justice Stephen Breyer argued in his dissenting opinion in *Hudson v Michigan*, 547 US 586, 624 (2006), 'if the Court fears that effective enforcement of a constitutional requirement will have harmful consequences, it should face those fears directly by addressing the requirement itself. It should not argue, "the requirement is fine, indeed a serious matter, just don't enforce it"'.

[107] Ho Hock Lai, '"National Values on Law and Order" and the Discretion to Exclude Wrongfully Obtained Evidence' (2012) *Journal of Commonwealth Criminal Law* 232, 252.

[108] ibid 253.

[109] Thaman, 'Balancing Truth Against Human Rights' (2013) 408. For a refined version of the 'constitutional right to truth discovery' argument see Leon and Ward who argue that '[t]hose whose rights have been violated [by the commission of a criminal offence] have an interest in seeing those rights vindicated and in seeing evidence that may incriminate those responsible publicly aired'. T Ward and C Leon, 'Excluding Evidence (or Staying Proceedings) to Vindicate Rights in Irish and English Law' (2015) 35 *Legal Studies* 571, 582. It can be quickly responded that these rights are vindicated when the police exercise powers in accordance with the outcome of the constitutional balancing exercise, but not when they cross the constitutional boundaries and obtain evidence unlawfully. On the other hand, truth can be viewed as implicit in a system of ordered liberty, as per Rawls for instance, or as part of natural justice at English common law, which is indeed a constitutional value (in a common law constitution). I am grateful to Paul Roberts for discussion on these issues.

[110] Dripps, 'The "New" Exclusionary Rule Debate' (n 102) 753.

This is simultaneously a response to a critique which points out that the criminal trial is not the right forum for providing a response to the impropriety leading to the obtaining of the evidence, because there exist – the argument goes – alternative remedies, such as tort claims or disciplinary proceedings, which can achieve this without the cost of 'lost evidence'.[111] This critique is empirically flawed, as alternative judicial remedies are virtually non-existent in Anglo-American and Continental law.[112] Surely, if they provided a genuine alternative to exclusionary remedies, more legal systems would have experimented with them. Jackson notes that the fact that 'these remedies have not proved particularly effective' provides an argument for strengthening them or finding more effective remedies.[113] I agree. But even if, or when, we found such effective remedies, it would not follow that these should substitute for rights-based exclusion. Exclusionary rules and alternative judicial remedies are not mutually exclusive. A legal system serious about protecting constitutional or human rights might choose to use the exclusionary rule to remedy the constitutional rights violated, and civil actions or disciplinary proceedings to deter police officers from repeating such violations in the future. Of course, the multiplication of remedies would be likely to create a risk of overcompensating for violations of individual rights, but the risk would arguably soon start to decrease as a result of enhanced deterrence (assuming that alternative remedies work), which would in its turn reduce the need to rely heavily upon the exclusionary rule in the future. The 'alternative remedies' critique is also counter-intuitive for suggesting that responses to improper behaviour that manifests itself in the context of the criminal process, interferes with principles that are central to it (through violations of substantive or procedural rights), implicates key parties in the process and can drastically affect its outcomes, should be dealt with in a forum unconnected with any of these.[114] Furthermore, it gives no consideration to situations where the use of improperly obtained evidence in court would in itself amount to a new violation of the relevant constitutional right, such as where unlawfully recorded private conversations are played again in court.[115]

[111] See generally AR Amar, 'Against Exclusion (Except to Protect Truth or Prevent Privacy Violations)' (1997) 20 *Harvard Journal of Law & Public Policy* 457; Laudan (n 13) 220; W Signorelli, *The Constable Has Blundered* (Durham, North Carolina, Carolina Academic Press, 2010) 189–99.

[112] See eg, Hardiman J's critique of the availability of alternative remedies in his dissenting opinion in *DPP v JC* [2015] IESC 31 [14], where he explains that 'in the whole history of the [Irish] State, no prosecution for breach of a citizen's constitutional rights has ever been taken against a public official'.

[113] J Jackson, 'Human Rights, Constitutional Law and Exclusionary Safeguards in Ireland' in Roberts and Hunter (n 47) 134.

[114] See, eg Dennis who explains that civil actions for damages or disciplinary proceedings would be 'inadequate to prevent the disadvantage [suffered by the defendant, with the denial of a right he is entitled to] being converted into the permanent form of conviction'. Dennis (n 14) 106. See also Ho Hock Lai (n 25) 126.

[115] Kamisar explained, back in 1983, that the idea that the use of unconstitutionally obtained evidence would 'inflict a second and distinct injury' upon the victim of the police illegality was 'out of favour' in American jurisprudence. He still saw considerable merit in it. The idea has been widely acceppted in Greek exclusionary rule scholarship. See, eg Th Dalakouras, 'The exclusionary rule for improper audio and video recordings under article 370Δ para 2 of the Criminal Code (article 31 of

In conclusion, to argue that excluding evidence to protect rights has substantial societal costs, and that breaches of fundamental rights should not be dealt with in the criminal process, is truly to envisage an evidence admissibility regime that would let constitutional or human rights violations go unpunished and treat truth-discovery and victims' rights as constitutionally protected interests that could outweigh the protection of individual rights.

It is also levelled against the rights theory that it is counter-intuitive, 'rather awkward', to speak like Zuckerman, because it ignores the 'crucial factor' that '[t]he evidence has been obtained, is now available and does tend to prove the accused's guilt';[116] 'the informational status quo can never, in reality, be retrieved once epistemic innocence is lost'.[117] 'Whatever happened, happened', seems to be the logic here.[118] But one may, first of all, reply that as far as the trier of fact is concerned – who will remain unaware of the unlawfully discovered evidence unless it is admitted in court, especially in common law jurisdictions, where there is generally no prior contact with the tainted evidence – the epistemic innocence remains intact.[119] Secondly, one may point towards a number of situations in the criminal justice system where the State may possess information indicating the guilt of the suspect, situations where the epistemic innocence has been lost, and yet the State does not act upon it as a result of giving way to other epistemic or non-epistemic considerations. To take a few examples only, the common law, in particular, has traditionally been reluctant to use evidence of bad character, to avoid prejudice not just to fact-finding, but sometimes also to 'basic precepts of fair trial and legitimate adjudication'.[120] Strict time limits for prosecution, particularly in Continental legal systems, and the double jeopardy rule, stop the State from pursuing (or pursuing

Law 1941/1991)' (1992) *Iperaspisi* 25, 26 (in Greek); D Spinellis, 'Evidential prohibitions in the criminal process' (1986) 36 *Poinika Chronika* 865, 879 (in Greek); Ch Satlanis, 'Tape recordings as evidence in the criminal process (a parallel contribution to the evidential prohibitions doctrine)', Poinika No 48 (Athens-Komotini, AN Sakkoulas, 1996) 20–22 (in Greek); G Triantafillou, 'Evidential prohibitions and the proportionality principle' (2007) 57 *Poinika Chronika* 295 (in Greek); *Informationsbeherrschungsrechte im Strafprozess* (Berlin, 1990) 11, cited by Dalakouras, ibid. In England and Wales, the argument was rejected in *R v Button* [2005] EWCA Crim 516.

[116] A Zuckerman, 'Illegally Obtained Evidence' (n 51) 57.

[117] Roberts and Zuckerman (n 1) 183. See also Androulakis, *Fundamental notions* (n 10) 211 (in Greek).

[118] See Karras, *Penal procedural law* (n 37) 690, who describes this argument by reference to German criminal procedure scholarship, eg Gössel, Bockelmann-FS (1979) 801. Karras refers to Art 15 of the UN Convention against Torture and Other Cruel, Inhuman or Degrading Treatment or Punishment that prohibits the use as evidence in any proceedings of 'any statement which is established to have been made as a result of torture', to illustrate the fallacy of the 'whatever happened, happened' logic. See also Redmayne, 'Review' (n 101) 184. *Cf* Roberts and Zuckerman (n 1) 183–84.

[119] The 'epistemic innocence' argument can also be read as referring to society at large, not just the trier of fact. If the result of excluding improperly obtained evidence is that somebody we know to be very dangerous is released back into the community, our 'innocence' is lost and the consequences are on our conscience. See eg, the complex moral dilemmas raised by *Gafgen v Germany* (2010) 52 EHRR 1. One might however counter-argue that the public's 'innocence', as to the moral foundations of the criminal justice system, would be equally lost if constitutional and human rights values central to liberal and democratic societies were sidestepped in order to pursue the search for truth.

[120] Roberts and Zuckerman (n 1) 587.

further) cases where strong evidence indicating the guilt of the accused may be available from the outset or may have come to the surface after the acquittal of the defendant.[121] The ban on the use of intercept evidence in UK courts means that we refrain from bringing perpetrators to justice to protect the secrecy of the intelligence gathering system.[122] In fact, we have gone so far as detain foreign suspected terrorists without trial for years,[123] and have subjected suspected individuals to house arrest (and then to Terrorism Prevention and Investigation Measures),[124] despite the fact that the epistemic innocence about their implication in terrorist activity had long been lost and the use of intercept evidence would have been likely to secure a conviction.[125] Taken to its logical extreme, the epistemic innocence thesis could provide support for the unexceptional use of unlawfully obtained, but reliable, evidence. If the fact that the evidence is now available prevails over the need to protect constitutional or human rights, why would the evidentiary outcome be any different if we rather sought – through exclusion, discretionary even – to safeguard the integrity of the proceedings or discipline the police? Those finding the 'epistemic innocence' argument a convincing critique of the rights thesis will inevitably consider it a convincing critique of excluding evidence on non-epistemic grounds more generally.

The chapter has so far claimed that Ashworth's rights thesis retains all of its normative force, and that critiques that focus on the need to balance (again) rights protection against the public interest are misguided. At the same time, it must be understood that the rights thesis is not a panacea, will not cover for all eventualities and is therefore vulnerable to critiques that explore admissibility against a broader set of circumstances that go beyond violations of individual rights. Thus, sceptics have rightly pointed out that the protective principle will *not* apply where there has been a breach of the fundamental rights of someone other than the defendant or where the evidence has been unlawfully obtained by a private party.[126] In the former set of circumstances, the defendant will lack 'standing' to object to the admission of the evidence, as *his* or *her* rights will not have been violated. In the latter, there will not even be a violation of a constitutional right, as – according to conventional constitutional law doctrine – constitutional rights apply only against the state, not individual parties.[127] By the same token, we can recognise

[121] In the UK, *cf* Criminal Justice Act 2003, Part 10.

[122] See, eg, House of Commons, *The Use of Intercept Evidence in Terrorism Cases*, SN/HA/5249, 24 November 2011; J Blackbourn and N McGarrity, 'Listening and Hearings: Intercept Evidence in the Courtroom' (2012) *Journal of Commonwealth Criminal Law* 257.

[123] See *A and others v Secretary of State for the Home Department* [2004] UKHL 56.

[124] See Terrorism Prevention and Investigation Measures Act 2011; Counter-Terrorism and Security Act 2015.

[125] See Prevention of Terrorism Act 2005, which introduced the power to impose 'control orders', including, in some cases, house detention for up to 18 hours a day.

[126] Duff et al (n 54) 232–33; Jackson, 'Human Rights' in Roberts and Hunter (n 47) 135.

[127] *Cf* Art 25 of the Greek Constitution, which makes constitutional rights applicable to private individuals, and how this is reflected in the constitutional exclusionary rule for privacy violations under Art 19, para 3 of the Constitution.

the difficulties in applying the rights thesis to cases of illegitimate entrapment,[128] though we should not forget that the admission of evidence obtained by entrapment triggers the right to fair trial under article 6 of the ECHR.[129] We must also accept that the rigorous rights-thesis we have described loses its ability to support exclusion where procedural violations do not amount to violations of constitutional or human rights, for example where evidence has been obtained by the use of deception, traps or tricks in custodial interrogation such as in cases where interrogating officers lead suspects to believe that a co-defendant has implicated them in the offence or where the police lie about the strength of the evidence that they may have obtained.[130] This is all the more the case where breaches of procedural provisions – not constitutional or human rights – have been committed, and they are deemed to be technical or venial. But all this takes nothing away from the rights thesis' unique ability to provide a solid normative justification for the exclusion of improperly obtained evidence in the wide range of situations covered in this book, namely violations, by *state officials*, of *defendants'* right to privacy and their right to custodial legal assistance. If there are gaps in the protection that the rights thesis can provide, it is logical to ask how these can be covered, not dismiss the value of rights-based exclusion altogether.[131]

At this point, the chapter appeals to using the judicial integrity thesis to provide protection where the rights thesis leaves the defendant without support. The chapter has already explained how integrity-based considerations can outweigh the search for truth, and distinguished between integrity-based accounts that allow for a balancing of the public interest with the protection of individual rights and other, non-instrumental, court-centred, accounts, that focus on the impact of the admissibility of evidence upon the rule of law, without reference to the attitudes or views of the public towards the use of improperly obtained evidence. Though it is beyond the scope of this chapter to provide a full account of judicial integrity as a rationale for exclusion in cases where the protective rationale does not apply, it can be contemplated that a court-centred, rule of law-based, account of integrity is going to be the best candidate for supplementing the rights thesis in situations,

[128] Duff et al (n 54) 232.

[129] See, eg, P Roberts, 'Normative Evolution in Evidentiary Exclusion: Coercion, Deception and the Right to a Fair Trial' in Roberts and Hunter (n 47) 177.

[130] See Jackson and Summers (n 1) 170.

[131] See also Chau, 'Excluding Integrity?' in Hunter et al, *Integrity* (n 2) 272. But Chau also insinuates that the fact that the protective principle does not apply to violations by private parties is a strength rather than a weakness. ibid 273. I disagree. From the normative angle of strict reparation, or returning the defendant to the status quo ante, *who* is responsible for the violation of the right should not make a difference to the defendant, in the sense that he is still denied 'something to which he is entitled' or 'he is subjected to treatment which is improper'. The fact that the protective principle does not apply here is simply the 'collateral damage' of reading constitutional rights narrowly, as applying to the actions of state actors only (and as being the result of requiring that a constitutional or human right violation has been committed before triggering the strict protective principle). Where this is not the case, as in Portugal, Greece or Italy, the protective principle also applies to violations of defendants' rights by private parties. See ch 2 and below at III A. Chau suggests, however, that evidence obtained unlawfully by private parties can be excluded on the basis of a no-profit principle which he distinguishes from the protective principle. ibid 277.

like the ones described above, where this might be needed. Here the chapter sees judicial integrity and the rights thesis as working together. The use of evidence obtained by violations of constitutional or international human rights necessarily impacts on judicial integrity, in its court-centred version. By excluding the tainted evidence, courts restore the defendant to the status quo ante and avoid a second violation when the evidence is used in court. They give effect to defendants' rights and ensure these will not become empty promises. They avoid the hypocrisy of saying one thing – in the constitutional charter or the subscribed international human rights convention – and doing another, when dealing with the evidentiary consequences of human rights violations. But they also safeguard judicial integrity and the rule of law, in accordance with moral imperatives of propriety and decency, unaffected by the mood of the public towards these rights.[132] To safeguard judicial integrity courts *may* therefore have to exclude evidence even where no violation of constitutional or human rights has been committed, such as in cases of unlawful entrapment or where the police have used deception, traps and tricks to obtain self-incriminating statements. The same applies to situations where the constitutional or human right violation concerns a third party or where it has been committed by a third party or, at the extreme, where the defendant has obtained evidence by violating the rights of others. The remedial approach may not require the exclusion of such evidence, but the judicial integrity approach could well do. The use of such evidence may well cross the moral threshold for admissibility set by particular criminal justice systems, even if this depends on a balancing exercise that will take into account competing values. French jurisprudence in relation to the unlawful obtaining of evidence by private parties provides an interesting case study: though the evidence is admissible in principle, the moral threshold is crossed, and exclusion is required, where it is established that the police have connived with the private party in the unlawful obtaining of the evidence in question.[133] To sum up the above, judicial integrity is conceived here as a supplement to the rights thesis, not the other way round. The rights thesis and the judicial integrity rationale are seen as providing standalone, complementary, normative foundations for the exclusion of improperly obtained evidence, in agreement with the idea that there is no need to seek explanatory unification between them.[134]

At this point we can change tack, again. Having described the rights (plus integrity) thesis as the normative foundation of this book, we can now revert back to comparative law analysis to inquire, from a pragmatic point of view, how much scope there might be in Anglo-American and Continental law for reinvigorating this thesis.

[132] As Young observes, it would be 'antithetical to the rule of law for courts to be swayed by popular opinion in all situations'. Young, 'A Public Law Conception of Integrity in the Criminal Process' in Hunter et al (n 2) 38.

[133] *Crim* 20 September 2016, *Bull crim* n 244. See also ch 4.

[134] M Redmayne, 'Review' (2009) 12 *New Criminal Law Review* 287, 310. *Cf* Duff et al (n 54) 235. See also Chau, 'Excluding Integrity?' in Hunter et al (n 2) 278.

III. Is There Support in Comparative Law for the Rights Thesis?

In juxtaposing English, French, Greek and United States law, and taking into account pivotal ECHR jurisprudence and EU legislation, the book has identified an emerging rapprochement on the exclusion of confessional evidence obtained in violation of custodial interrogation rights, such as the right to silence and the right to custodial legal assistance, even if the divergent exclusionary rationales that are in operation, and differences between categorical exclusionary rules and exclusionary discretion, generate important fluctuations as to the levels of protection afforded to these rights by exclusion. Rights theorists will find in these contextual studies significant developments to build upon, if they envisage breathing new life into the rights thesis as the normative basis for exclusion, at least in relation to self-incriminating statements obtained in violation of fair trial rights. In undertaking these contextual studies, the book has so far intentionally sacrificed breadth for depth of analysis. But the time is now opportune to paint with a broad brush, to situate these conclusions within a wider comparative law context. This will be done with the caveat that analysis here has not been shaped by direct observation or study in the systems examined, though, it does, in many cases, reflect interaction with scholars and legal professionals who are experts in the relevant domestic legal systems.

A. Exclusionary Rules for Rights Violations (and their Exceptions) in Southern Europe: Portugal, Italy and Spain

The preceding discussion of Greek exclusionary rules and nullities serves as a fitting prelude to analysis of other Southern European perspectives, considering similarities in Constitutional structures and the historic experiences that gave birth to them, including periods of dictatorship, whose ramifications for the law of the exclusion of improperly obtained cannot go unnoticed. Portugal is a perfect illustration, with the transition from dictatorship to liberal democracy, and the enactment of a new Constitution in 1976, coinciding with the end of the military junta and the return to democratic stability in Greece, culminating in the enactment of the Constitution of 1975 there.[135] With this historic backdrop in mind, it is fascinating to observe that Portugal, like Greece, has entrenched a categorical, rights-centred, exclusionary rule into its Constitutional charter, and

[135] See the Constitution of Portugal, adopted on 2 April 1976, and the Constitution of Greece, adopted on 9 June 1975. See also Kondilis, Intervention, Athens Bar Association debate on improperly obtained evidence, 19 January 2016, available at www.youtube.com/watch?v=5PPQGgAiocY (in Greek), who argued that the Portuguese Constitution is closer to the Greek Constitution than any other European constitutional charter, in putting the individual at the centre of its system of constitutional rights.

that the scope for its operation is even wider than that of its Greek counterpart. While the Greek constitutional exclusionary rule applies to privacy violations only, the Portuguese one prohibits the use of '[a]ny evidence obtained by torture, force, violation of the physical or moral integrity of the individual' in addition to evidence obtained by 'wrongful interference in private life, the home, correspondence, or telecommunications'.[136] The constitutional exclusionary rule is mirrored in the Portuguese Code of Penal Procedure by exclusionary rules applying to specific procedural acts, and by corresponding procedural nullities.[137] These rules and nullities apply at all stages of the criminal process, as well as to evidence obtained by private parties,[138] and they extend to derivative evidence, subscribing Portuguese law to the 'fruit of the poisonous tree' doctrine. Constitutional Court jurisprudence recognises, however, that the link between the unlawful act and derivative evidence can be attenuated to a degree that the illegality is cured and the fruits become admissible.[139] It also emerges from evidence by criminal defence practitioners in Portugal that, due to systemic secrecy in Portuguese criminal procedure, defendants seem to be routinely confronted with great amounts of derivative evidence 'several months (or years) after' the primary evidence has been gathered, and that it is at that point 'nearly impossible' to escape a finding that 'the chain of causation between the illegal action and the tainted evidence is too attenuated for the secondary evidence to be excluded'.[140] There is equal concern about the fact that improperly obtained evidence that may have been excluded at the pre-trial stage is rarely removed from the case file or destroyed, and that fact-finders therefore obtain access in reality to the supposedly excluded evidence.[141] A trial court practice whereby the decision on the 'exclusion' of the tainted evidence is postponed to the final judgment constitutes an even more blatant attempt to apply the existing exclusionary rules but only in theory.[142]

[136] Art 36, para 2 of the Constitution of Portugal. See MT Alves-Martins, 'Portugal' in M Delmas-Marty and JAE Vervaele, *The Implementation of the Corpus Juris in the Member States* (Antwerp, Intersentia, 2000) 768.

[137] See, eg, Art 58, para 5 Code of Penal Procedure (CPP) (Portugal), which prohibits the use of evidence obtained in violation of the rights of the suspect applying to custodial interrogation; Art 119 (c) CPP (Portugal), which imposes the pronouncement of a nullity for violations of the right to access to a lawyer when the suspect is questioned by the police.

[138] V Moreira, 'Portugal' in EU Network of Independent Experts on Fundamental Rights (CFR-CDF), *Opinion on the Status of Illegally Obtained Evidence in Criminal Procedures in the Member States of the European Union*, 30 November 2003, 22.

[139] Constitutional Court 198/2004, 24 March 2004; Acórdão do Tribunal Constitucional no 198/2004, de 24 de março de 2004 (Moura Ramos). See generally P de Souza Mendes, Comparative Exclusionary Rules – Portuguese and Brazilian perspective, available at www.carlospinteodeandreu.com; P Caeiro and M João-Costa, 'Portugal' in K Ligeti (ed), *Toward a Prosecutor for the European Union – A Comparative Analysis – volume 1* (Oxford, Hart/Beck, 2012) 540, 574–75. This decision also recognised the 'independent source' and 'inevitable discovery' exceptions. See M Gomes Ferreira, Fair Trials International questionnaire: 'Judicial remedies in the EU' working group, January 2017 (on file with author).

[140] Gomes Ferreira, ibid.

[141] ibid.

[142] ibid.

A similar pattern can be observed in Italy and Spain. Following a process of constitutionalisation of criminal procedure, both countries have transitioned from a position geared towards the general admissibility of improperly obtained evidence[143] to adopting categorical exclusionary rules for violations of constitutional and other procedural rights. But in both countries, there exist serious question marks about how effectively these rules are applied in practice. In Italy, the legislator embedded constitutional court jurisprudence[144] into the Code of Penal Procedure (CPP Italy). Article 191 provides that 'evidence obtained in violation of statutory provisions cannot be used'. It is regarded as 'intrinsically unlawful'.[145] In June 2017, the legislator added a new paragraph to this article, with a view to categorically prohibiting the use of any statements or information obtained from the defendant by the use of torture.[146] This now is in synergy with the prohibition to use evidence obtained by methods that can affect the defendant's ability for self-determination or his capacity to remember or evaluate events.[147] We can also take the example of the evidentiary prohibition of the use of unlawfully obtained wiretaps, to illustrate that Italy possesses a wide range of strict exclusionary rules,[148] which seemingly make it one of the European countries most favourable to keeping tainted evidence outside of the criminal process.[149] In practice, however, constitutional court jurisprudence has severely limited the application of these exclusionary rules, particularly in relation to search and seizure, notably on the basis that, where the unlawfully obtained evidence is material evidence that proves the commission of the offence (*corpo del reato*), the unlawfulness of the search does *not* contaminate the seizure and the evidence *can* be used in trial.[150] Recent empirical evidence on the operation of Italian exclusionary rules on search

[143] See generally W Pakter, 'Exclusionary Rules in France, Germany and Italy' (1985) 9 *Hastings International and Comparative Law Review* 1, 22; E Ruiz Vadillo, 'Spain' in C van den Wyngaert (ed), *Criminal Procedure Systems in the European Community* (London, Butterworths, 1993) 383, 384; Y Ma, 'Comparative Analysis of Exclusionary Rules in the United States, England, France, Germany and Italy' (1999) 22 *Policing: An International Journal of Police Strategies & Management* 280, 295; SC Thaman, *Comparative Criminal Procedure* (Durham, North Carolina, Carolina Academic Press, Comparative Law Series, 2002) 100.

[144] See, eg, *Corte Cost* 6 April 1973, 18 *Giur Cost* 316.

[145] G Trovato, Nullità, inutilizzabilità, inamissibilità delle prove penali, available at www.diritto.it/materiali/penale/trovato.html

[146] Art 191, para 2bis CPP (Italy), introduced with the Law of 23 June 2017.

[147] Art 188 CPP (Italy).

[148] Art 271 CPP (Italy).

[149] JR Spencer, 'Evidence' in M Delmas-Marty and JR Spencer (ed), *European Criminal Procedures*, Cambridge Studies in International and Comparative Law (Cambridge, Cambridge University Press, 2005) 608.

[150] See eg, Corte Cost, 27 March 1996, (1997) *Giust Penale* 138, quoted by Thaman, *Comparative Criminal Procedure* (n 143) 116–18. See also E Grande, 'Italian Criminal Justice: Borrowing and Resistance' (2000) 48 *American Journal of Comparative Law* 227, 249; R Van Cleave, 'Italy' in C Bradley (ed), *Criminal Procedure – A Worldwide Study*, 2nd edn (North Carolina, Carolina Academic Press, 2007) 303; G Illuminati and M Caianello, 'The Investigative Stage of the Criminal Process in Italy' in E Cape, J Hodgson, T Prakken and T Spronken, *Suspects in Europe – Procedural Rights at the Investigative Stage of the Criminal Process in the European Union* (Antwerp-Oxford, Intersentia, 2007) 129, 147.

and seizure reinforces this point, leading to the conclusion that the use of '[t]he law of evidence in Italy as an exclusionary mechanism is very limited'.[151] It nonetheless emerges from the same empirical source that evidence obtained by force, or by persons with no authority to do so, would not be admissible, and this, very interestingly, is also the case when material evidence has been unlawfully obtained by private parties.[152]

We can tell a similar story about the operation of the exclusionary rule in Spain. A story that starts with the enactment of the 1978 Constitution after the collapse of Franco's regime, continues with the gradual constitutionalisation of Spanish criminal procedure and culminates in Constitutional Court jurisprudence requiring the exclusion of evidence obtained in violation of constitutional rights.[153] This jurisprudence was translated into statutory law with article 11.1 of the Law on Judicial Power 1985, which mandates that '[e]vidence obtained, directly or indirectly, in violation of fundamental rights or liberties, shall have no effect'.[154] Jurisprudential applications of article 11.1 since then have shown that there is significant scope to exclude improperly obtained evidence in Spanish law, for instance where a search has been conducted without a warrant, in violation of the provisions of the constitutional right to privacy,[155] or where self-incriminating evidence has been obtained through the use of force.[156] At the same time, we can locate in Constitutional Court jurisprudence an effort to minimise the effect of what can otherwise be seen as 'a seemingly absolute exclusionary rule'.[157] In the law of search and seizure in particular, the Court has muddied the water by drawing a distinction between unconstitutional searches and searches where a valid warrant has been issued, but the search has not been undertaken in full conformity with it. In the first case the evidence will be excluded, in the second, it won't.[158] The Court has similarly been rigorously applying the 'fruit of the poisonous tree' doctrine at first, before, more recently, going on to recognise 'standing', 'independent source' and 'inevitable discovery' exceptions to it.[159]

Drawn together, Portugal, Italy and Spain could give us – if studied in detail – a captivating narrative of the constitutionalisation of criminal procedure going

[151] A Ryan, *Towards a System of European Criminal Justice – The problem of Admissibility of Evidence* (London and New York, Routledge, 2014) 207.

[152] ibid 205.

[153] See, eg, Tribunal Constitucional 114, 29 November 1984.

[154] Ley Orgánica del Poder Judicial 1985.

[155] See, eg, Tribunal Constitucional 9 July 1993, RJ 1993, cited by Thaman (n 143) 100. See also Tribunal Constitucional 123/2000, 20 May 2002; 167/2002, 18 September 2002; 205/2002, 11 November 2002, cited by T Freixes, 'Spain' in EU Network of Independent Experts on Fundamental Rights (CFR-CDF), *Opinion* (n 138) 24.

[156] See generally R Vogler, 'Spain' in C Bradley (ed), *Criminal Procedure – A Worldwide Study* (North Carolina, Carolina Academic Press, 1999) 361, 381.

[157] LB Winter, 'Spain: The Constitutional Court's Move from Categorical Exclusion to Limited Balancing' in Thaman (n 143) 209, 215.

[158] Vogler, 'Spain' in Bradley, *Criminal Procedure* (n 153) 383.

[159] LB Winter, 'Spain' in Thaman (n 143) 216.

hand in hand with the adoption of the rights thesis, and of simultaneous resistance to rights-centred exclusion, arguably born out of a perceived need to protect the public interest against excessive reliance on safeguarding individual rights.

B. Between the Protection of Rights and Truth Discovery in Central and Western Europe: Belgium, Switzerland and the Netherlands

Belgium provides an interesting counter-point to Southern European perspectives, with resistance to rights-centred 'exclusion' triggering a reversal of the automatic nullities previously in place and a transition to a model predominantly resting on balancing and judicial discretion. A critical step in this direction was taken with the introduction of legislation in October 2013[160] that gave a statutory footing to Cour de cassation (Belgian Court of Cassation) jurisprudence first established in 2003 (the *Antigoon* jurisprudence).[161] *Antigoon* 'substitut[ed] a prohibition in principle to use illegally obtained evidence with an authorisation in principle [to use such evidence], subject only to criteria specifically prescribed by the Court',[162] namely where 'nullities are provided for the respect of procedural requirements, where the irregularity has affected the reliability of the evidence and where the use of the evidence violates the right to fair trial'.[163] In *Antigoon* itself, where the firearm used in the offence had been discovered as a result of an unlawful search of the defendant's car, the Court did not consider that using the evidence would violate the right to fair trial.[164] Post-*Antigoon* Cour de cassation jurisprudence clarified that courts possess a wide discretion, which requires them to take into account (a) the bad faith of the police; (b) whether the gravity of the offence is more serious than the irregularity committed;[165] (c) whether the improperly obtained evidence constitutes material proof of the commission of the offence[166] and, finally, (d) whether the irregularity had no effect on the enjoyment of the right or freedom protected by the procedural rule breached.[167]

To fully appreciate the significance of Belgium's U-turn towards a balancing approach, we can take a closer look at pre-2003 Cour de cassation jurisprudence. A decision from 1986 is indicative of how widely the concept of illegally obtained

[160] Loi du 24 octobre 2013 modifiant le titre préliminaire du Code de procédure pénale en ce qui concerne les nullités, Moniteur belge, 12.11.2013, 84999.

[161] Cass 14 October 2003, RW 2003-2004, 814.

[162] F Kuty, 'Le droit de la preuve' in Conférence du Jeune Barreau de Mons, *Questions d'actualité de droit pénal et de procédure pénale*, Mons, 27 May 2005 (Bruylant, Bruxelles, 2005) 75.

[163] Cass 14 October 2003, RW 2003–2004, 814.

[164] ibid.

[165] Cass 2 March 2005, RG P 04 1644 F.

[166] Cass 23 March 2004, RABG 2004, 1061.

[167] Cass 2 March 2005, RG P 04 1644 F.

evidence was originally being interpreted: 'Evidence obtained not only by an act expressly forbidden by law but also by an act that is irreconcilable with substantial rules of criminal procedure or general principles of Law and more particularly respect for the rights of the defence is illegal'.[168]

An equally strong demonstration is provided by a 1994 decision where the Cour de cassation held that 'the judge cannot establish [the commission of] a criminal offence if the evidence has been obtained following an act punishable [by criminal law] or in other irregular manner',[169] such as where evidence has been obtained by illegal telephone intercepts[170] and other violations of the secrecy of correspondence,[171] the illegal search of a person[172] or the violation of postal secrecy.[173] This was in addition to excluding evidence where procedural violations had been committed, such as where telephone intercepts had not been authorised by the investigating judge,[174] where the provisions of the Code had not been followed in relation to search and seizure[175] or where self-incriminating statements had been obtained in violation of general principles of law.[176] In other words, 'in the old days, things were simple: any evidence obtained improperly was excluded'.[177]

Comparative law observers interested in the rights thesis will therefore be confronted with thought-provoking antitheses in Belgian law, between striking pre-*Antigoon* endorsement of automatic nullities and post-*Antigoon* rejection of 'rights violations' as a normative exegesis for removing improperly obtained evidence from the criminal process. The same antitheses characterise the Swiss approach to improperly obtained evidence following the enactment of the harmonised CPP in 2011, even if, conversely to the contemporary Belgian approach, Switzerland now takes automatic exclusion as its starting point. So, the Swiss CPP categorically prohibits the use of evidence obtained by 'coercion, violence, threats, promises, deception and methods that may compromise the ability of the person concerned to think or decide freely',[178] and the use of evidence declared inadmissible by the Code.[179] For other unlawfully obtained evidence, it provides

[168] Cass 13 May 1986, *Pas* 1986, I, 1107. See also R Declerq, *La preuve en matière pénale* (Brussels, Swinnen, 1988) 58–59; A de Nauw, 'Les règles d'exclusion relatives à la preuve en procédure pénale belge' (1990) *Revue de droit pénal et de la criminologie* 721–23.

[169] Cass 4 January 1994 (1994) *Revue de droit pénal et de la criminologie*, 80, conclusions of the general prosecutor J du Jardin, cited by O De Schutter, 'Belgique' in EU Network of Independent Experts on Fundamental Rights (n 138) 10.

[170] Ch mis Bruxelles 11 June 2003, JT 2004, 478.

[171] Cass 16 September 1974, *Pas* 1975, I, 48.

[172] Bruxelles 20 June 1997, RDP 1997, 1092.

[173] ibid.

[174] Cass 26 June 1996, *Pas*, 263. See also J de Kodt, 'Les nullités de l'instruction préparatoire et le droit de la preuve. Tendances récentes' (2000) *Revue de droit pénal et de la criminologie* 80, 24.

[175] de Kodt (ibid) 25–29.

[176] ibid 42.

[177] Sénat de Belgique, Proposition de loi modifiant le Code d'instruction criminelle en ce qui concerne les nullités, n 5-1666/1, session de 2011–12, 13 June 2012, 3.

[178] Art 140(1) CPP and Art 141(1) CPC (Switzerland).

[179] Art 141(1) CPP (Switzerland).

an admissibility exception, where it is 'essential' to use the evidence 'in order to secure a conviction for a serious offence'.[180] A second antithesis lies in the fact that the Code adopts, on the one hand, an absolute exclusionary rule for derivative evidence, resting the 'fruits of the poisonous tree' doctrine on a far reaching *conditio sine qua non* rationale,[181] whereas, on the other hand, Federal Supreme Court jurisprudence has begun to chip away at the doctrine's protective scope, even by 'disregard[ing] the wording of relevant provisions' in situations where these are considered 'too inflexible'.[182] In terms of practical enforcement, it is important to note that the Code also requires that tainted evidence be removed from the case file and held in safekeeping until the proceedings have been concluded and then destroyed.[183] On the other hand, the legislator takes care to avoid the potentially excessive outcomes of the strict application of the exclusionary rule. So, evidence is admissible where a trivial breach has been committed. Swiss law presumes this is the case where only administrative regulations have been violated.[184] Domestic law experts Gless and Martin interestingly visualise current jurisprudential trends in this area as 'water always find[ing] its way'. '[C]ourts have found a way around [the] new [exclusionary] rules as soon as they considered the regime too rigid for practical needs', they explain.[185] A more optimistic view might instead highlight that, despite setting out to undertake a balancing exercise between the protection of rights – the right to fair trial in particular, which appears to be the exclusionary rule's key rationale[186] – and the public interest in the conviction of the guilty, the Swiss legislator still opted for categorical exclusionary rules (and a 'serious criminality' exception) rather than discretion, and that jurisprudential efforts to bypass the rules have so far been limited to providing attenuation exceptions to the fruit of the poisonous tree doctrine.

We can contrast the Swiss exclusionary rules with discretionary exclusion in the Netherlands.[187] The enactment of article 359a of the CPP in 1996 gave Dutch courts a system with no real equivalent in comparative law, combining a variety of options: sentence reduction, exclusion of evidence and abandoning the prosecution altogether. But the architecture of the provision, and its foundation on combined 'trial fairness' (narrowly conceived) and deterrence rationales, made sure that these options would be predominantly used to admit improperly obtained evidence in the criminal trial, requiring courts to take into consideration the interest that the

[180] Art 141(2) CPP (Switzerland).

[181] Art 141(4) CPP (Switzerland).

[182] S Gless and J Martin, 'Water Always Finds Its Way – Discretion and the Concept of Exclusionary Rules in the Swiss Criminal Procedure Code' in Caianello and Hodgson, *Discretionary Criminal Justice* (n 96) 179.

[183] Art 141(5) CPP (Switzerland).

[184] Art 141(3) CPP (Switzerland).

[185] Gless and Martin, 'Water Always Finds Its Way' in Caianello and Hodgson (n 96) 179.

[186] ibid 162.

[187] For a detailed investigation of the operation of Dutch remedies for improperly obtained evidence see KM Pitcher, *Judicial Responses to Pre-Trial Procedural Violations in International Criminal Proceedings*, PhD thesis (2016) (on file with author).

breached rule serves,[188] the gravity of the breach and the harm it causes,[189] and to assess, by undertaking a cost–benefit analysis, whether the 'gravity of the breach' and 'seriousness of the harm' thresholds have been crossed.[190] Before reaching that stage, courts must inquire whether the procedural violation can be repaired.[191] Even where the violation is deemed to be 'irreparable', the court may determine that the prejudice caused to the accused is not significant enough to warrant applying one of the remedies enumerated in article 359a. The court may simply declare that a violation has occurred without attaching any further consequences,[192] a practice that the Supreme Court has expressed its preference for and lower courts have endorsed.[193] Furthermore, where the defendant *has* suffered actual prejudice, the default position is for the court to consider whether sentence reduction, not the exclusion of evidence, will be an appropriate remedy.[194] The prejudice must lend itself to 'compensation' in this way. Violations of the right to privacy can be compensated via sentence reduction, whereas violations of custodial interrogation rights cannot be.[195] So, it is only where the court establishes that sentence reduction will not be an appropriate remedy that it has to consider excluding the evidence. To apply the exclusionary remedy, a causality test must then be satisfied. The evidence must have been directly obtained by the breach.[196] A serious breach of the defendant's rights must have also occurred. A violation of the right to privacy is not seen as one. Here the Dutch Supreme Court finds support in the restrictive interpretation of the ECtHR on the interrelationship between Articles 8 and 6 of the Convention, accepting that a violation of the former does not necessarily lead to a violation of the latter.[197] Finally, the option of barring a prosecution or staying the proceedings is reserved for very exceptional cases.[198] Pitcher sums up the position of Dutch law with precision, though arguably rather understatedly: 'it appears to give precedence to the goal of truth-finding, and, by extension, the

[188] This means that the defendant will not have 'standing' to request the exclusion of the evidence where his rights have not been violated, for example where an unlawful search of a house has taken place and he is not the occupant. HR 19 February 2013, ECLI:NL:HR:2013:BY5322, para 2.4.1. See also M Borgers and L Stevens, 'The Netherlands: Statutory Balancing and a Choice of Remedies' in Thaman (n 81) 183, 187.

[189] Art 359a(2) CPP (Netherlands). The interest of the suspect that the offence is not detected is not regarded as an interest that would be 'harmed' by the admission of improperly obtained evidence. HR 19 February 2013 [2.4.1].

[190] Pitcher, *Judicial Responses* (n 187) 174. In undertaking this exercise, the court must take into account 'weighty interests' such as 'the discovery of truth and punishment of the perpetrator', the seriousness of the offence as well as 'the rights of victims or their survivors'. HR 19 February 2013 [2.4.5].

[191] For example, the court may be able to add an item to the case file or inform the defendant of the results of a DNA test, where the police have originally failed to do the above. See Borgers and Stevens, 'The Netherlands' in Thaman (n 81) 183, 186–87; Pitcher (n 187) 129.

[192] Pitcher (n 187) 131.

[193] ibid 134.

[194] Art 359a(1)(a) CPP (Netherlands).

[195] Pitcher (n 187) 133.

[196] ibid 135.

[197] HR 19 February 2013, para 2.4.2.

[198] Borgers and Stevens, 'The Netherlands' in Thaman (n 143) 188.

crime-control objective, over that of individual legal protection, save in exceptional circumstances'.[199]

Against the backdrop of a system so heavily weighted towards allowing the use of improperly obtained evidence, recent – previously discussed – Dutch Supreme Court jurisprudence requiring the exclusion of self-incriminating statements obtained in violation of the right to consult with a lawyer prior to interrogation[200] merits special attention, highlighting, once again, the unique ability of the ECtHR to instil rights-centred reform. But adherence to ECHR case law is far from being automatic, and local resistance is perhaps nowhere stronger than in relation to evidence admissibility matters.[201] The same Dutch Supreme Court decision that requires exclusion for violations of the right to consult with a lawyer also holds that, where the suspect has not been afforded the right to have the lawyer present during questioning, the remedy 'does not necessarily have to be exclusion from evidence' and that article 359a 'does not exclude the possibility of – depending on the circumstances of the case – a reduction of the sentence or a mere acknowledgement of the procedural error in question'.[202] This significantly diverges from what *Salduz* and its progeny require, and does not appear to rest on a rational criterion for distinguishing normatively between the two violations. The Dutch Supreme Court rather ambiguously asserts that non-consultation 'will generally be graver [a procedural error] than the non-attendance of a lawyer during the interview'.[203]

C. Ireland and New Zealand: Is the Rights Thesis in Retreat in Anglo-American Law?

Ireland and New Zealand provide fascinating case studies on the rights thesis. No common law system can demonstrate a more unambiguous attachment to the protective principle than Ireland. This country boasts 'one of the strictest exclusionary rules to be seen in the common law world when evidence has been obtained in breach of constitutional rights'.[204] But the Irish Supreme Court's recent decision in *DPP v JC* directly attacked the protective rationale, abruptly reorientating the rule towards a deterrent logic.[205] New Zealand was similarly adopting a rights-based prima facie rule of exclusion until the Court of Appeal substituted, in 2002, a discretionary test for it.[206] If these developments indicate that the rights

[199] Pitcher (n 187) 174.

[200] HR 22 December 2015, ECLI:NL:HR:2015:3608, r.o. 6.3 and 6.4.3, NJ 2016/52 m nt AH Klip.

[201] See generally D Giannoulopoulos, 'Custodial Legal Assistance and Notification of the Right to Silence in France: Legal Cosmopolitanism and Local Resistance' (2013) 24 *Criminal Law Forum* 291.

[202] HR 22 December 2015, ECLI:NL:HR:2015:3608, r o 6.3 and 6.4.3, NJ 2016/52 m n. AH Klip.

[203] ibid.

[204] Jackson, 'Human Rights' in Roberts and Hunter (n 47) 119, 122. See also Y Daly, 'Exclusion of Evidence: *DPP (Walsh) v Cash*' (2011) 15 *International Journal of Evidence & Proof* 62, 63.

[205] *DPP v JC* [2015] IESC 31.

[206] See *R v Shaheed* [2002] 2 NZLR 377.

thesis is in retreat in the common law world, how can we square them with our appeal to Anglo-American and Continental legal systems to place a new emphasis on rights protection when excluding improperly obtained evidence?

Let us start this line of argument with analysis of the Irish exclusionary rule. It was soon after *Mapp* that the Irish Supreme Court held, in the seminal case of *People (AG) v O'Brien*, that 'evidence obtained in deliberate conscious breach of the constitutional rights of an accused person should … be absolutely inadmissible',[207] save for 'extraordinary excusing circumstances';[208] while, for illegally (but not unconstitutionally) obtained evidence, it recognised an exclusionary discretion.[209] The Court stressed the 'far greater importance' of a breach of a constitutional right, pointing out 'the vindication and the protection of constitutional rights' as the rationale for exclusion. This was a fundamental duty of the courts that could not 'yield place to any other competing interest'.[210] The Court's 'strongly protectionist stance towards constitutional rights'[211] was categorically reaffirmed in *People (DPP) v Kenny*, where the Supreme Court rejected a possible good faith exception to the exclusionary rule. The Court recognised the exclusionary rule's 'negative deterrent' function, but underlined the importance of the 'absolute protection rule of exclusion' as 'a positive encouragement to those in authority … to consider in detail the personal rights of the citizens'.[212] The Court concluded that '[t]he detection of crime and the conviction of guilty persons, no matter how important', could not 'outweigh the unambiguously expressed constitutional obligation "as far as practicable to defend and vindicate the personal rights of the citizen"'.[213] *Kenny's* strong protective rationale must be seen in conjunction with other jurisprudential developments making real the promise of 'absolute protection', notably strict construction of the exceptions to automatic exclusion originally recognised in *O'Brien*.[214]

[207] *People (AG) v O'Brien* [1965] IR 142, 170. Charleton J noted in *DPP v Cash* [2007] IEHC 108 [52] that Ireland 'imported the [exclusionary] rule from the United States'.

[208] Such 'extraordinary excusing circumstances' existed where the destruction of vital evidence was imminent, where there was the need to rescue a victim in peril or where the evidence had been obtained by a search incidental to and contemporaneous with a lawful arrest although made without a valid search warrant. *People (AG) v O'Brien* [1965] IR 142, 170.

[209] ibid 160.

[210] ibid 170.

[211] Jackson, 'Human Rights' (2012) 131.

[212] *People (DPP) v Kenny* [1990] 2 IR 110, 133.

[213] ibid 134. The duty to defend and vindicate, as far as practicable, the personal rights of the citizen is provided by Art 40.3.1 of the Irish Constitution.

[214] As Heffernan illustrates, 'extraordinary excusing circumstances' are rarely invoked in practice, while the concept of a 'deliberate and conscious' violation of constitutional rights has been interpreted objectively so as not to relate 'to the violation of constitutional rights but to the conduct leading to the violation'. In addition, the constitutional protection of individual rights has grown to the extent that 'the distinction between illegally and unconstitutionally obtained evidence is negligible in practice', given that 'virtually every instance of misconduct involves a potential constitutional violation'. L Heffernan, 'The Fourth Amendment's Exclusionary Rule: Blurring the Line Between Rule and Exception' (2011) 9 *International Commentary on Evidence* article 3, 23–24. See also A Cras and YM Daly,

Not surprisingly, the Irish Supreme Court's strong preference for the rights thesis was not without its critics. In 2006 the Government established a review group which recommended abandoning automatic exclusion,[215] whilst politicians attacked the rule for letting the guilty get off on a technicality.[216] Equally noticeable was Supreme Court jurisprudence admitting, through the back door, unconstitutionally obtained evidence destined for exclusion.[217] Charleton J's critique in *DPP v Cash* can perhaps be read as a prelude to *DPP v JC*. He complained that the exclusionary rule's 'entire focus [was] on the accused and his rights' and that 'the rights of the community to live safely [had] receded out of view'.[218] Arguing that the exclusionary rule was 'remorselessly exclud[ing] evidence obtained through

'Ireland: A Move to Categorical Exclusion?' in Thaman (n 143) 33, 36–38, discussing *DPP v Madden* [1977] IR 336 (where the Court adopted a narrow test for a 'deliberate and conscious' breach), *People (DPP) v Shaw* [1982] IR 1 (which agreed with *Madden*), *People (DPP) v Kenny* [1990] 2 IR 110 (discussed above), *DPP v Balfe* [1998] 4 IR 50 (which adopted the subjective interpretation of 'deliberate and conscious' established in *O'Brien*) and *DPP v Laide and Ryan* [2005] 1 IR 209 (which confirmed *Kenny's* objective test and 'absolute protection rule of exclusion'). On the other hand, in *DPP v Balfe*, the Supreme Court created a dichotomy between mistakes on the face of a search warrant and search warrants made without lawful authority, with discretionary exclusion applying to the former and automatic exclusion applying to the latter. According to Daly, this distinction 'has provided the courts with something of an escape valve and has mitigated the hard edges of the strict rule to a notable extent'. YM Daly, 'Overruling the Protectionist Exclusionary Rule: *DPP v JC*' (2015) 19 *International Journal of Evidence & Proof* 270, 273.

[215] *Balance in the Criminal Law Review Group* (Dublin, 2007) 8, http://www.justice.ie/en/JELR/Pages/Balance_in_criminal_law_report. A majority of this Group concluded that the exclusionary rule in Ireland was 'too strictly calibrated' and recommended that it be substituted with a discretion to exclude 'having regard to the totality of the circumstances and in particular the rights of the victim' (p 161). In a way reminiscent of recent US Supreme Court jurisprudence, the Review Group also stressed that the need for the rule had been 'superseded by radical changes to the nature of policing in recent years', such as video taping and the creation of a Police Ombudsman (pp 159–60). Gerard Hogan, the chairman of the Group, wrote a separate note of dissent in defence of the strict exclusionary rule, observing that it was the 'logical corollary' of the Constitution and the 'occasional exclusion of otherwise relevant evidence' was 'a price society should be prepared to pay in the interests of upholding the values solemnly enshrined in [Ireland's] highest law' (p 288). The Irish Council for Civil Liberties expressed its agreement with this position. See Irish Council for Civil Liberties, *Taking Liberties: The Human Rights Implications of the Balance in the Criminal Law Review Report* (Dublin 2008) 25 www.iccl.ie/-taking-liberties-the-human-rights-implications-of-the-balance-in-the-criminal-law-review-group.html. On the other hand, the DPP, James Hamilton, argued that the exclusionary rule is irrational and distanced from reality. D McDonald, *Plea to relax 'loaded' laws on Evidence, The Sunday Times* (Ireland) 16 May 2006, www.thesundaytimes.co.uk/sto/news/world_news/article202218.ece. In another place, Hamilton pointed out that the exclusionary rule is 'a classic example of what is called "cutting off your nose to spite your face"'. J Hamilton, *Opening remarks – 7th annual prosecutors' conference,* 13 May 2006, www.dppireland.ie/filestore/documents/DIRECTOR_-_Opening_Remarks.pdf.

[216] See, eg, the comments of Richard Humphreys, the Labour councillor for the Stillorgan Ward in Dublin, in R Humphreys, *Miscarriage of justice as guilty get off on a technicality: the exclusionary rule has created a massive imbalance in our justice system, Sunday Independent* (Ireland), 28 July 2013.

[217] See *DPP v Cash* [2007] IEHC 108, which rejected application of the exclusionary rule to evidence obtained unconstitutionally in the pre-arrest period. Unlawfully retained DNA evidence had been used to ground reasonable suspicion for a lawful arrest.

[218] ibid [31]. See generally Daly, 'Exclusion of Evidence' (2011) 62.

an illegality occurring by mistake',[219] he advocated exclusion 'on the basis of a balancing of interests' instead.[220]

It is instructive to examine *JC* against the backdrop of these pressing calls for substantial reform. With this seminal judgment the Supreme Court introduced, in April 2015, an important exception to *Kenny's* robust exclusionary rule, but it nonetheless resisted the idea of a balancing test. More specifically, following *JC*, unconstitutionally obtained evidence will be admitted where the police have violated the relevant constitutional right inadvertently.[221] To exclude evidence even where violations of rights were inadvertent involved 'an inappropriate balancing of the interests concerned',[222] explained Clarke J. However, the evidence will still be excluded if it has been obtained 'in circumstances of recklessness or gross negligence',[223] he added, and where the police have knowingly violated the defendant's rights of course. Interestingly, this assessment requires analysis of the conduct or state of mind of the senior official or officials within the investigating or enforcement authority concerned and not just of the individual police officer who may have executed the warrant, which theoretically makes more unlikely a finding of inadvertence.[224] The evidence will also still be excluded where the unconstitutional obtaining affects the probative value of the evidence such as where confessional evidence has been obtained via oppression or the like.[225] In view of the above, Ward and Leon go so far as to argue that *JC* 'is a retreat from *Kenny* but quite a limited one' and the Irish rule 'remains an unusually rigid exclusionary rule'.[226] But one may be left wondering whether they are taking *JC* at face value. Daly is correct to point out that 'the nuances of operating the new rule will only become apparent as cases come through the trial and appellate courts'.[227]

Having said that, Hardiman J's thundering dissent leaves little room to doubt *JC's* detrimental effect on Ireland's rights-based exclusionary rule, and it is as resounding a defence of the rights thesis as can be found across Anglo-American and Continental law. Hardiman J has posthumously come to be lauded for his unfailing protection of 'civil liberties and individual freedoms'[228] and for

[219] ibid [65]. It is interesting to note the terminological borrowing from the House of Lord's decision in *AG's Reference (No 3 of 1999)* [2001] 2 AC 91, where Lord Cooke spoke of a 'remorseless principle of the exclusion of evidence unlawfully obtained'. Charleton J relied upon *AG's Reference* in *Cash*. See *DPP v Cash* [2007] IEHC 108 [48]–[51]. Using similar language, O'Donnell J made reference in *DPP v Gareth Mallon* [2011] IECCA 29 to '[t]he remorseless logic of the *Kenny* decision leading to the automatic exclusion of evidence sometimes as a result of quite trivial errors'.

[220] *DPP v Cash* [2007] IEHC 108 [66].

[221] *DPP v JC* [2015] IESC 31, per Clarke J [5.11].

[222] ibid [5.13].

[223] ibid [5.13].

[224] ibid [5.10].

[225] ibid [5.2]. On the other hand, *JC* has not clarified whether this will also be the case where confessional evidence has been obtained in violation of custodial interrogation rights.

[226] C Leon and T Ward, 'The Irish Exclusionary Rule after *DPP v JC*' (2015) 35 *Legal Studies* 590, 592–93.

[227] Daly, 'Overruling the Protectionist Exclusionary Rule' (2014) 279.

[228] *Supreme Court judge Adrian Hardiman dies, Irish Times*, 7 March 2016.

being 'a staunch defender of the rights of the accused'.[229] He wrote that *Kenny's* 'absolute exclusionary rule' marked how 'Ireland was a country in which the personal rights of the individual citizens [were] taken seriously' rather than being 'merely words on a page', adding that he 'was deeply proud that this [was] so'.[230] But the effect of *JC* on *Kenny*, 'a decision of major constitutional importance',[231] would be to relegate constitutional rights 'to mere shibboleths',[232] without even relying on 'any democratic process of legislation or referendum'.[233] Admission of unconstitutionally obtained evidence, even inadvertently obtained, would mean that 'the Constitution could be breached with impunity, the rights it assures not vindicated, and there would be no disincentive to a public authority or an individual public official simply ignoring the law and even defying the Constitution'.[234] Admission of the evidence would 'set the Constitution itself at nought' and 'infringe the Constitution a second time'.[235] Hardiman was 'ashamed' and 'appalled' that the majority opinion would bring about these consequences.[236]

So exceptional an attack upon the Court's majority opinion was not just premised on rights rhetoric though, but on a pragmatic basis as well. The strict exclusionary rule was the only choice, according to Hardiman's opinion. Criminal or disciplinary sanctions were an illusion. '[T]housands of hours of tape recordings of telephone calls to and from Garda stations [had been] illegally recorded in recent years', for instance, and yet '[n]ot one guard of any rank ha[d] been prosecuted for this',[237] noted the Supreme Court judge referring to the 'Gardagate' scandal. Courts had historically been 'very receptive' to claims about inadvertent breaches of constitutional rights and 'extremely credulous of them', he added.[238] Excusing a '"mistake"' would lead to many more '"mistakes"' being excused by the courts, Hardiman J concluded, until 'all content' of the constitutional right would 'be sucked out of it'.[239] In brief, Hardiman J's opinion displays admirable reflexes to counter efforts to substitute a deterrence logic for the rights thesis in Irish law. But the future of rights-orientated exclusion has been put significantly in doubt after *JC*, especially if Daly's observation is taken into account, that the Court's attack on the exclusionary rule is not an isolated incident, but rather forms part of a wider curtailment of due process rights in Irish criminal procedure.[240]

[229] C O'Mahony and S Ó Conaill, *Mr Justice Adrian Hardiman 1951-2016*, Constitution Project @ UCC, www.constitutionproject.ie/?p=573.
[230] *DPP v JC* [2015] IESC 31, per Hardiman J [5].
[231] ibid [6].
[232] ibid [5].
[233] ibid [6].
[234] ibid [14].
[235] ibid.
[236] ibid [16].
[237] ibid [14].
[238] ibid [16].
[239] ibid.
[240] Daly (n 214) 279. For the effect of the rise of penal populism on Irish criminal procedure see generally L Campbell, 'Criminal Justice and Penal Populism in Ireland' (2008) 28 *Legal Studies* 559.

From a rights perspective, it seems that within a period of less than three years from March 2014 to January 2017, the Court had come full circle. From adopting, in *DPP v Gormley*,[241] a paradigmatically cosmopolitan, pro-defendant interpretation of the right to custodial legal assistance, in line with (if not going further than) ECHR jurisprudence, to the decision in *DPP v Boyle*[242] denying suspects the fundamental right to have a lawyer present when questioned by the police, in blatant disregard of *Salduz* jurisprudence and its ground-breaking impact across Europe. The Court's change of heart in relation to suspects' rights provides a backdrop for further analysis of *JC*, and does not generally allow one to be optimistic about the ramifications of this seminal case for the future of the exclusionary rule in Ireland, at least from a rights theorist's point of view. It is also a useful reminder of the capricious ways in which the complex process of constitutionalisation can shape the content of exclusionary rules, particularly where law and order concerns have caught up with a Court's due process-orientated jurisprudence.

On the other hand, *JC* is another example where it might be useful to analyse domestic law developments through a 'simultanism' perspective. Compared to legal systems taking an inclusionary approach to evidence obtained by violations of the right to privacy, or legal systems where privacy-based exclusionary rules do not practically extend to frustrating search and seizure, the Irish exclusionary rule, even after *JC*, remains a robust, rights-based, strict exclusionary rule, at least unless and until domestic jurisprudence applying *JC* proves otherwise. This is obviously not an argument for playing down the seriousness of the Supreme Court's departure from its *Kenny* jurisprudence. The intention is the exact opposite; to highlight how deeply entrenched in rights protection the Irish exclusionary rule is, and, in this way, urge caution as to *JC's* effect in practice.

A few years prior to these critical jurisprudential developments in Ireland, a similar move in New Zealand – from a rights-based exclusionary rule to a balancing test – strengthens the view that, in the common law world, the rights thesis is in retreat. There are interesting qualifications to this view. It can also be argued that the story of the existence in New Zealand, for more than ten years, of a pure rights-based exclusionary rule, is worthy of attention in itself.

The operation and rationale of the now obsolete so-called prima facie rule of exclusion (a presumption of exclusion) was recognised in 1991 in *R v Butcher*, where the New Zealand Court of Appeal held that '[p]rima facie … a violation of rights should result in the ruling out of evidence obtained thereby'.[243]

[241] *DPP v Gormley* and *DPP v White* [2014] IESC 17. See generally D Giannoulopoulos, 'Strasbourg Jurisprudence, Law Reform and Comparative Law: A Tale of the Right to Custodial Legal Assistance in Five Countries' (2016) 16 *Human Rights Law Review* 103.

[242] *DPP v Boyle* [2017] IESC 1. See D Robinson, *Access to a Lawyer: Is Ireland turning back the clock?*, Fair Trials blog, 13 February 2017, available at www.fairtrials.org/access-to-a-lawyer-is-ireland-turning-back-the-clock.

[243] *R v Butcher* [1992] 2 NZLR 257, 266.

This was 'a strong presumption of inadmissibility',[244] rebuttable by the prosecution which would 'bear the onus of satisfying the Court that there [was] good reason for admitting the evidence despite the violation'.[245] Since *Butcher* the Court of Appeal stressed, on more than one occasion, that the prima facie rule was *not* a rule of automatic exclusion.[246] The rule was rather seen as 'an attempt to articulate a solution which would give primacy to the vindication of guaranteed rights but with some flexibility to recognise other societal interests'.[247] But, as the Court admitted itself, 'in reality', in the ten years of the application of the prima facie rule, 'the exclusion of evidence has followed almost automatically' from a breach of a constitutional right.[248] This was a time when from a strict vindication rationale derived 'severe remedial consequences' as 'a commensurate response' to violations of rights.[249]

An important qualification is that most of the cases in which the prima facie rule was examined by the Court of Appeal dealt with admissions and breaches of the right to custodial legal assistance, though privacy violations clearly also came within the rule's scope. In *R v Jefferies*, a case that related to a search of a car conducted in alleged breach of the constitutional right against unreasonable search and seizure,[250] McKay J opined that '[t]he evidence having been obtained in breach of the New Zealand Bill of Rights Act 1990, it should prima facie be excluded', though he then went on to argue that '[t]here [were] exceptions', for instance where the police gained no advantage from the breach or acted in good faith.[251] In *R v Grayson and Taylor*, the Court of Appeal reaffirmed the applicability of the prima facie rule to search and seizure, but emphasised the need for careful balancing of rights and remedies, the risks stemming from inflexibility as well as the consistency of 'a robust and rights-centred approach to individual rights … with flexibility of remedies where rights are breached'.[252] The seeds of doubt about presumptive exclusion had been sown in cases like these, which indeed formed part of the reasoning of the Court when, a few years later, it cast the prima facie rule into oblivion.

[244] S Optican and P Sankoff, 'The New Exclusionary Rule: A Preliminary Assessment of *R v Shaheed*' [2003] *New Zealand Law Review* 1, 2.

[245] ibid.

[246] See *Ministry of Transport v Noort* [1992] 3 NZLR 260, 285; *R v Goodwin* [1993] 2 NZLR 153, 206.

[247] *R v Shaheed* [2002] 2 NZLR 377 [140].

[248] ibid. The concept of 'good reason for admitting the evidence', such as where the breach was trivial or inconsequential, seemed to be interpreted narrowly. See Choo and Nash (n 55) 100. Optican and Sankoff note that, 'a few categorically defined exceptions' notwithstanding, evidence obtained in breach of the Bill of Rights 'tended commonly to be excluded'. Optican and Sankoff, 'The New Exclusionary Rule' (2003) 4.

[249] A Geddis and MB Rodriguez Ferrer, 'Judicial Innovation under the New Zealand Bill of Rights Act – Lessons for Queensland' (2016) 25 *University of Queensland Law Journal* 251, 261.

[250] Section 21 of the New Zealand Bill of Rights Act 1990.

[251] *R v Jefferies* [1994] 1 NZLR 290, 317. The majority of the Court had, however, concluded that the search of the car was not in violation of the right against unreasonable search and seizure. The majority opinion did not, as a consequence, discuss the prima facie rule.

[252] *R v Grayson and Taylor* [1997] 1 NZLR 399, 411–12.

This 'major paradigm shift in New Zealand criminal procedure'[253] happened with the seminal judgment in *R v Shaheed*, itself a case triggering the right against unreasonable search and seizure.[254] The Court undertook a review of the prima facie rule, which stressed, inter alia, the 'relatively narrow and almost mechanical approach by Judges',[255] the inability of the test to 'adequately [address] the interest of the community that those who are guilty of serious crimes should not go unpunished'[256] and to 'command the respect of the community'.[257] It also underlined the 'unbalanced and disproportionate' nature of the vindication as a remedy for violations of rights in cases where evidence is 'reliable and probative of a serious crime'.[258] Much was also made of the alleged tendency of the courts, in search and seizure cases, to 'avoid the issue [of exclusion] by concentrating on the reasonableness of the police actions', which 'may have led to some distortion – situations in which it would have been preferable to acknowledge that the search and seizure was unreasonable and then to determine by means of a balancing exercise whether the evidence ought nevertheless to be admitted'.[259] It was partly in view of these alleged defects of the prima facie rule that the Court reached the conclusion that the proper approach to exclusion was a balancing exercise that would give considerable weight to breaches of rights, but that might in the end be outweighed by other factors.[260] The new balancing test then obtained a statutory basis with section 30 of the New Zealand Evidence Act 2006, which requires judges to evaluate whether exclusion would be 'a proportional remedial response to the police misconduct in the case'[261] by taking into account a list of non-exclusive factors such as the importance of the right breached, the bad faith of the police, the nature and quality of the evidence, the seriousness of the offence and the availability of alternative investigatory techniques and alternative judicial remedies.[262]

Against the majority of six justices who dispensed with the prima facie rule in *Shaheed*, Elias CJ was alone in providing a defence, and a remarkably strong one at that. The Chief Justice drew attention to how the courts had read the prima facie rule into the Bill of Rights to protect the rights identified therein,[263] and how the balancing approach had been previously rejected.[264] She pointed out the risk of uncertainty and erosion of rights as inherent in the balancing approach, the latter

[253] J Ip, 'The End of the Prima Facie Exclusionary Rule' (2002) 9 *Auckland University Law Review* 1016, 1030.
[254] *R v Shaheed* [2002] 2 NZLR 377.
[255] ibid [140].
[256] ibid [143].
[257] ibid.
[258] ibid.
[259] ibid [141]. See also Optican and Sankoff (n 244) 3.
[260] ibid [144].
[261] Section 30(2)(b) Evidence Act 2006.
[262] Section 30(3) Evidence Act 2006.
[263] ibid [8].
[264] ibid [17], citing *R v Te Kira* [1993] 3 NZLR 257.

as a result of 'double-counting, in the balancing of remedy, other public interests already balanced in the determination of breach'.[265] She warned that abolition of the prima facie rule would 'deny the only effective remedy', endorse an 'ends justifies the means' doctrine and might 'co-opt the Court into completing breaches of rights',[266] explaining that 'if the Court admits the evidence, it effectively completes the breach'.[267] Finally, Elias CJ focused on how exclusion serves to vindicate the constitutional rights breached, 'rights fundamental to all citizens, and not simply as punishment of the officer for breach or as compensation to the person affected, who may be unworthy of much consideration'.[268]

There are impressive similarities in Elias CJ's defence of the rights thesis with normative justifications for rights-centred exclusion in Ireland and many of the Continental legal systems examined in this chapter, particularly those adopting a constitutional criminal procedure system. The significance of these similarities should not be underestimated. Irrespective of the turn to balancing in New Zealand, the deterrent principle coming to the surface in Ireland and legislative developments weakening, in some cases, rights-centred exclusionary rules in Continental legal systems, preceding observations demonstrate that support for the rights thesis can be generated across the Anglo-American and Continental law divide, subject to the appropriate conditions being in place. It is equally instructive to take note of resistance in these jurisdictions to efforts to move away from rights-based exclusionary rules. New Zealand offers an opportunity for a concluding thought in that respect. The Court of Appeal's decision in *Williams*, for instance, explained that a serious breach of defendant's rights would 'normally' lead to exclusion, 'even where the crime was serious', and that exclusion would be 'almost inevitable' where the violation of the right was 'deliberate, reckless or grossly careless'.[269] Furthermore, Choo's and Nash's jurisprudential study of the first few years of operation of the post-*Shaheed* balancing test concluded that the evidently pro-prosecution approach adopted with *Shaheed* did 'not appear to have decreased the extent of exclusion' in practice. With its new approach, the Court of Appeal had perhaps reflected crime control concerns of the public, 'rather than a desire to see more improperly obtained evidence in fact admitted'.[270] We must add, as a postscript, that post-*Shaheed* jurisprudence also draws attention to the risk of uncertainty inherent in balancing tests, as *Shaheed's* promise of 'clarity, certainty

[265] ibid [19].
[266] ibid.
[267] ibid [22].
[268] ibid [24], quoting from *R v Te Kira* [1993] 3 NZLR 257, 276.
[269] *R v Williams* [2007] NZCA 52 [251]–[52]. See S Optican, '"Lessons from Down Under": The Exclusion of Improperly Obtained Evidence in New Zealand as the Model for a Changing United States Exclusionary Rule' (2011–2012) *Journal of Commonwealth Criminal Law* 226, 235. *Cf Hamed v R* [2011] NZSC 101, whose effect has been to 'abandon *Williams* as the required or even preferred approach to the exclusion exercise'. S Optican, '*Hamed, Williams* and the Exclusionary Rule: Critiquing the Supreme Court's Approach to s 30 of the Evidence Act 2006' (2012) NZLR 605, 612.
[270] Choo and Nash (n 55) 104.

and intellectual rigour' in applying the proportionality-balancing test[271] does not seem to have been realised, despite the availability of a long list of factors that courts need to take into account and despite conscientious jurisprudential efforts to rationalise the operation of the test.[272] Recent Supreme Court jurisprudence seems to have abandoned the test to the 'largely unguided discretion of individual judges',[273] generating 'inconsistency, unpredictability and confusion' when excluding improperly obtained evidence.[274] Adoption of the rights thesis allows legal systems to avoid these consequences (where the impropriety in question involves infringing rights).

D. 'Taking Rights Seriously' in Judicial Integrity-based Exclusionary Systems?: Canada, Australia and International Criminal Courts

This section has so far surveyed exclusionary systems that adopt, or have at one point adopted, the rights thesis, and that employ, or have previously employed, strict exclusionary rules to give it effect. Examples from Anglo-American and Continental law that can serve as useful points of reference for legal systems that might consider adopting – or reinforcing, if they're already applying it – the rights thesis as their basis for exclusion. Drawing on the close links of the rights thesis with the judicial integrity thesis, this section will now briefly consider legal systems where the exclusion of improperly obtained evidence is determined by reference to the effect that the use of the tainted evidence has on the integrity of the proceedings. In doing so, this section will highlight examples of legal systems that strive to afford appropriate weight to rights protection within a discretionary, integrity-based, exclusionary system. The plasticity of the exclusionary rule doctrine in Anglo-American and Continental law, and its close links with broader political issues, partly explain continuous movements along the exclusionary-admissibility spectrum, from rights-centred, categorical exclusionary rules to judicial integrity-based balancing tests to invoking deterrence – and stressing reliability – in order to reduce exclusion in practice, if not endorse a fully inclusionary approach. With this mind, it is imperative to shed light on how, or whether, the judicial integrity principle, and discretionary exclusion, can be seen as an adequate substitute for the rights thesis, and whether discretionary exclusion can be a proper replacement for automatic exclusion, in circumstances where the political climate, or prevailing criminal justice principles, do not conduce to adopting the rights thesis or introducing categorical exclusionary rules.

[271] S Mount, '*R v Shaheed*: The Prima Facie Rule Re-Examined' [2003] *New Zealand Law Review* 45, 69–70.

[272] See *R v Williams* [2007] NZCA 52.

[273] Optican, '"Lessons from Down Under"' (n 269) 637.

[274] ibid 640.

Canadian law provides a useful prism for exploration of these issues. The entry point to understanding the theoretical foundations of Canadian law on improperly obtained evidence is that it emerged from a dynamic process of constitutionalisation of criminal procedure. Before Canada obtained a charter of constitutional rights, criminal procedure 'was subject to few constitutional constraints' and '[w]ith the exception of involuntary confessions, Canadian courts accepted all improperly obtained evidence in a criminal trial'.[275] Then, in 1982, the Charter of Rights and Freedoms was enacted. Section 24(2) mandated that evidence obtained in violation of any rights or freedoms guaranteed by the Charter 'shall be excluded if it is established that, having regard to all the circumstances, the admission of it in the proceedings would bring the administration of justice into disrepute'. The first major decision of the Canadian Supreme Court on section 24(2), *R v Collins*, distinguished between three groups of factors which courts needed to balance, taking into account how they affected the repute of the administration of justice: (a) the effect of admission on the fairness of the trial; (b) the seriousness of the Charter violation; and (c) the effect of excluding the evidence on the repute of the administration of justice.[276] The balancing exercise mandated by *Collins* was 'highly discretionary and fact specific',[277] 'broad and imprecise',[278] so even a summary of the extensive jurisprudence developing each factor lies beyond the scope of the concise comparative review undertaken in this chapter. It is rather instructive to observe that, within such a discretionary test, a virtually automatic rule of exclusion for evidence obtained in violation of the right against self-incrimination was until recently in operation. It is equally noteworthy to examine the Court's revisionist second thoughts.

Collins held that 'if the admission of the evidence in some way affect[ed] the fairness of the trial, then the admission of the evidence would *tend* to bring the administration of justice into disrepute and, subject to a consideration of the other factors, the evidence generally should be excluded'.[279] This would particularly be the case where 'the accused [was] conscripted against himself through a confession or other evidence emanating from him'. Admitting such evidence in court would strike 'at one of the fundamental tenets of a fair trial, the right against self-incrimination'.[280] *R v Stillman*, the other major point of reference in Canadian exclusionary rule jurisprudence, then settled the question of whether courts were indeed required to consider the second and third groups of factors once they had made a finding that the admission of the evidence would violate the right against self-incrimination. The *Stillman* majority held that they were not.

[275] K Roach, 'Canada's Experience with Constitutionalism and Criminal Justice' (2013) 25 *Singapore Academy of Law Journal* 656, 658.

[276] *R v Collins* [1987] 1 SCR 265 [36]–[39].

[277] J Milne, 'Exclusion of Evidence Trends Post *Grant*: Are Appeal Courts Deferring to Trial Judges?' (2015) 19 *Canadian Criminal Law Review* 373.

[278] *R v Grant* [2009] 2 SCR 353 [60].

[279] *R v Collins* [1987] 1 SCR 265 [36].

[280] ibid [37].

It explained that 'the primary aim and purpose of considering the trial fairness factor in the s. 24(2) analysis [was] to prevent an accused person whose Charter rights ha[d] been infringed from being forced or conscripted to provide evidence in the form of statements or bodily samples for the benefit of the state'.[281] The Court concluded that 'the admission of [such 'conscriptive'] evidence would generally tend to render the trial unfair',[282] and it should therefore be 'excluded without consideration of the other *Collins* factors'.[283] This was because the right to fair trial was a 'cornerstone' of the 'Canadian democratic society'. Upholding a conviction on the basis of a violation of the right to fair trial would be 'unthinkable', 'contrary to the [Canadian] concept of justice' and indeed 'a travesty of justice'.[284] The Court recognised only one exception: where conscriptive evidence was 'discoverable', its admission would 'not, as a general rule, render the trial unfair', so the court should proceed to examine the second and third groups of factors.[285]

Stillman 'treated the principle against self-incrimination as so fundamentally important that *it required* evidence to be excluded, regardless of other considerations such as the degree of police fault, the reliability of the evidence and the seriousness of the offence',[286] and all this within the context of a highly fact-specific discretionary test. This should not go unnoticed by exclusionary rule scholars on this side of the Atlantic. The *Collins–Stillman* jurisprudence resonates with *Salduz* and its progeny, as to reading into the privilege against self-incrimination an automatic (or near-automatic) exclusionary rule for evidence obtained in violation of the right against self-incrimination.[287] In the case of Canada, this near-automatic exclusionary rule was not even restricted to self-incriminating statements obtained in violation of custodial interrogation rights (as *Salduz* is), but also extended to bodily evidence obtained in violation of the right against self-incrimination. The *Collins–Stillman* jurisprudence strongly supports the narrative of converging rights-based approaches to excluding evidence obtained in violation of fair trial rights applying to custodial interrogation, which has been developed in this book. It reinforces the idea of focusing attention on the rights thesis particularly when dealing with confessional evidence obtained in violation of such rights.

But the quasi-automatic exclusionary rule for conscriptive evidence was abandoned in 2009, in the seminal case of *R v Grant*, which now constitutes the foremost Canadian authority on section 24(2). The Supreme Court found in *Grant* that *Stillman's* 'general rule of inadmissibility of all non-discoverable conscriptive evidence … seem[ed] to go against the requirement of s. 24(2) that the court

[281] *R v Stillman* [1997] 1 SCR 607 [73].

[282] ibid.

[283] ibid [72].

[284] ibid.

[285] ibid [107]. Evidence was 'discoverable' where 'a non-conscriptive means existed through which the evidence would have been discovered or … its discovery was inevitable …; it would have been discovered in the absence of the unlawful conscription of the accused' (ibid).

[286] J Dawe and H McArthur, 'Charter Detention and the Exclusion of Evidence after *Grant, Harrison* and *Suberu*' (2010) 56 *Criminal Law Quarterly* 376, 406.

[287] See ch 5.

determining admissibility must consider "all the circumstances"'.[288] The Court also challenged '[t]he underlying assumption that the use of conscriptive evidence always, or almost always, renders the trial unfair'.[289] Keen to square 'preserving basic procedural fairness to the accused' with satisfying 'the public interest in getting at the truth', it ended by reimagining 'trial fairness as a multifaceted and contextual concept' that could no longer accommodate 'a near-automatic presumption' of inadmissibility.[290] The groups of factors that courts needed to balance were therefore recalibrated. Courts' three lines of inquiries should start with 'the seriousness of the Charter-infringing conduct', proceed to whether 'the breach actually undermined the interests protected by the right infringed' (the 'Impact on the Charter-Protected Interests of the Accused') and conclude with analysis of 'whether the truth-seeking function of the criminal trial process would be better served by admission of the evidence, or by its exclusion' ('Society's Interest in an Adjudication on the Merits').[291]

Reaction to *Grant* was mixed. Dawe and McArthur pointed out, for instance, that in overturning '22 years of settled s. 24(2) jurisprudence that emphasized the importance of "trial fairness" and the principle against self-incrimination', the Court 'open[ed] the door to a considerable amount of evidence that would have been excluded under the *Collins/Stillman* approach now being ruled admissible'.[292] Jochelson and Kramar went further, arguing that 'the [new] test allow[ed] for the potential of a socio-legal trend towards inclusion and therefore [had] the potential to be aligned with, or subsumed within, conceptions of penal populism'.[293] On the other hand, empirical surveys of post-*Grant* case law have brought to the surface that Canadian courts continue to routinely exclude improperly obtained evidence,[294] as is also illustrated by recent Supreme Court jurisprudence.[295]

[288] *R v Grant* [2009] 2 SCR 353 [65].

[289] ibid.

[290] ibid.

[291] ibid [72]–[86].

[292] Dawe and McArthur, 'Charter Detention' (2010) 376.

[293] R Jochelson and K Kramar, 'Situating Exclusion of Evidence Analysis in its Socio-Legal Place: A Tale of Judicial Populism' (2014) 61 *Crime, Law and Social Change* 541, 554.

[294] See M Madden, 'Marshalling the Data: An Empirical Analysis of Canada's Section 24(2) Case Law in the Wake of *R. v. Grant*' (2011) 15 *Canadian Criminal Law Review* 229; A Asselin, 'Trends for Exclusion of Evidence in 2012' (2013) *Criminal Reports*, 7th series, cited by Milne, 'Exclusion of Evidence Trends' (2015) 373, 375–76. Madden has found an, impressive, overall exclusion rate of 70% in a survey of 100 cases.

[295] See, eg, *R v Paterson* [2017] 1 SCR 202, where the Supreme Court found that drugs and a firearm 'obtained as a result of the entry and search of [the defendant's] residence should be excluded', even though the police conduct was 'not egregious' (but 'it represented a serious departure from well-established constitutional norms'). See also *R v Marakah*, 2017 SCC 59, where the Supreme Court found that the defendant had a reasonable expectation of privacy in a text message conversation recovered on the accomplice's device, and therefore standing to challenge the unreasonable search and admission of evidence. The Supreme Court considered that Society's interest in the adjudication of the case on its merits was significant, as the SMS messages offered highly reliable and probative evidence in the prosecution of a serious offence. But the seriousness of the police conduct (accessing and searching the electronic conversation through the defendant's iPhone without a warrant two hours after his arrest) ultimately weighed in favour of excluding the evidence.

These observations must be examined in parallel with pre-*Grant* analysis demonstrating that, even when faced with non-conscriptive evidence, 'Canadian courts have been willing to use their exclusionary powers in s. 24(2)'.[296]

In summary, Canada offers an absorbing example of an exclusionary system, which may prioritise balancing and judicial integrity, yet gives serious consideration to the protection of constitutional rights. This is a fortiori the case in relation to confessional evidence obtained in violation of the right against self-incrimination. *Grant's* abandonment of the *Collins–Stillman* rule seems more likely to affect the admission of physical evidence, not statements obtained in violation of the right against self-incrimination. In relation to the latter, the Court accepted that there should still exist 'presumptive general, although not automatic, exclusion'.[297]

Exclusion in Canada post-*Grant* can be usefully contrasted with discretionary exclusion in Australia, especially in view of the rejection in the latter of the right to fair trial as an 'appropriate legal concept by reference to which to attempt to secure the exclusion of "what might loosely be called 'real evidence'", notably 'the result of breathalyzer tests, fingerprint evidence and so on'.[298] As in Canada, exclusion in Australia revolves around the balancing of competing considerations. In the seminal case of *Bunning v Cross*, the High Court of Australia explained that this process involved:

> the weighing against each other of two competing requirements of public policy, thereby seeking to resolve the apparent conflict between the desirable goal of bringing to conviction the wrongdoer and the undesirable effect of curial approval, or even encouragement, being given to the unlawful conduct of those whose task it is to enforce the law.[299]

Section 138 of the Uniform Evidence Acts now provides that evidence obtained 'improperly or in contravention of Australian law' and any derivative evidence 'is not to be admitted unless the desirability of admitting the evidence outweighs the undesirability of admitting evidence' obtained in this way.[300] Section 138(3) provides a non-exhaustive list of factors that courts may take into account, including whether individual rights protected under international human rights law have been violated:

> (a) the probative value of the evidence, and
> (b) the importance of the evidence in the proceeding, and
> (c) the nature of the relevant offence, cause of action or defence and the nature of the subject-matter of the proceeding, and
> (d) the gravity of the impropriety or contravention, and
> (e) whether the impropriety or contravention was deliberate or reckless, and

[296] Choo and Nash (n 55) 97.
[297] *R v Grant* [2009] 2 SCR 353 [92].
[298] Choo and Nash (n 55) 87, quoting from *Bunning v Cross* (1978) 141 CLR 54.
[299] *Bunning v Cross* (1978) 141 CLR 54, 74.
[300] Section 138(1) Uniform Evidence Acts.

(f) whether the impropriety or contravention was contrary to or inconsistent with a right of a person recognised by the *International Covenant on Civil and Political Rights*, and
(g) whether any other proceeding (whether or not in a court) has been or is likely to be taken in relation to the impropriety or contravention, and
(h) the difficulty (if any) of obtaining the evidence without impropriety or contravention of an Australian law.

It is notable that Australian law starts from a position of inadmissibility, and that the prosecution has the onus of persuading the court that improperly or unlawfully obtained evidence should nonetheless be admitted. But Choo and Nash have drawn attention to empirical research demonstrating that police lawlessness is tolerated to a significant degree, and improperly obtained evidence is widely admitted in practice.[301] They view the absence of human rights norms from Australian legislation as a possible explanatory factor, especially by reference to contrasting trends in Canada that have been generated, and continue to be influenced, by the strong constitutionalisation of Canadian criminal procedure.[302] The link between constitutionalisation and placing sufficient weight upon rights protection, in the context of a balancing approach, resonates fully with the link between constitutionalisation and the creation of categorical exclusionary rules, encountered in certain Anglo-American and Continental legal systems examined earlier on in this – and previous – chapters, and in detailed comparative analysis undertaken throughout the book. This remains true even if a number of qualifications demonstrate, in both cases, that the link may be 'less linear and more vacillating'[303] than first acquaintance with the idea suggests.

International criminal courts supply a final set of illustrations of judicial integrity-centred balancing exercises that strive to place sufficient emphasis on the protection of constitutional or human rights. Article 69(7) of the Rome Statute of the International Criminal Court (ICC) provides that:

> Evidence obtained by means of a violation of this Statute or internationally recognized human rights shall not be admissible if:
>
> (a) The violation casts substantial doubt on the reliability of the evidence; or
> (b) The admission of the evidence would be antithetical to and would seriously damage the integrity of the proceedings.

Similar provisions applied at the International Criminal Tribunal for the Former Yugoslavia (ICTY) and the International Criminal Tribunal for Rwanda (ICTR). On the exclusion of unreliable evidence, we can take the example of *Delalić* at the

[301] Choo and Nash (n 55) 87, quoting from *Bunning v Cross* (1978) 141 CLR 54 and citing B Presser, 'Public Policy, Police Interest: A Re-Evaluation of the Judicial Discretion to Exclude Improperly or Illegally Obtained Evidence' (2001) 25 *Melbourne University Law Review* 757, 777.
[302] ibid 104.
[303] See generally Geddis and Rodriguez Ferrer, 'Lessons for Queensland' (n 249) 282.

ICTY, where 'the Trial Chamber, in granting the motion, held that good cause had been shown as to why the relief should be granted, as it would be "unjust to deprive the accused of the right to challenge the admission of the Statements which [were] claimed to have been obtained in oppressive circumstances"'.[304] In elaborating guidelines on evidence admissibility in *Orić*, the Trial Chamber at the ICTY announced 'at the very outset that involuntary statements, obtained from witnesses by oppressive means, cannot pass the test' under the relevant exclusionary rule.[305] In analysing the 'shared approach' of the ICTY, the ICTR and the Special Court for Sierra Leone (SSLC) on interrogation safeguards for suspects, and the exclusion of improperly obtained statements, Fairlie notes the emergence of 'a robust precedent of exclusion' in the face of a system of discretionary exclusion.[306] She underlines that these Courts 'chose to avail of their discretionary authority by excluding wrongfully obtained statements',[307] finding the exclusionary outcome 'nearly self-evident'.[308]

Similarly, at the ICC, the Trial Chamber in *Katanga* automatically excluded statements obtained from the accused in violation of the right to silence and the right to custodial legal assistance.[309] According to Iontcheva Turner, the decision was an example of the ICC taking an 'absolutist approach to remedies', as it 'appear[ed] to assume that admission of evidence obtained in violation of international human rights is by definition "antithetical to and would seriously damage the integrity of the proceedings"', even if this interpretation of the exclusionary rule under the Rome Statute appeared 'inconsistent not only with the text, but also with the drafting history of Article 69(7)'.[310] The same author discerns, on the other hand, a 'more nuanced interest-balancing approach' emerging in *Lubanga*.[311] The evidence there had been obtained in disregard of the right to privacy, yet the seriousness of the violation was balanced against the reliability of the evidence and the evidence was admitted.[312] The Trial Chamber took into account, in particular, that 'the violation was not of a particularly grave kind', the 'rights violated related to someone other than the accused' and the illegal acts had not been committed by the prosecution, but by the national authorities, although an investigator from the prosecution was present during the illegal search.[313] The Trial Chamber

[304] *Prosecutor v Delalić*, 16 November 1998 [69].

[305] *Prosecutor v Orić*, 21 October 2004, IT-03-68-T [x].

[306] Fairlie, '*Miranda*' (2013) 42.

[307] ibid 38.

[308] ibid 39.

[309] *Prosecutor v Katanga*, 24 June 2009, ICC-01/04-01/06 Decision on the Admission of Material from the 'Bar Table'.

[310] J Iontcheva Turner, 'Policing International Prosecutors' (2012) 45 *New York University Journal of International Law and Politics* 175, 193.

[311] ibid 194.

[312] *Prosecutor v Lubanga*, 24 June 2009, ICC-01/04-01/06, Decision on the admission of material from the 'bar table'.

[313] ibid [47].

emphasised that the operation of section 69(7) was not intended 'to deter and punish illegal conduct by domestic law enforcement',[314] and distanced itself from the normative thesis that '*any* violation of internationally recognised human rights will necessarily damage the integrity of proceedings before the ICC'.[315] On the other hand, the Trial Chamber took the more rights-centred view that neither the probative value of the evidence,[316] nor the seriousness of the alleged offence,[317] should inform decisions on admissibility. It also drew attention to the fact that the search had not been conducted in violation of international human rights law, but in breach of national procedural laws only. It is arguable that the balance might have tipped in favour of exclusion had the Trial Chamber established a violation of an international human right.

The flexible discretionary exclusion test provided by the Rome Statute will take many years to mould into shape, but the early indications are that this will provide a stimulating case study of a discretionary system placing particular weight upon, if not prioritising, the protection of international human rights, particularly fair trial guarantees applying at the custodial interrogation stage.[318] The importance of this development for a reinvigorated rights thesis, even where this is seen as part of – or aligned with – a wider judicial integrity thesis, cannot be emphasised enough. As Roberts notes, with reference to the structure of s. 69(7)'s exclusionary rule, it is

> of considerable significance, if only as strong evidence of convergence in international attitudes, that 120 states with diverse legal traditions voted for an ICC Statute which not only prioritises rights and procedural propriety over truth-finding, but also contains something approximating a presumptive exclusionary rule for evidence obtained through serious breaches of human rights standards.[319]

IV. Concluding Thoughts

Taking Anglo-American and Continental law doctrine as its point of departure, this chapter first demonstrated that excluding evidence on non-epistemic grounds, notably to protect constitutional or human rights or the integrity of the criminal justice system, is consistent with the aims of the criminal process. It then revisited,

[314] Ibid [45], citing *Prosecutor v Radoslav Brđanin*, IT-99-36-T, Decision on the Defence Objection to Intercept Evidence, 3 October 2003 [63].

[315] ibid [41].

[316] ibid [43].

[317] ibid [44].

[318] McDermott already offers the view that '[w]here an accused has not been adequately informed of his or her rights, the statement in question will be excluded from the evidence', and that the same applies '[w]here interviews have been conducted without fully informing the accused of the case against him or her'. Y McDermott, *Fairness in International Criminal Trials* (Oxford, Oxford University Press, 2016) 47 and 63.

[319] P Roberts, 'Why International Criminal Evidence?' in P Roberts and M Redmayne, *Innovations in Evidence and Proof – Integrating Theory, Research and Teaching* (Oxford, Hart, 2007) 347, 361.

and provided a strong defence of, Ashworth's rights thesis, focusing on its application to violations of constitutional or international human rights. At the same time, the chapter accepted that the judicial integrity thesis could fill in the gaps left open by the rights thesis, for example where the rights of a third party have been violated or where a private party has acted unlawfully when obtaining tainted evidence.

The chapter explained that support for the rights thesis could be generated from analysis of many aspects of the operation of exclusionary rules in the legal systems that have been comprehensively examined throughout the book, particularly with regards to confessional evidence obtained in violation of custodial interrogation rights. Departing from this observation, it widened the comparative angle to provide a more holistic view of the law of improperly obtained evidence in Anglo-American and Continental law. By presenting succinct overviews of recent developments in Portugal, Italy, Spain, Switzerland, Belgium, the Netherlands, Ireland, New Zealand, Canada, Australia and the international criminal courts, it shed light on the fact that the rights thesis has underpinned the development of a wide range of exclusionary rules in comparative law; albeit that some recent developments may indicate wavering support for rights protection as the normative basis for exclusion, especially in common law jurisdictions. It was equally important to take note of strong resistance to attacks on the rights thesis. The dissenting opinions of Hardiman J in *JC* and Elias CJ in *Shaheed* deserve particular attention when reflecting upon the risks of moving away from rights-based exclusionary rules. The chapter also provided further evidence for the existence of a link between the constitutionalisation of criminal procedure and rights-based exclusion, stressing that this is not a linear link and much depends on the political and human rights context within which exclusionary rules are generated and apply.

The preceding discussion refocuses attention on the rights thesis. By presenting comparative case studies in which the development of strict exclusionary rules has been underpinned by constitutional or human rights protection, and in drawing attention to discretionary exclusion systems that prioritise the protection of constitutional or human rights within a balancing of competing considerations context, this chapter further developed the argument for legal systems across the Anglo-American and Continental law world to place renewed emphasis on rights protection when excluding improperly obtained evidence.

7

Epilogue: The Future

This book primarily attempts to reinvigorate the idea of excluding evidence to protect constitutional or human rights (the rights thesis), arguing that there is significant scope for Anglo-American and Continental legal systems to place a renewed emphasis on it, particularly in relation to confessional evidence obtained in violation of custodial interrogation rights. It has located an emerging rapprochement in this area, at a comparative, transnational and regional human rights protection level, in view of a growing realisation of the importance of custodial interrogation rights and the risks inherent in the use of potentially unreliable self-incriminating evidence. It has also identified unique potential, in Europe, for ECtHR jurisprudence and EU legislation to build consensus in this respect, by tying the protection of novel custodial interrogation rights with the deployment in Europe of common exclusionary remedies. Conversely, the book points to the risk of asymmetry between legislating rights and giving them effect in practice, if the Court succumbs to the temptation of reverting back to its longstanding position that the admissibility of evidence is primarily a matter for regulation under national law and if EU institutions continue uncritically to defer to national rules and systems on the admissibility of evidence. In marked contrast to observations about improperly obtained confessional evidence, the book has unearthed significant divergence with regards to the exclusion of evidence obtained by privacy violations, and found little momentum for the adoption of a revived rights thesis more widely. It also makes the claim that the rights and integrity theses should be working together. Though the book takes rights as its starting point, it deploys judicial integrity as a supplemental principle, which can fill in the gaps left open by the rights thesis and can provide the elastic solutions that this does not allow for. In other words, the book advances a 'rights plus integrity' thesis, and calls for the building of synergies between them.

Moving forward, it would be useful to examine the thesis advanced in this book against the backdrop of the 'enormous growth' of human rights in, and their 'profound impact' upon, modern legal systems.[1] As Roberts notes with regards to English law, '[t]he protective principle's rights-based rationale for excluding

[1] Lord Thomas of Cwmgiedd, former Lord Justice of England and Wales, 'Judicial Independence: The Need for Constant Vigilance', British Academy conference on 'Challenges to Judicial Independence in Times of Crisis', 8–9 March 2018, British Academy, London (on file with author).

improperly obtained evidence is perfectly attuned to the language and judicial culture of the post-HRA [Human Rights Act] era'.[2] We can take this line of thinking further by reflecting on the close link between the constitutionalisation and internationalisation of criminal procedure and the emergence of constitutional, mandatory, exclusionary rules, which has been explored in detail in this book. By taking the constitutionalisation and internationalisation of criminal procedure as a historic exegesis for the emergence of automatic exclusionary rules in Anglo-American and Continental law, we might thus be able to envisage a promising future for the rights (plus integrity) thesis. Put simply, the historic and comparative review undertaken in this book could provide support to the observation – about the future of the exclusionary rule – that the more criminal procedure becomes infused with human rights principles, the more scope there will be to advance the rights thesis. But caution is required, as the link between constitutionalisation or internationalisation and automatic exclusion is not linear. It rather fluctuates vis-à-vis constantly changing socio-political conditions, transformations of institutional structures and the increasing politicisation of debates around criminal justice. This means that, while the influence of a growing human rights culture upon the exclusionary rule debate cannot be emphasised enough, a range of countervailing factors retain the capacity to offset its impact: indicatively we can mention the persisting 'law and order' politics that generate wave after wave of attack upon human rights claims in the criminal justice arena; post-Brexit, post-Trump, populist attacks upon human rights and the idealisation of isolationist trends as means to defend national sovereignty against external, international, pressures for human rights reform;[3] or the 'politics of othering', which brands unpalatable individuals as 'undeserving beneficiaries of the law and of human rights in particular',[4] including, historically, those suspected of the commission of criminal offences.

In this environment, if the 'law and order', anti-human rights, pressures on the exclusionary rule cannot be avoided, perhaps something can be done to alleviate their effect. A pragmatic way forward would be to place heavier emphasis on the effective protection of substantive rights *ex ante* as opposed to strictly applying the exclusionary rule ex post facto. Put simply, concentrate on averting violations of suspects' rights to avoid the public interest-centred dilemmas that surround

[2] P Roberts, 'Excluding Evidence as Protecting Constitutional or Human Rights?' in L Zedner and JV Roberts, *Principles and Values in Criminal Law and Criminal Justice – Essays in Honour of Andrew Ashworth* (Oxford, Oxford University Press, 2012) 171, 189.

[3] See generally C Gearty, *On Fantasy Island: Britain, Europe and Human Rights* (Oxford, Oxford University Press, 2016); D Giannoulopoulos, *Britain in Europe – What Lies Ahead?*, 13 October 2016, available at www.youtube.com/watch?v=UGP6w5aVSz8; M Spurrier, *UK government's spin project on human rights (and why Theresa May is intent to weaken them)*, launch of Knowing Our Rights research project, available at https://www.youtube.com/watch?time_continue=1&v=leIhQyFi7CI; G Nice, 'Human Rights: Whether in Europe or Out?' in G Nice, *Justice for All and How to Achieve It – Citizens, Lawyers and the Law in the Age of Human Rights* (London, Scala, 2017) 257.

[4] N Mavronicola, *The ECHR, Euroscepticism and the politics of othering*, video interview, 23 February 2017, 'Knowing Our Rights' research project, available at www.knowing-our-rights.com/dr-natasa-mavronicola-on-the-echr-euroscepticism-and-the-politics-of-othering.

the application of the exclusionary rule to remedy violations of these rights. The electronic recording of police interrogations is a primary example.[5] The presence of a judicial officer,[6] or a court clerk who will act as a 'judicial notary', during search and seizure operations,[7] or the use of body-worn cameras by police officers to record encounters with civilians,[8] may also prove effective in taking some pressure off the exclusionary rule as the be-all and end-all mechanism for the protection of the right to privacy, even if such measures will fit different legal systems to varying degrees. Putting in place 'training programmes' and establishing 'resources and incentives to motivate officials to establish best-practice investigative protocols' is equally indispensable.[9] The idea here is that the 'exclusion of evidence should be viewed as just one of a basket of measures'.[10] This line of argumentation inevitably leads to consider whether alternative remedies, such as claims for damages, criminal prosecution or disciplinary proceedings, could also be relied upon to relieve pressure from the exclusionary rule. However, it can be observed, from a wide comparative angle, that such measures, where they exist, have generally failed to provide adequate levels of protection. We must also take note of a potential logical flaw in the above. The systemic, cultural, institutional and political reasons that may underpin resisting a rights-centred approach to excluding improperly obtained evidence in the first place, as an ex post method for the protection of suspects' rights, can equally obstruct placing emphasis – and allocating resources – on protecting rights *ex ante*. For these solutions to succeed, a certain level of political and institutional will is needed.

When considering the future of the exclusionary rule, vis-à-vis the rights-centred approach taken in this book, it is equally important to note that no attempt is made here to develop, let alone impose, a model exclusionary rule (reflecting the rights-centred logic). The book recognises that domestic solutions about how to respond to the use of improperly obtained evidence in criminal trials often echo

[5] The audio recording of police questioning is part and parcel of police interrogation in the UK, while audio-visual recording has, more recently, been enacted into legislation in France and its use has grown exponentially in Australia and the United States. See generally TP Sullivan, 'Electronic Recording of Custodial Interrogations: Everybody Wins' (2005) 95 *The Journal of Criminal Law and Criminology* 1127; D Dixon, '"A Window into the Interviewing Process?" The Audio-visual Recording of Police Interrogation in New South Wales, Australia' (2006) 16 *Policing and Society* 323; R Leo, *Police Interrogation and American Justice* (Cambridge, Harvard University Press, 2009) 320. See also Loi n 2007-291 du 5 mars 2007 tendant à renforcer l'équilibre de la procédure pénale; Police and Criminal Evidence Act 1984, Code of Practice E 2016 on audio recording interviews with suspects.

[6] See Art 9 of the Constitution in Greece.

[7] In relation to the presence of a court clerk in entry and search of dwellings in Spain, see LB Winter, 'Spain: The Constitutional Court's Move from Categorical Exclusion to Limited Balancing' in SC Thaman (ed), *Exclusionary Rules in Comparative Law* (New York, Springer, 2013) 209, 215. In relation to Greece see Art 9 of the Constitution.

[8] American Civil Liberties Union Foundation of Massachusetts and University of California, Berkeley, School of Law's Samuelson Law, Technology & Public Policy Clinic, *No Tape, No Testimony – How Courts Can Ensure the Responsible Use of Body Cameras*, 29 November 2016, available at www.law.berkeley.edu/wp-content/uploads/2016/11/SLTPPC_ACLU_BodyCameras_Final.pdf.

[9] J Jackson, 'Human rights, Constitutional Law and Exclusionary Safeguards in Ireland' in Roberts and Hunter, *Criminal Evidence and Human Rights* (Oxford, Hart Publishing, 2012) 119, 120.

[10] ibid.

moral and political choices, and correspond to specific institutional and procedural arrangements, within particular legal systems and wider legal traditions, and are therefore affected by the weight such legal systems and traditions attach to constitutional and human rights in the hierarchy of criminal justice values. Rather the book calls upon Anglo-American and Continental legal systems to review existing solutions, and adjust them accordingly if needed, with a view to ensuring that rights are given due consideration in the exclusion of improperly obtained evidence, whatever the domestic framework might be. The book gives priority to rights-centred exclusionary rules as the ideal way to achieve this, but recognises that rights *may* also be effectively protected within discretionary models, not least when the judicial integrity principle comes into play to complement the protective principle in all these cases where the latter cannot be triggered.

On the other hand, the book reveals intrinsic weaknesses in the operation of (unstructured) discretion to exclude improperly obtained evidence. The contextual studies in point (France and England and Wales) bring to light that judicial discretion is exercised unduly narrowly in practice, and that insufficient weight is given to human rights or judicial integrity considerations, leading appellate courts to routinely uphold decisions allowing the use of evidence – notably real, non-confession, evidence – on reliability grounds alone, even where they have been obtained in violation of human rights. This happens despite the fact that courts in the legal systems compared have been invested with significant, wide-encompassing, discretionary powers. This offers a useful counterpoint to critiques of automatic exclusion that tend to idealise discretion as an effective alternative to categorical exclusionary rules.

The book also demonstrates that the choice between automatic and discretionary exclusion is ultimately not determinative of how much exclusion there will be in practice, as the level of enforcement often varies depending on changing political priorities in the criminal justice system or the simple change of personnel in appellate and supreme courts. Similarly, the book brings to the fore intriguing variations as to the unconstitutional methods of obtaining evidence that generate appellate court jurisprudence in different jurisdictions, which invites further investigation into the procedural, cultural and institutional factors that produce this effect. The different focus between United States and Greek exclusionary jurisprudence, on search and seizure and telephone taps and other means of electronic surveillance respectively provides a key illustration.

From a broader, macro-comparative, angle, the book's main ambition was to move the scholarship away from rough generalisations about Anglo-American and Continental law approaches to improperly obtained evidence, and place it on contextual inquiries with the ability to generate a more nuanced view about what separates Anglo-American and Continental legal systems in this area and what brings them together. The book identifies significant, surprising, convergence and divergence between pairs of Anglo-American and Continental legal systems around automatic or discretionary exclusion, in the face of procedural, institutional and cultural factors that seemingly militate against such convergence and divergence. It particularly draws attention to the constitutionalisation and internationalisation of criminal evidence and procedure as factors allowing rapprochement (or divergence) beyond the traditional Anglo-American and Continental law divide. This is in tune with contemporary theoretical attempts to 'find a "common grammar" for building consensus' between the Anglo-American and Continental traditions, while 'not seek[ing] to deny that there are important institutional and cultural differences' between them.[11] Perhaps more importantly, through the analysis of a range of Continental law perspectives on the exclusion of improperly obtained evidence, including in relation to normative justifications for exclusion well-rehearsed in Anglo-American doctrine – such as the 'protective' or 'judicial integrity' rationales – the book challenges the conventional view that exclusionary rules are idiosyncratic of Anglo-American law and that, in Continental legal systems, 'free proof' reigns supreme. Not only this, but the two key examples from Continental criminal procedure studied in this book – Greece and France – strongly point to indigenous attitudes as the source for the development of the improperly obtained evidence doctrine there. This challenges another conventional view, that the exclusionary rule was exported to Europe from the United States.[12]

This book has a wider ambition. It was the direct effect of a cosmopolitan process that inspired its author to undertake study, research or professional work in four different legal systems, and endeavours to be read as an enthusiastic endorsement of cosmopolitan legal thinking. At the centre of such thinking is an intrinsic openness to legal cultures and to comparative law as the key that can unlock their secrets;[13] a desire for the mutual exchange of ideas that can 'bring down the walls of ignorance and avoid that legal systems withdraw back to [their] sterile tropisms'.[14] Such thinking echoes Delmas-Marty's pluralist conception of law; legal systems are inevitably interconnected in a world where it has become impossible to isolate oneself from external influences.[15] To pretend otherwise and close our eyes to the unlimited opportunities that exist beyond our domestic law borders is to bury our head in the sand. Cosmopolitan law insists that we don't. In this book, it finds its inspiration in the view that 'human well-being is not defined by geographical or cultural locations … and that all human beings require equal moral respect and concern',[16] and in Tom Bingham's fifth principle of the rule of law, that '[t]he law must afford adequate protection of fundamental human rights'.[17]

[11] JD Jackson and SJ Summers, *The Internationalisation of Criminal Evidence – Beyond the Common Law and Civil Law Traditions* (Cambridge, Cambridge University Press, 2012) 13. See also M Delmas-Marty, 'Réflexions sur l'hybridation en procédure pénale: nécessité du droit comparé à l'heure de l'internationalisation pénale' in Mélanges Bernard Bouloc, *Les droits et le droit* (Paris, Dalloz, 2007) 313.

[12] See, eg, C Bradley, '*Mapp* Goes Abroad' (2001) 52 *Case Western Law Review* 375.

[13] J-C Marin, 'La culture de l'ouverture et du droit comparé' in B Fauvarque-Cosson, *Le droit comparé au XXIe siècle*, Journées internationales de la société de législation comparée 8–9 avril 2015 (Paris, Société de législation comparée, 2015) 15.

[14] ibid.

[15] M Delmas-Marty, *Les forces imaginantes du droit (II), Le pluralisme ordonné* (Paris, Seuil, 2006) 40.

[16] D Held, *Cosmopolitanism – Ideals and Realities* (Cambridge, Polity Press, 2010) 95.

[17] T Bingham, *The Rule of Law* (London, Penguin Books, 2011) 66.

BIBLIOGRAPHY

Accomado, G and Guéry, C, 'La sonorisation: un mode légal de preuve' (2002) *Recueil Dalloz*, 2001.

Alix, J, 'Les droits de la défense au cours de l'enquête de police après la réforme de la garde à vue: état de lieux et perspectives' (2011) *Recueil Dalloz* 1699.

Allen, F, 'Federalism and the Fourth Amendment: A Requiem for Wolf' (1961) *Supreme Court Review* 1 (in Greek).

Alves-Martins, MT, 'Portugal' in M Delmas-Marty and JAE Vervaele, *The Implementation of the Corpus Juris in the Member States* (Antwerp, Intersentia, 2000) 768.

Amann, DM, 'Harmonic Convergence? Constitutional Criminal Procedure in an International Context' (2000) 75 *Indiana Law Journal* 809.

Amar, AR, 'Against Exclusion (Except to Protect Truth or Prevent Privacy Violations)' (1997) 20 *Harvard Journal of Law & Public Policy* 457.

American Civil Liberties Union Foundation of Massachusetts and University of California, Berkeley, School of Law's Samuelson Law, Technology & Public Policy Clinic, *No Tape, No Testimony – How Courts Can Ensure the Responsible Use of Body Cameras*, 29 November 2016, available at www.law.berkeley.edu/wp-content/uploads/2016/11/SLTPPC_ACLU_BodyCameras_Final.pdf.

American Enterprise Institute, 'From the Bench: Judge Brett Kavanaugh on the Constitutional Statesmanship of Chief Justice William Rehnquist', 18 September 2017, www.aei.org/wp-content/uploads/2017/08/from-the-bench.pdf.

Anagnostopoulos, I, 'The Right of Access to a Lawyer in Europe: A Long Road Ahead?' (2014) 4 *European Criminal Law Review* 3.

Anagnostopoulos, I, *Improperly obtained evidence in the criminal trial and (the state's duty to respect) fair trial guarantees*, Public debate at the Athens Bar Association, 19 January 2016, Hellenic Criminal Bar Association, *Press release on improperly obtained evidence in the criminal trial (art. 65 Law 4356/2015)*, http://www.hcba.gr/news/announcements (in Greek).

Anagnostopoulos, I, 'Defendants' Rights in the European Union – The Directives 2010/64/EU and 2012/13/EU' (Athens, PN Sakkoulas, 2017) (in Greek).

Androulakis, N, 'Concerning the problem of confessions obtained in police interrogations' (1974) 22 *Nomiko Bima* 1345 (in Greek).

Androulakis, N, *Fundamental notions of the criminal process*, 2nd edn (Athens-Komotini, AN Sakkoulas, 1994) (in Greek).

Androulakis, N, *Fundamental notions of the criminal process*, 3rd edn (Athens, PN Sakkoulas, 2007) (in Greek).

Androulakis, N, 'A change of paradigm in the criminal trial?' (2016) 7 *Poiniki Dikeosini* 545 (in Greek).

Archbold: Criminal Pleading, Evidence and Practice 2015 (London, Sweet & Maxwell-Thomson Reuters, 2015).

Archbold: Criminal Pleading, Evidence and Practice (London, Sweet & Maxwell-Thomson Reuters, 2017).

Aristotle, *Rhetoric*, 1375b, 20 (Athens, Kaktos, 1995).

Ashworth, A, 'Excluding Evidence as Protecting Rights' [1977] *Criminal Law Review* 723.

Ashworth, A, 'Should the Police Be Allowed to Use Deceptive Practices' (1998) 114 *Law Quarterly Review* 108.

Ashworth, A, *Human Rights, Serious Crime and Criminal Procedure* (London, Sweet & Maxwell, 2002).

Ashworth, A and Redmayne, M, *The Criminal Process*, 3rd edn (Oxford, Oxford University Press, 2005).

Ashworth, A, 'Four Threats to the Presumption of Innocence' (2006) 10 *International Journal of Evidence & Proof* 241.

Ashworth, A and Redmayne, M, *The Criminal Process*, 4th edn (Oxford, Oxford University Press, 2010).

Ashworth, A, 'The Exclusion of Evidence Obtained by Violating a Fundamental Right: Pragmatism Before Principle in the Strasbourg Jurisprudence' in P Roberts and J Hunter, *Criminal Evidence and Human Rights – Reimagining Common Law Procedural Traditions* (Oxford, Hart Publishing, 2012) 145.

Asselin, A, 'Trends for Exclusion of Evidence in 2012' (2013) *Criminal Reports*, 7th series.

Auld LJ, *Review of the Criminal Courts of England and Wales* (London, Stationary Office Books, 2001).

Australian Law Reform Commission, Evidence (Interim Report) [1985] ALRC 26.

Bakas, C, *The preparatory phase of the criminal process*, Poinika n 50 (Athens-Komotini, AN Sakkoulas, 1995) 17 (in Greek).

Balance in the Criminal Law Review Group (Dublin, 2007), http://www.justice.ie/en/JELR/Pages/Balance_in_criminal_law_report.

Barbaretos, G, *Code of Penal Procedure*, 6th edn (Athens, Sakkoulas, 1982) (in Greek).

Barrett, C and Aglionby, J, *Famous names had HSBC Swiss accounts, Financial Times*, 9 February 2015, www.ft.com/cms/s/0/c4f77d36-b04e-11e4-a2cc-00144feab7de.html#axzz48kkiRKPu.

Barrett Jr, E, 'Exclusion of Evidence Obtained by Illegal Searches – A Comment on *People v Cahan*' (1955) 43 *California Law Review* 565.

Barrett Lain, C, 'Countermajoritarian Hero or Zero? Rethinking the Warren Court's Role in the Criminal Procedure Revolution' (2004) 152 *University of Pennsylvania Law Review* 1409.

Bateman, C, '*Dickerson v United States*: *Miranda* is Deemed a Constitutional Rule, but Does it Really Matter?' (2002) 55 *Arkansas Law Review* 177.

Beccaria, *Des délits et des peines* (Paris, Flammarion, 1991).

Beling, *Die Beweisverbote als Grenzen der Wahrheitserforschung im Strafprozeß*.

Béliveau, P and Pradel, J, *La justice pénale dans les droits canadien et français* (Brussels, Bruylant, 2007).

Bell, J, *French Legal Cultures* (London, Butterworths, 2001).

Belloni, F and Hodgson, J, *Criminal Injustice – An Evaluation of the Criminal Justice Process in Britain* (London, Macmillan Press, 2000).

Benelli-de Bénazé, C, 'Garde à vue: conséquences de l'omission de la notification du lieu de l'infraction', *Dalloz actualité* 15 June 2015.

Benillouche, M, 'Les objectifs du procès pénal' in G Giudicelli-Delage (ed), *Les transformations de l'administration de la preuve pénale: perspectives comparées* (Paris, Société de législation comparée, 2006) 19.

Bingham, T, *The Rule of Law* (London, Penguin Books, 2011).

Blackbourn, J, and McGarrity, N, 'Listening and Hearings: Intercept Evidence in the Courtroom' (2012) *Journal of Commonwealth Criminal Law* 257.

Blackstock, J, 'Procedural Rights in the European Union: a Road Well Travelled?' (2012) 2 *European Criminal Law Review* 23.

Blackstock, J, Cape, E, Hodgson, J, Ogorodova, A and Spronken, T, *Inside Police Custody: An Empirical Account of Suspects' Rights in Four Jurisdictions* (Cambridge, Intersentia, 2014).

Bloom, R, and Massey, H, 'Accounting for Federalism in State Courts: Exclusion of Evidence Obtained Lawfully by Federal Agents' (2008) 79 *University of Colorado Law Review* 381.

Bloom, RM and Dewey, E, 'When Rights Become Empty Promises: Promoting an Exclusionary Rule that Vindicates Personal Rights' (2011) 46 *Irish Jurist* 38.

Blum, B, 'Doctrines without Borders: The "New" Israeli Exclusionary Rule and the Dangers of Legal Transplantation' (2008) 60 *Stanford Law Review* 2131.

Blum, B, '"Exclude Evidence, You Exclude Justice": A Critical Evaluation of Israel's Exclusionary Rule After *Issacharov*' (2010) 16 *Southwestern Journal of International Law* 385.

Boerman, B, 'Beyond the Wire: An Analysis of Non-Telephonic Conversations under Title III' (2008) 3 *New York University Journal of Law & Liberty* 599.

Bohlander, M, *Principles of German Criminal Procedure* (Oxford, Hart Publishing, 2012).

Borgers, M and Stevens, L, 'The Netherlands: Statutory Balancing and a Choice of Remedies' in SC Thaman (ed), *Exclusionary Rules in Comparative Law* (New York, Springer, 2013) 183.

Bouloc, B, 'Les abus en matière de procédure pénale' (1991) *Revue de sciences criminelle* 221.

Bouloc, B, 'Observations sur les nullités en matière de procédure pénale' in Mélanges offerts à Pierre Couvrat, *La sanction du droit* (Paris, PUF, 2001).

Bouloc, B, *Procédure pénale*, 25th edn (Paris, Dalloz, 2016).

Bouzat, P, 'La loyauté dans la recherche des preuves' in *Recueil d'études en hommage à M Louis Hugueney* (Paris, Pédone, 1964) 155.

Bouzat, P and Pinatel, J, *Traité de droit pénal et de criminologie*, 2nd edn (Paris, Dalloz, 1970).

Bradley, C, 'The Exclusionary Rule in Germany' (1983) 96 *Harvard Law Review* 1032.

Bradley, C, *The Failure of the Criminal Procedure Revolution* (Philadelphia, University of Pennsylvania Press, 1993).

Bradley, C, *Criminal Procedure – A Worldwide Study* (Durham, Carolina Academic Press, North Carolina, 1999).

Bradley, CM, '*Mapp* Goes Abroad' (2001–2002) 52 *Case Western Law Review* 375.

Bradley, CM, 'Mixed Messages on the Exclusionary Rule' (2006) 42 *Trial* 56.

Bradley, CM, *Criminal Procedure: A Worldwide Study*, 2nd edn (Durham, North Carolina, Carolina Academic Press, 2007).

Bradley, CM, 'Is the Exclusionary Rule Dead?' (2012) 102 *Journal of Criminal Law & Criminology* 1.

Bridges, L and Cape, E, *CDS Direct: Flying in the Face of the Evidence* (London: Centre for Crime and Justice Studies, King's College, 2008).

Brooks, P, *Troubling Confessions: Speaking Guilt in Law and Literature* (Chicago, Chicago University Press, 2000).

Brouillaud, JP, 'Les nullités de procédure: des procédures pénales et civiles comparées' (1996) *Recueil Dalloz* 99.

Buisson, J, 'La légalité dans l'administration de la preuve pénale' (1998) *Procédures* 3.

Buisson, J, 'Principe de loyauté dans la recherche de preuves et constat d'infractions' in Journées d'études Dalloz, Dossiers, *Le nouveau procès pénal après la loi Perben II* (Paris, Dalloz, 2004).

Buisson, J, 'L'annulation suppose le constat préalable de la violation d'une norme ou d'un principe' (2007) *Procédures*, comm 21.

Buisson, J, 'Perquisition – saisie: nullité à grief – Pesée des stupéfiants: nullité d'ordre public' (2008) *Revue de sciences criminelle* 645.

Buisson, J, 'Perquisition dans un local de presse: régie par les conditions de nécessité et de proportionnalité' (2008) *Revue de sciences criminelle* 648.

Burger, W, 'Who Will Watch the Watchmen?' (1964) 14 *American University Law Review* 12.

Caeiro, P and João-Costa, M, 'Portugal' in K Ligeti (ed), *Toward a Prosecutor for the European Union – volume 1* (Oxford, Hart/Beck, 2012) 540.

Caianiello, M, 'To Sanction (or not to Sanction) Procedural Flaws at EU level? A Step Forward in the Creation of an EU Criminal Process' (2014) 22 *European Journal of Crime, Criminal Law and Criminal Justice* 317.

Caianello, M, 'Procedural Sanctions in the EU Framework: Toward a Harmless Error Doctrine and Practice?' in M Caianello and J Hodgson, *Discretionary Criminal Justice in a Comparative Context* (North Carolina, Carolina Academic Press, 2015) 207.

Calabresi, G, 'The Exclusionary Rule' (2003) 26 *Harvard Journal of Law & Public Policy* 113.

Campbell, L, 'Criminal Justice and Penal Populism in Ireland' (2008) 28 *Legal Studies* 559.

Canivet, G, 'The Practice of Comparative Law by the Supreme Courts: Brief Reflections on the Dialogue Between the Judges in French and European Experience' in B Markesinis and J Fedtke (eds), *Judicial Recourse to Foreign Law: A New Source of Inspiration* (London, UCL Press, 2006) 308.

Canter, E, 'A Fourth Amendment Metamorphosis: How Fourth Amendment Remedies and Regulations Facilitated the Expansion of the Threshold Inquiry' (2009) 95 *Virginia Law Review* 155.

Capdeville, JL, 'Possibilité pour les services de police d'accéder aux parties communes librement accessibles d'un immeuble' (2014) *Actualité juridique pénal* 138.

Cape, E, 'The Rise (and Fall?) of a Criminal Defence Profession' [2004] *Criminal Law Review* 401.

Cape, E, Namoradje, Z, Smith, R, and Spronken, T, *Effective Criminal Defence in Europe* (Antwerp, Intersentia, 2011).

Cape, E and Hodgson, J, 'The Right to Access to a Lawyer at Police Stations – Making the European Union Directive Work in Practice' (2014) 5 *New Journal of European Criminal Law* 4.
Caplan, G, 'Questioning Miranda' (1985) 38 *Vanderbilt Law Review* 1417.
'Cardiff murder appeal man "beaten over head" verbally', *The Guardian*, 10 December 1992, available at www.theguardian.com/uk/1992/dec/10/cardiff-three-wales.
Carney, D, 'Covert surveillance of suspects in police vehicle' (2013) *Police Journal* 340.
Case Comment, '*Cadder v HM Advocate*' (2010) *Scottish Criminal Law* 1265.
Case Comment, 'Terrorist Suspects' Procedural Rights' [2017] *European Human Rights Law Review* 75.
Cassel, P and Hayman, B, 'Police Interrogation in the 1990s: An Empirical Study of the Effects of *Miranda*' (1996) 43 *UCLA Law Review* 839.
Chalmers, J and Leverick, F, '"Substantial and Radical Change": A New Dawn for Scottish Criminal Procedure?' (2012) 75 *Modern Law Review* 837.
Charalampakis, A, 'Constitution and criminal law'(2000) *Syntagma* 93 (in Greek).
Charalampakis, A, 'The punishable nature of interceptions' (2002) 50 *Nomiko Bima* 1061 (in Greek).
Chardouvelis, GA, *The biggest challenge for Greece of the 21st century*, To Vima, 24 December 2000 (in Greek).
Chau, P, 'Excluding Integrity? Revisiting Non-Consequentialist Justifications for Excluding Improperly Obtained Evidence in Criminal Trials' in J Hunter, P Roberts, SNM Young and D Dixon, *The Integrity of the Criminal Process – From Theory Into Practice* (Oxford and Portland, Oregon, Hart Publishing, 2016) 267.
Chilcot, J, *Privy Council Review of Intercept as Evidence*, 30 January 2008, Cm 7324.
Choo, A L-T, *The Law of Evidence, Text and Materials* (London, Longman, 1998).
Choo, A L-T, 'The Legal Aspects of Undercover Police Operations in England and Wales' (1998) 2 *International Journal of Police Science and Management* 144.
Choo, A L-T, *Comments on the Auld Report* (on file with author).
Choo, A L-T, *Abuse of Process and Judicial Stays of Criminal Proceedings*, 2nd edn (Oxford, Oxford University Press, 2008).
Choo, A L-T, *Evidence*, 3rd edn (Oxford, Oxford University Press, 2012).
Choo, A L-T, 'England and Wales: Fair Trial Analysis and the Presumed Admissibility of Physical Evidence' in S Thaman (ed), *Exclusionary Rules in Comparative Law* (Dordrecht, Springer, 2013) 352.
Choo, A L-T, *The Privilege Against Self-Incrimination and Criminal Justice* (Oxford, Hart Publishing, 2013).
Choo, A L-T, *Evidence*, 4th edn (Oxford, Oxford University Press, 2015).
Choo, A L-T and Nash, S, 'Evidence Law in England and Wales: the Impact of the Human Rights Act 1998' (2003) 7 *International Journal of Evidence & Proof* 31.
Choo, A L-T and Nash, S, 'Improperly Obtained Evidence in the Commonwealth: Lessons for England and Wales? (2007) 11 *International Journal of Evidence & Proof* 75.
Chopin, F, 'Vers un nouveau modèle de justice pénale' in *Mélanges offerts à Raymond Gassin – Sciences pénales et sciences criminologiques* (Aix-Marseille, Presses universitaires d'Aix-Marseille III, 2007) 135.
Chrisogonos, K, *Individual and social rights*, 2nd edn (Athens-Komotini, AN Sakkoulas, 2002) (in Greek).
Clancy, TK, 'The Fourth Amendment Exclusionary Rule as a Constitutional Right' (2013) 10 *Ohio State Journal of Criminal Law* 357.
Clément, G, 'De la règle, pas de nullité sans grief, en droit judiciaire privé et en procédure pénale' (1984) *Revue de sciences criminelle* 433.
Cloud, M, 'A Conservative House United: How the Post-Warren Court Dismantled the Exclusionary Rule' (2013) 10 *Ohio State Journal of Criminal Law* 477.
Cohen, A, 'Is the Supreme Court about to kill off the exclusionary rule?' *The New York Times*, 15 February 2009.
Cole, GF and Smith, CE, *The American System of Criminal Justice*, 8th edn (Belmont, West/Wadsworth, 1998) 116.

Colson, R and Field, S, *The Transformation of Criminal Justice: Comparing France with England and Wales; Les transformations de la justice pénale: une comparaison franco-anglaise* (Paris, L'Harmattan, Bibliothèques de droit, 2011).

Colson, R and Field, S, *EU Criminal Justice and the Challenges of Diversity – Legal Cultures in the Area of Freedom, Security and Justice* (Cambridge, Cambridge University Press, 2016).

Colvin, E, 'Fairness and Equality in the Criminal Process' (2006) 6 *Oxford University Commonwealth Law Journal* 1.

Commaret, D, 'Les métamorphoses de la preuve' (2004) *Revue pénitentiaire et de droit pénal* 735.

Commaret, D, 'La procédure pénale vue comme modèle éthique et déontologique des professions judiciaires' in Cour de cassation, *La procédure pénale en quête de cohérence* (Paris, Dalloz, 2007) 313.

Commission for the Revision of the Constitution, Proceedings of September 13, 2000.

Commission nationale de contrôle des interceptions de sécurité, 22e rapport d'activité, Années 2013–2014 (La Documentation Française, January 2015) 86.

Conchon, H, *L'évolution des nullités de l'instruction préparatoire* (Paris, L'Harmattan, 2002).

Conte, P and Maistre du Chambon, P, *Procédure pénale*, 4th edn (Paris, Armand Collin, 2002).

Corker, D, 'Lawyers should be able to use spy material in court', *The Times*, 12 September 2018.

Costa Ramos, V, 'The Rights of the Defence According to the ECtHR – An Illustration in the Light of *A.T. v. Luxembourg* and the Right to Legal Assistance' (2016) 7 *New Journal of European Criminal Law* 397.

Cotte, B, discours de rentrée du TGI de Paris, *Gazzette du Palais*, 1 May 1993, 42.

Council of Europe, The Stockholm Programme – An Open and Secure Europe Serving and Protecting the Citizens, 2 December 2009, 17024/09.

Coutant, MF, *Essai d'une théorie générale des nullités en procédure civile, pénale et administrative*, Doctoral thesis (Aix-Marseille, 1996).

Couvrat, P, 'Les méandres de la procédure pénale: commentaire de la loi n° 75. 701 du 6 août 1975' (1976) *Recueil Dalloz*, 43.

Cox, R, 'Crime, Employment and Incarceration in Light of the Great Recession' (2010) 37 *Review of Black Political Economy* 283.

CPS, *Confessions, Unfairly Obtained Evidence and Breaches of PACE*, available at https://www.cps.gov.uk/legal-guidance/confessions-unfairly-obtained-evidence-and-breaches-pace.

Cras, A and Daly, YM, 'Ireland: A Move to Categorical Exclusion?' in SC Thaman (ed), *Exclusionary Rules in Comparative Law* (Heidelberg, Springer, 2013) 33.

Crawford (ed), A, *International and Comparative Criminal Justice and Urban Governance: Convergence and Divergence in Global, National and Local Settings* (Cambridge, Cambridge University Press, 2011) 1.

Crocker, L, 'Can the Exclusionary Rule Be Saved?' (1993) 84 *The Journal of Criminal Law & Criminology* 310.

Crown Prosecution Service, *Selection of Prosecuting Advocates*, available at http://www.cps.gov.uk/legal/p_to_r/prosecuting_advocates_-_selection_of.

Dalakouras, Th, 'Prohibited evidence: doctrinal foundations of evidential prohibitions in the criminal process' in Hellenic Association of Criminal Law (ΕΕΠΔ), *Evidence in the criminal process*, Proceedings of the 6th panhellenic conference (PN Sakkoulas, Athens, 1998) 60 (in Greek).

Dalakouras, Th, 'The exclusionary rule for improper audio and video recordings under article 370Δ para 2 of the Criminal Code (article 31 of Law 1941/ 1991)' (1992) *Iperaspisi* 25 (in Greek).

Daly, Y, 'Exclusion of Evidence: *DPP (Walsh)* v *Cash*' (2011) 15 *International Journal of Evidence & Proof* 62.

Daly, YM, 'Overruling the Protectionist Exclusionary Rule: *DPP v JC*' (2015) 19 *International Journal of Evidence & Proof* 270.

Damaška, M, 'Free Proof and its Detractors' (1995) 43 *American Journal of Comparative Law* 343.

Damaška, M, *Evidence Law Adrift* (New Haven, Yale University Press, 1997).

Damaška, M, 'The Competing Visions of Fairness: The Basic Choice for International Criminal Tribunals' (2011) 36 *North Carolina Journal of International Law and Commercial Regulation* 365.

Daoud, E and Bouche, B, 'Interceptions judiciaires: "mais qui gardera les gardiens?"', Actualité juridique pénal 2014, 333.

Davies, SL and Scanlon, AB, '*Katz* in the Age of *Hudson v Michigan*: Some Thoughts on "Suppression as a Last Resort"' (2008) 41 *University of California Davis Law Review* 1035.

Dawe, J and McArthur, H, 'Charter Detention and the Exclusion of Evidence after *Grant, Harrison* and *Suberu*' (2010) 56 *Criminal Law Quarterly* 376.

de Golian, E, '*Davis* and the Good Faith Exception: Pushing Exclusion to Extinction?' (2011–2012) 63 *Mercer Law Review* 751.

de Gouttes, R, 'L'encadrement de la procédure pénale par la norme internationale: quelle norme? quelle cohérence? quel encadrement?' in Cour de cassation, *La procédure pénale en quête de cohérence* (Paris, Dalloz, 2007) 171.

de Kodt, J, 'Les nullités de l'instruction préparatoire et le droit de la preuve. Tendances récentes' (2000) *Revue de droit pénal et de la criminologie*, 80.

de Lamy, B, 'De la loyauté en procédure pénale. Brèves remarques sur l'application des règles de la chevalerie à la procédure pénale' in Mélanges offerts à Jean Pradel, *Le droit pénal à l'aube du troisième millénaire* (Paris, Cujas, 2006) 97.

de Nauw, A, 'Les règles d'exclusion relatives à la preuve en procédure pénale belge' (1990) *Revue de droit pénal et de la criminologie*, 721.

De Schutter, O, 'Belgique' in EU Network of Independent Experts on Fundamental Rights, *Opinion on the Status of Illegally Obtained Evidence* (2003) 10.

de Souza Mendes, P, Comparative Exclusionary Rules – Portuguese and Brazilian perspective, available at www.carlospinteodeandreu.com.

Declerq, R, *La preuve en matière pénale* (Brussels, Swinnen, 1988).

Decocq, A, Montrevil, J and Buisson, J, *Le droit de la police* (Paris, Litec, 1998).

Dedes, X, *Criminal procedure*, 9th edn (Athens-Komotini, AN Sakkoulas, 1989) (in Greek).

Delage, JP, 'La sanction des nullités de la garde à vue: de la sanction juridictionnelle à la sanction parquetière', *Archives de politique criminelle* 2006, 137.

Delève, E, *Écoutes de Sarkozy: Les juges sont allés trop loin (bâtonnier)*, France Info, 2 July 2014.

Deligianni-Dimitrakou, X, *Introduction to comparative law* (Athens-Thessaloniki, Sakkoulas, 1997) (in Greek).

Delmas-Marty, M, 'La preuve pénale' (1996) *Droits* 52.

Delmas-Marty, M, 'Necessity, legitimacy and feasibility of the Corpus Juris' in M Delmas-Marty and JAE Vervaele, *The Implementation of the Corpus Juris in the Member States*, volume I (Antwerp, Intersentia, 2000).

Delmas-Marty, M, 'Introduction' in M Delmas-Marty and C Lucas de Leyssac, *Libertés et droits fondamentaux: introduction, textes et commentaires*, 2nd edn (Paris, Seuil, 2002).

Delmas-Marty, M, 'The Contribution of Comparative Law to a Pluralist Conception of International Criminal Law' (2003) 1 *Journal of International Criminal Justice* 13.

Delmas-Marty, M, *Les forces imaginantes du droit (II), Le pluralisme ordonné* (Paris, Seuil, 2006).

Delmas-Marty, M, 'Le paradigme de la guerre contre le crime: légitimer l'inhumain' (2007) *Revue de sciences criminelle* 461.

Delmas-Marty, M, 'Réflexions sur l'hybridation en procédure pénale: nécessité du droit comparé à l'heure de l'internationalisation pénale' in Mélanges Bernard Bouloc, *Les droits et le droit* (Paris, Dalloz, 2007) 313.

Dennis, I, 'Reconstructing the Law of Criminal Evidence' (1989) *Current Legal Problems* 21.

Dennis, I, 'Miscarriages of Justice and the Law of Confessions: Evidentiary Issues and Solutions' (1993) *Public Law* 291.

Dennis, I, *The Law of Evidence*, 2nd edn (London, Thompson, Sweet & Maxwell, 2002).

Dennis, I, 'Editorial – Legal Advice in Police Stations: 25 Years on' [2011] *Criminal Law Review* 1.

Dennis, I, *The Law of Evidence*, 5th edn (London, Sweet & Maxwell, 2013).

Dimitratos, N, *Evidential Prohibitions in the Criminal Process*, Poinika No 35 (Athens-Komotini, AN Sakkoulas, 1992) (in Greek).

Dimitratos, N, 'The evolution of the institution of evidential prohibitions in Hellenic penal procedural law – simultaneously, a comparative review of the correspondent American and German law' (2001) 51 *Poinika Chronika* 5 (in Greek).

Dixon, D, '"A Window into the Interviewing Process?" The Audio-visual Recording of Police Interrogation in New South Wales, Australia' (2006) 16 *Policing and Society* 323.

Doak, J and McGourlay, C, *Criminal Evidence in Context* (Exeter, Law Matters Publishing, 2005).

Doherty, M, 'Judicial Discretion: Victimising the Villains?' (1999) 3 *International Journal of Evidence & Proof* 44.

Dorange, A and Field, S, 'Reforming Defence Rights in French Police Custody: A Coming Together in Europe?' (2012) 16 *International Journal of Evidence and Proof* 153.

Dorin, D, 'Marshalling Mapp: Justice Clark's Role in Mapp v. Ohio's Extension of the Exclusionary Rule to State Searches and Seizures', Symposium on the fortieth anniversary of *Mapp v Ohio* (2001) 52 *Case Western Law Review* 402.

Downes, D and Morgan, R, 'The Skeletons in the Cupboard: the Politics of Law and Order at the Turn of the Millenium' in M Maguire, R Morgan and R Reiner (ed), *The Oxford Handbook of Criminology*, 3rd edn (Oxford, Oxford University Press, 2002).

Dripps, D, 'Beyond the Warren Court and Its Conservative Critics: Toward a Unified Theory of Constitutional Criminal Procedure' (1989–1990) 23 *University of Michigan Journal of Law Reform* 591.

Dripps, D, 'Constitutional Theory for Criminal Procedure: Dickerson, Miranda, and the Continuing Quest For Broad – But Shallow' (2001) 34 *William & Mary Law Review* 1.

Dripps, D, 'The "New" Exclusionary Rule Debate: From "Still Preoccupied with 1985" to "Virtual Deterrence"' (2010) 37 *Fordham Urban Law Journal* 743.

Duff, A, *Trials and Punishments* (Cambridge, Cambridge University Press, 1986).

Duff, A, Farmer, L, Marshall, S and Tadros, V, *The Trial on Trial – Volume One: Truth and Due Process* (Oxford, Hart Publishing, 2004).

Duff, A, Farmer, L, Marshall, S and Tadros, V, *The Trial on Trial – Volume Two: Judgment and Calling to Account* (Oxford and Portland, Hart Publishing, 2006).

Duff, A, Farmer, L, Marshall, S and Tadros, V, *The Trial on Trial – Volume Three: Towards a Normative Theory of the Criminal Trial* (Oxford, Hart Publishing, 2007).

Duff, P, 'Irregularly Obtained Real Evidence: The Scottish Solution?' (2004) 8 *International Journal of Evidence & Proof* 77.

Dumont, J, *Nullités de l'information, Juris-Classeur Procédure Pénale*, arts 170–174 CPP (1997).

Dumont, Juris-Classeur Procédure pénale, art 802, n 35.

Dworkin, R, *Taking Rights Seriously* (London, Duckworth, 1977).

Dworkin, R, *The Supreme Court Phalanx, The New York Review of Books*, 27 September 2007.

Dyson Heydon, Justice at the High Court of Australia, *The Common Law of Evidence and Human Rights*, seminar at the School of Law, University of Nottingham, 21 February 2008 (on file with author).

Dzioras, D, *The System of Hellenic Criminal Procedure*, Tome I (Athens, 1973) (in Greek).

Editorial, 'Chipping away at the Constitution', *Los Angeles Times*, 27 January 2009.

Edwards, A, 'Legal Aid, Sentencing and Punishment of Offenders Act 2012 – the Financial Procedural and Practical Implications' [2012] *Criminal Law Review* 584.

Esen, R, 'Intercepting Communications "in Accordance with the Law"' (2012) *Journal of Criminal Law* 164.

Euller, S, 'Private Security and the Exclusionary Rule' (1980) 15 *Harvard Civil Liberties-Civil Rights Law Review* 649.

European Commission, Impact assessment accompanying the Proposal for a Directive on the right of access to a lawyer in criminal proceedings and on the right to communicate upon arrest, 8 June 2011, SEC (2011) 686.

Fadaei-Tehrani, R, and Green, T, 'Crime and society' (2002) 29 *International Journal of Social Economics* 781.

Fair Trials, *Right of Access to a Lawyer Directive*, Fair Trials practitioner training on the Roadmap Directives, Athens, 4–6 March 2016.

Fairlie, MA, '*Miranda* and its (More Rights-Protective) International Counterparts' (2013) 20 *University of California Davis Journal of International Law & Policy* 1.

Fansten, E, *Écoutes de Sarkozy: un rapport accablant, Libération*, 22 September 2014.

Farrar, S, 'Degrading Searches and Illegally Obtained Evidence in the Malaysian Criminal Justice System' in Roberts and Hunter (ed), *Criminal Evidence and Human Rights – Reimagining Common Law Procedural Traditions* (Oxford, Hart Publishing, 2012) 113.

Faustin Hélie, *Traité de l'instruction criminelle*, vol 1(Brussels, éd belge de Nupels, 1863).

Faustin-Hélie, *Traité de l'instruction criminelle*, vol IV, 2nd edn (1866).

Favoreu, L, 'Le Conseil constitutionnel et la protection de la liberté individuelle et de la vie privée. À propos de la décision du 12 janvier 1977 relative à la fouille des véhicules', Études offertes à Pierre Kayser, vol 1, 411.

Feldman, D, *Civil Liberties and Human Rights in England and Wales* (Oxford, Clarendon Press, 1993).

Feldman, D, *Civil Liberties and Human Rights in England and Wales*, 3rd edn (Oxford, Oxford University Press, 2002).

Feldmann, C, Das Tonband als Beweismittel in Strafprozeß, NJW 1959.

Fenwick, H, *Civil Liberties and Human Rights* (London-Sydney, Cavendish Publishing, 2002) 880.

Ferguson, PR, 'The Right of Access to a Lawyer' (2009) *Scots Law Times* 107.

Ferguson, PR, 'Repercussions of the *Cadder* Case: The ECHR's Fair Trial Provisions and Scottish Criminal Procedure' [2011] *Criminal Law Review* 743.

Ferguson, PR and Raitt, FE, 'A Clear and Coherent Package of Reforms? The Scottish Government Consultation Paper on the Carloway Report' [2012] *Criminal Law Review* 909.

Fettig, DT, 'When "Good Faith" Makes Good Sense': Applying *Leon's* Exception to the Exclusionary Rule to the Government's Reasonable Reliance on Title III Wiretap Orders' (2012) 49 *Harvard Journal on Legislation* 373.

Finielz, R, 'Loyauté et liberté de preuves' (2007) *Revue de sciences criminelle*, 331.

Fitzpatrick, B and Taylor, N, 'Human Rights and the Discretionary Exclusion of Evidence' (2001) 65 *Journal of Criminal Law* 349.

Fletcher, G and Sheppard, S, *American Law in a Global Context: The Basics* (Oxford, Oxford University Press, 2005).

Flynn, A, Hodgson, J, McCulloch, J and Naylor, B, 'Legal Aid and Access to Legal Representation: Redefining the Right to a Fair Trial' (2016) 40 *Melbourne Law Review* 207.

Foster, N, and Sule, S, *German Legal System*, 3rd edn (Oxford, Oxford University Press, 2002).

Fraenkel, O, 'Concerning Searches and Seizures' (1920–1921) 34 *Harvard Law Review* 361.

Frase, R, 'France' in C Bradley, *Criminal Procedure – A Worldwide Study* (Carolina Academic Press, Durham, North Carolina, 1999) 143.

Freixes, T, 'Spain' in EU Network of Independent Experts on Fundamental Rights (CFR-CDF), *Opinion on the Status of Illegally Obtained Evidence in Criminal Procedures in the Member States of the European Union*, 30 November 2003, 24.

Fricker, R, 'The Warren Court: A Retrospective' (1995) 22 *Human Rights* 46.

Friedman, D, 'From Due Deference to Due Process: Human Rights Litigation in the Criminal Law' (2002) 2 *European Human Rights Law Review* 216.

Gallaway, J, *The Supreme Court and the Rights of the Accused* (New York, Facts on File, 1973).

Gallaway, J, *The Criminal Justice and the Burger Court* (New York, Facts on File, 1978).

Garapon, A and Papadopoulos, I, *Juger en Amérique et en France* (Paris, Odile Jacob, 2003).

Garcia, A, 'Is *Miranda* Dead, Was It Overruled, or Is It Irrelevant' (1998) 10 *St Thomas Law Review* 461.

Garé, T, 'L'admission de la preuve illégale: la Chambre criminelle persiste et signe' (2000) *Recueil Dalloz*, 391.

Garraud, R, *Traité théorique et pratique d'instruction criminelle et de procédure pénale*, tome premier (Paris, Librairie du Recueil Sirey, 1907).

Gauthier, J, 'Quelques remarques sur la liberté des preuves et ses limites en droit pénal' (1990) 2 *Revue pénale suisse* 184.

Gearty, G, *On Fantasy Island: Britain, Europe and Human Rights* (Oxford, Oxford University Press, 2016).

Geddis, A and Rodriguez Ferrer, MB, 'Judicial Innovation under the New Zealand Bill of Rights Act – Lessons for Queensland' (2016) 25 *University of Queensland Law Journal* 251.

Gendrel, M, 'Garde à vue et droit de l'individu. La défense doit-elle commencer dans les locaux de gendarmerie ou de police?', *Ed Techniques, Droit pénal*, March 1992, 1.

Gershowitz, AM, 'Is Texas Tough on Crime but Soft on Criminal Procedure?' (2012) 49 *American Criminal Law Review* 31.

Giannoulopoulos, D, Comment on *Khan* v *United Kingdom* (2001) 6 *Poiniki Dikeosini* 614 (in Greek).

Giannoulopoulos, D and Parizot, R, 'La preuve technologique des interceptions et surveillances' in Giudicelli-Delage (ed), G, *Les transformations de l'administration de la preuve pénale: perspectives comparées* (Société de législation comparée, Paris, 2006) 245.

Giannoulopoulos, D, 'The Illusion of Privacy' (2006) 156 *New Law Journal* 572.

Giannoulopoulos, D, 'Protecting the Right to Secrecy of Correspondence: Constitutional Myths and Reality in Modern Greece' (2006) 9 *Mediterranean Journal of Human Rights* 119.

Giannoulopoulos, D, 'The Exclusion of Improperly Obtained Evidence in Greece: Putting Constitutional Rights First' (2007) 11 *International Journal of Evidence & Proof* 181.

Giannoulopoulos, D, 'Custodial Legal Assistance and Notification of the Right to Silence in France: Legal Cosmopolitanism and Local Resistance' (2013) 24 *Criminal Law Forum* 291.

Giannoulopoulos, D, '"North of the Border and across the Channel": Custodial Legal Assistance Reforms in Scotland and France' [2013] *Criminal Law Review* 369.

Giannoulopoulos, D, 'Strasbourg Jurisprudence, Law Reform and Comparative Law: A Tale of the Right to Custodial Legal Assistance in Five Countries' (2016) 16 *Human Rights Law Review*, 103.

Giannoulopoulos, D, *Britain in Europe – What Lies Ahead?*, 13 October 2016, available at www.youtube.com/watch?v=UGP6w5aVSz8.

Giannoulopoulos, D, '"Falling on Deaf Ears": Looking for the *Salduz* Jurisprudence in Greece' in JD Jackson and SJ Summers (eds), *Obstacles to Fairness in Criminal Proceedings: Individual Rights and Institutional Forms* (Oxford, Hart Publishing, 2018) 155.

Gilday, BJ, 'The Exclusionary Rule: Down and Almost Out' (1977) 4 *Northern Kentucky Law Review* 1.

Giudicelli-Delage, G, 'Conclusion' in Giudicelli-Delage (ed), *Les transformations de l'administration de la preuve pénale: perspectives comparées* (Paris, Société de législation comparée, 2006) 327.

Gless, S, and Martin, J, 'Water Always Finds Its Way – Discretion and the Concept of Exclusionary Rules in the Swiss Criminal Procedure Code' in M Caianello and J Hodgson, *Discretionary Criminal Justice in a Comparative Context* (Durham, North Carolina, Carolina Academic Press, 2015) 179.

Glover, R and Murphy, P, *Murphy on Evidence*, 13th edn (Oxford, Oxford University Press, 2013).

Glover, R, *Murphy on Evidence*, 15th edn (Oxford, Oxford University Press, 2017).

Godsey, M, 'Rethinking the Involuntary Confession Rule: Toward a Workable Test for Identifying Compelled Self-Incrimination' (2005) 93 *California Law Review* 466.

Goldberg, A, 'The Warren Court and Its Critics' (1980) 20 *Santa Clara Law Review* 831.

Gomes Ferreira, M, Fair Trials International questionnaire: 'Judicial remedies in the EU' working group, January 2017 (on file with author).

Gorman, MJ, 'Survey: State Search and Seizure Analogs' (2007) 77 *Mississippi Law Journal* 417.

Goss, R, 'Out of Many, One? Strasbourg's *Ibrahim* Decision on Article 6' (2017) 80 *Modern Law Review* 1137.

Gössel, Bockelmann-FS (1979).

Grande, E, 'Italian Criminal Justice: Borrowing and Resistance' (2000) 48 *American Journal of Comparative Law* 227.

Grano, J, 'Introduction – The Changed and Changing World of Constitutional Criminal Procedure: The Contribution of the Department of Justice's Office of Legal Policy' (1988–1989) 22 *University of Michigan Journal of Law Reform* 395.

Grant, R, 'The Exclusionary Rule and the Meaning of Separation of Powers' (1991) 14 *Harvard Journal of Law & Public Policy* 173.

Gray, D, 'A Spectacular Non Sequitur: The Supreme Court's Contemporary Fourth Amendment Exclusionary Rule Jurisprudence' (2013) 50 *American Criminal Law Review* 1.

Greenblatt, R, 'Violations of Electronic Eavesdrop Procedures Under Title III and the Exclusionary Rule' (1976–1977) 43 *Brooklyn Law Review* 1271.

Grevling, K, 'Fairness and the Exclusion of Evidence Under Section 78(1) of the Police and Criminal Evidence Act' (1997) 113 *Law Quarterly Review* 667.

Gudjonsson, G, 'Unreliable Confessions and Miscarriages of Justice in Britain' (2002) 4 *International Journal of Police Science & Management* 332.

Gudjonsson, G, *The Psychology of Interrogations and Confessions*, Wiley Series in Psychology of Crime, Policing and Law (New Jersey, Wiley, 2003).

Guerrier, C, *Les écoutes téléphoniques* (Paris, CNRS Droit, 2000).

Guerrier, C, *Étude de droit comparé en matière d'organismes de contrôle pour les interceptions téléphoniques* (Paris, IDEFIS, 2009).

Guerrin, M, 'Les changements opérés par la loi relative à la présomption d'innocence sur les nullités de procédure dans la phase préalable au jugement pénal' (2000) *Revue de sciences criminelle* 757.

Guerrin, M, *Les irrégularités de procédure sanctionnées par la nullité dans la phase préalable au jugement pénal*, Doctoral thesis, Université Strasbourg III – Robert Schuman (1999).

Guinchard, S and Buisson, J, *Procédure pénale* (Paris, Litec, 2000).

Guinchard, S and Buisson, J, *Procédure pénale*, 4th edn (Paris, Lexis-Nexis Litec, 2008).

Gutin, DA, 'Technical Knockout: *Hudson v. Michigan* and the Unfortunate Demise of the Knock-and-Announce Rule' (2007) 44 *American Criminal Law Review* 1239.

Habermas, J, *The Divided West* (Cambridge, Polity, 2006).

Habibullah, MS, and Baharom, AH, 'Crime and Economic Conditions in Malaysia' (2009) 36 *International Journal of Social Economics* 1071.

Halmenschlager, T, 'Du problème politique et juridique de la légalité des écoutes dites fortuites', *Dalloz actualité*, 25 March 2014.

Hamilton, J, *Opening remarks – 7th annual prosecutors' conference*, 13 May 2006, www.dppireland.ie/filestore/documents/DIRECTOR_-_Opening_Remarks.pdf.

Hammack, J, 'Turning Miranda Right Side Up: Post Waiver Invocations and the Need to Update the Miranda Warnings' (2011) 87 *Notre Dame Law Review* 421.

Hart, HLA, *The Concept of Law*, 2nd edn (Oxford, Oxford University Press, 1997).

Hassemer, W, 'Human Dignity in the Criminal Process: The Example of Truth-Finding' (2011) 44 *Israel Law Review* 185.

Heffernan, L, 'The Fourth Amendment's Exclusionary Rule: Blurring the Line Between Rule and Exception' (2011) 9 *International Commentary on Evidence* article 3, 2.

Held, D, *Cosmopolitanism: Ideals and Realities* (Cambridge, Polity, 2010).

Hennion-Jacquet, P, 'Les nullités de l'enquête et de l'instruction. Un exemple du déclin de la légalité criminelle' (2003) *RPDP* 7.

Hennion-Jacquet, P, 'L'encadrement relatif de la liberté de la preuve par la Convention européenne des droits de l'homme' (2005) *Recueil Dalloz* 2575.

Hock Lai, Ho, '"National Values on Law and Order" and the Discretion to Exclude Wrongfully Obtained Evidence' (2012) *Journal of Commonwealth Criminal Law* 232.

Hock Lai, Ho, 'The Criminal Trial, the Rule of Law and the Exclusion of Unlawfully Obtained Evidence' (2016) 10 *Criminal Law and Philosophy* 109.

Hodgson, J, 'Tipping the Scales of Justice: The Suspect's Right to Legal Advice' [1992] *Criminal Law Review* 854.

Hodgson, J and Bridges, L, 'Improving Custodial Legal Advice' [1995] *Criminal Law Review* 101.

Hodgson, J, 'Codified Criminal Procedure and Human Rights: Some Observations on the French Experience' (2003) *Criminal Law Review* 165.

Hodgson, J, *French Criminal Justice – A Comparative Account of the Investigation and Prosecution of Crime in France* (Oxford, Hart Publishing, 2005).

Hodgson, J, 'Conceptions of the Trial in Inquisitorial and Adversarial Procedure' in A Duff, L Farmer, S Marshall and V Tadros, *The Trial on Trial – Volume Two: Judgment and Calling to Account* (Oxford and Portland, Hart Publishing, 2006) 223.

Hodgson, J, 'The French Prosecutor in Question' (2010) 67 *Washington & Lee Law Review* 1361.

Hodgson, J, 'Safeguarding Suspects' Rights in Europe: A Comparative Perspective' (2011) 14 *New Criminal Law Review* 611.

Horowitz, M, 'The Warren Court and the Pursuit of Justice' (1993) 50 *Washington and Lee Law Review* 5.

House of Commons, *The Use of Intercept Evidence in Terrorism Cases*, SN/HA/5249, 24 November 2011.

Huitema, D, 'Miranda: Legitimate Response to Contingent Requirements of the Fifth Amendment' (2000) 18 *Yale Law & Policy Review* 261.

Humphreys, R, *Miscarriage of justice as guilty get off on a technicality: the exclusionary rule has created a massive imbalance in our justice system, Sunday Independent* (Ireland), 28 July 2013.

Hunter, J, 'Government May Not Introduce Evidence Derived from Illegal Private Wiretaps Despite Its "Clean Hands" – *United States v Crabtree*, 565 F3d 887 (4th Cir 2009)' (2009–2010) 43 *Suffolk University Law Review* 767.

Hunter, M, 'Judicial Discretion: Section 78 in Practice' [1994] *Criminal Law Review* 558.

Illuminati, G, and Caianello, M, 'The Investigative Stage of the Criminal Process in Italy' in E Cape, J Hodgson, T Prakken and T Spronken, *Suspects in Europe – Procedural Rights at the Investigative Stage of the Criminal Process in the European Union* (Antwerp-Oxford, Intersentia, 2007) 129.

Imwinkelried, EJ, 'The Liberalisation of American Criminal Evidence Law – A Possibility of Convergence' (1990) *Criminal Law Review* 790.

Informationsbeherrschungsrechte im Strafprozess (Berlin, 1990).

Iontcheva Turner, J, 'Policing International Prosecutors' (2012) 45 *New York University Journal of International Law and Politics* 175.

Iontcheva Turner, J, 'The Exclusionary Rule as a Symbol of the Rule of Law' (2014) 67 *SMU Law Review* 821.

Ip, J, 'The End of the Prima Facie Exclusionary Rule' (2002) 9 *Auckland University Law Review* 1016.

Irish Council for Civil Liberties, *Taking Liberties: The Human Rights Implications of the Balance in the Criminal Law Review Report* (Dublin 2008) 25 www.iccl.ie/-taking-liberties-the-human-rights-implications-of-the-balance-in-the-criminal-law-review-group.html.

Jackson, H, '*Arizona v Evans*: Expanding Exclusionary Rule Exceptions and Contracting Fourth Amendment Protections' (1996) 86 *The Journal of Criminal Law & Criminology* 1201.

Jackson, J, 'Analysing the New Evidence Scholarship: Towards a New Conception of the Law of Evidence' (1996) 16 *Oxford Journal of Legal Studies* 309.

Jackson, J, 'Managing Uncertainty and Finality: The Function of the Criminal Trial in Legal Inquiry' in A Duff, L Farmer, S Marshall and V Tadros, *The Trial on Trial – Volume One: Truth and Due Process* (Oxford, Hart Publishing, 2004) 121.

Jackson, J, 'Human Rights, Constitutional Law and Exclusionary Safeguards in Ireland' in P Roberts and J Hunter (ed), *Criminal Evidence and Human Rights – Reimagining Common Law Procedural Traditions* (Oxford and Portland, Hart, 2012).

Jackson, JD, Langer, M and Tillers, P (eds), *Crime, Procedure and Evidence in a Comparative and International Context* (Oxford, Hart Publishing, 2008).

Jackson, JD and Summers, SJ, *The Internationalisation of Criminal Evidence – Beyond the Common Law and Civil Law Traditions* (Cambridge, Cambridge University Press, 2012).

Jackson, JD and Summers, SJ, 'Confrontation with Strasbourg: UK and Swiss Approaches to Criminal Evidence' [2013] *Criminal Law Review* 114.

Jackson, JD, 'Responses to *Salduz*: Procedural Tradition, Change and the Need for Effective Defence' (2016) 97 *Modern Law Review* 987.

Jean, JP, 'Politique criminelle et nouvelle économie du système pénal' (2006) *Actualité juridique pénal* 473.

Jimeno-Bulmes, M, 'The EU Roadmap for Strengthening Procedural Rights of Suspected or Accused Persons in Criminal Proceedings' (2009) *Eucrim* 157.

Jochelson, R and Kramar, K, 'Situating Exclusion of Evidence Analysis in its Socio-Legal Place: A Tale of Judicial Populism' (2014) 61 *Crime, Law and Social Change* 541.

Juris-Classeur, *Procédure pénale*, Art 170–174-1, fasc 20 (2003).

Justice AJ Goldberg, 'The Warren Court and Its Critics' (1980) 20 *Santa Clara Law Review* 831.

Justice TC Clark, 'Some Notes on the Continuing Life of the Fourth Amendment' (1977) 5 *American Journal of Criminal Law* 275.

Justice TJ Saylor, 'Fourth Amendment Departures and Sustainability in State Constitutionalism' (2012) 22 *Widener Law Journal* 1.

Justice WJ Brennan Jr, 'State Constitutions and the Protection of Individual Rights' (1977) 90 *Harvard Law Review* 489.

Kaisaris, P, *Code of Penal Procedure*, tome III, articles 127–179 (Athens-Komotini, Sakkoulas, 1984) (in Greek).

Kalfelis, G, 'Violations of privacy and cameras (in reflection of the amendments introduced with article 10 para 5 of Law 3674/2008)' (2008) 58 *Poinika Chronika* 865.

Kaminis, G, 'Secrecy of telephone communication: constitutional protection and its application from the criminal law legislator and the courts' (1995) 43 *Nomiko Bima* 505 (in Greek).

Kaminis, G, *Illegally obtained evidence and constitutional guarantees of human rights* (*the exclusion of evidence in criminal and civil proceedings*) (Athens-Komotini, AN Sakkoulas, 1998) (in Greek).

Kaminis, G, 'The problem of illegally obtained evidence in the criminal process after the revision of Article 19 of the Constitution' in volume in honour of Ioannis Manoledakis, *Democracy – Liberty – Security* (Athens-Thessaloniki, Sakkoulas, 2005) 337 (in Greek).

Kamisar, Y, 'The Exclusionary Rule in Historical Perspective: The Struggle to Make the Fourth Amendment More than "an Empty Blessing"' (1979) 62 *Judicature* 337.

Kamisar, Y, 'Does (Did) (Should) the Exclusionary Rule Rest on a "Principled Basis" Rather Than an "Empirical Proposition"' (1983) 16 *Creighton Law Review* 565.

Kamisar, Y, 'Remembering the "Old World" of Criminal Procedure – A Reply to Professor Grano' (1989–1990) 23 *University of Michigan Journal of Law Reform* 537.

Kamisar, Y, 'On the Fortieth Anniversary of the Miranda Case: Why We Needed It, How We Got It – And What Happened to It' (2007–2008) 5 *Ohio State Journal of Criminal Law* 163.

Kamisar, Y, 'The Rise, Decline and Fall (?) of *Miranda*' (2012) 87 *Washington Law Review* 965.

Kaplan, J, 'The Limits of the Exclusionary Rule' (1974) 26 *Stanford Law Review* 1027.

Karras, A, *The 'judicial process' principle in the criminal process*, Poinika 29 (Athens-Komotini, Sakkoulas, 1989).

Karras, A, 'Procedural sanctions for violations of defendants' rights' in Hellenic Association of Criminal Law, *Defendants' rights in the criminal process in general* (Athens, PN Sakkoulas, 1989) 103.

Karras, A, 'Free evaluation of proof and "Cassation Court" review' in Hellenic Association of Criminal Law (ΕΕΠΔ), *Evidence in the criminal process*, Proceedings of the 6th panhellenic conference (Athens, PN Sakkoulas, 1998) (in Greek).

Karras, A, *Penal procedural law*, 2nd edn (Athens-Komotini, AN Sakkoulas, 1998) (in Greek).

Karras, A, *Penal procedural law*, 4th edn (Athens, Nomiki Bibliothiki, 2011) (in Greek).

Karsenty, D, 'L'article 63-1 du Code de procédure pénale dans la jurisprudence récente de la chambre criminelle' (2000) *Droit pénal*, 6 June, 4.

Kassin, S, and Gudjonsson, G, 'The Psychology of Confessions: A Review of the Literature and Issues' (2004) 5 *Psychological Science in the Public Interest* 33.

Kassin, M, Drizin, S, Grisso, T, Gudjonsson, G, Leo, R and Redlich, A, 'Police-Induced Confessions: Risk Factors and Recommendations' (2010) 34 *Law and Human Behaviour* 3.

Katrougkalos, G, 'Revision of classic rights and guarantees' in D Tsatsos, E Venizelos and X Kontiadis, *The new Constitution* (Athens, AN Sakkoulas, 2001) 55 (in Greek).

Katz, L, 'Mapp After Forty Years: Its Impact on Race in America', Symposium on the Fortieth Anniversary of *Mapp v Ohio* (2001) 52 *Case Western Law Review* 471.

Keane, A and McKeown, P, *The Modern Law of Evidence*, 10th edn (Oxford, Oxford University Press, 2014).

Keane, A and McKeown, P, *The Modern Law of Evidence*, 12th edn (Oxford, Oxford University Press, 2018).

Kemp, V and Balmer, N, *Criminal Defence Services: User's Perspectives* Research Paper No. 21 (London, Legal Services Research Centre, 2008).

Kioupis, D, Comment on Arios Pagos 1317/2001, 1 *Poinikos Logos* 1822 (in Greek).

Klein, S, '*Miranda's* Exceptions in a Post-*Dickerson* World' (2001) 91 *The Journal of Criminal Law & Criminology* 3, 567.

Knowing our Rights, *Human rights and abuse of power by the press*, available at www.knowing-our-rights.com/human-rights-abuse-power-press.

Kokkinakis, K, 'The importance of article 19 para 3 for the criminal process' (2001) 4 *Poiniki Dikeosini* 876 (in Greek).

Kollias, C and Paleologou, SM, 'Labour Market Conditions and Crime in Greece' (2012) 39 *International Journal of Social Economics* 983.

Kondilis, Intervention, Athens Bar Association debate on improperly obtained evidence, 19 January 2016, available at www.youtube.com/watch?v=5PPQGgAiocY (in Greek).

Konstadinides, T and O'Meara, N, 'Rebalancing Judicial Protection in Criminal Matters after Lisbon and Stockholm' in C Murphy and D Acosta Arcarazo (eds), *EU Security and Justice Law: After Lisbon and Stockholm* (Oxford, Hart Publishing, 2014) 77.

Konstantinidis, K, *Criminal law and human dignity* (Athens-Komotini, AN Sakkoulas, 1987) (in Greek).

Kontiadis, X, *The new constitutionalism and fundamental rights after the revision of 2001* (Athens-Konotini, AN Sakkoulas, 2002) (in Greek).

Kostaras, A, 'Do the ends justify the means? Or the procedural evaluation of illegally obtained or illegally used criminal evidence' (1984) *Efimerida Ellinon Nomikon* 169 (in Greek).

Kostaras, A, *The search for truth in the criminal process* (Athens, AN Sakkoulas, 1998) 15 (in Greek).

Kouvelis, F, Parliamentary debates archives, Period I, Session A, 24 January 2001, 106.

Krapac, D, 'Some Trends in Continental Criminal Procedure in Transition Countries of South-Eastern Europe' in J Jackson, M Langer and P Tillers (ed), *Crime, Procedure and Evidence in a Comparative and International Context* (Oxford, Hart Publishing, 2008) 119.

Kurland, A, *Politics, the Constitutions and the Warren Court* (Chicago, The University of Chicago Press, 1970).

Kuty, F, 'Le droit de la preuve' in Conférence du Jeune Barreau de Mons, *Questions d'actualité de droit pénal et de procédure pénale*, Mons, 27 May 2005 (Bruxelles, Bruylant, 2005) 75.

La Forge, N, 'Hands Off: *United States v Crabtree* and the Proper Application of Title III of the Omnibus Crime Control and Safe Streets Act of 1968' (2011) 37 *New England Journal on Criminal and Civil Confinement* 123.

LaFave, W, Israel, J and King, N, *Criminal Procedure*, Hornbook Series (St Paul, Minnessota, West Group, 2000).

LaFave, W, 'The Smell of *Herring*: A Critique of the Supreme Court's Latest Assault on the Exclusionary Rule' (2009) 99 *The Journal of Criminal Law & Criminology* 757.

LaFave, WR, *Search and Seizure: a Treatise on the Fourth Amendment*, 4th edn Minnesota, Thomson West, 2011–12).

Laffranque, J, Keynote speech, Fair Trials Legal Experts Advisory Panel (LEAP), Annual conference, Athens, 3–4 March 2017 (contemporaneous notes on file with author).

Langbein, J, *Comparative Criminal Procedure: Germany* (St Paul, Minnesota, West Pub Co, American Casebook Series, 1977).

Laudan, L, *Truth, Error and Criminal Law - An Essay in Legal Epistemology* (Cambridge, Cambridge University Press, 2006).

Leclerc, H, 'La loi du 15 juin 2000 (Gaz. Pal, Bull. lég. 13 juillet, p. 263 et circ. P. 287) renforçant la présomption d'innocence et les droits des victimes', *Gazette du Palais*, 29–30 September 2000.

Lempert, R, 'The New Evidence Scholarship: Analyzing the Process of Proof' (1986) 66 *Boston University Law Review* 439.

Leo, R, *Police Interrogation and American Justice* (Cambridge, Massachusetts, Harvard University Press, 2008).

Leo, R, and White, W, 'Adapting to *Miranda*: Modern Interrogators' Strategies for Dealing with the Obstacles Posed by *Miranda*' (1999–2000) 84 *Minnesota Law Review* 397.

Leo, R, Drizin, S, Neufeld, P, Hall, B and Vatner, A, 'Bringing Reliability Back In: False Confessions and Legal Safeguards in the Twenty-First Century' [2006] *Wisconsin Law Review* 480.

Leon, C and Ward, T, 'The Irish Exclusionary Rule after *DPP v JC*' (2015) 35 *Legal Studies* 590.

Liberopoulos, L, *The flaws of the procedural act and sanctions in the criminal process: nullities in criminal procedure* (Athens-Komotini, Sakkoulas, 1993) (in Greek).

Liptak, A, *American Exception – US is Alone in Rejecting All Evidence if Police Err, The New York Times*, 19 July 2008.

Liptak, A, *Justices step closer to repeal of evidence ruling, The New York Times*, 30 January 2009.

Livos, N, 'The criminal protection of traffic data of telecommunications' (1997) 47 *Poinika Chronika* 737 (in Greek).

Livos, N, 'Evidentiary use of derivative evidence' in Volume in honour of GA Magkakis (Athens, AN Sakkoulas, 1999) 525.

Lord Thomas of Cwmgiedd, 'Judicial Independence: The Need for Constant Vigilance', British Academy conference on 'Challenges to Judicial Independence in Times of Crisis', 8–9 March 2018, British Academy, London (on file with author).

Ma, Y, 'Comparative Analysis of Exclusionary Rules in the United States, England, France, Germany and Italy' (1999) 22 *Policing: An International Journal of Police Strategies & Management* 280.

MacDougal, DV, 'The Exclusionary Rule and Its Alternatives: Remedies for Constitutional Violations in Canada and the United States' (1985) 76 *Criminal Law & Criminology* 608.

Maclin, T, *The Supreme Court and the Fourth Amendment Exclusionary Rule* (Oxford, Oxford University Press, 2013) 85.

Maclin, T, and Rader, J, 'No More Chipping Away: The Roberts Court Uses an Axe to Take Out the Fourth Amendment Exclusionary Rule' (2012) 81 *Mississippi Law Journal* 1183.

Madden, M, 'Marshalling the Data: An Empirical Analysis of Canada's Section 24 Case Law in the Wake of *R. v. Grant*' (2011) 15 *Canadian Criminal Law Review* 2, 229.

Madden, M, 'A Model Rule for Excluding Improperly or Unconstitutionally Obtained Evidence' (2015) 33 *Berkeley Journal of International Law* 442.

Madison, James, Speech proposing the Bill of Rights, 8 June 1789 in *American History – From Revolution to Reconstruction and Beyond*, www.let.rug.nl/usa/documents/1786-1800/madison-speech-proposing-the-bill-of-rights-june-8-1789.php.

Maher, G, 'Natural Justice as Fairness' in DN McCormick and PBH Birks (eds), *The Legal Mind: Essays for Tony Honore* (Oxford, Clarendon Press, 1985) 115.

Maistre du Chambon, P, 'Propos critiques et désabusés sur une réforme mort-née de la procédure pénale' in Mélanges en l'honneur de J Larguier (Fontaine, PUG, 1993).

Marin, J-C, 'La culture de l'ouverture et du droit comparé' in B Fauvarque-Cosson, *Le droit comparé au XXIe siècle*, Journées internationales de la société de législation comparée 8–9 avril 2015 (Paris, Société de législation comparée, 2015) 15.

Markezinis, B, 'Learning from Europe and Learning in Europe' in B Markezinis (ed), *The Gradual Convergence – Foreign Ideas, Foreign Influences, and English Law on the Eve of the 21st Century* (Oxford, Clarendon Press, 1994) 30.

Marsat, C, 'La flagrance, la liberté et la loyauté de la preuve', *Droit pénal*, October 1999, 6.

Martin-Chenut, K, and De Melo e Silva, F, 'La constitutionnalisation/ conventionnalisation du droit de la preuve' in Giudicelli-Delage (ed), G, *Les transformations de l'administration de la preuve pénale: perspectives comparées* (Paris, Société de législation comparée, 2006) 31.

Matsopoulou, H, *Les enquêtes de police*, Bibliothèque des sciences criminelles (Paris, LGDJ, 1996).

Maurice-Hersant, A, 'Réflexions sur l'Article 802 du code de procédure pénale, loi n° 75. 701 du 6 août 1975 art. 19' (1976) *Recueil Dalloz*, 117.

Mavronicola, N, *The ECHR, Euroscepticism and the politics of othering*, video interview, 23 February 2017, 'Knowing Our Rights' research project, available at www.knowing-our-rights.com/dr-natasa-mavronicola-on-the-echr-euroscepticism-and-the-politics-of-othering.

May, R, 'Fair Play at Trial: An Interim Assessment of Section 78 of the Police and Criminal Evidence Act 1984' [1988] *Criminal Law Review* 722.

Mayer, D, 'Y-a-t-il une place pour l'hypnose en procédure pénale?' (2001) *Recueil Dalloz*, 1340.

McCluskey, J, 'Supreme Error' (2011) 15 *Edinburgh Law Review* 276.

McConville, M, and Wilson, G, (ed), *The Handbook of the Criminal Justice Process* (Oxford, Oxford University Press, 2002).

McDermott, Y, *Fairness in International Criminal Trials* (Oxford, Oxford University Press, 2016).

McDonald, D, *Plea to relax 'loaded' laws on Evidence, The Sunday Times* (Ireland), 16 May 2006, www.thesundaytimes.co.uk/sto/news/world_news/article202218.ece.

McEwan, J, *Evidence and the Adversarial Process – The Modern Law*, 2nd edn (Oxford, Hart Publishing, 1998).

McEwan, J, 'Ritual, Fairness and Truth: The Adversarial and Inquisitorial Models of Criminal Trial' in A Duff, L Farmer, S Marshall and V Tadros, *The Trial on Trial – Volume One: Truth and Due Process* (Oxford, Hart Publishing, 2004) 51.

McLean, J, 'From Empire to Globalization: The New Zealand Experience' (2004) 11 *Indiana Journal of Global Legal Studies* 161.

Meintjes-Van der Walt, L, 'Tracing Trends: The Impact of Science and Technology on the Law of Criminal Evidence and Procedure' (2011) *South African Law Journal* 147.

Merle, R and Vitu, A, *Traité de droit criminel, Procédure pénale*, Volume, 4th edn (Paris, Cujas, 1989).

Milne, J, 'Exclusion of Evidence Trends Post *Grant*: Are Appeal Courts Deferring to Trial Judges?' (2015) 19 *Canadian Criminal Law Review* 373.

Mirfield, P, *Silence, Confessions and Improperly Obtained Evidence*, Oxford Monographs on Criminal Law and Justice (Oxford, Clarendon Press, 1997).

Mirfield, P, 'Miranda Exclusionary Rule Re-affirmed: *US v Dickerson*' (2001) 5 *International Journal of Evidence & Proof* 61.

Mirfield, P, 'Regulation of Investigatory Powers Act 2000: Part 2: Evidential Aspects' (2001) *Criminal Law Review* 91.

Mirfield, P and Smith, R, *Essays for Colin Tapper* (London, Lexis-Nexis Butterworths, 2003).

Mitsilegas, V, 'The Future of European Criminal Justice', paper prepared for the Commission Expert Group on EU Criminal Law Policy, 12 March 2014.

Molina, E, *La liberté de la preuve des infractions en droit français contemporain* (Aix-en-Provence, Presses Universitaires d'Aix-Marseille, 2001).

Molina, E, 'Réflexion critique sur l'évolution paradoxale de la liberté de la preuve des infractions en droit français contemporain' (2002) *Revue de sciences criminelle* 266.

Montana, R, 'Procedural Tradition in the Italian Criminal Justice System – The Semi Adversarial Reform in 1989 and the Inquisitorial Cultural Resistance to Adversarial Principles' (2016) 20 *International Journal of Evidence & Proof* 289.

Montesquieu, *De l'esprit des lois* (Paris, Garnier-Flammarion, 1979).

Moran, DA, 'The Supreme Court 2005 Term: Leading Cases' (2006) 120 *Harvard Law Review* 125.

Moran, DA, 'The End of the Exclusionary Rule, Among Other Things: The Roberts Court Takes On the Fourth Amendment' [2006] *Cato Supreme Court Review* 283.

Moran, DA, 'Waiting for the Other Shoe: *Hudson* and the Precarious State of *Mapp*' (2008) 93 *Iowa Law Review* 1725, 1726.

Moran, DA, 'Hanging on by a Thread: The Exclusionary Rule (Or What's Left of It) Lives for Another Day' (2011) 9 *Ohio State Journal of Criminal Law* 363.

Moreira, V, 'Portugal' in EU Network of Independent Experts on Fundamental Rights (CFR-CDF), *Opinion on the Status of Illegally Obtained Evidence in Criminal Procedures in the Member States of the European Union*, 30 November 2003, 22.

Morgan, C, 'Where Are We Now with EU Procedural Rights?' (2012) 4 *European Human Rights Law Review* 428.

Morissey, LA, 'State Courts Reject *Leon* on State Constitutional Grounds: A Defense of Reactive Rulings' (1994) 47 *Vanderbilt Law Review* 917.

Morrison, A, 'Application of the Canadian Section 24(2) Exclusionary Rule in U.S. Cases: Would It Make a Difference?' (2002–2003) 9 *Southwestern Journal of Law & Trade in the Americas* 149.

Mount, S, '*R v Shaheed*: The Prima Facie Rule Re-Examined' [2003] *New Zealand Law Review* 45.

Munday, R, 'Exclusionary Rules of Criminal Evidence in English Law' in JP Gardner, *UK Law in the 1990's*, UK Comparative Law Series (United Kingdom National Committee of Comparative Law, 1990) 360.

Munday, R, *Evidence*, 8th edn (Oxford, Oxford University Press, 2015).

Myers II, RE, 'Fourth Amendment Small Claims Court' (2013) 10 *Ohio State Journal of Criminal Law* 567.

Naintos, CD, *Evidential prohibitions in the criminal trial* (Athens-Salonica, Sakkoulas, 2010) (in Greek).

Nash, S, Comments on the Auld Report (on file with author).

Nash, S and Choo, A L-T, 'What's the Matter with section 78?' [1999] *Criminal Law Review* 929.

Nelken, D, *Comparative Criminal Justice* (London, Sage, 2010).

Newburn, T and Reiner, R, 'From PC Dixon to Dixon PLC: Policing and Policing Powers since 1954' [2004] *Criminal Law Review* 601.

Nice, G, 'Human Rights: Whether in Europe or Out?' in G Nice, *Justice for All and How to Achieve It – Citizens, Lawyers and the Law in the Age of Human Rights* (London, Scala, 2017).

Nioré, V, 'Splendeurs et misères de la mission du bâtonnier au cours d'une perquisition chez l'avocat' (2013) *Dalloz avocats* 336.

Nioré, V, 'Le secret professionnel de l'avocat à l'épreuve de l'interception et de la captation de données informatiques à distance: un secret en lambeux?' (2013) *Dalloz avocats*, 92.

Nolasco, CA, del Carmen, RV and Vaughn, MS, 'What *Herring* Hath Wrought: An Analysis of Post-*Herring* Cases in the Federal Courts' (2011) 38 *American Journal of Criminal Law* 221.

Norton, J, 'The Exclusionary Rule Reconsidered: Restoring the Status Quo Ante' (1998) 33 *Wake Forest Law Review* 261.

Nouskalis, G, 'Some reflections on the extent of the protection of the secrecy of correspondence and private life, after amendment of articles 370A of the Penal Code and 7A of Law 2472/1997 and with Law 3090/2002' (2003) 6 *Poiniki Dikeosini* 8 (in Greek).

O'Mahony, C and Conaill, SÓ, *Mr Justice Adrian Hardiman 1951–2016*, Constitution Project @ UCC, www.constitutionproject.ie/?p=573.

Office of Legal Policy, *Report to the Attorney General on the Search and Seizure Exclusionary Rule*, Truth in Criminal Justice Report No 2, 26 February 1986, available in (1988–1989) 22 *University of Michigan Law Reform* 573.

Okechukwu Benjamin, V, 'Interception of Internet Communications and the Right to Privacy: An Evaluation of some Provisions of the Regulation of Investigatory Powers Act Against the Jurisprudence of the European Court of Human Rights' (2007) 6 *European Human Rights Law Review* 637.

Optican, S and Sankoff, P, 'The New Exclusionary Rule: A Preliminary Assessment of *R v Shaheed*' [2003] *New Zealand Law Review* 1.

Optican, S, '"Lessons from Down Under": The Exclusion of Improperly Obtained Evidence in New Zealand as the Model for a Changing United States Exclusionary Rule' (2011–2012) *Journal of Commonwealth Criminal Law* 226.

Optican, S, '*Hamed, Williams* and the Exclusionary Rule: Critiquing the Supreme Court's Approach to s 30 of the Evidence Act 2006' (2012) NZLR 605.

Ormerod, D, 'Case Comment – Evidence: Entry on Premises to Ascertain Next of Kin – Drugs Found There – *R v Veneroso*' [2002] *Criminal Law Review* 306.
Ormerod, D, 'ECHR and the Exclusion of Evidence: Trial Remedies for Article 8 Breaches' [2003] *Criminal Law Review* 61.
Ormerod, D and Birch, D, 'The Evolution of the Discretionary Exclusion of Evidence' [2004] *Criminal Law Review* 767.
Ormerod, D, and McKay, S, 'Telephone Intercepts and Their Admissibility' [2004] *Criminal Law Review* 15.
Osmer, JD, Der Umfang des Beweisverwertungsverbotes nach § 136a StPO (Hamburg, 1966).
Owen, PD, 'Painting', *Encyclopaedia Britannica*, www.britannica.com/art/painting#ref364642.
Packer, H, *The Limits of the Criminal Sanction* (California, Stanford University Press, 1965).
Pakter, W, 'Exclusionary Rules in France, Germany and Italy' (1985) 9 *Hastings International and Comparative Law Review* 1.
Papadamakis, A, *Penal procedure: theory, practice, jurisprudence* (Athens-Thessaloniki, Sakkoulas eds, 2002) (in Greek).
Papadamakis, A, 'Evidential prohibitions and "fair" trial' (2016) *Poiniki Dikonomia* 449 (in Greek).
Papadimitrakis, G, 'The arrest of the suspect and house searches through the prism of the Fourth Amendment of the United States Constitution' (2007) *Poiniki Dikeosini* 1051 (in Greek).
Papageorgiou-Gonatas, S, 'The problem of illegally obtained indirect evidence in the criminal process' (1989) 39 *Poinika Chronika* 545 (in Greek).
Papageorgiou-Gonatas, S, 'Evidential prohibitions as expressions of constitutional mandates' (2003) 3 *Poinikos Logos* 17 (in Greek).
Parienté, J, Vaudano, M and Laurent, S, *Affaire des écoutes: ce qui est reproché à Nicolas Sarkozy*, Le Mondre.fr, 13 March 2014.
Parliamentary Debates (Greece), Proceedings of May 7, 1996, 6042; May 9, 1996, 6149.
Parrish, AL, 'Storm in a Teacup: The US Supreme Court's Use of Foreign Law' (2007) *University of Illinois Law Review* 637.
Patrick Glenn, H, *Legal Traditions of the World*, 2nd edn (Oxford, Oxford University Press, 2004).
Pattenden, R, 'The Exclusion of Unfairly Obtained Evidence in England, Canada and Australia' (1980) 29 *International and Comparative Law Quarterly* 664.
Pattenden, R, and Skinns, L, 'Choice, Privacy and Publicly Funded Legal Advice at Police Stations' (2010) 73 *Modern Law Review* 349.
Pattenden, R, 'Case Comment – Unlawfully Obtained Evidence – *R (Cook) v Serious Organised Crime Agency*' (2011) 15 *International Journal of Evidence & Proof* 82.
Paulopoulos, P, 'Technological evolution and constitutional rights: the modern adventures of secrecy of correspondence' (1987) 35 *Nomiko Bima* 1511 (in Greek).
Paulou, S, Fountedaki, A and Dimitrainas, G, 'Evidential prohibitions and adoption' (2002) 5 *Poiniki Dikeosini* 915 (in Greek).
Perelman, C, 'La preuve en droit, essai de synthèse' in C Perelman and P Foriers, *La preuve en droit* (Brussels, Bruylant, 1981) 358.
Piquet, C, *Affaire des écoutes: pourquoi l'enquête visant Sarkozy a été suspendue*, LeFigaro.fr, 24 September 2014, available at http://www.lefigaro.fr/actualite-france/2014/09/24/01016-20140924 ARTFIG00159-affaire-des-ecoutes-pourquoi-l-enquete-visant-sarkozy-a-ete-suspendue.php.
Pitcher, KM, *Judicial Responses to Pre-Trial Procedural Violations in International Criminal Proceedings*, PhD thesis (2016) (on file with author).
Pitoun, A, 'Appréciation judiciaire *a minima* d'un contrôle d'identité et de l'information d'un placement en garde à vue incident' (2004) *Actualité juridique pénal* 160.
Pizzi, W, *Trials Without Truth: Why our System of Criminal Trials has Become an Expensive Failure and What we Need to Do to Rebuild it* (New York and London, New York University Press, 1999).
Pleasence, P, Kemp, V and Balmer, N, 'The Justice Lottery? Police Station Advice 25 years on from PACE' [2011] *Criminal Law Review* 6.
Porteron, C, 'Nullité des perquisitions au cours de l'instruction' (2005) *Actualité juridique pénal*, 143.

Porteron, C, 'Le secret professionnel de l'avocat' (2009) *Actualité juridique pénal* 158.

Powe Jr, L, *The Warren Court and American Politics* (Cambridge, Massachussets and London, The Belknapp Press of Harvard University Press, 2000) 199.

Pradel, J, *Procédure pénale*, 5th edn (Paris, Cujas, 1990).

Pradel, J, 'Un exemple de restauration de la légalité criminelle: le régime des interceptions de correspondances émises par la voie des télécommunications (commentaire de la loi nº 91-646 du 10 juillet 1991)' (1992) *Recueil Dalloz* 49.

Pradel, J, *Droit pénal comparé* (Paris, Dalloz, 1995).

Pradel, J, *Procédure pénale*, 10th edn (Paris, Cujas, 2001).

Pradel, J, 'Le parloir n'a plus de secret pour le juge d'instruction en matière de criminalité organisée' (2006) *Recueil Dalloz* 1504.

Pradel, J, 'Nullité d'une procédure pour défaut d'enregistrement de l'interrogatoire d'un mineur en garde à vue' (2007) *Recueil Dalloz* 2141.

Pradel, J, 'Procédure pénale: septembre 2010 – août 2011' (2011) *Recueil Dalloz* 2231.

Pradel, J, 'Panorama – Procédure pénale juin 2013 – juin 2014' (2014) *Recueil Dalloz* 1736.

Pradel, J and Varinard, A, *Les grands arrêts du droit criminel, Tome II – Le Procès, la sanction* (Paris, Dalloz, 1995).

Presser, B, 'Public Policy, Police Interest: A Re-Evaluation of the Judicial Discretion to Exclude Improperly or Illegally Obtained Evidence' (2001) 25 *Melbourne University Law Review* 757.

Privy Counsellor Review Committee, *Anti-Terrorism, Crime and Security Act Review: Report*, 18 December 2003 [209], available at www.statewatch.org/news/2003/dec/atcsReport.pdf.

Psarouda-Benaki, A, 'The tape recorder in the criminal trial and the need to protect oral speech' (1965) 15 *Poinika Chronika* 397 (in Greek).

Rassat, ML, *Manuel de procédure pénale* (Paris, Presses universitaires de France, 2002).

Reiner, R, *Law and Order – An Honest Citizen's Guide to Crime and Control* (Cambridge, Polity Press, 2007).

Renucci, JF, 'L'avocat et la garde à vue: exigences européennes et réalités nationales' (2009) *Recueil Dalloz* 2897.

Renucci, JF, 'Garde à vue et CEDH: la France condamnée à Strasbourg' (2010) *Recueil Dalloz* 2950.

Reynolds, M, 'Why Stop Halfway?' (1995) *National Review* 59, 60.

Rhodes, A, (Deputy Chief Constable, Lancashire Constabulary), *Blog: The professionals*, available at http://www.college.police.uk/News/College-news/Pages/the_professionals.aspx.

Ritz, W, 'Twenty-Five Years of State Criminal Confession Cases in the U.S. Supreme Court' (1962) 19 *Washington and Lee Law Review* 35.

Roach, K, 'Dialogue or Defiance – Legislative Reversals of Supreme Court Decisions in Canada and the United States' (2006) 4 *International Journal of Constitutional Law* 347.

Roach, K, 'Unreliable Evidence and Wrongful Convictions: The Case for Excluding Tainted Identification Evidence and Jailhouse and Coerced Confessions' (2007) 52 *Criminal Law Quarterly* 210.

Roach, K, 'Canada's Experience with Constitutionalism and Criminal Justice' (2013) 25 *Singapore Academy of Law Journal* 656.

Robert, J, Intervention in conference on 'force ou faiblesse de la constitutionnalisation du droit pénal' in Cour de cassation, *La procédure pénale en quête de cohérence* (Paris, Dalloz, 2007) 103.

Robert, P, 'Ordre, insécurité, liberté: les incertitudes de la procédure pénale' in Cour de cassation, *La procédure pénale en quête de cohérence* (Paris, Dalloz, 2007) 37.

Roberts, A, 'Case Comment – *R. v Plunkett (Daniel)*: evidence – admissibility – suspects' conversations in police van covertly recorded' [2013] *Criminal Law Review* 766.

Roberts, P, 'Science, Experts and Criminal Justice' in M McConville and G Wilson (ed), *The Handbook of the Criminal Justice Process* (Oxford, Oxford University Press, 2002).

Roberts, P, 'Theorising Procedural Tradition: Subjects, Objects and Values in Criminal Adjudication' in A Duff, L Farmer, S Marshall and V Tadros, *The Trial on Trial – Volume Two: Judgment and Calling to Account* (Oxford and Portland, Hart Publishing, 2006) 37.

Roberts, P, 'Rethinking the Law of Evidence: a Twenty-First Century Agenda for Teaching and Research' in P Roberts and M Redmayne, *Innovations in Evidence & Proof – Integrating Theory, Research and Teaching* (Oxford, Hart Publishing, 2007) 19.

Roberts, P, 'Why International Criminal Evidence?' in P Roberts and M Redmayne, *Innovations in Evidence and Proof – Integrating Theory, Research and Teaching* (Oxford, Hart, 2007) 347.

Roberts, P, 'Normative Evolution in Evidentiary Exclusion: Coercion, Deception and the Right to a Fair Trial' in P Roberts and J Hunter, *Criminal Evidence and Human Rights – Reimagining Common Law Procedural Traditions* (Oxford, Hart Publishing, 2012) 163.

Roberts, P, *Expert Evidence and Scientific Proof in Criminal Trials* (London, Routledge, 2014).

Roberts, P, and Hunter, J, 'Introduction – The Human Rights Revolution in Criminal Evidence and Procedure' in P Roberts and J Hunter (ed), *Criminal Evidence and Human Rights – Reimagining Common Law Procedural Traditions* (Oxford and Portland, Hart, 2012) 1.

Roberts, P and Zuckerman, A, *Criminal* Evidence, 2nd edn (Oxford, Oxford University Press, 2010).

Roberts, P, 'Excluding Evidence as Protecting Constitutional or Human Rights?' in L Zedner and JV Roberts, *Principles and Values in Criminal Law and Criminal Justice – Essays in Honour of Andrew Ashworth* (Oxford, Oxford University Press, 2012) 171.

Robinson, D, *Access to a lawyer: is Ireland turning back the clock?*, Fair Trials blog, 13 February 2017, available at www.fairtrials.org/access-to-a-lawyer-is-ireland-turning-back-the-clock.

Robinson, P and Cahill, M, *Law Without Justice – Why Criminal Law Doesn't Give People What They Deserve* (Oxford, Oxford University Press, 2006).

Rogall, K, *Gegenwärtiger Stand und Entwicklungstendenzen der Lehre von den strafprozessualen*, ZStW 91 (1979).

Rome, F, Éditorial – Les indignés, *Recueil Dalloz*, 20 March 2014.

Roussel, Y, 'Le régime des nullités de la procédure pénale après les lois du 4 janvier 1993 et du 24 août 1993' (1996) *Gazzette du Palais* 72.

Roxin, Strafverfahrensrecht (1998).

Royal Commission on Criminal Procedure, *The Investigation and Prosecution of Criminal Offences in England and Wales, The Law and Procedure*, Cmnd 8092 (1981).

Ruiz Vadillo, E, 'Spain' in C van den Wyngaert (ed), *Criminal Procedure Systems in the European Community* (London, Butterworths, 1993) 383.

Ryan, A, *Towards a System of European Criminal Justice – The Problem of Admissibility of Evidence* (London and New York, Routledge, 2014).

Rychlak, RJ, 'Replacing the Exclusionary Rule: Fourth Amendment Violations as Direct Criminal Contempt' (2010) 85 *Chicago-Kent Law Review* 241.

Safferling, C, *Towards an International Criminal Procedure* (Oxford, Oxford University Press, 2001).

Saint-Pierre, F, 'Les droits de la défense dans la loi Perben II' in Journées d'études Dalloz, *Le nouveau procès pénal après la loi Perben II* (Paris, Dalloz, 2004) 429.

Saint-Pierre, F, 'Le véritable enjeu des contrôles juridictionnels de la légalité des procédures pénales: la "sûreté" des justiciables' (2005) *Actualité juridique pénal* 177.

Samatas, M, 'Studying Surveillance in Greece: Methodological and Other Problems Related to an Authoritarian Surveillance Culture' (2005) 3 *Surveillance & Society* 181.

Sandby, SE, 'Everyman's Exclusionary Rule: The Exclusionary Rule and the Rule of Law (or Why Conservatives Should Embrace the Exclusionary Rule)' (2013) 10 *Ohio State Journal of Criminal Law* 393.

Sanders, A, Young, R and Burton, M, *Criminal Justice*, 4th edn (Oxford, Oxford University Press, 2010).

Saripolos, N, *Constitutional law system*, vol B (Athens, 1923) (in Greek).

Saripolos, N, *Constitutional law system* (Athens-Komotini, Classic Legal Library, 1987) (in Greek).

Satlanis, Ch, 'Tape recordings as evidence in the criminal process (a parallel contribution to the evidential prohibitions doctrine)' Poinika No 48 (Athens-Komotini, AN Sakkoulas, 1996) (in Greek).

Sayers, D, 'Protecting Fair Trial Rights in Criminal Cases in the European Union' (2014) 14 *Human Rights Law Review* 733.

Schmidt, Eb, Lehrkommentar zur Strafprozeßordnung und zum Gerichtsverfassungsgesetz (Göttingen, Auflage, 1964).

Schroeder, W, 'Restoring the Status Quo Ante: The Fourth Amendment Exclusionary Rule as a Compensatory Device' (1983) 51 *George Washington Law Review* 633.

Schünemann, B, 'Der Richter im Strafverfahren als manipulierter Dritter? Zur empirischen Bestätigung von Perseveranz- und Schulterschlusseffect' (2000) 3 *Strafverteidiger* 159.

Schwendener, VM, 'L'action de la police judiciaire confrontée à l'exigence de la loyauté' (2005) *Actualité juridique pénal* 267.

Seet, M, 'Case Comment – Suspected Terrorists and the Privilege against Self-Incrimination' (2015) 74 *Cambridge Law Journal* 208.

Sénat de Belgique, Commission de la Justice, Rapport 'Les suites de l'arrêt Salduz', 2 March 2011.

Service de la politique criminelle, Évaluation de la 'loi Salduz', available at www.dsb-spc.be/web/index.php?option=com_content&task=view&id=152.

Seuvic, J-F, 'Forces et faiblesses de la constitutionnalisation substantielle et formelle du droit pénal' in Cour de cassation, *La procédure pénale en quête de cohérence* (Paris, Dalloz, 2007) 111.

Sharpe, C, *Search and Surveillance – The Movement from Evidence to Information* (Ashgate-Dartmouth, Aldershot, 2000).

Sharpe, S, 'Covert Policing: A Comparative View' (1996) 25 *Anglo-American Law Review* 163.

Shrock, T and Welsh, R, 'Up from Calandra: the Exclusionary Rule as a Constitutional Requirement' (1974) 9 *Minnsessota Law Review* 251.

Sieghart, P, *Human Rights in the United Kingdom*, Human Rights Network (London and New York, Pinter Publishers, 1988).

Signorelli, W, *The Constable Has Blundered* (Durham, North Carolina, Carolina Academic Press, 2010).

Simmons, S, 'The Warren Court and Civil Liberties' (1973–1975) 18 *Howard Law Journal* 610.

Singer, J, Miller, K and Adya, M, 'The Impact of DNA and Other Technology on the Criminal Justice System: Improvements and Complications' (2007) 17 *Albany Law Journal of Science & Technology* 87.

Siyuan, C, 'The Judicial Discretion to Exclude Relevant Evidence: Perspectives from an Indian Evidence Act Jurisdiction' (2012) 16 *International Journal of Evidence & Proof* 398.

Skeen, A, 'The Admissibility of Improperly Obtained Evidence in Criminal Trials' (1988) 1 *South-African Journal of Criminal Justice* 389.

Skinns, L, 'The Right to Legal Advice in the Police Station: Past, Present and Future' [2011] *Criminal Law Review* 19.

Slobogin, C, 'An Empirically Based Comparison of American and European Regulatory Approaches to Police Investigation' (2001) 22 *Michigan Journal of International Law* 423.

Slobogin, C, 'The Exclusionary Rule: Is it on Its Way Out? Should It Be?' (2013) 10 *Ohio State Journal of Criminal Law* 341.

Soo, A, '(Effective) Remedies for a Violation of the Right to Counsel during Criminal Proceedings in the European Union: An Empirical Study' (2018) 14 *Utrecht Law Review* 18.

Soyer, J-C, *Droit pénal et procédure pénale* (Paris, LGDJ, 1994).

Spencer, JR, 'Les limites en matière de preuve – Aspects actuels' (1992) *Revue de sciences criminelle* 42.

Spencer, JR, 'Bugging and Burglary by the Police' (1997) *Cambridge Law Journal* 6.

Spencer, JR, 'Evidence' in M Delmas-Marty and JR Spencer (ed), *European Criminal Procedures*, Cambridge Studies in International and Comparative Law (Cambridge, Cambridge University Press, 2005) 608.

Spencer, JR, Deleuze, B and Vorms, D, 'La preuve: une question inclassable' (1993) *Archives de politique criminelle* 37.

Spencer, ML, 'Suppress or Suspend: New York's Exclusionary Rule in School Disciplinary Proceedings' (1997) 72 *New York University Law Review* 1494.

Spinellis, D, 'Legal values and their importance in the modern teaching of criminal law' (1971) 21 *Poinika Chronika* 812 (in Greek).

Spinellis, D, 'Evidential prohibitions in the criminal process' (1986) 36 *Poinika Chronika* 865 (in Greek).
Spirakos, D, 'The secrecy of correspondence – basic principles and choices to deal with the right to secrecy in law and politics' (1993) 3 *To Sintagma* 526 (in Greek).
Spitieri, A, *The right to access to a lawyer in Malta: a few steps forward, a few steps back*, 21 December 2016, Fair Trials blog, available at www.fairtrials.org/the-right-to-access-to-a-lawyer-in-malta-a-few-steps-forward-a-few-steps-back.
Spronken, T, 'EU Policy to Guarantee Procedural Rights in Criminal Proceedings: an Analysis of the First Steps and a Plea for a Holistic Approach' (2011) *European Criminal Law Review* 212.
Spurrier, M, *UK government's spin project on human rights (and why Theresa May is intent to weaken them)*, launch of Knowing Our Rights research project, available at https://www.youtube.com/watch?time_continue=1&v=leIhQyFi7CI.
Stefani, G, Levasseur, G and Bouloc, B, *Procédure pénale*, Précis Dalloz, 17th edn (Paris, Dalloz, 2000).
Stenson, K, 'Making Sense of Crime Control' in K Stenson and D Cowell (ed), *The Politics of Crime Control* (London, SAGE, 1991).
Stewart, P, 'The Road to Mapp v. Ohio and Beyond: The Origins, Development and Future of the Exclusionary Rule in Search-and-Seizure Cases' (1983) 83 *Columbia Law Review* 1365.
Stone, G, 'The Miranda Doctrine in the Burger Court' (1977) *Supreme Court Review* 99.
Stone, R, *The Law of Entry, Search and Seizure*, 4th edn (Oxford, Oxford University Press, 2005).
Stribopoulos, J, 'Lessons from the Pupil: A Canadian Solution to the American Exclusionary Rule Debate' (1999) 22 *Boston College International & Comparative Law Review* 77.
Stuntz, W, 'The American Exclusionary Rule and Defendants' Changing Rights' [1989] *Criminal Law Review* 117.
Sudre, F, 'La dimension internationale et européenne des libertés et droits fondamentaux' in Cabrillac, R, Frichon-Roche, MA and Revet, T (ed), *Libertés et droits fondamentaux*, 11th edn (Paris, Dalloz, 2005) 32.
Sullivan, TP, 'Electronic Recording of Custodial Interrogations: Everybody Wins' (2005) 95 *The Journal of Criminal Law and Criminology* 1127.
Sundby, E, 'Everyman's Exclusionary Rule: The Exclusionary Rule and the Rule of Law (or why Conservatives Should Embrace the Exclusionary Rule)' (2013) 10 *Ohio State Journal of Criminal Law* 393.
Svolos, A and Vlachos, G, *The Constitution of Greece*, vol B (Athens, 1955) (in Greek).
Sweet, AS and Matthews, J, 'Proportionality Balancing and Global Constitutionalism' (2008) 47 *Columbia Journal of Transnational Law* 72.
Symeonidou-Kastanidou, E. 'Journalism and secrecy of correspondence' (2006) 9 *Poiniki Dikeosini* 1297 (in Greek).
Symeonidou-Kastanidou, E, 'Article 370A Penal Code and recent announcements regarding its amendment' (2008) 4 *Poiniki Dikeosini* 462, 463 (in Greek).
Tapper, C, 'Overhearing and Oversight' (1996–1997) 1 *International Journal of Evidence & Proof* 162.
Tapper, C, *Cross & Tapper on Evidence*, 10th edn (London, LexisNexis Butterworths, 2004).
Tapper, C, 'The Law of Evidence and the Rule of Law' (2009) 68 *Cambridge Law Journal* 67.
Taslitz, AE, 'Hypocrisy, Corruption and Illegitimacy: Why Judicial Integrity Justifies the Exclusionary Rule' (2013) 10 *Ohio State Journal of Criminal Law* 419.
Thaman, SC, '*Miranda* in Comparative Law' (2001) 45 *Saint Louis University Law Journal* 581.
Thaman, SC, *Comparative Criminal Procedure* (Carolina Academic Press, Comparative Law Series, 2002).
Thaman, SC, '"Fruits of the Poisonous Tree" in Comparative Law' (2010) 16 *Southwestern Journal of International Law* 333.
Thaman, SC, 'Balancing Truth Against Human Rights: A Theory of Modern Exclusionary Rules' in SC Thaman (ed), *Exclusionary Rules in Comparative Law* (Springer, 2013).
Thaman, SC (ed), *Exclusionary Rules in Comparative Law* (Heidelberg, Springer, 2013).
Thayer, JB, *A Preliminary Treatise on Evidence at the Common Law* (Boston, Little, Brown, 1898).

Theuman, JE, 'State Constitutional Requirements as to Exclusion of Evidence Unlawfully Seized – post-Leon case', 19 *American Law Reports* 5th 470.

Thomas III, GC, 'The End of the Road for *Miranda v Arizona*? On the History and Future of Rules for Police Interrogation' (2000) 37 *American Criminal Law Review* 1.

Thomas III, GC, 'Stories About *Miranda*' (2004) 102 *Michigan Law Review* 1959.

Thomas III, GC and Leo, R, *Confessions of Guilt – From Torture to Miranda and Beyond* (Oxford, Oxford University Press, 2012).

Tomkovicz, J, '*Hudson v. Michigan* and the Future of Fourth Amendment Exclusion' (2008) 93 *Iowa Law Review* 1819.

Tomkovicz, J, *Constitutional Exclusion* (Oxford, Oxford University Press, 2011).

Tomlinson, E, 'Non-adversarial Justice: The French Experience' (1983) 42 *Maryland Law Review* 131.

Tonini, P, *Lineamenti di diritto processualle penale* (Milan, Giuffrè Editore, 2004).

Totten, C and Cobkit (Cheurprakobkit), S, 'The Knock-and-Announce Rule and Police Searches after *Hudson v. Michigan*: Can Alternative Deterrents Effectively Replace Exclusion for Rule Violations' (2012) 15 *New Criminal Law Review* 414.

Traest, P, 'The Putting into Perspective of the Exclusionary Rule: Some General Remarks and the Belgian Experience' in C Breur, M Kommer, J Nijboer, J Reijntjes, *New Trends in Criminal Investigation and Evidence*, vol 2 (Antwerpen – Groningen – Oxford, Intersentia, 2000) 649.

Traynor, R, 'Mapp v. Ohio at Large in the Fifty States' (1962) 3 *Duke Law Journal* 319.

Trechsel, S, 'Why Must Trials Be Fair' (1997) 31 *Israeli Law Review* 94.

Triantafillou, G, 'Evidential prohibitions and the proportionality principle' (2007) 57 *Poinika Chronika* 295 (in Greek).

Trovato, G, Nullità, inutilizzabilità, inamissibilità delle prove penali, available at www.diritto.it/materiali/penale/trovato.html.

Tsakirakis, S, 'Secrecy of correspondence: absolutely inviolable or a wish of the legal order' (1993) 41 *Nomiko Bima* 995 (in Greek).

Tsatsos, D, 'Constitutional revision and interpretation of the Constitution – the necessity for an interpretative theory preceding the Constitution of 2001' in D Tsatsos, E Venizelos and X Kontiadis, *The new Constitution* (Athens, AN Sakkoulas, 2001) 55 (in Greek).

Tsimpoukis, P, *Amendment for the use as evidence of the Lagarde list by financial crime prosecutors*, Proto Thema, 22 December 2015, www.protothema.gr/politics/article/538586/tropologia-gia-tin-axiopoiisi-tis-listas-lagard-os-apodeiktikou-mesou-apo-tous-oikonomikous-eisaggeleis (in Greek).

Tsiplakis, K, Parliamentary debates archives, Period I, Session A, 24 January 2001, 142.

Tsiris, P, *The constitutional protection of the right to secrecy of correspondence* (Athens-Komitini, AN Sakkoulas, 2002) (in Greek).

Tsolias, G, Comment on Arios Pagos 1568/2004, (2005) 8 *Poiniki Dikeosini* 295 (in Greek).

Tsolka, O, *The 'nemo tenetur se ipsum prodere/accusare' principle in the criminal process*' (Athens, PN Sakkoulas, 2002) (in Greek).

Twining, W, *Theories of Evidence, Bentham and Wigmore* (London, Weidenfled and Nicholson, 1985).

Twining, W, *Rethinking Evidence* (Cambridge, Cambridge University Press, 1990).

Twining, W, *Rethinking Evidence – Exploratory Essays*, 2nd edn (Cambridge, Cambridge University Press, 2006).

Tzannetis, A, 'Evidential prohibitions and alternative legal obtaining of evidence' (1995) 35 *Poinika Chronika* 5 (in Greek).

Tzannetis, A, 'The unlawful obtaining of evidence (interpretative approach of article 177 para 2 of the Code of Penal Procedure)' (1998) 48 *Poinika Chronika* 105 (in Greek).

Uglow, S, 'The Human Rights Act 1998: Part 4: Covert Surveillance and the European Convention on Human Rights' [1999] *Criminal Law Review* 287.

Uglow, S, *Evidence – Text and Materials*, 2nd edn (London, Thomson, Sweet & Maxwell, 2006).

Uviller, R, *Virtual Justice: The Flawed Prosecution of Crime in America* (New Haven and London, Yale University Press, 1996).

Van Cleave, R, 'Italy' in C Bradley (ed), *Criminal Procedure – A Worldwide Study*, 2nd edn (North Carolina, Carolina Academic Press, 2007) 303.

Van de Laar, T and de Graaf, RL, '*Salduz* and *Miranda*: Is the US Supreme Court Pointing the Way? (2011) *European Human Rights Law Review* 304.

Vanderhallen, M, van Oosterhout, M, Panzavolta, M and de Vocht, D, *Interrogating Young Suspects – Procedural Rights from an Empirical Perspective* (Cambridge, Intersentia, 2016).

Varvitsiotis, I, Parliamentary debates archives, Period I, Session A, 24 January 2001, 96.

Venizelos, E, 'The topical character of the constitutional phenomenon and the 2001 Greek revision approach' in D Tsatsos, E Venizelos and X Kontiadis, *The New Constitution* (Athens, AN Sakkoulas, 2001) 31 (in Greek).

Venizelos, E, Parliamentary debates archives, Period I, Session A, 24 January 2001, 94.

Venizelos, E, '*The constitutional acquis' – The constitutional phenomenon in the 21st century and the contribution of the revision of 2001* (Athens-Komotini, AN Sakkoulas, 2002) (in Greek).

Vergès, E, 'Loyauté et licéité, deux apports majeurs à la théorie de la preuve pénale' (2014) *Recueil Dalloz* 407.

Vitiello, M, '*Herring v. United States: Mapp's* Artless Overruling' (2009) 10 *Nevada Law Journal* 164.

Vlamynck, H, 'Droit de ne pas s'auto-incriminer et loyauté de la preuve' (2014) *Actualité juridique pénal* 194.

Vogler, R, 'Spain' in C Bradley (ed), *Criminal Procedure – A Worldwide Study* (North Carolina, Carolina Academic Press, 1999) 361.

Vrellis, S, *Comparative law* (Athens-Komotini, AN Sakkoulas, 1988) (in Greek).

Vroom, C, 'La liberté individuelle au stade de l'enquête de police en France et aux Etats-Unis' (1988) *Revue de sciences criminelle* 487.

W White, 'What Is an Involuntary Confession Now?' (1998) 50 *Rutgers Law Review* 2001.

Walker, S, *Taming the System: The Control of Discretion in Criminal Justice 1950–1990* (Oxford, Oxford University Press, 2000).

Ward, T and Leon, C, 'Excluding Evidence (or Staying Proceedings) to Vindicate Rights in Irish and English Law' (2015) 35 *Legal Studies* 571.

Warren, E, *The Memoirs of Chief Justice Earl Warren* (Lanham, New York and Oxford, Madison Books, 1977) 316.

Warren, S, and Brandeis, L, 'The Right to Privacy' (1890) 5 *Harvard Law Review* 193.

Wasik, M, Gibbons, T and Redmayne, M, *Criminal Justice: Text and Materials* (London and New York, Longman, 1999).

Weigend, T, 'Should We Search for the Truth, and Who Should Do It' (2011) 36 *North Carolina Journal of International Law & Commercial Regulation* 389.

Weigend, T, 'Throw It All Out? Judicial Discretion in Dealing with Procedural Faults' in M Caianiello and J Hodgson, *Discretionary Criminal Justice in a Comparative Context* (North Carolina, Carolina Academic Press, 2015) 185.

Weisselberg, C, 'Saving Miranda' (1998) 84 *Cornell Law Review* 109.

Weisselberg, C, 'Exporting and Importing *Miranda*' (2017) 97 *Boston University Law Review* 1235.

Wenzelburger, G, 'Parties, Institutions and the Politics of Law and Order: How Political Institutions and Partisan Ideologies Shape Law-and-Order Spending in Twenty Western Industrialized Countries' (2015) 45 *British Journal of Political Science* 664.

Wenzelburger, G, and Staff, H, 'The "Third Way" and the Politics of Law and Order: Explaining Differences in Law and Order Policies between Blair's New Labour and Schröder's SPD' (2017) 56 *European Journal of Political Research* 553.

White, S, 'Miranda's Failure to Restrain Pernicious Interrogation Practices' (2001) 99 *Michigan Law Review* 1211.

White, RM and Ferguson, PR, 'Sins of the Father? The "Sons of *Cadder*"' [2012] *Criminal Law Review* 357.

Whitebread, C, and Slobogin, C, *Criminal Procedure – An Analysis of Cases and Concepts* (New York, University Textbook Series, 2000).

Wigmore, JH, 'Using Evidence Obtained by Illegal Search and Seizure' (1922) 8 *American Bar Association Journal* 479.

Wilkey, MR, 'A Call for Alternatives to the Exclusionary Rule: Let Congress and the Trial Courts Speak' (1979) 62 *Judicature* 351.

Wilson, B, *Enforcing the Fourth Amendment – A Jurisprudential History* (New York and London, Garland Publishing, 1986).

Winter, LB, 'Spain: The Constitutional Court's Move from Categorical Exclusion to Limited Balancing' in SC Thaman (ed), *Exclusionary Rules in Comparative Law* (Heidelberg, Springer, 2013) 209.

Woolworth, A, 'The Good Faith Exception: "What is it Good For?" The Michigan Supreme Court Overturns Twenty Years of Precedent Holding it Was Worth "Absolutely Nothing"' (2006) 83 *University of Detroit Mercy Law Review* 441.

Yeo, MH, 'The Discretion to Exclude Illegally and Improperly Obtained Evidence: A Choice of Approaches' (1981–1982) 13 *Melbourne University Law Review* 31.

Young, SNM, 'A Public Law Conception of Integrity in the Criminal Process' in J Hunter, P Roberts, SNM Young and D Dixon, *The Integrity of the Criminal Process – From Theory Into Practice* (Oxford and Portland, Oregon, Hart Publishing, 2016) 46.

Zigouras, A, 'Evidentiary use by private parties of improperly obtained evidence after the latest legislative reform' (2008) 58 *Poinika Chronika* 1013 (in Greek).

Zimianitis, D, 'Unlawful video or audio recordings and use of their products by the mass media' (2010) 13 *Poiniki Dikeosini* 1028 (in Greek).

Zuckerman, A, 'Illegally Obtained Evidence – Discretion as a Guardian of Legitimacy' [1987] *Current Legal Problems* 55.

Zuckerman, A, *The Principles of Criminal Evidence* (Oxford, Clarendon Press, 1989).

Zygouras, A, 'The procedural use by private parties of illegally obtained evidence after the latest legislative reform' (2008) 58 *Poinika Chronika* 1013 (in Greek).

INDEX

www.ingramcontent.com/pod-product-compliance
Lightning Source LLC
LaVergne TN
LVHW050301210926
848481LV00014BA/307